ENDOR

Michael Brown is one of the most gifted and truly anointed-by-God individuals I've ever known. It is indescribably amazing how much he writes and how powerfully he communicates. I believe he is delivering prophetic words from God to help save the future of faith, family, and freedom in the United States and around the world. In recent years, we have grown very close. We not only share our hearts with one another but seek to share God's heart. Although strong, I find Michael to be very teachable, with a desire to present truth with unconditional, redemptive love and uncompromising courage and conviction. His personal testimony is profound, and I trust you'll find this book to be a great source of inspiration. Thank you, God, for Michael Brown.

James Robison
Founder and President, LIFE Outreach International
Fort Worth, Texas

Michael is a man of Spirit and fire who is tirelessly consumed with passion for the gospel. He's like a human blowtorch—and those around him cannot help but get zinged by his zeal for the Lord and his compassion for others. In a time of cultural turmoil, there are very few people speaking with such moral clarity and biblical wisdom. Michael may be turning 70, but he isn't slowing down—in fact, he's picking up the pace!

John L. Cooper
Singer for Skillet
Author of *Awake and Alive to Truth*

In my opinion, the greatest need of the Church today, speaking generally, is to experience both the Word and the Spirit. In most churches, it seems to me like it's one or the other! Dr. Michael Brown is a gifted scholar who has the exceedingly rare combination of being equally open to both the Word and the Spirit. That makes this book essential reading.

R. T. Kendall
Minister, Westminster Chapel (1977-2002)

How Michael gets everything done that he does—in the time available and with the resources available—is truly a testament to God's power. Michael is one of my dearest friends, but reading his story has helped me get to know him in a whole new way. Yet this book not only helps us get to know Michael Brown better—as we follow his relationship with the Lord, we witness God graciously fulfilling His promises. In short, this book invites us to get to know not just Michael but God better, to learn from the model of this man of God's struggles and blessings. Beyond all that, the story is hard to put down!

Craig Keener
F. M. and Ada Thompson Professor of Biblical Studies
Asbury Theological Seminary

There are very few people in my life whose influence I would label as "profound," and Michael Brown is one of them. We have traveled together in ministry, served together in a Messianic congregation, prayed and worshiped in each other's home, wept over the passing of loved ones, wrestled with difficult and sensitive spiritual issues, and celebrated great victories. Yes, he is my friend for more than four decades, but he is also a teacher and mentor of extreme personal discipline and exceptional insight. He is competitive to the bone, and yet I have seen him be remarkably kind to those with whom he is diametrically opposed. For me, Dr. Michael Brown is a unique and valued treasure who has been, and continues to be, one of life's unexpected blessings.

Paul Wilbur
International Recording Artist
Songwriter and Worship Leader

Michael has been my go-to expert on answering Jewish objections to Jesus for almost 40 years. His scholarship, hunger for revival, and whole-hearted commitment to serve the Lord at any cost has been a true inspiration in my life. His tireless efforts to bring spiritual reformation to our nation and speak truth into the most controversial issues of our day never ceases to amaze me. He is a true warrior for the Lord! It's a great honor and joy to call him my friend.

Jonathan Bernis
President & CEO
Jewish Voice Ministries International

Living in the Line of Fire by Dr. Michael Brown is a powerful and deeply personal testimony of a life transformed by God's grace and dedicated to His service, even in the face of intense challenges. Dr. Brown has been an immense blessing to my life and ministry, offering wisdom, encouragement, and a steadfast example of faithfulness under fire. One story that particularly stands out is Dr. Brown's harrowing account of nearly losing his life as a teenager, only to be miraculously saved by God's intervention—a moment that set him on the path to becoming the fearless leader and voice for truth that he is today. This book, much like Dr. Brown himself, is a beacon of hope and resilience for those who are navigating the pressures and persecutions of living boldly for Christ. His story reminds us that, no matter the opposition, standing firm in our faith will always lead to victory in God's Kingdom.

Vladimir Savchuk
Senior Pastor, Author, and Speaker

Michael Brown's *Living in the Line of Fire,* is an amazing, interesting, inspiring book. Dr. Brown's books have been a boon to the Charismatic, Pentecostal, and Third Wave movements. It has been my privilege to have him as one of our teachers in the doctoral program of Global Awakening Theological Seminary. What an amazing teacher who is not only brilliant but also passionate for the glory of the Father, the Son, and the Holy Spirit. As I read the book, I was drawn into the story of Dr. Brown's life and the story of the redemptive purposes of God in his life. I highly recommend *Living in the Line of Fire*.

Randy Clark
DD, DMin, ThD, MDiv, BS Religious Studies
Overseer of the Apostolic Network of Global Awakening
President of Global Awakening Theological Seminary

Many people speak of the "fire" of the Spirit. I know of no one who has walked more in such a fiery lifestyle than my dear friend Michael, whom I have had the privilege to serve together now exactly 40 years. I guarantee your soul will be charged with divine electricity as you read this book or receive from any other of his teachings as well.

Asher Intrater
President, Tikkun Global
Jerusalem, Israel

Dr. Michael Brown's life story is a powerful testament to God's transforming grace and the impact of a fully surrendered life. From drug-addicted teenager to respected scholar, revivalist, and cultural commentator, Dr. Brown's journey inspires us to pursue intimacy with God and to boldly proclaim truth in love. His unwavering commitment to revival, ministry to the Jewish community, and equipping the next generation challenges us all to live with purpose and passion for the Kingdom.

Pastor Mike Signorelli
Founder and Lead Pastor
V1 Church, New York City

For more than two decades, Dr. Michael Brown has been more than an influential figure in my life—he's been a steady, guiding presence from my time as a student at the Brownsville Revival School of Ministry to walking beside me during some of life's most trying moments. He's not just a teacher; he's been a trusted friend and mentor, anchoring me in biblical truth. Though not everyone can know him personally as I have, his autobiography, *Living in the Line of Fire*, offers the next best thing: a window into his life and journey. With honesty and vulnerability, Dr. Brown invites us to witness the trials and triumphs that have shaped him into the man he has become. What a precious gift! I have no doubt this book will become an instant classic memoir, inspiring and guiding generations to come.

Daniel Kolenda
Evangelist/President of Christ for all Nations
Lead Pastor of Nations Church

LIVING IN THE LINE OF FIRE

Rom. 8:28!

DESTINY IMAGE BOOKS BY MICHAEL L. BROWN

The End of the American Gospel Enterprise
How Saved Are We?
*Whatever Happened to the Power of God: Is the Charismatic Church
Slain in the Spirit or Down for the Count?*
*Our Hands Are Stained with Blood: The Tragic Story of the Church and
the Jewish People*
*It's Time to Rock the Boat: A Call to God's People to Rise Up and Preach a
Confrontational Gospel*
From Holy Laughter to Holy Fire: America on the Edge of Revival
Let No One Deceive You: Confronting the Critics of Revival
The Fire That Never Sleeps
*Donald Trump Is Not My Savior: An Evangelical Leader Speaks His
Mind About the Man He Supports as President*
Revival or We Die: A Great Awakening Is Our Only Hope

LIVING IN THE LINE OF FIRE

*How God Can Turn
Rebels Into Revivalists
and Broken People Into
World-Changers*

MICHAEL L. BROWN, PhD

© Copyright 2025– Michael L. Brown

All rights reserved. This book is protected by the copyright laws of the United States of America. This book may not be copied or reprinted for commercial gain or profit. The use of short quotations or occasional page copying for personal or group study is permitted and encouraged. Permission will be granted upon request. Scripture quotations marked KJV are taken from the King James Version. Scripture quotations marked NIV are taken from the HOLY BIBLE, NEW INTERNATIONAL VERSION®, Copyright © 1973, 1978, 1984, 2011 International Bible Society. Used by permission of Zondervan. All rights reserved. Scripture quotations marked ESV are taken from The Holy Bible, English Standard Version® (ESV®), copyright © 2001 by Crossway, a publishing ministry of Good News Publishers. Used by permission. All rights reserved. Scripture quotations marked NET are taken from The NET Bible®, New English Translation copyright © 1996 by Biblical Studies Press, L.L.C. NET Bible® is a registered trademark. All rights reserved. Scripture quotations marked CSB are from The Christian Standard Bible. Copyright © 2017 by Holman Bible Publishers. Used by permission. All rights reserved. Take note that the name satan and related names are not capitalized. We choose not to acknowledge him, even to the point of violating grammatical rules.

DESTINY IMAGE® PUBLISHERS, INC.
P.O. Box 310, Shippensburg, PA 17257-0310
"Publishing cutting-edge prophetic resources to supernaturally empower the body of Christ"

This book and all other Destiny Image and Destiny Image Fiction books are available at Christian bookstores and distributors worldwide.

For more information on foreign distributors, call 717-532-3040.
Reach us on the Internet: www.destinyimage.com.

ISBN 13 TP: 979-8-8815-0230-0
ISBN 13 eBook: 979-8-8815-0231-7

For Worldwide Distribution, Printed in the U.S.A.
1 2 3 4 5 6 7 8 / 29 28 27 26 25

DEDICATION

To Nancy, my beautiful bride since 1976 and my very best friend since 1974; to Jen and Meg, our wonderful, special daughters; to Jimmy and Ryan, our terrific, devoted sons-in-law; and to Elianna, Andrew, Connor, and Riley, our absolutely amazing grandkids.

CONTENTS

Preface		xv
1	From a Happy Childhood to Shooting Heroin	1
2	Saved!	19
3	Meeting Nancy and Starting a Family	41
4	The Lure of Academics and the Reawakening of My First Love	57
5	The Outpouring, Full-Time Ministry, and the Call to the Nations	75
6	The Refiner's Fire, Ravenhill, and Wilkerson	95
7	Revival!	117
8	Revolution Rising	143
9	The Painful Birth of FIRE	169
10	The Culture Wars, Radio, and My Calling to Be a Voice	191
11	To the Jew First	219
12	Adventures in the Spirit	245
13	Called to Be a Lightning Rod	269
14	Time to Meet Nancy for Yourself	291
15	Lessons Learned and Lessons Still Being Learned	311
16	The Best Is Yet to Come	335
Endnotes		351
About the Author		359

PREFACE

Why would someone write their own life story? Isn't that a little self-aggrandizing? In my own case, wouldn't it be better to wait until others chose to write about me? To be candid, I hardly think my life has been important for enough for someone (let alone more than one person) to write a book about me.

Then why write my own story? It is to testify to the amazing goodness and faithfulness and mercy and power of God, to encourage others with what He can do through a frail, human vessel, to demonstrate that all things are possible to the one who believes. This book is written to the glory of the Lord!

It is true that two old friends, both from New York, chastised me for not putting my own testimony and story in print. One asked me if I had ever put my full conversion story in writing, and when I told him I had not, he literally rebuked me to my face (in love). The other friend sent me a message one day, saying he strongly felt from the Lord I was to write out my life story. When I basically pooh-poohed his suggestion, he wrote back quite surprised. He felt deeply that this was the Lord's idea, not his.

A few years later, the idea started to germinate in me, and I felt it would be right and pleasing to the Lord to write this tribute to my Savior and God in conjunction with turning seventy years old in March 2025. (As you read the book, you'll realize that just turning seventy is a further testimony to His goodness.) Then, once I started writing, I was literally shocked by the sense of divine destiny on me, experiencing a powerful sense of His presence as I wrote, with the words pouring out as fast I could type. I was also staggered with the realization of how many times He sent just the right person to me at the right time, altering the course of my life, and how many times He intervened to save me from going down the wrong path, at times literally saving my life.

LIVING IN THE LINE OF FIRE

I was also blown away when I went back to review decades of my detailed journals, often bringing back vivid memories (both the good and the bad), at other times helping me convey the miraculous nature of what I was experiencing. What an amazing God we serve! The gospel is totally and completely real, and all His promises are true. They are!

Reliving my journey so far ultimately reminded me how totally, completely, utterly I am indebted to Jesus. I recognize this to the core of my being, and I pray from the heart that your love and appreciation for Him will be increased as you read.

I so appreciate Larry Sparks and the Destiny Image family for taking hold of this vision with me and helping me infuse a generation of readers with faith, truth, and courage so that they—meaning you, as you read!—can stand strong on the front lines. If the book blesses you, please let me know at TheLineofFire.org (click Contact). I'd be blessed to hear from you!

Thankfully, because I give credit to whom credit is due throughout the rest of this book, I don't need to go through lengthy acknowledgments here in the Preface, other than to say once more to my bride of almost fifty years, "You are the most amazing person I know on the planet, and I wouldn't be who I am or where I am—not within a million miles—without you. I love you more than words can say! I'm so glad the whole world will get to hear more about you too."

When I told a younger ministry colleague about the book, he seemed slightly surprised, saying, "You're going to need an addendum. The best is yet to come." I told him he was right and that the last chapter of the book carried those very words. In Jesus, the best, indeed, is yet to come!

May all glory and honor and praise and adoration be given to the only One who deserves it—the One who created us, redeemed us, and made us His very own children forever. I love You, Lord, with every fiber of my being! May I walk worthy of You all the days and years ahead. May You receive the maximum honor and glory possible through me!

October 2, 2024
(the beginning of the Jewish New Year)

CHAPTER 1

FROM A HAPPY CHILDHOOD TO SHOOTING HEROIN

"I'm burning in hell! I'm burning in hell!"

It was 1:30 in the morning on Saturday, September 4, 1971. I was only sixteen years old, but already I had earned the nicknames "Drug Bear" and "Iron Man." I could do greater quantities of drugs than any of my friends—and live to brag about it! Whether I was shooting heroin or using hallucinogenics like LSD and mescaline, taking mega-doses of drugs had become my lifestyle. But this time I went too far. *I took enough mescaline for thirty people*, and my friends put me on a bus alone, sending me home to fend for myself. They thought it was a big joke! Actually, it was a matter of life and death.

I became delirious on the bus and got off two stops too soon, more than a mile from my family's home in Island Park, New York. As I walked slowly toward the house, I thought the journey would never end. I became disoriented and got lost just two blocks from home. I sat down on the ground in mental torment, feeling like I had entered a maze from which I could never get out. I thought I had died and gone to hell.

Then, at that late hour of the night, a neighbor came by, walking his dog. He looked at me with shock as I screamed, "I'm burning in hell!" I was shocked too. "Why is he walking his dog in hell?" I wondered.

As soon as he walked away, I made a decision: "I'm going to jump in front of the next car that comes by. I can't take it any longer." I felt like I was losing my mind.

1

Within minutes, a car came racing around the corner, partially obscured by bushes. I jumped into the road directly in front of the car and threw my hands in the air. The car came to a screeching halt just inches from my body. It was my parents! The man with the dog had gone to my house and deeply shaken, woke them up in the middle of the night and told them what he had seen. They came looking for me. They were ready to stop at that very corner. *If it had been any other car I would have been hit and could have been killed.*

But what I was doing there anyway, stoned out of my head? How did a nice Jewish boy like me get so messed up? And why was I thinking about hell? Let me tell you the story. I think you'll be interested to hear what happened!

BACK TO THE BEGINNING

I was born in New York City in 1955. My father, Abe, worked as a lawyer in the New York Supreme Court (ultimately becoming the senior law clerk to the judges), and he and my mother, Rose, were as happily married as any couple that I have ever known. So, life was peaceful with my parents, along with one sibling, my sister Melissa, who was three-and-a-half years older than me. Nothing unique or out of the ordinary.

My upbringing was also fairly typical for many New York Jewish families. We moved to Long Island, I did well in school, I played lots of sports; and, like all my friends, I basically stayed out of trouble. But something changed. It all began innocently enough.

When I was eight years old, I started playing drums. There was no question that I had ability. In fact, by the time I was fifteen I had played on a studio album. But my favorite music was rock, and after my bar mitzvah in 1968, I got interested in playing in a band. I wanted to be a rock drummer, and all my role models were known for their heavy drug use, rebellion, and flagrant immorality. I wanted to be like them!

In fact, the event that had the most spiritual impact on me in 1968 was not my bar mitzvah, which was more of a social event than a spiritual event because we were not a religious family. It was seeing Jimi Hendrix

From a Happy Childhood to Shooting Heroin

in concert on November 28, 1968, at the New York Philharmonic. I was mesmerized by the power of the moment—the screeching, incredibly loud sounds; the visual impact of Hendrix and his bandmates; their open defiance of the status quo. They were my new heroes.

And so, in 1969, at the age of fourteen, when a friend asked me if I wanted to try smoking pot, I was only too happy to oblige. Not only did the rock stars use drugs, but at that time smoking pot was against the law, so there was that lure of touching something that was forbidden. But the pot didn't affect me at all, to the surprise of my friend, who instantly got high from the drug. Soon I tried smoking hash, a more potent drug than pot. But that, too, had no effect on me, despite others in the room saying it was very potent. So I immediately went to harder drugs—ups, downs, and then LSD. "But I'll never do anything worse than that," I thought. Yet I was deceived. Soon I starting using speed, then I started shooting speed. (Of course, I had been *sure* I would never put a needle in my arm!) Then I got the opportunity to try heroin. I loved it! *I was fifteen years old—just one year after smoking pot for the first time.*

By the time I was sixteen, my grades began to go down in school, and drugs and rock music completely dominated my life. For fun, my friends and I even broke into some homes and even a doctor's office. We experimented with the drugs we stole from the doctor's office and almost killed ourselves. But after all, we were cool! We were doing "our thing." And one day we would be famous rock stars!

Less than one year after these crazy events, I was living for God and telling people about Jesus, the Messiah and Lord of both Gentile and Jew. But before I tell you the incredible story of how the Lord intervened so miraculously in my life, let me paint a fuller picture of just how lost I was.

FROM MANHATTAN TO LONG ISLAND

I have limited memories of living in New York City, where I was born on March 16, 1955, since we moved to Long Island when I was about seven. But I do remember living in an apartment in Knickerbocker Village in Manhattan, and I remember on some occasions going to the Supreme

LIVING IN THE LINE OF FIRE

Court with my father, who was loved and respected there. The building had such a hallowed feeling to it, but it was austere rather than warm, fitting for a courthouse. It was also within walking distance of the apartment building, which was one reason we lived there.

We would also frequently walk over to Chinatown to eat at our favorite Chinese restaurant. As I recall, I always got the same meal, never trying anything else. This became the pattern for years once I started school, eating the same meal every day, without variation and never trying anything new.

During my years in elementary school, I had a peanut butter sandwich for lunch—just peanut butter, without jelly, and with the crust removed—*every single day*, including weekends. (Why I didn't like crust, I cannot tell you. Crust was simply not for me. As for jelly, I never tried it, so of course, I didn't like it. That also became a lifelong pattern: I had a dread of trying new foods.)

For breakfast, I had four Oreo cookies (honestly!), taking regular bites of the first and third Oreos, then opening up the second and fourth, licking off the white filling, then eating the outside cookie part. When I came home from school in the afternoon, I would have pretzels with grape juice—*every single day*. (How I grew to 6' 3" is quite the mystery with nutrition like that.)

During junior high school (called middle school today), I had a hamburger and fries every day for lunch during the school week. (I don't recall what I ate on the weekends.) Many nights my mother would also make burgers and fries, meaning that I ate that "nutritious" meal twice a day. (Yes, we serve a merciful God.)

Speaking of my mom, she and my father loved each other deeply, got along wonderfully, and were incredibly affirming as parents, always making me feel as if I was special. They did this with my sister Melissa too. But my mom was not known for her cooking skills, and when she made spaghetti and meatballs (one of my favorites!), she used *Campbell's Tomato Soup* for the sauce. I thought it was delicious! The first time I had the real thing—eating spaghetti and meatballs at the home of an Italian family in

From a Happy Childhood to Shooting Heroin

Pennsylvania when I was nineteen or twenty—I almost gagged. I'm sure it was amazing, but to me having grown up with tomato soup for sauce, it was disgusting. (Do I hear some connoisseurs of Italian food groaning?)

I also hated pizza the first couple of times I tried it (probably before my early teens, if I recall), almost gagging on that too. But once I took a liking to it, I became a pizzaholic, often eating pizza every day during much of my adult life, sometimes even twice a day. In fact, I once estimated that, while teaching at Bible school on Long Island from 1983-1987, I ate 3,000 slices of pizza from the local (amazingly good) pizzeria.

Since 2014, when God intervened in my life and helped me to make a radical diet change (which is why I'm alive to write this book today!), I have a massive salad every single day, without fail, using the same ingredients, creature of habit that I am, and only changing the dressing. And I look forward to it, *every single day*.

But getting back to my childhood in New York, I remember taking walks on Saturdays with my family and my grandmother on my father's side, the only grandparent I knew. My dad's parents came over from Russia at the turn of the twentieth century, with their last name being shortened to Brown when they arrived at Ellis Island. This was a common occurrence for immigrants with longer names, but to this day, I don't know what our original family name was. What I do know, on the spiritual side of things, is that either my father's grandparents (or, possibly, great-grandparents) were Orthodox Jews, based on the one picture that was preserved. But my dad's own mother and father were quite secular, and neither he nor his two brothers were bar mitzvahed themselves.

Sadly, my dad's father died at the age of forty-four, contracting cancer due to the fumes he breathed in as a painter. My father, the middle of the three brothers, became the responsible breadwinner for the family at the age of eleven and remained incredibly responsible until his dying day. As for my grandmother, I do not remember a single conversation we had, just recalling how sweet she was to me and how she spoke other languages better than English (at least Russian and Yiddish if not Polish too).

LIVING IN THE LINE OF FIRE

My mom's family background also had some early tragedy. She was born in England but the family moved to the United States when she was young. Then, when her mother died in her early forties, her dad remarried and his new wife would not take in his children. So my mom, just nine years old, and her two siblings were effectively orphaned, to be raised by their aunt and uncle who had to take on extra jobs to care for them. (Providentially, as I was writing this chapter, I heard from a cousin on my mother's side whose existence I had totally forgotten about. We had not been in touch for more than fifty years, but she found me through a DNA website, and she helped me piece together some of these details, also sending me a picture of our mothers arriving in America by ship.)

The amazing thing is that my mother never once complained about the difficulties of her childhood, nor did she carry any visible baggage into her relationship with my dad, who passed away suddenly at the age of sixty-three in 1977. My mom passed away at the age of ninety-four in 2016, but during all those years alone, I cannot remember her speaking of her own needs. She only wanted Melissa and I (and our spouses, and, of course, our kids—her grandkids!) to be happy. She was remarkably unscarred despite all she went through, so different from the prevalent, self-focused attitudes of today.

As for other childhood memories back in New York City, I do recall throwing a tantrum on the way into the apartment when I was quite little, perhaps as young as three. My parents simply went inside and let me scream and pound my fists on the floor for a few minutes until I sobered up. The tantrum didn't work.

In 1962, we moved to Long Island after spending the summers there the previous years in a little house we owned in the small town of Island Park, which was surrounded by water and was next to Long Beach, famous for its beach on the Atlantic Ocean. The house we bought in 1962 was in a neighborhood within Island Park called Harbor Isle, also surrounded by water, and with about 300 families living there, almost all of them Jewish. But I only knew of one Jewish family that was observant enough to light the Sabbath candles.

From a Happy Childhood to Shooting Heroin

The rest of us were quite nominal in our Judaism. But that was the only Judaism I knew. In other words, I thought that Judaism was a lifeless, wishy-washy religion, not realizing that it was the form of Judaism I was exposed to that was so shallow. Once I came to faith, I knocked on every single door in Harbor Isle, wanting to talk about Jesus or at least leave a tract.

As for the local synagogue, on some Saturday mornings my dad would get an emergency call, asking if he could hurry over to the shul (another name for a synagogue). On those occasions, they only had nine men there, including the rabbi, but in order to have an official service, you need a minyan (which is a minimum of ten men). My dad would wash up quickly, get dressed, and drive over.

Jewish law, however, forbids driving a car on the Sabbath, so some of the men would park their cars one block from the shul and walk the rest of the way. That was the level of their observance. Only the rabbi would walk the whole way rather than drive. Yet when the High Holidays came (in the Spring and Fall), the synagogue, which seated perhaps 150-200 people at most, was not big enough. Everyone got religious at that time of year to the point that they actually had to build an annex to seat the crowds that came just a few days a year. That was the type of Judaism in which I was raised.

When it came to Hebrew School, once we got to about ten years old (boys only), we had to attend classes a couple of days a week after public school. We learned a little Jewish history and some basic Hebrew, enough for us to read the portion of Scripture we would be required to chant at our bar mitzvah. But our level of spirituality was such that no one bothered to tell me what I was reading. In other words, I was reciting Hebrew words without knowing what they meant—and no one suggested that I read the passage in English too. For my part, it never dawned on me to do so. That was how shallow my own Jewish faith was.

Still, even though we went to school with our Gentile friends and all played together, we knew that we were Jews, which made us different. They—meaning Gentiles, Christians, Catholics, which were all synonyms

7

LIVING IN THE LINE OF FIRE

to us—had their own religion. It was "them" and "us," but not in a hostile, negative way. That was just the nature of being Jewish, and I do not recall any antisemitism expressed by those friends back then.

One day before Hebrew school, I asked my Jewish classmates if they knew if Jesus was Jewish. I had heard someone mention it, but I didn't know if it was true. We debated it for a few minutes (no one was totally sure either way), and then I came up with what I thought was a very clever quip. I asked, "So when did Jesus become Catholic? After He rose from the dead?"

As for what Christians believed, I had no idea. Sometimes, in New York City, while riding the subway with my dad, I saw words scrawled on the wall, "Jesus saves." But I had no clue what it meant. Not the slightest. There was even the Jewish joke, "Jesus saves, Moses invests." Funny to me, but meaningless.

As for my knowledge of the cross, my dad once told me a joke about a Jewish kid who got into all kinds of trouble in public school, getting kicked out of one school after another. So his father got him into a private Jewish school, but he was quickly expelled from there. Finally, in desperation, his dad enrolled him in a Catholic school, and he came home on his best behavior the first day. When his father asked him what happened, the boy said, "Dad, in those other schools, they may threaten to hit you if you misbehave. But in this school, they've got someone nailed to the wall!" That's how much I knew about Jesus or the gospel. And when my cousin Andy began to let his hair and beard grow long, as one of the first hippies in the city, we nicknamed him J.C., short for Jesus Christ. He was that guy with long hair and a beard.

THE PLUNGE INTO DRUGS

There was really nothing distinct about my childhood. I was not deeply motivated to learn, getting by with minimum effort in school but getting good grades, and I was not asking any existential questions about the meaning of life. I was simply enjoying a fairly innocent childhood, not hanging out with any lawbreakers or social rebels. (We had very few

From a Happy Childhood to Shooting Heroin

troublemakers in our little community back then.) What motivated me was playing drums and listening to rock music, and it was only then, once I started doing drugs, that the "iron man" part of my personality emerged, that tendency to take on too much, do too much, push too hard, and go too far.

The first time I took LSD (or as we would say, "dropped acid"), I was supposed to meet up with my friends, but we got our signals crossed. So I had the scary experience of taking my first trip while home alone, having to make it through dinner without my parents knowing that something was wrong. I still remember trying to figure out how to chew and swallow the pieces of chicken as if I was eating rubber. Everything felt so weird.

Soon enough, I was dropping acid as often as I could, along with using all the other drugs I could get my hands on, with pot and hash now affecting me too. As for tripping, I thought that it literally expanded my mind, giving me incredible insights, sharpening my senses, and massively enhancing the sound and feel of music. And when I discovered that I could do larger quantities of drugs than my friends, up to five times as much on one occasion, that became part of my identity. Then, with my tendency to push the boundaries, I would take the highest dose of LSD I could, seeing if I could make it through the trip without losing my mind. (I subsequently knew of some young people who *did* lose their minds on "bad trips," never becoming normal again.)

Sitting at home and hallucinating, I would keep looking at my hand until it disappeared into a blur of brightly painted, imaginary images. That's how high I was. And when I would walk outside at nighttime while tripping heavily, I was unable to distinguish between reality and fantasy, holding my hand in front of my face so as not to bump into anything. Was that a real, cartoonish-looking tree, or an imaginary one? Were those actual, bizarre-looking people coming my way or was I simply seeing things? I was also unable to determine the temperature, strolling around with my coat wide open during the freezing New York winter weather.

One night while using LSD, I drew an incredible picture of a man skiing down the side of a mountain, creating the image using only a series

LIVING IN THE LINE OF FIRE

of dots formed by the tip of my pen. I was blown away at my enhanced drawing skills. When I woke up the next morning and looked at the paper, I saw a bunch of random dots and nothing more. So much for the mind-expanding power of LSD.

When I first tried speed, snorting powdered methedrine (or amphetamine), which created a burning sensation in my nostrils, I immediately discovered my new, favorite drug. It was instant euphoria, instant joy, instant excitement and jubilation. I wanted to run down the streets telling the whole world how incredible it was. Suddenly, I loved everyone! But when I saw some of my new friends shooting speed, I was repulsed. A needle? That was wicked. That was lowlife. That was inner city kind of stuff. That was not for me.

But as my heart got harder, I decided to try it out, and now my love affair with speed only deepened. Shooting it into my veins produced an even more dramatic and instantaneous high. And then to play with our band—the other guys used speed with me too—was incredible. I drummed faster. We played better.

Oddly enough, despite all this craziness, I never smoked a cigarette or had a cup of coffee (even though I loved coffee candy). I took one puff of a cigarette and didn't like it and one sip of coffee and didn't like it, and that was that. At least there were two addictions I did *not* have. This has also opened the door for me to share my testimony over the years when I'm asked if I'd like to have a cup of coffee. I explain that I never had a cup in my entire life. "Really?" people reply. I then say, "And I've never had a cigarette either." Now they think I'm really holy. Then I say, "But I was shooting heroin at age fifteen."

As for our band, despite having no official name (other than the three-man band, in contrast with our previous band, which we subsequently dubbed, "The Incredibly Notorious Five-Man Band," featuring two guitarists, *two bassists*, and me), we were quickly becoming legends in our own minds. One day we would be famous too. Oddly enough, we were entirely instrumental at that point (in other words, without any vocals), with Jon Kavajian on bass, Kerry Chaplinsky on guitar, and me on drums.

From a Happy Childhood to Shooting Heroin

But we did write our own music, and every song featured extensive jams (meaning unscripted, free-flowing musical improvisations). In keeping with the spirit of the day, the song that became everyone's favorite was called, "Dance of the Mushroom Man." Enough said? (For the benefit of those for whom "mushrooms" are only something that you eat, in hippie culture, they were used as hallucinogenics as well.)

FROM BAD TO WORSE

My life now consisted of going to school (but often skipping classes and paying no attention while there), getting high, playing with my band, going to rock concerts, and partying. I saw Jim Morrison and the Doors, Janis Joplin, Led Zeppelin, the Who, the Grateful Dead, Hendrix again, Jethro Tull, Ten Years After, Chicago, Johnny Winter, the Chambers Brothers, and more, seeing some of these bands multiple times. Once I was fully entrenched in drugs, I always made sure I was high during the concerts, with the Fillmore East becoming my favorite venue, replete with the famous Joshua Light Show (with pulsating, hallucinogenic type images which synchronized with the music), and the whole building, which seated about 2,000, smelling like pot. And on a personal level, I was always looking for a new buzz and chasing a more exotic high.

Still, there was one drug that was off-limits—heroin. In fact, when I heard that some students in my high school were shooting dope, I was shocked. In our school, on Long Island? But as time went on, I became curious about heroin too, in keeping with the old saying that sin will take you farther than you planned to go, keep you longer than you planned to stay, and cost you more than you planned to pay.

That's because sin doesn't satisfy. Instead, it leads to more sin, which in turn leads to worse sin, and then it enslaves. Soon enough, you're not controlling your sin—your sin is controlling you. The downward descent is inevitable.[1] But I didn't know anyone personally who was shooting dope. There was quite a big gulf between being a hippie and a junkie, and so I had no way to obtain it (or "cop" it, as we would say).

11

LIVING IN THE LINE OF FIRE

How, then, did I start shooting dope? You've probably heard of (or experienced) a divine appointment, where the Lord providentially sets things up for you to meet someone and share the gospel with them (or, make some kind of significant life connection). Well, this was a satanic appointment, straight from the pit of hell.

I was taking the bus home one day from West Hempstead, where I went to high school and where many of my friends lived. On this particular day, I really stood out with my long hair, as there were no other hippies on the bus (not even close).

A man said to me, "Do you know where I could cop some mescaline?" This was similar to LSD but much harder to come by. It just so happened that I had some in my possession, a white powder wrapped in tin foil. By that time I was dealing drugs too, but even so, I rarely obtained mescaline. Yet it was *that* drug he asked me about.

I thought to myself, "He could be an undercover cop, a narc" (meaning, a narcotics policeman). Should I say anything to him?

Stupidly, I replied, "Sure, I have some on me. Do you know where I could cop some dope?"

He replied, "I have some on me." (Do you see why I said this was a satanic appointment? Talk about a setup from hell!)

And so, right there, with people on the bus looking right at us, we both took out our tin foil, exchanged enough white powder for one dose, instructing one another to shoot it all, and that was that. I don't recall saying another word to anyone the rest of the ride.

When the bus arrived at my stop about twenty minutes later, I was so excited that I ran all the way home—well over a half mile—calling a friend to come over and help me, since I was still getting used to putting a needle in my arm. And that is how I shot heroin for the first time. For all I knew, the man could have given me rat poison. But I was that lost and that foolish. (Remember, I was still only fifteen here.)

As for the drug experience, it was totally different from LSD, as there were no hallucinations or "mind expanding" sensations; and it was the opposite of speed, since it was a downer not an upper. Instead, it produced

12

From a Happy Childhood to Shooting Heroin

a different kind of euphoria, one in which you felt like all was well and you were the king. It quickly got a grip on me.

Yet I never became a junkie. That's because I found heroin to be too expensive. The first day, I could get high for five dollars. The second day, because of my high tolerance of drugs it cost me ten. By the fifth day, it cost me twenty-five dollars, and with limited funds, I would switch over to a different drug that would be cheaper.

You might say, "But weren't you addicted?" Actually, I had thought that heroin was instantly (or very quickly) addicting. But for most people, it took more than a few days to get physically hooked, and for me, it might have taken a full month. At the same time, I could actually see my personality changing and my morals getting even worse. I was becoming harder, and I knew it. My addiction was to drugs in general and, more specifically, to putting a needle in my arm. I loved the needle.

HOW LOW IS LOW?

To paint a picture of just how heavily I was into drugs and foolish living, allow me to share a few stories with you, forming some of the backstory to the life of "Dr. Michael L. Brown." The mercy of the Lord is great!

One time, while hanging out with some friends in Long Beach, I decided to take some barbiturates (downers) as well as shoot heroin, which made for a lethal combination. But I was expected at a party in West Hempstead at my bandmate Kerry's house while his parents were away. So, I started staggering down the street, walking to the bus stop.

A car pulled up next to me, offering me a ride, so I got in the back seat, with a young man driving the car and his girlfriend in the passenger seat. He said to me, "I thought you were hitchhiking." I responded, "No, I was afraid of the pigs" (our derogatory way of speaking of the police, since they represented the authority structure, and as hippies, we were rebels). He replied, saying something about cops. I answered, "Yeah, cops, pigs, the same thing." He then said sternly, "I said my father is a cop."

LIVING IN THE LINE OF FIRE

Right then, I knew that I was in big trouble, especially with his girl-friend there, before whom he wanted to look good. He said angrily, "Get out of the car and start running."

I got out of the car immediately, trying my best to move my feet. He yelled out the window, "Run faster!" I replied with my slurred speech, "I'm going as fast as I can!" Thankfully, he drove off rather than come after me. (Despite being so drugged, I remember this all vividly.)

I made it onto the bus, then walked over to Kerry's house, but I was so out of it that when someone opened the door for me, I collapsed inside. And all this while I had been traveling with heroin and a needle in my pockets. That's why I was "afraid of the pigs."

A little while later, I decided to shoot more dope, and when one of my friends expressed a concern I might overdose, I said, "If I do, just give me mouth to mouth resuscitation until the ambulance arrives." Talk about being a complete idiot. But because I was so out of it, I wasn't sure if I had the needle properly inserted in the vein; and so before I pumped the drug in, I pulled the needle out, and blood began gushing onto the white refrigerator door. So I tried again, and the second time, I succeeded. Drug Bear was doing his thing.

Perhaps even more depraved was our habit of huffing diesel gas, something that some of my other bandmate Jon's previous friends had been doing for a number of years, with disastrous effects. I had noticed that their speech seemed a little slow and that they were not that sharp mentally. Jon told me that it was the effect of huffing lots of diesel gas.

Jon, Kerry, and I would walk behind the train tracks of the Long Island Railroad in Island Park where some trucks were parked. It was dark and isolated there and we would unscrew the gas caps and take a sample huff until we found one that smelled the strongest, breathing in deeply with our hands cupped around the opening. Almost instantly, we were in another realm, one that is very difficult to describe. Some nights, to enhance the high, we would get high first, smoking pot or using LSD or mescaline, meaning that our judgment became totally impaired.

From a Happy Childhood to Shooting Heroin

Then the three of us would sit on the ground in a circle, fantasizing that we were demonic spirits who had left people's bodies, plotting out destruction on the earth. We called ourselves the Demon Meeting Council, but I don't recall a single thing we talked about. It was just plain sick.

I do remember, though, that I discovered the secret of the universe while huffing diesel gas, which was the secret of all motion (really!). Talk about being delusional.

More seriously, after Jon and Kerry started going to church—but were still doing drugs with me, a story I'll share in the next chapter—and they started talking to me about Jesus, I had a horrific experience one night after ingesting a hallucinogenic drug and then huffing diesel gas. It was an out-of-body experience in which I found myself caught up in what we called "the machine." We could all hear this "machine" passing by when we were high on diesel gas (we would even see it coming, riding on the electrical wires). But this time, I was sucked into it, finding myself in what looked like a small train compartment along with three or four other people. But they were lifeless and looked almost grey, making me wonder what they had gone through as the compartment moved and bumped along.

I said to myself, "No problem, I'll just put on some music." But there was no music. "Well, I'll just do more drugs." But there were no drugs. "Well, I'll just hang out with my friends." But there were no friends! Suddenly, to my absolute terror, I realized that I was alone and that I would be alone forever. I was in hell!

When I came out of the experience a few minutes (or seconds?) later, I thought I was in a sewer, looking up at Jon and Kerry through the grating, before suddenly standing next to them. I was frightened out of my wits. And although this terrifying experience brought about no change in my life at that point, it made the fear of hell very real to me.

As for looking for thrills, after a while, just getting high wasn't enough, so we found some oil storage units in my neighborhood, sneaking in at night and climbing over the outside steel wall, then getting high in the

LIVING IN THE LINE OF FIRE

area between the wall and the tank. We also spray painted the walls, even writing "666" on one of the walls, as by then we were hearing more about the Book of Revelation and the end times and the antichrist, because of Jon and Kerry's church attendance. But that thrill quickly faded. We needed something higher to climb.

So we decided to sneak into the field surrounding the two LILCO towers (LILCO was the acronym for the Long Island Lighting Company, which went out of business in 1998). The taller tower was about 300 feet high, and on two occasions I scaled it with my friends (the first time with Jon and Kerry), slowly climbing up the ladder to the top. (After the first few feet, the ladder was enclosed with steel grating, so you could fall straight down but not backward.) When we made it to the top, we could feel it swaying in the wind, which definitely spooked us. But it was made to do this, and we were actually quite safe.

Of course, we had to get high while up there, trying to smoke a joint, but this was very hard to light because of the wind. Jon said to me, mainly in jest, "If you fall, say, 'I receive Jesus Christ as my Savior' before you hit the ground." Little by little, he was starting to believe, but he still had a long way to go, which is why he had broken the law with me that night and climbed the tower.

One night, well before Jon's transformation, he and I decided to really go for it, breaking into a little doctor's office in town. We were doing it both for the thrill and for drugs and needles. (The doctor's office was about a half mile from where I lived too. Crazy!) We cut into a screen window which was about eye-level on the side of the building, and surprisingly enough, we found the window itself unlocked and I helped Jon crawl through. He then opened the back door and we turned on the lights. (Even as I write this, I can feel the fear of being caught. What first-class jerks we were.) We then grabbed all the drugs that looked good along with a bunch of needles, then we took off and ran for cover. No one saw a thing, and back then, there were no surveillance cameras nearby.

Remarkably, perhaps because it was such a small town, there was not even an alarm system in the little building. Still, we were ethical thieves,

From a Happy Childhood to Shooting Heroin

and the next night, we went back there again. The screen had not been repaired and the window was still not locked, so we tossed inside the items we didn't need. But we did keep the bottle of adrenaline, which had a stern warning on the outside, stating that this should only be administered when the patient's heart stopped beating. "Cool!" we thought to ourselves. We need to try this.

The next day, we were upstairs in my house in the room where our band practiced, with my parents right downstairs. I was with Jon and another fellow named Eddie who just happened to be with us that day. First it was Eddie's turn, and so I put about 30 percent of the adrenaline into the syringe for him to shoot into his vein. (Yes, sheer insanity!) He was instantly flat on his back and in distress. Next, it was Jon. Within moments, he was laying on his back, barely able to say the words, "Heavy speed rushes" as he held on for dear life. Then it was my turn, and of course, I had to do more than the others. After all, I was Iron Man!

Instantly, I was flat on my back too, feeling as if my heart was about to beat out of my chest. This was no high. This was flirting with death, and Jon was worried that he would have to run downstairs and get my dad, telling him what happened. But all of us survived.

This gives just a small glimpse of how lost I was. To my shame, I even stole money from my father on a few occasions, helping out my friends with some of his cash (perhaps about sixty dollars at a time). He realized, of course, what was happening, even when I tried to make it look as if someone had broken in through one of our doors, concocting a story about them stealing money. My dad knew I was guilty, even as I blamed some of my friends. To punish me, he banned those friends from the house.

Still, I never learned the art of being a thief or a criminal, which I'll illustrate with this last story. A junkie friend told me that when you break into a house, you should put toothpicks in the keyhole of the front door. That way, when the homeowners arrived and tried to open the door with their key, they would be delayed because of the toothpicks.

I decided to try this one night, calling the house of one of my friends who lived down the block to be sure that he and his family were out

LIVING IN THE LINE OF FIRE

before trying to break in and look for something valuable. My drug use was getting out of hand and I needed some extra income.

I put the toothpicks in the front door keyhole and then went around to the back of the house to look for a window where I could try to climb in. Suddenly, I heard my friend's father blurt out, "Toothpicks! Who put toothpicks in the lock?" They had already come home. Absolutely terrified, I took off running before I could be seen.

As for the toothpicks, I failed to realize that I was supposed to break them off once I inserted them in the keyhole. That way, it would take the homeowner a long time to open the door. I just thought the toothpicks were a momentary distraction! When I shared this story one night during the Brownsville Revival, Steve Hill, the evangelist and my dear friend, found it absolutely hysterical as a former junkie and thief himself.

I was not just a rebellious, proud sinner. I was a stupid sinner. Talk about being lost! And because I was so reckless, had the Lord not saved me before I got my driver's license, I don't believe I would have made it to my eighteenth birthday, likely the victim of a fatal accident due to me driving while high on LSD and unable to distinguish fantasy from reality. Great is the mercy of the Lord!

CHAPTER 2

SAVED!

You might be wondering if I felt guilty for the way I was living and if I recognized that I needed help. Quite the contrary. I actually boasted about my abusive lifestyle and dishonesty. As for needing help, not a chance. Despite some bumps in the road and my life going downhill because of heroin, I was still enjoying drugs and rock music. It was my whole identity.

As for my band members Jon and Kerry, they liked two girls in our high school who were sisters, Kathy and Geri. Their dad, Rudy Nuzzolo, who was a strong Pentecostal believer, had been praying for Kathy and Geri's salvation all their lives, and Rudy's brother, George, their uncle, was the pastor of the Pentecostal church that Rudy attended. In answer to their dad's prayer, the sisters began to attend services at the church, and in order to spend time with the girls, Jon and Kerry decided to attend as well.

The church was located in Queens, New York, about thirty minutes from where we lived, and it was called the Springfield Assembly of God. But it was not actually part of the Assembly of God denomination. Instead, it was part of the CCNA—Christian Church of North America—which was entirely Italian. Its mission was "to the Italian first," and its original charter required its senior leader, the General Superintendent, to speak Italian. It came out of early Italian Pentecostalism, which was birthed out of Azusa Street, and one stream from which the CCNA emerged was originally called the Unorganized Italian Christian Church. Having come out of Catholic backgrounds, the founders were scandalized by the concept of church organization.

LIVING IN THE LINE OF FIRE

As to the religious backgrounds of Jon and Kerry, Jon was raised Methodist while Kerry had been raised Russian Orthodox, but they were completely nominal, and Jesus had no more role in their lives than He had in mine. For them, going to these services was a way to spend time with Kathy and Geri. It also was really interesting for them, as the Pentecostal beliefs of speaking in tongues, praying for the sick, and driving out demons struck them as really novel. This church was cool!

Not only so, but the pastor, who was known as Brother George (in keeping with everyone being called "brother" or "sister"), was teaching a lot out of the Book of Revelation, which Jon and Kerry found totally fascinating. They would come to my house at night after attending a service and share what they heard. (The church had services Sunday morning, Tuesday night, and Friday night with a prayer meeting Monday night as well. The building, which was very small, seated a little over 100 people.)

Jon and Kerry weren't believers yet, so we would get high together when they returned from church, play our instruments quietly, with the amps set to a really low volume and with me playing on my drum pad, and they would give me highlights from the sermon. "Yes," they said with bated breath in between puffs on a joint, "there's going to be a beast that comes out of a bottomless pit with seven heads and ten horns!"

"That's in the Bible?" I asked? "Wow!" We even wondered aloud about the authors of the Bible, asking, "What were they smoking?"

But little by little, Jon and Kerry started to change, not wanting to party with me or get high and even becoming concerned about my heroin use. To me, this was a threat to our band, so I decided to attend a service with them—as a Jew, marking the first time I had ever set foot in a church building—in order to show them how ridiculous the whole thing was and pull them out.

It was August 1971, and I was sixteen years old, with shoulder-length hair, wearing my typical outfit of jeans, a long-sleeve shirt (to cover my arms, which showed some signs of shooting up) with small holes in it (the result of "roaches"—the butts of marijuana joints—burning through the

20

Saved!

shirt when they fell out of my hand) and cowboy boots, for some odd reason.

Some years after Nancy and I were married (I'll introduce her in the next chapter), she saw an old picture of me from about that time, and she burst into laughter. I said to her, "You're laughing because I look like a woman." She replied, "No, I'm laughing because you look like an *ugly* woman." She was right!

MY FIRST NIGHT IN CHURCH

When the service started, I was surprised to see the pastor, a short, balding man, standing behind the pulpit in a suit and tie, without any type of clerical robes. It seemed quite secular to me and not what I expected, based on my synagogue experience and my images of Christian clergy. I was also surprised to hear people praying spontaneous prayers out loud, as I was used to liturgical recitation. They raised their hands too, which was odd. As for the music, it consisted only of the pastor's wife, Marie, playing piano, although on some nights she was joined by her brother-in-law Frank, a former jazz guitarist and nightclub entertainer. (I don't remember if he was there that first night.)

Frank was one of the four Nuzzolo brothers I knew who came to faith (there were thirteen siblings in all), along with George, the pastor. There was also Rudy, Geri, and Kathy's dad, and Al, who was a pastor as well. George, for his part, had also been a nightclub entertainer before he was a believer, playing accordion and singing. Every so often, he would bless the congregation by playing a hymn on accordion, most memorably, "Meeting in the Air," which also featured an accordion solo. The congregants used to say that he had angels in his fingers.

I don't remember a word Brother George said that first night, other than at the end, when he gave a strong warning, saying there was someone there and it was their last chance to repent. It was urgent that they raised their hand and respond! I was sure he meant me—after all, I was the "big sinner" in the church that night, to the point that Geri's diary entry for the day said, "Antichrist comes to church." That was me!

21

LIVING IN THE LINE OF FIRE

Jon whispered to me, "I'll raise my hand if you raise yours." I agreed, but waiting for him to raise his hand first. If it wasn't him, I would then raise mine, although it was only a game to me. Jon raised his hand (thinking I was doing it at the same time), and Brother George exclaimed, "That's the one!" Jon went forward and Brother George asked everyone to come up and pray for him. Afterward, Jon was upset that I hadn't raised my hand at the same time, as if that would have changed things.

What really struck me, though, was the love of the people. They were almost all older, some even in their sixties, which seemed ancient to me, including Brother Nick and Brother Trixie. (Almost everyone in the church was of Italian descent, including these two men.) Once I was a believer, I found out that Nick had been in a chain gang before he was saved, and before that was thrown into the trunk of a car to be killed during his days as a criminal. Trixie was given that nickname as a boy because he used to love to play tricks, most notoriously grabbing some stray cats on the streets, opening the door of the local church, and throwing the cats in. His son, Tommy, became a prominent Assembly of God missionary to Italy before returning to pastor in the States, ultimately becoming pastor of that very same congregation where I came to faith (it had relocated to Long Island by then). While staying at Tommy's house years later, he told me that his father prayed for me every single day until he died in his eighties. I am indebted to these saintly men.

As I left the building that first night, Nick and Trixie were full of energy and life, greeting me warmly. I remember Nick saying to me, "And remember, no matter how close the devil is, the Lord is always closer!" I had no idea what he meant, but I was so impressed with them, along with some of the others, that I decided not to argue with Jon and Kerry anymore, saying to them, "You have your religion and I have mine," as if being Jewish was even a factor in my life.

For the believers in this little church, though, my visit was their signal to start praying for me, which they did faithfully, burdened by the Lord. The pastor's oldest daughter, Sharon—who has been a lifelong friend of Nancy and mine and who married Kerry the guitarist—told me a few

Saved!

years ago that they prayed for me at the services, at the prayer meetings, and in their homes. This moves me deeply to this day.

THE HOLY SPIRIT STARTS WORKING ON ME

Over the next few months, while Jon and Kerry stopped getting high, I continued plunging downward, still proud of my sin, still glorying in my identity as a budding rock drummer and heavy drug user, having absolutely no desire to change. And while many people hearing my story from a distance might say, "You were obviously strung out and looking for help," the reality is that I loved my sin and hated the thought of giving it up.

But those prayers were working, and out of the blue, something began to happen. I vividly remember lying in bed at night, high on some drug, thinking about all my sinful exploits, including stealing money from my father and my friends, yet feeling great about who I was. What a crafty guy! Then, without any change in circumstances, just days later, I found myself lying in bed at night, high on some drug and unable to sleep, but now feeling absolute torment for these very same deeds. What a wretch I was! If I could have crawled out of my skin, I would have.

I had never heard of the conviction of the Holy Spirit, but without a doubt, this is what I was experiencing. My remedy, though, was simply to use different drugs with the hope that they would not keep me up at night. But God was chasing me down.

The second week of November, John called me on the phone asking me to attend a church service with him. I said, "You haven't partied with me in weeks. So, you come and party with me, and I'll go to church with you." He said he couldn't do that, so I hung up the phone on him. But hanging up on him was nothing for me. I had become a cruel person, and discarding someone in that way was no big deal. In fact, when my terrible, jealous temper would take over, I became a different person entirely. Jon actually gave this super-angry version of me the nickname "Crag the Evil Genie." That should say it all.

To my surprise, though, I felt guilty for hanging up on Jon and told him that I would go to the service with him. That was November 12,

LIVING IN THE LINE OF FIRE

1971, which was the next step in this radical and dramatic change in my life.

Once again, though, I don't remember a single thing that was preached that night, nor do I remember the songs that were sung. But at the end of the night, Brother George gave a call for people to receive Jesus, as was his custom. Jon nudged me, saying that I should really do it. I thought to myself, "These people think I'm a really big sinner, so I'll go up to the front and say a prayer. They'll get all excited about it, and I'll go home." I really didn't mean anything by it.

But my friends had been preaching to me for months, and the gospel was starting to sink in, more than I realized. I went to the front and the pastor asked me to repeat a prayer after him. I said the words, "I believe that Jesus died for my sins." To my surprise, I *did* believe this. Jesus really did die for me! "And I believe He rose from the dead." Surprisingly, I believed that too! Then, the clincher, as I repeated the words, "And I promise to live for You all the days of my life." The pastor said to me, "Did you mean that?" I responded with a yes, and he said, "I believe you."

But in my heart, I was lying about the promise to live for God. I had no intention of changing at that moment, even though I said those words out loud. To the contrary, I had just purchased a sizable batch of cocaine, which was the new, big drug in town and which I was going to use and sell, and I had definite plans for the night. When I got home from church, I was going to smoke a large quantity of PCP (also called "Angel Dust"), enough for several people, followed by shooting a large quantity of cocaine.

But now I had a conflict. I knew that the gospel was real, but I didn't want to give up my sin. So I silently prayed this prayer as the church members came forward to pray as well: "God," I said, "You know that I'm planning on getting high tonight when I get home. So if You don't want me to do it, don't let it have any effect on me when I do." (Yes, this was a dangerous and even ridiculous prayer to pray, but I was brand-new, and God met me in His mercy.)

24

Saved!

Jon, Kerry, and I went back to my house, courtesy of Rudy ("Brother Rudy" to us), who for many months drove us to every service, multiple times a week, making different stops along the way to pick us up and drop us off. (We were still too young to drive.) I proceeded to smoke the large PCP joint as they watched, and then, immediately afterward, to mainline a substantial amount of cocaine, just as I had planned. For a moment, my heart started to pound, and then nothing. Nothing at all! The drugs had zero effect on me. I realized that something supernatural was up.

THIS GOD STUFF WAS REAL.

Over the next five weeks there was an intense battle for my soul. I would shoot dope one day and go to church the next, or smoke pot morning, noon, and night (my dad said I was becoming a pothead), then be back at church the next night. All the while, the conviction was getting deeper. Yet under no circumstances did I go to church high. It was one or the other, until I got a call from another friend, John F., who was also a heavy drug user. He had just purchased some really powerful heroin, and he wanted to give me some for free. The problem was that I was supposed to go to the church service that night.

Too weak to say no his offer, I told him to come over with the drugs, but he arrived late and Brother Rudy arrived early to pick me up. There was no time to turn the powder into liquid (heating it up in a spoon mixed with water, held over a match) and shoot it. (Can you imagine that I was going to do this and then go to church?) There was not even time for John to finish the process of injecting the drug. And so, with the needle still stuck in his arm, I ordered him to leave, making my way to Brother Rudy's car. This night, Jesus, not drugs, came first. That, in turn, led to the night of transformation. I can never forget it!

THE NIGHT WHEN EVERYTHING CHANGED

It was Friday night, December 17, 1971. I could not wait to get to the service. I was enjoying the meetings more and more, but this night something

25

LIVING IN THE LINE OF FIRE

happened. As we sang those old songs, tunes like, "Power in the Blood" and "Make Me a Blessing" and "Draw Me Nearer," songs I would have characterized as silly little ditty hymns, I became overwhelmed with a joy I had never experienced before. It was extraordinary, even though we only sang two or three hymns, and each were just three or four stanzas long with a chorus. That meant that this entire "worship experience" was just a few minutes long. Plus, there was no contemporary music, no special effects, no video screen, no smoke machines, not even a worship team—just the pastor's wife playing piano (and maybe her brother-in-law on guitar). Yet I encountered God!

In a moment of time, my mind raced to every other joyful or euphoric experience I had ever had: a drug high (and remember, I got *very* high), a music high, a sports high, a friendship high. In a split second, I realized that this was of a different quality from those other experiences. This must be what they called "the joy of the Lord," something the pastor talked about a lot and something we sang about. (I think back to one hymn that started with, "There's within my heart a melody, Jesus whispers sweet and low.")

Immediately, I saw a clear picture in my mind's eye, depicting the back and forth nature of what had been taking place in my life. In the vision, I was filthy from head to toe, but Jesus washed me with His blood, making me perfectly clean. He then put white robes on me. How beautiful! This was a picture of the grace I had experienced, as the Lord had given me faith and was slowly pulling me out of my sin. But the internal vision didn't end there. Instead, shockingly, I got up and went back to playing in the mud, depicting my severe ungratefulness and double-mindedness. At that moment the love of God was revealed to me, and I said to the Lord, "I will never put a needle in my arm again." And that was it! At that moment, I was instantly set free, for life. Praise You, Jesus!

You see, over these weeks, I knew it was sinful for me to shoot drugs, and I was even willing to say that I would stop for a while. But to say, "Never again for life" seemed impossible. Surely, I needed to keep that door open. But now, seeing how ungrateful I was to the Lord and how

Saved!

I was spitting on His mercy, and filled to overflowing with joy and gratitude, I made a full surrender. "Never again!"

I returned to my house with Jon and Kerry, we went up to our practice room where I had hidden all the needles and drugs, gathering them together. Then we walked a few blocks to the neighborhood bridge and we threw everything into the water. (My apologies for the pollution, but that was the last thing on my mind right then.) I was free! Praise God, totally free! It was not hard and there was no withdrawal. That is the power of the gospel!

Two days later, I got high with some friends in West Hempstead, smoking hash with them. But as I rode the bus back home, I realized that this too was displeasing to the Lord—not just shooting drugs, but all drugs—and I vowed never to get high again. And the rest, as they say, is history. Thank You, thank You, Lord!

What's amazing, though, about my December 17 transformation is that I had been listening to hard rock music day and night for years, along with playing loud and intense music with my band. When I would go to a concert, I would measure the volume by screaming at the top of my lungs, and if I could hear my voice, the music wasn't loud enough. And I loved Led Zeppelin's "Dazed and Confused" and Jimi Hendrix's "Purple Haze." Yet here I was in this little church, singing those little ditty hymns, with the pastor's wife playing piano, and that holy joy overtook my soul. How extraordinary!

As to the moment I was saved, God knows. Did He meet me that first night, November 12, as my faith came alive? Or was it in the intervening weeks, leading up to December 17? Only God knows for sure, but I can say this with certainty: I left the building a child of God on December 17, 1971, and one of the greatest proofs to me was that the guilt was gone. Totally gone! Even when I looked for it, thinking back to when I stole money from my father, a sin for which I felt most deeply convicted, there was no guilt. None!

Five weeks later, at a Monday night prayer meeting with about ten others present, I was filled with the Spirit and began speaking in tongues.

LIVING IN THE LINE OF FIRE

Then, on February 4, I was baptized in water, and I remember one of the young ladies in the church, Anna, saying to me with a smile, "Mike, when you came out of the water, it was filthy." She was speaking metaphorically. All my sins had been washed away.

TAKING MY FIRST STEPS

Of course, even though I was radically set free from drugs, I was not yet fully sanctified. Not quite! And so, just two weeks after my night of deliverance, which was the night of our New Year's Eve service, I lost my temper badly—and I mean badly. I was so angry with Geri over some silly incident, that her dad, Rudy, decided not to pick me up for the service. But because I was being so unreasonable, no one called to let me know. So I waited and waited, getting angrier by the minute.

When I realized I was not getting picked up, I called the church, demanding to speak with the pastor while the service was going on, as if he was going to stop preaching, step down from the pulpit, and come talk to me. One of the deacons, Al M., answered the phone and said Brother George was busy with the service and could not speak. I called back. Again he answered, telling me the same thing. I called again, but this time, the line was busy. They had taken the phone off the hook. I was furious!

Only later did I find out that the phone rang in the tiny office just a few feet from the pulpit, so everyone could hear it ringing during the service, and Al had to get up and walk to the front to answer it. As the story goes, I threatened to blow up the building. Although I don't personally recall this, it wouldn't surprise me, given how worked up I got when I became "Crag."

Of course, I immediately humbled myself and repented before the Lord, going back to the next service and seeking out Al, asking him to forgive me. He just smiled at me as if nothing had happened. That made a deep and lasting impression on me, as I recognized how full of grace these people were. Having received mercy from the Lord, they showed mercy to me, recognizing how absolutely raw I was.

28

Saved!

On another occasion, I got really angry with Sharon, also because of some silly incident, and waited in the church vestibule to give her a piece of my mind after prayer meeting. (Think of *that*. I prayed for an hour solid without subduing my anger.) She went downstairs to the bathroom but never came back up. Eventually, I found her outside the building, and I let her have it. She had been so afraid of me that she climbed out the bathroom window (and she managed to do this while wearing a dress).

That was a Monday night and the next night, I was back in church. After we sang a couple of hymns, the custom was to take prayer requests. Sharon's mom, Sis. Marie, the piano player, raised her hand and said, "Special unspoken." That referred to a prayer request that we preferred to keep silent.

By then, our whole band brought our equipment to the church service three times a week, playing quietly along with Sis. Marie and Frank. (No, I did not bring my full, double-bass drum set. But three times a week, I would take down some of the set, carry it into Brother Rudy's station wagon sometimes with the help of Jon or Kerry, set things up to play a few songs, take it down, bring it back home, and put the set back together.) I was sitting on my drum stool, just a few feet from Sister Marie, and as soon as I heard her make that prayer request, I said to myself, "That's me she's talking about! She wants prayer for me because I was so mean to her daughter. Why doesn't she just say it!" I was still upset. Years later, I found out that the request *was* for me!

Then it was time for the message and Brother George, who was more of a preacher than a teacher, spoke quietly and gently from 1 Corinthians 13, the love chapter (or in the King James Version, the chapter about "charity"). As he read those words, arrows of conviction cut into my heart: "Charity suffereth long, and is kind; charity envieth not; charity vaunteth not itself, is not puffed up, doth not behave itself unseemly, seeketh not her own, is not easily provoked, thinketh no evil; rejoiceth not in iniquity, but rejoiceth in the truth; beareth all things, believeth all things, hopeth all things, endureth all things" (1 Corinthians 13:4–7 KJV).

LIVING IN THE LINE OF FIRE

Silently, I prayed, "Lord, I repent! I am so sorry! I am guilty as charged! I yield! Please stop the message!" I felt like I was going to explode, just wanting the message to end so I could go up to Brother George and apologize to him too. Finally, the message ended and I went to apologize, but when I did, it was just the same as with Al. Brother George simply smiled at me with forgiving eyes. This was the mercy of the Lord.

Still, I knew that I had to get the victory over my temper, and one day, meditating on Proverbs 16:32, the light went on. The text said, "He that is slow to anger is better than the mighty; and he that ruleth his spirit than he that taketh a city" (Proverbs 16:32 KJV). That meant that I had to rule my strong, self-willed nature. I didn't need to cast out a demon, I needed to get the mastery over my strong spirit. And by God's grace, spending quality time in His presence daily, the victory was won. Crag was crucified.

As for the process of sanctification, I had grown my hair long as part of the hippie scene, not just to be cool but as a sign of rebellion, yet the Lord had not convicted me about this before I was baptized in water on February 4. I was still quite proud of my long hair, but because it was thick and would curl on the end, people didn't really know how long it was. Now, as I came out of the water, everyone could see the real length of my hair. I was proud of it. The sanctifying process was not quite complete, and of course, it is still ongoing to this day!

It became my habit to attend every service, which meant three services a week, plus Sunday school, plus prayer meeting. Eventually, when we bought property in Oceanside, Long Island, the town next to Island Park, we added a Wednesday night service and then a Sunday night service. Under no circumstances, sick or not, did I ever miss a service, always sitting on the front row, even when we had special services entirely in Italian.

You see, in order to minister to the Italian speakers in our congregation, for a period of time the Monday night prayer meeting was turned into an Italian service once a month. The hymns were sung in Italian, testimonies were in Italian, and a passionate, older pastor named Frank

Saved!

Catanzarro preached in Italian. I remember him being so short that when he stood behind the pulpit, you could barely see him. But what he lacked in stature, he made up for in fire. I knew this because I attended these Italian services without fail, along with Jon and Kerry, even though we didn't understand a word. But if the doors were open, we were there!

Years later, as I preached in hundreds of services in Italy with an Italian interpreter, I was reminded of those Monday nights, saying to myself, "This is my way of repaying my debt to the Italian church." Not surprisingly, in the providence of God, more of my books have been translated into Italian than any other language.

TIME TO GO DEEPER

Getting back to 1972, I was totally in and fully committed, but it was time to go deeper, and I needed to be more disciplined in redeeming the time. Before we were saved, we would waste endless hours getting high and, in our stupefied state, listening to rock music. Now that we were believers, we had more time on our hands, and we started to get bored.

One night that winter (this was early in 1972), with nothing to do, Jon, Kerry, and I decided to go ice skating. It was out of complete boredom, since none of us were into skating. Not long after that, I made a decision. I could lead a clean but empty life, or I could give myself to God the same way I gave myself to drugs and rock music, with absolute abandon and with the totality of my being. In fact, years later, I realized that was one of the things I loved about rock—the band members put themselves totally into the music. It was an extension of their souls—often, a demonic and destructive extension—an expression of their inmost being, and the power of that music swallowed them up. Now, I wanted to give myself fully and entirely to serving and knowing the Lord, without reservation of any kind.

I began to read the Word more and pray more. I became even more zealous about sharing my faith, looking for one new person every day to tell about Jesus—not as a burden, but out of joy. When we didn't have a church service, I would sometimes visit a congregant who had a need

LIVING IN THE LINE OF FIRE

or was home sick, and sometimes on Saturdays, I would knock on doors and share the gospel. Often, on Monday nights before the prayer meeting, even in blizzard-like weather, we would stand on street corners a few miles from the church building and hand out tracts. This was my new life in the Lord, and it was wonderful.

But spending more time in the Word and prayer only deepened my hunger. I began to memorize scripture, getting to the point where I would memorize one verse per day. Then I added more. And then more again. And then still more. By the time I was saved for one year, I would memorize *twenty verses a day*, without fail, and I did so for six straight months, never missing a day and retaining most of the verses I had memorized.

Having realized years earlier while doing a school lesson that writing things out helped you to memorize, I developed a method of looking at a verse until I could write it out once from memory. Then I would repeat it seven times perfectly, then write it again, and then it was locked in. My mind, which had been so fried from drugs, was now sharper than ever. It took me exactly one hour a day to memorize those twenty verses. By God's grace, I was engaged—fully and totally engaged.

I also read the Word two hours each day, reading the Bible cover to cover about five times in my first two years in the Lord. And I would pray at least three hours daily, including at least one hour straight in tongues, plus two hours of other types of praying, including praying for every member of our church and their families, all my friends at school, all my extended family members, and every new person I met with whom I shared the gospel. This often meant praying for "the man with the red hat" and "the woman with the black coat," since I didn't even know their names. Eventually, I was praying for about 3,000 people daily in rapid fire, perhaps somewhat legalistically, but as part of my devotion to the Lord.

At night, prior to going to sleep, I would kneel by my bed and pray in tongues for an hour, often meditating on the verses I had been memorizing. Then I would quote to the Lord passages such as 1 Corinthians 13:4–7 (the very verses I just cited) or 2 Peter 1:5–7, which speak of the

Saved!

virtues we are to add to our faith. I would also pray over myself from head to toe—thoughts that I thought, things I saw and heard, words I spoke, what my hands touched, where my feet went—consecrating my life to the Lord and asking for His Spirit to transform my life. And as I would lay in bed before falling asleep, overflowing with that holy, intimate joy, I would say to myself, "If any of my friends at school could walk in my shoes for twenty-four hours, they would never go back to their old ways."

Speaking of my school, during the spring of 1971, about six months before I was born again, I joined with a group of student rebels to protest school policies, acting at one point as a ringleader. (This was the thing to do in the late 1960s and early '70s, when students on college campuses even took buildings hostage.) To our surprise, the administration yielded to our demands, allowing us to form a school of our own design. (I kid you not.) The new program began in the fall of 1971 and was called S.A.F.E. School, which stood for Student and Faculty Education, since it was going to be a learning experience for everyone. And rather than having to call the teachers by their last names, we used their first names. We were really breaking with the status quo.

S.A.F.E. School was given four rooms in the corner of one of the buildings, and while all the rest of the windows in the school were clean, ours were covered with graffiti. Out of the student body of 1,200, we had between sixty and seventy, for the most part the druggies and rebels and hippies of the student body.

For the rest of the school, classes ended at 3:00 p.m. For us, classes got out at noon. We also did not have formal class requirements with normal tests and assignments. We could simply request a passing grade and not even show up. In fact, our most radical teacher said to us, "If your education is to go out in the field and get high every day and you'd like an A for that, I will give it to you." This was my kind of school!

A few months into this new program, I was gloriously born from above, and once I got really serious about the Lord, I had those extra free school hours to spend with Him every day. It was all part of His plan to lay deep biblical and spiritual foundations in my life at this early stage in

33

LIVING IN THE LINE OF FIRE

my walk with Him, a major part of preparation for my life calling to the ministry. Not only so, but S.A.F.E. School was an incredible harvest field since there was so much spiritual speculation and searching among us. It was the time of the Jesus Revolution, also known as the Jesus People Movement, when so many from my generation were radically and dramatically saved.

Prior to coming to the faith, my friends and I would get high and speculate about spiritual things, knowing that there had to be more than the typical American dream. Something was in the air and the Spirit was at work. Not surprisingly, at the end of my first year in the Lord I counted forty different people from my school who had attended one of our church services, including one of our teachers.

As for my zeal, it was boundless. As for my wisdom, it was in its infancy, to say the least. As for my compassion, it was still to come. And so, when I witnessed, I could mow you down with scriptures, which I could recite with machine gun speed and precision. (Yes, I also used the Bible to argue for whatever position I was taking; but here, I'm talking about using it for the right purposes.) I was certainly lacking in sensitivity and love, to put it mildly, but if you were part of a cult or into some false teaching, I could nail you with the Word.

But I was zealous, and I did want to see people come to faith, and my custom in high school was to look for someone new to talk to in the cafeteria. I would say, "Can I talk to you for a minute?" If the person said yes, I would ask, "Are you saved?" (I know, not the best strategy.) Remarkably, some of those classmates came to faith and are serving the Lord to this day. But not everyone was willing to talk, especially once my reputation preceded me. When I would ask, "Can I talk to you for a minute?" the student would say, "No!" and get up and walk away.

One day I came home from school to see a woman walking down the driveway of our house as I was about to pull in (by then I had my driver's license!). She was a neighbor from down the street named Judy, a Jewish woman who was a Jehovah's Witness. (I had actually broken into her house before I was saved, stealing some fake jewelry!) Judy had knocked

Saved!

on the door to talk about her faith with my mother, who wasn't at all interested, but I was more than eager to talk.

By then, I had spoken with a number of Jehovah's Witnesses, and when I did, I could see that they were not truly engaging me. They would hear my words outwardly but not inwardly, just responding with the next verse they had been taught to use. But things were different with this woman. I could see that my answers jarred her for a moment, and for every verse she threw at me, I had a scriptural response, and it was solid.

Some months later, she left the Jehovah Witnesses as a result of the many discussions we had. Out of curiosity, I asked her, "What did my mother say when you knocked on the door?" Judy replied, "She said to me, 'I'm not interested in religion, but wait for my son to come home. He'll convert you. He converts everybody.'" That was my proud Jewish mom!

THE HAND OF GOD

There were also some amazing signs of God's hand in those early days, confirming the miraculous nature of my new life in Him, beginning with the healing of my body. Before I came to faith, I came down with a bad case of hives, with a miserable itch spreading all over my body. I would wake my mom at night, tormented by what felt like fire in my skin, and she would prepare a bath with some formula to help reduce the itch, but it barely helped.

My mom and dad finally took me to a doctor, who prescribed medicine for me, telling me it would take about 24 hours to take effect, and then, over the course of a week, the hives should entirely disappear. No more red blotches. No more itch. And after several days, it worked.

But right after I came to faith, the hives came back with a vengeance, yet I was so new in the Lord I didn't think God would hear me if I prayed alone. That's because I would regularly hear in church services, "Where two or three are gathered in His name, He is in our midst." I thought I needed someone else to pray with me, but I was home alone! Talk about being brand-new. So, not thinking my prayers would be heard since I

LIVING IN THE LINE OF FIRE

was alone in my bedroom at night, I took the medicine again. And once more, over time, the hives disappeared, to the point that I didn't even carry any pills with me just for security.

Not long after that, I was on the bus going to school when I noticed my arms starting to itch. To my dismay, when I rolled up my shirt (this was in the middle of the winter, so I was wearing long sleeves), I saw the ugly red blotches starting to appear. And I had no pills! Even if I had some, it could take a full day before they made a difference. I started to panic.

When I got to S.A.F.E. school, I went into our homeroom, but no one else was there, so I pulled up my sleeves to check on things. The hives had spread rapidly, covering my arms, and the blotches were big and swollen. At that moment another new believer walked in the room, and now I had someone to agree with in prayer. Yes! We agreed for my healing, I pulled my sleeves back down, just as the other students filled the little room. Perhaps two minutes later, I realized the itching had stopped, and to my amazement, when I checked, *all the blotches were gone*. Gone! The Lord was making Himself real to me!

During this same period of time, those early "honeymoon" days in the Lord, a friend named Johnny was at my house. He and his twin brother Jimmy were pretty notorious in our school for drinking and drugs, but for a brief moment, Johnny had come to faith. That day, he gouged his finger on a sharp piece of wood, literally taking out a chunk of flesh. Jon and Kerry were there as well, and we immediately prayed for his healing. When we saw him a couple of days later, we were all amazed. Not only was he healed, but there was no sign that he had lost some flesh. What a divine sign!

I understand that these were not incidents of raising the dead or opening the eyes of the blind, but there was no doubt that God heard us and even cared about the little things of everyday life. Our heavenly Father was real.

There were even the odd but very personal signs, like the night Jon and Kerry left my house to walk over to Jon's around 11:00 p.m., well after all the stores in Island Park had closed, including their favorite deli where

Saved!

they often bought sandwiches made a particular and somewhat unusual way, just to their liking. Late this night, they were hungry, but there were no food options. As they walked home, they noticed a small brown bag, carefully folded, sitting in the middle of the road, right between the yellow lines and under the traffic light. Intrigued, they opened the bag and found two sandwiches, also carefully wrapped and obviously untouched.

Even more intrigued now, they opened the sandwiches, only to find that these were the two exact sandwiches they would order from the deli, made to their precise specifications. Convinced that this was a gift from God, they ate the sandwiches with joy (although, to be sure, they did think twice, since it's not recommended to eat food found on the road!). God was showing us He was very near!

MY FIRST SERMON, AND THEN TIME FOR COLLEGE

As I spent hour after hour in God's presence in prayer and the Word, my only desire was to preach the gospel, and I had no intention of going to college. Why would I? For what purpose? As for the idea of going to a Bible school, that was quite foreign to our church and we used to say, "Seminary, cemetery" when it came to formal ministerial training. Plus, when it came to secular education, the whole college scene was part of the status quo I had rejected as a hippie, and I saw no reason to pursue college now. My parents, on the other hand, really wanted me to go, but I declined.

One Sunday morning, we had a guest speaker, which was incredibly rare. He was also Italian, and we knew him by his last name, "Brother Callela." He preached a message on Jesus being a teenager (I can still hear him say, "Think of it! Jesus was a teenager!") and how He honored His father and mother. When I came home from the service, my dad inquired about the service, as he was now used to me going to church. He asked, "Michael, what was the sermon about today?" I gave him the main sermon points, and he said, "How do you reconcile that with the fact that your mother and I want you to go to college more than anything, and you're not willing?" Being convicted by the Word, without hesitation, I

LIVING IN THE LINE OF FIRE

said, "Okay. I'll go." Little did I know how much academics would play a role in my life.

The summer of 1973, before starting college, my dad helped me get a full-time job, working with a crew that cleaned up trash at a local beach. While this gave me a new group of people with whom I could share my faith, I had much less free time each day, meaning less time in prayer and the Word. I'll share how that affected me in another chapter, shortly.

It was also in the summer of 1973 when I preached my first sermon on August 21. Two weeks before that, Jon preached his first sermon, and the next week it was time for Kerry. The pastor believed that all three of us were called to preach, and so we preached in the order in which we had come to faith, Jon, Kerry, then me.

It was an unwritten tradition in our church that if you were truly anointed to preach, you didn't use notes. This meant that not only did we have the pressure of preaching our first message, but we had to do so without notes. Jon got up to speak on August 7 and shared spontaneously, speaking whatever came into his mind for about twenty minutes. Afterward, he and I named his sermon, "Random Thoughts on Christianity."

The next week was Kerry's turn, and he started to preach a great message for about five minutes. Suddenly he realized what he was doing, speaking in front of maybe forty or fifty people, and he panicked. It was like a boy riding a bicycle for the first time, and he didn't realize his dad had let go of the bike. Dad screams out, "You're doing great," at which point the child realizes he's on his own, and he panics and falls over. That is what happened to Kerry. He got red in the face, stopped speaking, and sat down.

Then it was my turn, and because of the calling on my life to preach, coupled with the fact that I had memorized about 4,000 verses in the previous months, the Word just exploded out of me, point for point and backed by scripture. (My text was Acts 26:18.) I probably preached a forty-minute message in twenty minutes, and when I was done, Brother Gorge went up to the pulpit and said, "If Mike Brown is not called to preach, no one is called to preach." It was an extraordinary feeling.

38

Saved!

To this day, it is my habit to preach without notes, sometimes even teaching full classes at a seminary or Bible school without any notes (although, if possible, in school settings, I do my best to prepare notes for the benefit of the students). It's simply the way the Lord wired me and is part of His calling on my life, and it was a result of my upbringing in that Italian Pentecostal church.

More than one year earlier, I had attended a youth rally in the Bronx along with the kids from my church and young people from other CCNA churches. At the end of the service, as we were up at the altar on our knees praying, the pastor of that congregation, a respected, older man of God named Brother Bavarra, came over to me and began weeping over me in prayer.

Now at this time, as a new believer, I still had my long hair, so I hardly looked like some preacher in the making. Yet this man saw something in the Spirit, so I went up to him after the meeting and asked him what the Lord was showing him, having been moved by how intensely he prayed and wept over me. He told me that God showed him that I would be greatly raised up and one day they—meaning he and the other leaders— would all be looking up to me.

When we got in the car to drive home, Geri asked me to share what Brother Bavarra had said, since she had noticed him weeping over me at the altar and saw me speaking with him afterward. Brother George was driving, I was in the passenger seat, and Geri and some other young people were in the back seat. As I shared what Brother Bavarra said, I could see from Brother George's expression that he wasn't entirely happy. It wasn't that he disbelieved the prophecy. Instead, for good reason, he was concerned that it could go to my head. At that moment, though, I can honestly say that I was deeply humbled by the love and kindness of the Lord and did sense some kind of holy calling and destiny.

Yes, the Lord had plans for this former heroin-shooting, LSD-dropping, diesel gas-huffing, foul mouthed, "evil genie." How He delights in taking the foolish and worthless things of the Lord to accomplish His purposes! This way, no flesh can glory in His presence—and we are still flesh. All praise and honor and adoration go to Him alone.

CHAPTER 3

MEETING NANCY AND STARTING A FAMILY

Because our congregation was so small, there were not a lot of dating options, but pretty quickly, just months after we were saved, different couples paired up, including Jon and Kathy, and soon thereafter Kerry and Sharon. They would often go out together, and if my other friends were busy too, this left me alone. On the one hand, it was a gift from God, as I would shut the door to my bedroom and spend even more hours with the Lord. But I wanted to meet someone and eventually get married, and so it became my custom to pray this prayer every day: "Lord, give me the one You have for me when You have her for me, and give me patience until You do."

At one point, I asked the Lord to give me a vision of me walking down the aisle with my bride, showing me her face ahead of time. This way, I figured, I wouldn't even think of getting involved with anyone else. I would just wait for her. Needless to say, God did not give me that vision.

I prayed that same prayer daily during my final year of high school, and I continued to pray this prayer every day once I was in college; overall, praying those same words for more than two years. Then in the spring of 1974, that prayer was answered, and I am eternally grateful to the Lord. Simply stated, outside of my salvation, my wife Nancy is the greatest gift God has given to me. I can't imagine life without her! We have been together since 1974 and married since 1976, celebrating forty-nine years of marriage when this book is released. But it was hardly love at first sight—that is, not on her part.

41

LIVING IN THE LINE OF FIRE

To start at the beginning, Nancy was born November 30, 1954, making her two-and-a-half months older than me. Nancy's mom and dad were also Jewish, but she grew up in a very different environment than I did. Her mother was married four times, having no children with her first husband, then having both Nancy and her older sister Robin (born in 1952) with her second husband (Bruce), and then no more children with husbands three (Bill) and four (Ted).

Bill (stepfather number one) had three daughters of his own, all high achievers, along with being stepfather to Robin and Nancy, with Nancy being the youngest. (His other daughters lived with their mother on Central Park West in New York City but came to visit regularly.) Bill himself was a brilliant man, a certified genius, part of the Mensa Club. By profession he was an engineer, but he also served as a professor at several universities. Later in life, he made a career as a sought-after sculptor. But Nancy didn't mix well with him personally—he was a stern, exacting man who insisted on perfection, especially scholastically, and there was a constant stream of screaming and yelling between Bill and Lillian, Nancy's mother. It was anything but a peaceful environment. Nancy would wake up in the middle of the night hearing them fighting. Terrified, she would sneak out of bed and go to the stairwell to listen to the arguments downstairs, not knowing what was going to happen. Every family vacation was ruined because of the constant arguing between them.

Being the youngest child, and with little scholastic interest, Nancy knew that she always came up short in her stepfather's eyes. Although she had no aspirations to please him, she felt like an outsider and loser. Not surprisingly, she always felt like she never had a real father and a stable happy home. And although she did see Bruce, her biological father, regularly, she pined to see him more and live with him, even into her early teen years.

Interestingly, while Bill was not a religious man, he was active in the local synagogue, even serving as president. Nancy's mother, who also was not a person of faith, was active in synagogue life as well. But this is because it was a Reform synagogue, meaning very liberal and quite

42

Meeting Nancy and Starting a Family

humanistic in its approach to the Bible, Jewish tradition, and God. In such settings, you could be a committed Jew without firmly believing in the existence of God, and Nancy doesn't ever remember hearing the mention of God in the home. Going to the synagogue was a social thing rather than a spiritual thing, and the only thing Nancy enjoyed was the Jewish pastries served after the service on Saturday.

But even as a little girl, Nancy recognized there was something wrong with going to a supposed house of God that had none of the reality of God. The rabbi actually told her parents not to send her to Hebrew school anymore. She had no interest in what they were offering. And because she did not sense any semblance of God in the synagogue, by the time she was eight, she concluded that He did not exist. In her recollection, when she came to that conclusion, she felt sad, since the concept of a God seemed like a wonderful idea. Alas, it was just a myth! The older she got, the harder she became. In her mind, religious people were ignorant and weak, not willing to face reality, believing in a convenient fantasy. But not her. She was a realist to the core. And what once seemed like a wonderful idea now seemed absolutely stupid.

After ten years of marriage to Bill, Lillian divorced him and sent Robin and Nancy off to summer camp while the divorce proceedings were taking place and the home was being vacated. Nancy was about twelve then, and to add to the trauma of yet another major life upheaval, she had to leave behind their home which was situated on five wooded acres and was a sanctuary for her, where she would play and run and talk to the trees as a little girl. Now, Nancy's new home was a small, one-bedroom apartment together her mother and Robin. And who moved in next door? Bill!

Yet there's more. It was at that time when Lillian got involved with Ted, and he and Lillian would sleep on the pull-out in the apartment's living room, while Robin and Nancy, now fifteen and thirteen, shared a bedroom. An interesting arrangement! After a year or two, the four of them moved into a townhome as a "family"—but this was still *before* Ted and Lillian were married. Eventually they tied the knot.

43

LIVING IN THE LINE OF FIRE

In her teen years, Nancy got caught up in the counterculture lifestyle like millions of other American kids, drinking (Southern Comfort was her favorite), doing drugs, and living in sin and rebellion, also taking on a very strong feminist mentality. Then for some reason at the age of nineteen, she stopped drinking, stopped doing drugs, stopped smoking cigarettes (she was up to two packs a day), and broke up with her boyfriend. Shortly after that, we met. How that happened is a story in itself.

WE MEET FOR THE FIRST TIME

When Nancy and I met in the spring of 1974 we were both nineteen-years-old, but our lives had been radically different for the previous two-and-a-half years. I had been seeking God in prayer and studying the Word and sharing the gospel and attending church services day and night. Nancy was living in sin and mocking the very concept of God, believing fully that He was a figment of people's imagination.

One of my good friends whom I met in church, Danny, had just started working at a veterinary clinic, but he came down sick the first week and was fired. Talking with him a few days later, he said to me, "Mike, I know God gave me that job." I said to him, "You got sick and missed work. They fired you." Well, he turned out to be right, and shortly after that, the office called him and he was rehired.

Nancy had been working as a cashier and wanted a second job, going to that same veterinarian's office and applying for work. They told her, "We haven't hired a woman yet and never will." Shortly after that, to her surprise, they changed their mind, called her, and said she was hired. And that is how the Lord, in His sovereignty, initiated the plan to bring us together. (For all of you wondering if God can really bring the right person into your life, I'm telling you He can.)

Danny began to talk to Nancy about the Lord, but the subject didn't interest her. In fact, one day when she asked him why he believed a particular doctrine, Danny cited the writings of Paul, to which she asked, "Who the [expletive] is Paul?" Yet for some reason, when he invited her

Meeting Nancy and Starting a Family

to a church service, she agreed to go. (To this day, she really can't say why she agreed to it. She just did—as a hardcore, religion-mocking atheist.)

When she walked into our little church building on a Sunday morning, she noticed a tall guy standing in the first row of pews, instantly saying to herself, "I could never go out with someone that looked like him." (Yes, you guessed it, I was that guy!) So rather than love at first sight, it was more like rejection at first sight. (Seriously now, how many people see someone for the first time and say, "I could never go out with someone like that"? But that was Nancy's first reaction to me.) At the same time, it seemed as if God prevented this very foreign spiritual environment—people raising their hands and speaking in tongues and praising God—from penetrating into her consciousness. Had He not done that, she would have made her way to the door in disgust, because in her mind, displays of this kind were utter foolishness.

At the end of the service, I went up to talk with her. She was one foot shorter than me (she still is!), cute, with red hair, blue eyes, and freckles. And—you're not going to believe this—I asked for her phone number. (To this day I remember her personal phone number and her family phone number. She says I have no way of proving it since she doesn't remember what the numbers were.)

You might say, "Wasn't that a little brazen on your part? And since she wasn't a believer at that point, why would you do that?"

Well, I did that with virtually every new person who came to one of our church services. I would talk with them about the Lord and ask for their phone number so I could follow up with them. Young or old, male or female, that was my practice. (And yes, I remembered all the phone numbers back then.)

For some unknown reason (call it the Lord!) she gave me her number, we began to talk over the phone, and I invited her back to church. The question is why she would agree to go a second time, since she had no interest in God (or me). Once again it was the Lord! From that point, we began to speak for hours on the phone, and I kept inviting her to the services, and she kept coming.

LIVING IN THE LINE OF FIRE

But one night before I was going to drive her to service, I had a dream in which I was starting to like her. This scared me, since our church taught strongly against believers dating non-believers. So I immediately prayed about this, wanting to guard my heart. She, for her part, still had no interest in me, but she was fascinated by our conversations, where we somehow ended up talking a lot about demons.

Then one day while walking from her house, she was struck by the reality that personified evil existed—there was absolutely such a thing as evil in the world, and she could see it. Immediately, she thought to herself, "If there is evil, there has to be good. And if there is a devil"—whom she recognized was real—"then there has to be the opposite of that, a God. There cannot only be evil and satan in the world." Something just snapped into her consciousness, and she knew God was real. It was that simple.

Not long after that, on May 31, 1974, we attended a Friday night service in our church, and the speaker (not the pastor, who almost always spoke), gave a call for the lost to respond. She didn't go forward, but as we sat in my car on the way home and talked about what happened at the service, I asked her, "Did you want to go forward?" She said, "Yes."

I asked, "Do you believe the people wanted you to go forward?" Her answer again was yes. "Do you believe God wanted you to go forward?" Once more, yes. That meant it was the enemy who did not want her to take that step.

She was resolved to get right with God that night and put her faith in Jesus, but we had been having such a good time, talking and laughing, that it didn't feel right for us to pray together. More importantly, this was between her and the Lord alone. And so she went to her room and, in the midst of a very intense, very supernatural, even terrifying experience (which is her story to tell, not mine), she committed her life to the Lord and received forgiveness of sins. The process took several hours, as she wanted to be sure that she articulated to Him everything that needed to be articulated. No outside prodding. It was Nancy alone with God.

Meeting Nancy and Starting a Family

One week later, we became a couple, and one week after that, we knew we were in love and would spend the rest of our lives together. Now, fifty years later, I write these words with tears of gratitude in my eyes. There is no one like my bride, the very one I needed to help me run the race the Lord has called me to, my most wonderful, very best friend, the most loyal person I know on the planet.

We were married on March 14, 1976, two days before I turned twenty-one (She had just turned twenty-one on November 30, 1975, meaning she had to sign for the rental car when we got to California for our honeymoon; I wasn't old enough. This is something she has also enjoyed pointing out over the years.) I was still in college, and we lived on a very low budget, initially with the help of funds my dad had put away for me as I was growing up. By December 1978 both of our daughters were born, meaning that we had two children while I was still twenty-three and Nancy had just turned twenty-four.

And where did Nancy give birth to our girls? She had both babies at home (our first apartment was in Hempstead and our second in Long Beach, both on Long Island), saying to me bluntly one day, "Hospitals are for sick people, and I'm not sick." But that was a long time before home births were popular, and we had to go through a circuitous, quasi-underground system to find a midwife who would come to our apartment and deliver the babies. It also meant no pain-relieving meds of any kind. This was natural childbirth all the way—and yes, the labor was long and intense, twenty-three hours for Jen and fifteen hours for Meg.

I remember Nancy saying to me part way through the first agonizing labor, "Do something"—meaning, pray that the pain will let up. But no sooner did I begin to appeal to the Lord in prayer than I immediately thought of verses saying things like, "Howl like a woman in labor." Somehow, I couldn't muster up the faith, despite quoting to the Lord many of the verses I had memorized in the previous years. The intensity never let up.

One of the books Nancy read back then in preparation for childbirth (and in conjunction with our Bradley Method, natural childbirth classes)

LIVING IN THE LINE OF FIRE

was titled, *The Joy of Natural Childbirth*. I can assure you that after giving birth to Jen, she did not recommend that book to others.

But this is who Nancy is. If she has a conviction, she acts on it, come hell or high water, and in her mind, hospitals were for sick people, not for healthy moms about to give birth. And so, despite the intense first labor, Meg was born at home too.

To say that Nancy is not easily moved is a massive understatement. In fact, a prophetic brother once said to her, "You're the most stubborn person in the Spirit I've ever met." But then wanting her to understand that this was not an insult, he said to her, "Jesus was stubborn too."

For Nancy, though, it's not a matter of being stubborn. It's about being unable to deny the reality of something that seems clear to her, as if someone said to you, "Deny that you are a human being." It's not stubbornness to say you can't deny it. It's reality. That's how she is with deep-seated convictions: utterly immovable, and her immovability has strengthened mine as well.

This is not to say that Nancy can't be stubborn in the flesh too—after all, she has said that her theme song is Frank Sinatra's "I Did It My Way," which really describes her well. But when it comes to moral and spiritual convictions, it's a sanctified stubbornness that has helped me too.

More than forty years ago, I faced a very challenging situation as one of seventeen leaders in a church. About half of us, including most of the younger leaders and me, felt very deeply that the senior leader was not fit to lead the church at that time, but most of the older leaders were standing by him. And so, those of us who believed that the pastor was not able to fulfill his duties agreed that we would respectfully ask him to step down. Our entire leadership team met to lay out our viewpoints, in the presence of the senior leader, and to my shock, one by one, the other younger brothers who believed the pastor was unfit to lead, caved in on the spot, yielding to peer pressure or a man-pleasing spirit. In the end, we took a vote, and it was sixteen-to-one. (Yes, I was the "one.")

An older brother there, wanting to give me another opportunity to see the light, changed the nature of the vote, reversing the question we

Meeting Nancy and Starting a Family

were voting on. Now it was one against sixteen. I was still the holdout. But I could not move from my position for two reasons: first, spiritually speaking, I could not have been able to look God in the eyes if I had compromised; second, I could not go home to Nancy and look her in the eyes. The issues were too clear, and she could never have accepted me caving in just to get along.

More than a decade later, that same senior leader had lunch with me and said candidly, "Mike, you were right. I had no business leading the ministry then." It turns out the "one" was right and the sixteen were wrong. Nancy's clarity of heart and mind were a strength to me even though she was not physically present. Her presence was felt in other, just as tangible ways.

She is also quite singularly focused to the point that it's almost impossible to get her attention when her focus is elsewhere. She could be talking with someone on the phone and the house could start shaking because of an earthquake—this is hypothetical, for the record—and she would stay locked in on the conversation. It's not that she wouldn't notice the house shaking. It's just that the phone call would have her whole attention. (In contrast, when I asked her while writing this chapter how she would describe me in one word, she replied, "Distracted." That's my bride!)

More than twenty years ago, Nancy really wanted to learn how to do video editing on her Apple computer, having mastered lots of aspects of photo editing (using Photoshop). So she purchased Final Cut Pro, which I understand is quite advanced and highly technical. The software came with three, 500-page manuals, and she dug right in, starting on page one and reading every single page and reviewing every single example. I was away at that time, so she was totally undistracted, reading through the entire 1,500 pages during my absence that week. One night, she got so absorbed in going through the manual and understanding the software that she lost track of time. When she looked up, the sun was rising. She worked through the entire night without even knowing it. She was that locked in.

LIVING IN THE LINE OF FIRE

This intense, single-minded focus can also be seen when she has given herself to extended seasons of seeking God, spending all day and all night before Him, sometimes not moving from one place for hours (either sitting or kneeling), worshiping and praying and weeping and meditating on the Word. These seasons have been extraordinarily sacred and life-impacting, in some instances, changing her to the core of her being. (I'm an eyewitness to this.)

This is in keeping with the one-word description for Nancy given by our son-in-law Ryan (Meg's husband): tenacious (as he added, "in a good way"). Similar was our grandson Andrew's description of her as steadfast (he added, "for what means the most to her"). At key times in her life when she had to break through to a deeper place in God, she has taken hold of His promises with a holy tenacity and refused to let go no matter how many weeks (or months) it took. The intensity of these seasons has deeply moved and challenged me.

As for Nancy's toughness, my dad somehow picked up on this early on, telling her that she would have made a good pioneer woman in a previous century. The problem is that I would not have made a good pioneer man, so it's good we were born in the mid-20th century rather than in the 1700s or 1800s. To this day, Nancy has her own tool closet and a massive array of gardening equipment, from a tiller to huge augurs for drilling big holes in the ground. She also has kneepads and goggles and all kinds of saws. Not that long ago, I came home from a trip to see that she had installed a large mount for a long retractable hose. It was attached to a metal pipe used for gas lines which she had cemented into the ground, drilling the hole with one of her giant augurs and mixing the concrete. She did this all on her own.

Of course, I sometimes help her too, doing the grunt work and getting tools for her. (The good Yiddish word for this is "schlepper.") But since I don't know the names of many of the tools, she has to describe them to me. Often (perhaps most of the time?), I come running back with the tool, quite proud of myself for getting it right, only for her to say something like, "Does that look like a hand pruner?" Usually, by the second

50

Meeting Nancy and Starting a Family

or third time, I come back with the correct tool. Trust me. It's a *lot* of pressure (and a lot of exercise too!).

In the late 1980s when we lived in Maryland, I came home from an overseas trip to see that she had dug out a massive hole in the backyard—about 3½ feet deep and 11 feet by 9 feet, all with a shovel—put down a special rubber lining, and turned it into a small pond for koi fish and aquatic plants, replete with a little waterfall and stone edging. (She ran the electric under the ground to power the waterfall.) She did this all on her own, without any outside labor help. And although our house sat on just one-third of an acre, her landscaping was so beautiful that neighbors would bring their friends by for a tour. You can only imagine what she has done with the large piece of property where we now live in North Carolina. (Our last mulch order, delivered to the house, was 780 bags. And yes, I get to schlep them around to different parts of the property where she then painstakingly lays out the mulch throughout all the beds.)

One day, while working outside here in our current home, Nancy commented to me that I would not have survived as a caveman. My hands were too soft and I have no outdoor skills. (I told her I would have figured out a way to get others to work for me!) Another day, after I lifted and carried six very heavy stone planters, I asked her with a smile if she was proud of my muscles. She replied, "It's nice to have a husband." More recently, she texted me while I was on the road, telling me that the weather had gotten warm and that she spent the entire day outside gardening, cleaning up her large hosta bed. But, she wanted me to know, she missed me. That's because I wasn't there to dump the wheelbarrow for her. It's nice to be missed!

When Hurricane Helene devastated parts of North Carolina in October 2024, Nancy loaded her truck with supplies and went to help the hurricane victims, together with our younger daughter Megan. She did this twice, and then, the night before she left for another weekend of volunteer service, she needed me to run to the store and get her a big squeegee to help with the cleanup. Before she turned in very early (having to leave the next morning at 3:30 a.m.), I told her how deeply I loved her,

LIVING IN THE LINE OF FIRE

saying, "What would I do without you?" She replied, "What would I do without you? I would have to go to the store and get the squeegee myself." She said it in jest (well, partial jest!), but that is vintage Nancy. But when she returned home after four more days working in the muck and mud and contaminated waters, she posted her genuine appreciation for my care for her on social media: "Thanks to my faithful husband who served me a late dinner in bed and waited on me hand and foot when I arrived home." It was the least I could do![2]

OUR FIRST BIG TEST OF FAITH

Nancy does look to me as the head of the home, meaning the one on whom ultimate responsibility falls, the one who must carry the spiritual burden of caring for our family, the one who must face the crises head-on. So even though she is the strongest person I know and she runs everything in our home, from managing the finances to keeping every nook and cranny running smoothly (don't ask me where or what the main water shut off is or how to reset the electrical system after a power outage or how to maintain the well—handyman is not my middle name), it's my responsibility to bear the spiritual weight of our marriage and family.

This became clear when Nancy was pregnant with Jen, especially since the doctor who served as a backup for the midwife had a strict rule that if she went into labor more than two weeks before the due date or two weeks after the due date, she had to give birth in the hospital. The midwife had to honor this, and it seemed to be the better part of wisdom.

Nancy needed my support to be sure that this would happen, often asking me, "Am I going to have the baby at home?" It was tremendously important to her not to have the baby in the hospital, and she wanted to be sure that she would be able to have the baby at home, since she was very concerned that she wouldn't meet the deadlines. I had an assurance that she would have our baby at home, but I had no assurance she would give birth within the deadline. She said to me one day, "You're not planning on delivering the baby!" I really wasn't, but I simply felt sure that we would have the baby at home.

Meeting Nancy and Starting a Family

Our first child was due around May 19, so that meant Nancy could not go into labor before May 5, or after June 1. At that time, I was taking exams at college, and the moment the test was over, I would find a pay phone and call home, making sure she had not gone into labor. She had not. All good so far.

Thankfully, there were no problems of any kind with the pregnancy, and we kept speculating as to whether the baby was a boy or a girl, as did our friends. (For the younger readers, these were the days before ultrasounds, meaning that you didn't know if you were having a boy or girl until the baby was delivered.)

Nancy would continue to ask me, "Am I going to have the baby at home?" and I would give the same answer: "I'm sure you will, but I don't know if we'll make the deadline," which was now creeping up on us. Less than two weeks and counting until Nancy would be required to give birth in the hospital. The clock was ticking. What could we do?

We took long walks, but no baby. We took drives on bumpy roads, but no baby. Nancy even drank a lot of castor oil, which was supposed to clear out her system. It did, but no baby. Now the pressure was building. It was time for me to step up and be the head of our home and stand tall as a man of God.

I decided to fast for a breakthrough, not letting up until Nancy went into labor, but I failed miserably, getting a headache by mid-morning and feeling that I had to eat *now*, although I never ate breakfast and normally had no food before noon. So much for the fast. I couldn't even make it a few hours.

Now we were at the deadline. Two weeks past the due date! We didn't bring it up to the midwife, hoping she wouldn't notice, but this was becoming the worst-case scenario for Nancy, since it not only meant having the baby in the hospital but being induced and having the risk of extra chemicals in her body. A good friend came over, and I wanted to pray with him all night, determined to break through. He went home early and I fell asleep. So much for my persevering faith!

We went to see the doctor for a checkup, and he saw that things looked fine and was ready to send us home until he realized that Nancy was

53

LIVING IN THE LINE OF FIRE

almost three weeks late. That was it. He said, "If you're not in labor by Friday morning," which was June 10, just a couple of days away, "you're coming to the hospital and being induced." Some hours later—I don't recall the exact moment—but I got the assurance. I told her, "We'll meet the deadline! You'll be in labor by June 10."

Still, nothing had happened by midnight on June 9, so with Nancy lying down in our bedroom, I got on my knees in the living room of our little apartment, reading from Luke 11, where Jesus gave an example about bold persistence in prayer and then said this:

> So I say to you: Ask and it will be given to you; seek and you will find; knock and the door will be opened to you. For everyone who asks receives; the one who seeks finds; and to the one who knocks, the door will be opened. Which of you fathers, if your son asks for a fish, will give him a snake instead? Or if he asks for an egg, will give him a scorpion? If you then, though you are evil, know how to give good gifts to your children, how much more will your Father in heaven give the Holy Spirit to those who ask him! (Luke 11:9–13 NIV)

With tremendous faith rising in my heart, I prayed boldly, saying, "Father, You knew that at this very moment I would read these words and believe that they were true. That means that, unless You intended to deceive me, You must answer. Let Nancy go into labor!"

I was ready to stay on my knees all night, not letting go until the answer came, fully assured that the Lord would come through. And He did! Just thirty minutes into the prayer time, Nancy came out to tell me that she was having contractions. In fact, it had happened about fifteen minutes earlier, but she wanted to wait to be sure. Praise God!

Jen was delivered without incident about twenty-three hours later on June 10, just as the doctor required. And with the invigoration that only a mother can understand, after the agony of labor and missing one night's sleep, she stayed up the entire night with Jen laying on her chest, counting

Meeting Nancy and Starting a Family

her fingers and toes and amazed at the new life. There's something quite miraculous about the birth of a child.

Eighteen months later, on December 23, 1978, our second daughter Megan was born. This time, there was much less drama around the timing of the delivery (Meg was late, but only about nine days) but plenty of drama around the experience of the delivery. The midwife (a different woman this time around) was becoming impatient and wanted to go Christmas shopping. Nancy's slow delivery was spoiling her plans. At one point, she threatened to leave, and one of our friends, Patty, who was there to help out, assured Nancy that we could handle things on our own.

Nancy, for her part, was totally incredulous. The midwife, the woman responsible for bringing this new child into the world, was going to abandon her to go Christmas shopping? What a horrible moment. The whole purpose of a home birth is to have your child in the peace and security of your own home. Now Nancy was about to be abandoned, and to add insult to injury, the midwife made Nancy feel as if it was her fault. Thankfully she stayed for the delivery and Megan was born without incident (and at a whopping nine pounds).

One night later, on Christmas Eve, Nancy decided to go to her mom's house for the annual family gathering, taking Meg with her, despite the freezing temperatures and a winter storm. She dressed our newborn warmly and wrapped her up so just her little, reddened face was showing, before realizing that this was not a good idea. But Nancy was ready to go, with Meg actually in the car seat. As my dad said, she would have made a good pioneer. She definitely had (and still has) the spunk.

Later in the book I'll share more with you about my extraordinary wife, but bear this in mind as you read: I would not be who I am or where I am today without her.

CHAPTER 4

THE LURE OF ACADEMICS AND THE REAWAKENING OF MY FIRST LOVE

Very early in my walk with the Lord, when my dad saw that the conversion was real and that I was completely free from drugs, he said to me, "Michael, I'm glad you're off drugs. But we're Jews. We don't believe this. You need to talk to the rabbi." I was very happy to do this, since this gave me another opportunity to share my faith.

A new rabbi had taken over our little synagogue in Island Park, New York. He was twenty-seven and fresh out of seminary, and this was his first congregation. His name was William Berman. He was quite brilliant and had received his ordination through the Jewish Theological Seminary in New York City, and he took a real interest in me. We have stayed in contact on and off over the decades, as recently as 2019, and he actually wrote an endorsement for my 1992 book on Christian antisemitism, *Our Hands Are Stained with Blood*.[3]

We were scheduled to get together for the first time on January 24, 1972, after the Monday night prayer meeting at church, but that particular night was the night I was filled with the Spirit and spoke in tongues for the first time. And that called for celebration—pizza at Geno's in Long Beach! But since he and my dad were expecting me, I stopped by the shul and said to them with excitement (and without the slightest clue about how to express things to Jewish men), "I was just baptized in the Holy Ghost and can't meet tonight."

Rabbi Berman smiled and said, "Mazal tov!" (the Jewish phrase for "congratulations"), taking it all in stride and agreeing to postpone our

LIVING IN THE LINE OF FIRE

meeting for a few more days. I liked him! In the weeks and months that followed, he and I met face to face and talked often by phone. He was committed to seeing me come back to Judaism and began to introduce me to other rabbis, realizing that the spirituality of our local synagogue was lacking. But he did challenge me head-on, saying to me one day, "How can you tell us what to believe when you can't even read Hebrew and I've been studying it all my life?"

I told him I planned to study Hebrew in college, but in the meantime, I was using the Hebrew dictionary in the back of Strong's Concordance. He replied, "Meantime, shmeantime. If you don't know Hebrew, it doesn't mean a thing."

Sometime later, in the summer of 1973, Rabbi Berman drove me to Brooklyn to spend the day with two ultra-Orthodox Hasidic rabbis, part of the Lubavitch sect. This has become the most influential Jewish movement in the world today in terms of Jewish education and outreach but was fairly small back then. Rabbi Berman had realized that, in his words, I was a much more pious person than he was. Consequently, he reasoned, if we had both been Buddhists, I would have been a more pious Buddhist than he. So he said to me, "You need to meet Jews who are just as spiritual as you are, the difference is that their beliefs are right."

He was definitely on to something, as these rabbis also spent hours every day in study and prayer, which deeply resonated with me. And as I peeked into their synagogue, they certainly looked much more authentically Jewish than I did, not to mention that this synagogue certainly seemed like a more appropriate place for a Jew than a church. Rabbi Berman even joked with me saying, "They don't have a box with yarmulkes in the front" like we had in our synagogue. That's because the men here were deeply committed Jews who wore their skullcap all the time. In the circles in which I was raised (along with most American Jews), you only wore the yarmulke in the synagogue or for special Jewish celebrations, and if you didn't have one of your own, you could find one in the box.

Those hours I spent with those rabbis rattled me. I would quote my verses to them in English, but they would reply, "Oh, that English translation is so bad. You need to see what the Hebrew says."

58

The Lure of Academics and the Reawakening of My First Love

They would then point at the words, letter by letter, which made me feel like a little child, not because they were demeaning but because I had forgotten the little Hebrew I had learned in Hebrew school. How could I tell them what to believe? And contrary to my dealings with cult members and others, they had an answer for every argument I raised. Even if the argument wasn't entirely satisfying, it still stymied me for the moment. I knew without a doubt that Jesus had changed my life, but I had no answer for some of their challenges. For the first time, I felt shaken. I had to follow the truth, wherever it led. There was no other choice.

That's why I took a Hebrew class my first semester in college, attending Queensboro Community College in Queens, New York, where I enrolled as a Music Major. As I explained in Chapter 2, I had no intention of going to college and only went to honor my parents. In fact, I had skipped taking the PSATs during the eleventh grade and only took the SATs in twelfth grade. And although I scored well on the exams (especially on the math, getting a score of 720), because I had no formal grades my last two years of high school (because of S.A.F.E. School!), other than my grades for Band and Orchestra, I had to enroll in a community college. After two years, the plan was for me to transfer over to Queens College, which had an excellent music program.

But Queensboro only had classes in Modern Hebrew, the kind spoken every day in Israel, whereas my interest was in biblical Hebrew, an ancient language which is no longer spoken. So while taking that first class in "Ivrit" (that's the word for "Hebrew" but used to mean contemporary, spoken Hebrew), I asked Rabbi Berman to recommend a textbook I could use to teach myself biblical Hebrew. He recommended Thomas Lamdin's *Grammar of Biblical Hebrew,* not the easiest introduction to use but one that I dove into with zeal, working through every chapter and lesson.

But I wasn't interested in learning to speak Hebrew, so while I did fine in the class, I never went to the language lab to listen to the tapes, as we were encouraged to do. In fact, the Hebrew accent sounded odd to me, and I didn't try to master it. That's why, to this day, my spoken Hebrew is way behind my biblical Hebrew.

LIVING IN THE LINE OF FIRE

As for being a music major, by the second semester I realized that while I was a good drummer and percussionist and had even shared the musician of the year award in my senior year of high school, I was clearly lacking in other musical areas. So I changed my major to Liberal Arts, which I absolutely hated. I wanted to read the Bible and pray, not read these other books! By the end of my second year, I couldn't take it anymore, dropping out of most of my classes—I didn't have the heart to write the papers and prepare for the tests due to my massive lack of interest—leaving a note for the various professors, requesting that they give me a "Withdraw Passing" grade. I would not get credit for the classes (which I had to make up later), but I wouldn't get an "F" on my transcript. Thankfully, they complied.

But things changed dramatically when I transferred over to Queens College, which was not far away. They had so many Hebrew classes! And since I had already taken two years of Hebrew, I decided to become a Hebrew major. There was only one minor problem. Because the program there was more advanced, third and fourth-year Hebrew classes were all taught in Hebrew, meaning that I had to get by with my imperfect hearing and speaking of modern Hebrew. But I knew enough to manage, and with my solid reading and writing and grammatical skills, I did well enough to earn an Honors in Hebrew award when I graduated. Now I was starting to feel academically at home.

MY HORIZONS EXPAND

When I started college, my only church experience had been my own home congregation and some meetings with other CCNA churches. I had also been deeply immersed in the Word and prayer, to the point that when I saw a poster on the wall at college one day, I mistook the word "job" for the biblical book of "Job," thinking that perhaps the sign offering "Job Opportunities" (which I pronounced in my mind like Job in the Bible) was an invitation to a Bible study on Job. Seriously!

Sometime during my first semester in my freshman year, I heard about an actual Bible study on campus led by a Christian fellowship.

The Lure of Academics and the Reawakening of My First Love

I attended with interest, and listened as one of the students shared his thoughts on a passage of Scripture. I wasn't impressed by him, waiting for my turn to share my perspective, which I did, quoting many verses in the few minutes I had. Afterward, one of the students came up to me, saying that he was impressed with my fluency in the Word, and as we talked, I found he was Pentecostal too, a member of the Assemblies of God denomination.

I explained to him that while I knew we agreed on a lot, I had heard that in some ways the Assemblies of God were a little bit off. He probed me, trying to see where we disagreed, and I could not find any fault in his positions. But hey, it wasn't *my* church, and my church was the really special one, of course.

Soon enough, my horizons began to expand, especially when I was strongly challenged by a professor of ancient history who had written a 700-page doctoral dissertation on ancient Akkadian literature (that is the language of the ancient Assyrians and Babylonians) and who did not hide his disdain for us incoming freshmen at a community college. He was above teaching ignorant young people like us!

But I had no answers for his challenges. How did I know the Torah was written by Moses? What made me so sure biblical history was accurate? What about the seeming contradictions? What about the apparent historical and archeological conflicts?

No one in my local church could help, since these were sincere people but with a very simple, non-academic faith, and that meant going to the one Christian bookstore I knew on Long Island and trying to find some solid books on biblical subjects, among which were R. K. Harrison's *Introduction to the Old Testament* and Alfred Edersheim's *The Life and Times of Jesus the Messiah*. It turns out these were good places to start. And once I became a Hebrew major, rather than college being a drudgery to be endured, it became a place to expand my knowledge base.

After enrolling at Queens College for my junior year, I saw that they also offered Classical Arabic, so I added that in, believing that the more I could understand languages that were similar to Hebrew, the better

LIVING IN THE LINE OF FIRE

I could understand Hebrew itself and increase my knowledge of the Hebrew Bible. And, having taken all my required classes during the first two years of college, I was free to take whatever subjects I desired.

So not only did I take multiple Hebrew classes during my junior and senior years, but I took two years of Classical Arabic, one year of New Testament Greek (this was by correspondence, for credit, since it was not offered by the school), one year of Latin (I knew this was an important theological language), one year of Yiddish (the colloquial language of many Jews worldwide for the past 1,000 years or so), and one year of German (to read, not to speak, since many of the most important theological and linguistic books were written in German). This meant that I took *six languages at the same time*, not the best course of action if you really want to lay good foundations.

As far as my spiritual zeal, I was still going to church regularly, hardly missing a service. But Nancy and I were now married with our first child, I needed to take responsibility for paying the bills, and what really moved me now was not so much the desire to preach as the desire to study. I was ready for grad school!

My dad was actually a bit surprised to hear this, since in his mind, college was sufficient. Plus, he had paid for my college (thankfully, as a commuting student to a city college, the tuition wasn't high) and now he would be paying for my graduate schooling. In my mind, though, while I knew I needed to get a full-time job to support our family, grad school was calling my name.

But something else happened while I was in college. My theological horizons began to expand as well. In the church where I came to faith, we had a very negative view of Calvinism. It was one of the few doctrinal systems that Brother George would actually speak against, and I inherited his negative view. Now, as I began to read more and more academic books from Christian scholars, from commentaries to systematic theologies, I discovered that most of the scholars were Calvinists. They were also *not* Pentecostal, quite decidedly. This made me wonder, "Could it be that they know something I don't know?"

62

The Lure of Academics and the Reawakening of My First Love

I also met a learned pastor who was a staunch Calvinist and very excited about helping me become one as well. And so, over the course of a couple of years, after much study and reflection, I became a Calvinist, although Nancy did not agree at all. This brought about a serious fallout between Brother George and me, because of which we left the church to find a new spiritual home. (This was 100 percent my responsibility. I was the one who changed, not Brother George.) But it was a terribly traumatic experience for us, since this was the only home we knew, and we revered our pastor. Still, I could not stay there, and this meant another new beginning.

With the help of one of my friends, who had also left our home church because he too became a Calvinist, we found another congregation to attend named Community Bible Church in Inwood, still on Long Island but right on the border to Queens and just a few miles from JFK Airport. Nancy wasn't happy with the move, and she never embraced Calvinism—not in the least. The night she got saved, she received an incredible revelation of how Jesus died for every human being, whereas Calvinism teaches He died only for the elect. But this was where we were going to attend church, and I was quite excited by it. On the one hand, the church was barely charismatic and didn't have a clear understanding of what the baptism of the Spirit was. On the other hand, this was a church that was very active in doing good works, even standing for pro-life issues back in the late '70s.

This was a church that cared for the poor in the community, a church that urged every family to take in refugees from Vietnam during the boat people crisis in the late 1970s and early '80s. Nancy and I joined in this effort too, first taking in a Vietnamese couple with their baby boy, and then a number of Vietnamese and Cambodian men over the years, all of them becoming part of our family with Jen and Meg. We also took in an American baby after her mom, who was single, got into a motorcycle accident and eventually took in the mother as well.

I also played drums in a band called The New York Salt and Light Company that was part of our congregation, and when we would perform

63

LIVING IN THE LINE OF FIRE

at local churches and coffee shops, our final song began with the words, "Jesus has a church, and it's militant." At a certain point in the song, when I sensed the unction, I would then preach a short message, challenging the believers to stand for life and to care for the poor and the refugee.

As a congregation, we were definitely rich in good works. We could have intelligent discussions about world issues, we fought against racism and injustice, and the pastor, Bud Woodward, a silver-haired (although only in his thirties), theologically educated, southerner, fully embraced my calling to academics. At last, I was in an environment that recognized who I was and what my gifting was. The problem was that all this time I was gradually leaving my first love, but I didn't realize it.

Back in the summer of 1973, before I even met Nancy, when I worked full time before college and didn't have six or seven hours to spend in prayer and the Word every day, rather than recognizing that this was a new season in my life, I felt condemned. I did not understand that those previous months, when I was able to spend so much time in the Word and prayer, were not going to be the norm. Instead, every day, I felt like I was falling short and not doing enough, and that produced a feeling of condemnation, as if God was not happy with me. (For the record, this was the only time as a believer when I ever struggled with a feeling of condemnation. I realize that is not the norm with most believers.)

I also had a sense from the Lord as a new believer that I was called to write, and I remember writing one or two paragraphs about faith after I was saved just a few months. I was so excited about it that I showed it to my dad and to Brother George. And even though we really didn't talk much about being "called to write" back then, I remember Brother George saying to me, "Maybe you're called to write."

I was certainly called to preach, but as time went on and I tried to write, I found that things did not flow the same way as when I was preaching. I could preach with passion and clarity and simplicity, and the words just poured out of me. But when it came to writing, I didn't have that same flow, and after a page of writing with passion and fire, my writing style quickly changed, becoming very technical, and that feeling

The Lure of Academics and the Reawakening of My First Love

of inspiration abated. This also frustrated me and helped to move me away from my first calling, especially when academic writing seemed to come so naturally.

There was one other thing that negatively affected me in terms of understanding my calling. In the church where I came to faith, we recognized the ministry of the pastor or the evangelist. If you were called overseas, you were a missionary. But within the States, the only ministry options were pastor or evangelist.

I was clearly not called to be a pastor, so Brother George and I concluded that I was called to be an evangelist, since my messages were stirring and called for strong responses, and in my spirit I saw myself preaching to crowds. But being an evangelist meant traveling to different churches, calling the lost to be saved, and praying for the sick. That's what evangelists did, and I sometimes felt pressure (totally self-imposed) to see sick people healed in the meetings.

After Nancy and I were engaged, while still in our first church, we drove to Connecticut where I preached for a congregation of about 100 people, which was pretty big for me back then. When I gave the call for full surrender to the Lord, every person in the building responded. Praise God! But as Nancy and I talked later in the afternoon, something was missing, and I didn't know what. During the night service, in keeping with what I thought I was supposed to do, I prayed for the sick, with some apparent healings. But when we got back home, I questioned whether they were real. It was only years later that I understood that, while I'm called to be an evangelist to my Jewish people, my main calling to the church was to bring a prophetic wake-up call—as a revivalist more than an evangelist, undergirded by solid teaching.

But not understanding this back in the mid-1970s and not having the grace to write with passion and power, I concluded that I was called to be a scholar, working to improve translations of the Bible and teaching at a seminary. I still envisioned myself preaching from time to time, since I always wanted to keep the fire burning, but now I realized my true calling. It was to be a scholar.

LIVING IN THE LINE OF FIRE

In 1977, right after I got out of college and before leaving our first church, I heard the Spirit say to me clearly one day, "Preach the Word!" Immediately, I knew exactly what it meant. It meant that I would travel from place to place and preach the gospel and be rejected for my faith and even suffer some level of persecution. But now, this was the exact opposite of what I felt my calling had become. I had come to the conclusion that I was not to be a preacher. I was to be a professor. I was on my way to grad school. So rather than embrace this "Preach the Word" message from the Lord with all its implications, due to my growing emphasis on academics more than intimacy (I was starting to leave my first love without even knowing it), I turned God's word to me into a nice sermon for others and preached a message at my home church titled, "Preach the Word!" God didn't speak to me about this subject again for the next five years.

NYU

That same year, in 1977, I was accepted at both Columbia University, which had a well-known program in Middle Eastern Languages and Literatures led by Professor Moshe Held, and at New York University, where their program in Near Eastern Languages and Literatures was led by Professor Baruch Levine. Because the classes at NYU were a little cheaper, I decided to go there, speaking with Professor Levine by phone and getting an immediate open door from him to come and study. And study I did, completely immersing myself in the classes there, taking either one or two per semester as my schedule would allow since I was working a full-time job. By my second semester, I was such a prodigious and promising student that I was granted a full academic scholarship, with even a minor stipend of a couple of thousand dollars a year to help with living expenses. In the end, NYU paid my way through grad school all the way through my Ph.D.

Every week, I came home from a class in New York City supercharged. I couldn't wait to dig into my books and study languages more and get into the biblical text. But rather than reading the Word to feast on the riches

66

The Lure of Academics and the Reawakening of My First Love

and treasures that were there, I was reading it more to master Hebrew and Greek. As for studying new languages, that continued to be my focus, adding Ugaritic, Akkadian (meaning Babylonian and Assyrian), Aramaic and Syriac, taking another year of classical Arabic, plus also working with various Semitic dialects. I also took classes in rabbinic Hebrew and medieval Hebrew, continuing also to study biblical Hebrew, maintaining a grade point average of 4.0 all through my years at New York University, culminating in my Ph.D. in 1985.

These studies were also very important for my Jewish calling, as I didn't want to have to rely on a commentary or dictionary (or rabbi) to tell me what the Hebrew said. Now I could study it on my own, in its original context and against its original linguistic backdrop. This would help me reach my people with the good news as well. (I'll return to my Jewish calling later in the book.)

I seemed to have such a knack for Semitic studies that I started working on my first scholarly article before I even earned my M.A., ultimately finishing it in 1987 after I graduated. (It was published by the Semitic journal *MAARAV* and is titled, "'Is it Not?' or 'Indeed!': *hl* in Northwest Semitic.") It was clear that I was cut out for this kind of work, and I felt quite sure about my future calling to scholarship. But Nancy, for her part, wasn't entirely happy with my new academic direction. Her biggest heart for me was—and still is—that I be a man filled with God, and that is what would change the world.

As for life in our Calvinist church, while Nancy did her best to adapt to the spiritual climate there, she knew things were missing—we were rich in good works but really lacking in spiritual intimacy and power—and she saw that I was drifting more and more into an intellectual religious faith and further away from being a man of the Spirit. That's why, when I finished my dissertation in 1985, we joked that in the Dedication at the beginning of the work, I should have said, "This thesis was completed with no help from my wife, who opposed me every step of the way."

I did manage to work and provide for the family during this time, even taking one semester off after our second daughter Meg was born in 1978,

LIVING IN THE LINE OF FIRE

first selling baby pictures to new moms (what a job!), then selling equipment for industrial boilers to improve their efficiency before actually selling the boilers themselves, despite my complete lack of knowledge of the field. All these jobs were straight commission sales jobs, and meeting new people and trying to persuade them to buy something came quite naturally. Soon enough, rather than selling boilers and baby pictures, I would be lecturing full time at a seminar and doing scholarly research. Everything seemed set until God interrupted it all.

PERSONAL REPENTANCE AND THE ROAD BACK TO MY FIRST LOVE

In 1976, when we were still at our first church, the Pentecostal church, Nancy and I were able to lead her sister Robin to the Lord. (Robin, if you recall, is two years older than Nancy.) Robin quickly became a passionate, faith-filled believer. Several years later, after we had joined Community Bible Church, she also became a member, but she and I had some strong theological clashes. She was way too Pentecostal for me at that point (and worse still, she was Word of Faith), since not only had I become a Calvinist, but I also tried to become a cessationist, denying the gifts of the Spirit for today. (For the record, as Nancy was reading this manuscript, this caught her by surprise. She didn't know I had gone that far!) This was partly because we had some bad experiences at our first church (being tricked by a Pentecostal charlatan), partly because I was studying the writings of so many non-Pentecostal scholars, and partly because of my pride. After all, it sounded much more sophisticated to tell my fellow-students and professors at NYU that I held to the Reformed Faith—the theologically orthodox faith!—rather than admit that I was a tongue-talking Pentecostal. They all knew that I was a believer, and I was quite unashamed of my faith. But being a bit more moderate was much more appealing to the flesh.

I bought books such as Robert Gromacki's *The Modern Tongues Movement* and B. B. Warfield's classic book *Counterfeit Miracles*, but the more I read, the less convinced I was of their positions. The Word was

The Lure of Academics and the Reawakening of My First Love

just too clear. Plus, on those rare times when I would really meet with the Lord in prayer, I would begin to speak in tongues, and I knew it was real. I reasoned that the gifts of the Spirit *were* for today but that much of what we were witnessing in the contemporary Charismatic Church was not the real deal, especially some of the TV stuff. As for my own spiritual life, suffice it to say that I could go one entire year without praying for a solid hour in any one day or without fasting a single day. I was absolutely not the man I used to be, and I had become quite critical of others, using my growing knowledge base to rip apart other preachers and teachers.

I was particularly harsh on those who taught that healing was always the will of God. In fact, when the pastor asked the elders (which included me, as an elder in training) to write up a paper summarizing our views on healing, my paper concluded that God could be expected to smite rather than heal based on Old Testament texts. He was the Lord our Smiter, not the Lord our Healer. (How ironic that, just a few years later, I wrote my doctoral dissertation on the Hebrew word for healing and then, a decade after that, wrote a scholarly book on God being our Healer, coming to the opposite conclusion of my paper when I was an elder. More on that later.)

Robin, for her part, was listening to teaching that affirmed healing as God's will and emphasized positive confession of faith. While attending a meeting in New York City, she was instantly healed of a serious elbow injury after the speaker had a word of knowledge about that condition. She returned to our church zealous to share her testimony and to proclaim that it was always God's will to heal the sick. I said in response (while teaching a home Bible study), "Well, Joni Eareckson prayed for a sign from God and broke her neck and is crippled for life." That's how hardened I had become.

To make matters even worse, when Robin continued to share her views with our church members, despite our warning her not to, even inviting our folks to some of these Word of Faith meetings, which was in strict violation of our directives to her, we excommunicated her for being divisive. That's right. I participated in the excommunication of my

LIVING IN THE LINE OF FIRE

sister-in-law for being divisive. She even had the audacity to tell me that I had lost my anointing!

But rather than react with anger, Robin began to pray for me all the more, and the Lord burdened her to intercede with real travail, beyond her understanding. The folks in her new church were praying for me, as was Nancy, as she too knew that I was heading in the wrong direction. Then the breakthrough began.

It was early in January 1982 when Robin visited our house with a young man named Chris. He struck me as very odd (with a funny-sounding last name too), and I was totally unimpressed by him. At a certain point in the night, though, after speaking well of my academic studies, he began to talk to Nancy and me as if he had lived in our home, referring to conversations we had and things that only the Lord knew. Nancy had not been impressed with him either and at one point, Chris spoke demeaningly to her when she scorned his words. Right at that moment, the Lord spoke to her, saying, "You prayed for Me to work but You don't like the person I sent!" (This came directly from the Lord to her heart; these were not Chris's words.)

On my end, I was glad that Chris recognized my calling to academics, but I, too, was rattled by how the Spirit spoke through him. What *was* this? Little by little, the Lord started dealing with my pride and hardness.

Four months later, in May, one of my close friends, named Mike, was at the house when Chris visited again, and this time, we began to pray for revival and outpouring, something our church believed in theoretically, based on past revivals in America, but something we hardly pursued. We prayed into the early hours of the morning, and I prayed with more passion and fervor than I had prayed in years.

But something else happened that night as I prayed with my friends. I saw myself preaching a message at our church, going through Acts and saying, "Forget your theology for a moment and just ask yourself the question: Have we experienced what is written here?" Over the years, this is how I received sermons from the Lord. I would hear myself preaching the words and then hear myself giving an altar call at the end, and when

70

The Lure of Academics and the Reawakening of My First Love

it came time to preach, I would do what I had seen in my spirit, even if it seemed counterintuitive. And every single time, it would happen as I had seen and heard in advance.

This time, in my internal vision, I heard myself saying, "We need to move the chairs from the front because there won't be enough room for the people to respond." This was something that had *never* happened in one of our services, where altar calls were rare and hardly any people responded when they were given. But now, in my mind's eye, I saw the altars full and people being baptized in the Spirit—something that was unprecedented in our church. I knew we were going to have an outpouring, and I was going to preach the message that ignited it.

When I woke up the next morning after praying with Mike and Chris, I felt embarrassed at how fervently I had prayed the night before. I thought to myself, "You're in worse shape than you realized!" How telling that I felt embarrassed simply for praying with fervor. What an indictment.

Over the months that followed after that night of prayer in May, Pastor Bud and the rest of our leadership team began to talk more and more about the need for an outpouring, especially when we encountered some people with demonic strongholds and did not have the spiritual authority to set them free. Something was clearly missing in our midst. Within me, it was as if layer after layer was being peeled off as the Lord brought me into a season of repentance for my coldness and pride. Each time I thought the repentance was over, another layer was uncovered. And with each month that went by, I longed more deeply to see an outpouring of the Spirit in our midst. But there was more work to be done inside of me.

FROM MADISON SQUARE GARDEN TO THE NASSAU COLISEUM

In September of 1982, I attended a huge gospel rally in Madison Square Garden together with almost 20,000 people, going to hear a well-known evangelist. I had always loved this man's preaching, and this was a great time to see him in person. As we all stood together singing, "Let's Just Praise the Lord," I *faintly* sensed the presence of God, which immediately

LIVING IN THE LINE OF FIRE

jarred me. I thought to myself, "I used to experience His presence every time I attended a church service in those early years, and it was much more intense than what I'm experiencing now. Yet here I am with 20,000 other believers, the presence of God is faint, and this small glimmer of His presence is the strongest I have felt it in years." Once again, I realized that I had fallen further than I had understood.

I thought, "But what can I do? I can fast and pray for a few days, and I'll get all revved up again. But it will quickly fade. Then what?" So I made a resolution. I would take a little step every day. If I wasn't praying at all, I would pray five minutes. If I was going to pray or read the Word for fifteen minutes, I'd make it twenty. I would draw near to the Lord, one realistic step at a time, until the Lord visited me.

The next month, October 1982, Keith Green had been scheduled to be in concert at the Nassau Coliseum on Long Island. But Keith had been killed in a tragic plane crash in July 1982, something that affected me deeply. I really mourned over the loss. So the concert was changed to a memorial concert, and God used it to change my life. It was my joy to tell the story to Melody, Keith's widow, when we met in 1989.

The first thing that struck me was the video footage they played of Keith in concert. He threw himself into the music! I was reminded of the passion I once had for the Lord, but it was no longer there. What impacted me even more deeply was seeing Melody worshiping the Lord with love and adoration, just months after losing not just Keith but two of their children as well. And I was deeply moved when she said, "If more people can be reached by his death than by his life, so be it."

Years earlier, that had been my attitude too. By life or death, Lord, be glorified in me! I had no agenda other than to preach the gospel. But now, I felt called to scholarship. Surely, I thought, I had to finish my studies at NYU and get my doctorate and become a top scholar. Was it possible that this calling had become an idol in my life?

Along with thousands of others, I responded to the altar call that night and made a fresh surrender to the Lord, giving everything over to Him, including my scholarship. In the days that followed, to my shock, He

The Lure of Academics and the Reawakening of My First Love

burned it all up. The calling to be a world-class Semitic scholar went up in smoke! Months later, when He gave me the go-ahead to finish my doctoral work, everything had changed. Scholarship had become a tool, not an idol, and that is how it remains to this day.

By God's grace, I have served as a visiting or adjunct professor at more than seven major seminaries, as well as given lectures at others, written commentaries on Old Testament books, served as the general editor of a massive, Messianic study Bible, delivered papers at high-level scholarly conferences (even at Harvard University), contributed to world-famous encyclopedic works as well as academic journals, conducted debates at some of the most famous universities in the world (including Oxford University), and written watershed books in Old Testament studies and Jewish apologetics. But all this came about *after* I died to scholarship as an idol, and to this moment, it remains a tool and nothing more.

So, I served as a Visiting Professor at Trinity Evangelical Divinity School (among other, top-notch academic institutions), contributed twenty-eight articles to the *Oxford Dictionary of Jewish Religion* (and other, highly esteemed scholarly publications), and delivered outreach lectures at Yale University and the Hebrew University in Jerusalem *after* I died to the idolatry of scholarship and embraced it as a tool. Who can fathom the ways of the Lord?

Over the years, the Lord has reminded me of this, making sure I never forget what comes first. And so, when I contributed a chapter to the honorary volume compiled for my academic mentor at NYU, Professor Baruch Levine, whereas all the other scholars had affiliations including Harvard and Yale and the Hebrew University in Jerusalem listed by their names, my affiliation was "Brownsville Revival School of Ministry." It was embarrassing for the flesh but good for the heart!

There has also been a steady pattern over the decades where I am cited incorrectly by another scholar. Either my name will be spelled incorrectly (Brown should be pretty easy to get right!). Or I'll be quoted in a book, but the footnote referencing me is gone. Or the reference citing my work will confuse me with someone else, making for a meaningless

73

LIVING IN THE LINE OF FIRE

citation. I have seen it happen again and again. It is certainly the Lord's doing.

But I digress. By the fall of 1982, the fire was burning again in me. I was fasting one day a week along with some of the other leaders from our church, I was praying more daily, and I had shared with Bud my vision of a coming outpouring. He believed it was coming too. Then it was announced that he would be stepping down because of burnout due to the many ministries the church had taken on (we kept adding more programs to help more people in need). He would step down on November 14, 1982. But which of the elders would preach the next Sunday, November 21?

There was a previously scheduled leadership retreat set for the weekend of the 21st, meaning that Bud and the other elders would be at the retreat together, but I couldn't attend because our band was playing that Saturday night. And so, because I was the only one on the leadership team who would be at the service on that Sunday, I was asked to take the service.

I knew this was it. The Spirit was coming on November 21.

CHAPTER 5

THE OUTPOURING, FULL-TIME MINISTRY, AND THE CALL TO THE NATIONS

On November 20, the night before I was to preach my Sunday message, as our band, the New York Salt and Light Company played and ministered at another church, there was a stronger presence of the Spirit than we had ever experienced. Something was clearly happening. But the next morning—the morning I had been looking forward to since May—I was under the weather, and when I got up to preach, I had no special sense of the anointing. Still, I preached the message as I received it back in May and I did just as I had heard in my spirit, telling the people at the end of the message to move the chairs because we would not have enough room for everyone to respond. And respond they did! The altar was full, and people stayed on their knees seeking God for a long time, longer than I had ever seen. Later in the day, to the thrilling of my soul, I started to get phone calls, such as this one: "Mike, when I was at the altar today, I began to weep before the Lord, then I started laughing for joy, then I started speaking in tongues." It was happening!

That night, at our monthly Sunday night prayer meeting, we had a powerful visitation lasting four hours. Prior to this, these prayer meetings were incredibly dry and boring, not to mention powerless, and even as leaders, we looked for excuses not to attend. But this night, the people came with expectation after encountering God in the morning service. They were stirred, and something was happening. We had four straight hours of fervent prayer, with much repenting and crying out to the Lord. Not only so, but the gifts of the Spirit were in operation, as if we had

LIVING IN THE LINE OF FIRE

become an entirely new congregation overnight, and more people were baptized in the Spirit. (And remember: this was not a tongues-talking church.) I felt like I was dreaming, and I was personally being transformed. I was on fire again!

The next day I was scheduled to get a haircut by a family friend. She did haircuts at the house that she and her husband shared with another couple from our church, along with their kids and Vietnamese refugees. As she was cutting my hair, I told her what the Lord was doing and how He had touched their friends who lived upstairs. She herself had been touched on Sunday, but she wasn't aware of the full impact of what was happening to others, including her friends upstairs. Suddenly, she came under conviction, going through the house and bringing out packs of cigarettes and then cartons of cigarettes, tearing them up and throwing them away. She wanted to break the habit. My haircut was interrupted before she was done as I prayed for her to be filled with the Spirit. She dropped everything and went off alone to pray—that's how gripped she was—and I left for my business appointment with a slightly unusual hairdo.

That night, a friend named Bobby F. called me, asking, "Mike, would you like to go pray for people?" This was *not* the normal thing we did in our church, but everything was different now. I called the woman who had cut my hair and asked if she had broken through in her prayer time and been filled with the Spirit and spoken in tongues. She had not, but she and her husband wanted to receive prayer. I said, "We'll come over!"

Shortly before the outpouring, Bobby had been filled with the Spirit, and over the years he had been more spiritually oriented than many others in the church. That Sunday, when the outpouring began after my message, he was sitting at the altar in a cross-legged position, looking at his hands. He told me later that his hands felt like they were on fire, and when he began to lay hands on people at the altar, they began to weep. I was watching as it happened but didn't know what he was experiencing at that time.

76

The Outpouring, Full-Time Ministry, and the Call to the Nations

As we sat in his truck ready to drive over to this couple's house, talking about what he had experienced the day before, I asked him about one man he was praying for at the altar. I asked him, "What do you feel is hindering him spiritually?" He replied, "I believe he's still holding on to his former unsaved girlfriend." I said, "I agree." He then asked, "Is her name Ellen?" I said to him, "You didn't know what her name was, did you?" He acknowledged that he not previously known her or her name. I had known her name, but the Spirit just revealed it to him. He began to tremble in holy fear. I was overwhelmed as well.

When we got to the couple's house, a younger friend named Frank was there. He was the one who called me to report how he had been dramatically filled with the Spirit at the service the day before. Also there was Bobby B., a dyed-in-the-wool Pentecostal who had gone to R.W. Shambach's Bible school and who rented a room in the couple's house. He always seemed a little out of place in our congregation, but he was committed to stay and was a man of prayer.

Several months earlier, he had seen a vision of our church building with the word "Ichabod" written over it, symbolizing that the glory had departed. He said to the Lord, "What glory?" (Remember that Bobby was thinking in Pentecostal terms, and there had certainly been no Pentecostal glory in our church.) The Lord said to him, "My glory will come to this church, but if My people reject it, I will write 'Ichabod' over the doors."

I had heard about this prophecy from Bobby before the outpouring, confirming the word the Lord had given me about a coming visitation but also bringing a sense of reverential awe. We did not want to play games with the moving of the Spirit.

Immediately after arriving at the house, I laid hands on the woman who had cut my hair, and she was instantly baptized in the Spirit and began to speak in tongues loudly and fluently. It was so instant and so intense that I was shocked. Then I prayed for her husband, and he was slain in the Spirit, falling on his back and confessing his sin out loud before the Lord. Then, with hands raised and a smile on his face, he too began to speak in

LIVING IN THE LINE OF FIRE

tongues. No one was prodding them to do this or telling them what to say or how to do it. This was a spontaneous response to the Spirit.

Frank was also pacing around the room, praying in tongues. Bobby F. was laying on his face, trembling under the power of God, and Bobby B. was marching around the room, worshiping the Lord in tongues and moving his arms in a manner that reminded me of an Indian war dance. It seemed like holy mayhem.

On my end, I was having a crisis. This was the stuff I had walked away from, except what was happening this night was much more intense. I used to see people slain in the Spirit in my first church as well as when I would travel and preach (the phenomenon was somewhat unusual back then compared to today), but I had written it off years ago. I even had a little teaching on why being slain in the Spirit was not from God. Now, in a congregation that never saw this happen, this man was slain in the Spirit. I didn't like that!

And the way everyone else in the room was responding was embarrassing to me. I had become sophisticated in my faith. I was a respectable Christian. This stuff was so emotional! But I knew to the core of my being it was from the Lord. When we have a powerful encounter with the Creator of the universe, our emotions *will* be stirred and sometimes our bodies overpowered in response to the Spirit's touch. So I said to my Father, "If this is what it takes for these people to be touched and for me to get back on fire, I welcome it." This meant more death to the flesh but so much life in the Spirit.

After a while, Bobby F. said to me, "It's time to pray for Bev," a dear sister in our congregation who was battling a serious illness. She was a friend of Bobby B.'s who was also more Pentecostal than most of the congregation. The problem was that Bobby F. was so overcome by the Spirit he couldn't drive. I got in the driver's seat of his truck, but because it had an unusual stick shift, we had to coordinate our actions. When it was time to shift, I pressed down on the clutch, he moved the stick in the right position, and on we would go. It was a memorable ride.

When we arrived at Beverly's house, Bobby went straight inside like a man on a mission. He had a prophetic word for her that was right on, and

The Outpouring, Full-Time Ministry, and the Call to the Nations

she began to weep. We prayed together with her and some others who were there until 3:00 a.m. The outpouring was real!

The next scheduled service was Wednesday, the night before Thanksgiving, and by then, three days into the outpouring, a number of congregants had either been delivered from sinful habits or filled with the Spirit and spoken in tongues or both. I knew they planned to testify at the service, but when the time came for testimonies, they were ashamed to say what really happened, with one after another downplaying their experiences. I was devastated. The Lord had moved powerfully in each one of their lives, but they were embarrassed of the Spirit's work.

Overwhelmed with a burden to pray, I went into an adjoining room with another brother, crying in tongues for the first time in my life because of what I had just witnessed. I heard the Spirit say, "As quickly as I came I will leave because My people are ashamed to give Me glory." We were already on the verge of Ichabod!

I went back into the service devastated and gripped, rocking back and forth in my seat. The assistant pastor was preaching that night, and when he finished the message, he dismissed everyone saying, "I know you've got preparation for Thanksgiving, but if you'd like to stay and pray, the altar is open." He, too, believed God was ready to move, but he didn't want to push anything.

I ran to the pulpit—literally—and began to shake from head to toe as I spoke in tongues and then interpreted. To this day, I can't remember another time when I was gripped quite like that. And then the prophetic message: "If you have anything more important to do than seek Me, you need to run out of this building."

Instantly, the altar was full as conviction cut through the congregation like a knife, with some people staying on their knees for three hours, weeping before the Lord and encountering Him afresh. One of Nancy's best friends was sobbing so deeply that she was choking on her tears, continuing to cry in her home the next three days. God was visiting us!

From that point on, we had to open the church building every Sunday night for prayer. Each prayer meeting would last for three, focused, intense hours, without music or teaching. No props. People were even

LIVING IN THE LINE OF FIRE

saved and delivered at these gatherings. Spontaneous prayer meetings would also break out at various homes after meals, with deep repentance, supernatural spiritual encounters, and baptisms in the Spirit.

But some of the leaders were not happy with what was happening, feeling it divided the congregation into the "haves" (who had been powerfully touched by God and baptized in the Spirit) and the "have nots" (who had not). And not everyone welcomed the intensity of the repentance message, with some of the leaders putting the brakes on the Spirit's moving in our services, leaving no room for God to speak and act. It was back to business as usual. How utterly heartbreaking.

And so, on March 27, 1983, after weeks of the Spirit being quenched, the outpouring ended, to my absolute devastation. I could not stop sobbing, but I realized it was over. (Nancy realized it before I did, motioning with her hands to me from the back of the church that the dove had flown on the evening of the 27th at our Sunday night prayer meeting.) For me, though, a lasting change had occurred. I could never go back! From here on, wherever God would send me, I would seek to carry the fires of revival.

Although Pastor Bud wanted me to stay on despite our disagreements, I felt it was best to resign and leave the church. I wanted to honor his authority, not undermine him, so Nancy and I resigned our membership. But when one of my friends said he wanted to launch a coup against the pastor, I told him, "You need to leave. He's the pastor, and if you differ with him, then *you* go." He, in turn, went to the pastor and said, "Mike Brown is trying to pull me out of the church."

This resulted in us being excommunicated—what goes around, comes around; we had excommunicated Nancy's sister Robin and now we were excommunicated—and so some of our dearest, closest friends wouldn't even talk to us. Nancy and I immediately joined another congregation, wanting to be in submission to authority—it was the church that Robin attended—even though I didn't fully agree with the theology. But the pastor, a fairly young, blond-haired man named Frank Mangialomini, recognized the validity of the outpouring, and saw God's calling on my life, which was a great encouragement to me.

The Outpouring, Full-Time Ministry, and the Call to the Nations

It was during this time when the Spirit began to move on me in deep travail, with agonizing groanings of intercession. I had experienced this for the first time during the outpouring, resulting in dramatic deliverances for those we prayed for, but now this prayer experience was deepening. On April 4, 1983, gripped by the Lord, I wrote down these words: *"The call to wake up a sleeping Church; to prophetically call God's people to repentance; the time is at hand."* (Pastor Frank had asked me if I journaled, and when I told him no, he told me I needed to start. How thankful I am for his counsel. This was the first word that I officially journaled, and since 1995, I have been journaling daily. I could not have written much of this book without these journal entries.)

During the outpouring, a number of us read books by Leonard Ravenhill (1907-1994), especially *Why Revival Tarries* and *Revival Praying*. We went to hear him preach at Brooklyn Tabernacle in April 1983, and we were amazed to see hundreds of believers rushing to the altar to cry out in prayer and repentance, just as we had seen during the outpouring. We also listened to tapes by Art Katz (1929-2007), a deeply spiritual Jewish believer, and his messages brought searching conviction. When Art and I became friends years later, I told him jokingly, "If there's any flesh in heaven, you'll find it!" As for Leonard Ravenhill, he would play a very key role in my life, as would David Wilkerson. I'll share more about my relationship with them in Chapter 6.

In the early spring of 1983, I was gripped in intercession again, literally rolling back and forth on the floor as I laid on my face, groaning and travailing. The Spirit said to me, "You will be used in a revival that will touch the whole world." Immediately I thought to myself, "You're crazy. You have lost your mind. Your friends are right. You're deceived."

I thought of men like William Branham and John Alexander Dowie. I had heard that before they died, each of them imagined themselves to be Elijah the prophet. "That's what happened to me," my mind said. "You have gone off the deep end." I didn't think I was Elijah—let me make that very clear!—but I thought to myself, "You are obviously deceived."

Yet the more I prayed, the more God confirmed this word to me, even bringing confirmation of this calling through a respected elder who

LIVING IN THE LINE OF FIRE

had been part of excommunicating me and was a friend of my previous church. I shared the word I had received with him in order to test it (and test myself), assuming he would tell me I was off my rocker. But I didn't dare tell him that the revival I would be part of would touch the entire world. So I softened it to say that the revival would touch America. To my shock, he said to me that the only thing that mattered was the roll call in heaven—meaning, what God said, not what people thought—then asking me, "Why just America? Why not the whole world?" Amazing!

Thirteen years later, God brought this word to pass, calling me to serve as a leader in the Brownsville Revival, which saw a cumulative attendance of roughly three million people from more than 150 nations over a five-and-a-half-year period, including 300,000 different individuals who responded to the altar calls. (I'll share more about that extraordinary happening in Chapter 7.)

As for the pastor of the church which excommunicated me, we became friendly again in the years that followed. He was always gracious in our personal interaction, even if our relationship was a bit formal and strained. More than a decade later, he said to me with tears as we sat face to face, "Mike, the next time God moves, I don't want to miss it." He was acknowledging that the outpouring had been real. He was also able to visit Brownsville several times and was like a kid in a candy shop. His second daughter, Susanna, graduated from the Brownsville Revival School of Ministry, and I performed the wedding for her and husband James.

"QUIT YOUR JOB AND GO TEACH AT CHRIST FOR THE NATIONS"

As a new believer with Brother George as my pastor (1971-1977), I learned the importance of spiritual foundations: godly living, intimacy with God through the Word and prayer, and the joyful sharing of my faith. With Bud as my pastor (1977-1983). I learned to appreciate the broader Body of Christ and saw the importance of engaging culture with the gospel. With Frank as my pastor (1983-1986), I was now a bit older in the Lord and enjoyed more of a peer relationship, with him as my

The Outpouring, Full-Time Ministry, and the Call to the Nations

senior. Still, from Frank I learned the importance of hearing the voice of God and stepping out in the Spirit.

In the immediate aftermath of the outpouring and the excommunication in the spring of 1983, Frank encouraged me to sit back and be renewed in the Lord for a season, and I knew that he was right. At the same time, the fire was burning within me in greater and greater intensity, and I sensed that soon, the Lord would be calling me into full-time vocational ministry. Frank mentioned to me one day that a new Bible school was opening in Stony Brook, Long Island, Christ for the Nations Institute of Biblical Studies (CFNIBS), an extension of a well-known school based in Dallas. (I was not familiar with the Dallas school at that time, but it has a wonderful history.) He told me I should pray about the new school. I replied, "Why do I need more education?" Wouldn't this be a step backward educationally? I was also thinking to myself that I already knew the basics I would learn at a school like that. He answered, "I meant for you to teach there."

Nancy and I decided to attend one of the meetings at CFNIBS during an inaugural seminar the school was holding in June; and as we drove home after the meeting, she began to sing, "We're moving to Stony Brook." Somehow, she knew we'd be back there. Our daughters Jen and Meg absolutely loved the children's service too. Just days later, on July 5, 1983, I was attending a midweek service at our church. One of the congregants taught that night about tithing, and at the end of the message, Frank stood behind the pulpit and dangled the Bible over it, saying, "Sometimes I feel as if God is saying to us, 'I dare you to believe it.'"

Immediately, I felt stirred by the Lord, hearing Him say to me, "Go out on the street and find someone to witness to." I found a middle-aged couple about to go into a restaurant and said to them, "If you want to find out how to receive eternal life and forgiveness of sins, check out the church that meets in that building" (pointing to where we met). They politely smiled at me and quickly went into the restaurant, but I knew I had obeyed the Spirit's voice, as if it had been a test.

LIVING IN THE LINE OF FIRE

When I got back into the building, my heart was leaping. I said to the Lord silently, "It's time to quit my job." I heard the Lord reply, "Yes!" "I'll start knocking on doors and the Lord will pour in the funds." Again, that divine, "Yes!" Then, as a question rather than a statement, "What about CFNI?" One more time, "Yes!" My Father was cheering me on and directing me.

I went home and told Nancy I was going to quit my job and teach at CFNI. She burst out laughing, not out of unbelief but at the suddenness of the announcement. I called my mom to tell her the news. We would be moving further out on the Island, about an hour from her house, but we'd bring the grandkids over once a week for dinner and to hang out. The next day, I called my boss at the secular job where I worked, telling him that it would be sometime in the fall when I would be leaving my job to teach at a Bible school. He was happy for me. The only problem, of course, was that the school had no idea I was coming. But that was God's problem, not mine!

Pastor Frank had enrolled in a class at CFNI that summer, so I decided to visit the school with him shortly after receiving that word from the Lord. The man leading the meeting that day, a faculty member from the Dallas school who was overseeing things until the director arrived, had a prophetic word over me, confirming that God was about to call me about of my job (which I told him involved selling industrial boilers). Soon, he said, I would be heating people up for Jesus. On the way home, Frank and I rejoiced, saying to each other, "He's alive!" The Spirit was active and speaking.

This faculty member told me that he would leave my information with the incoming director of the school, Alastair Geddes, an imposing Scotsman, over 6' 5" tall. Alastair was in the first class at CFNI in Dallas in 1973 and then served in Zimbabwe where he led a prominent church and ministry. I read his testimony in the CFNI magazine as he was enroute to the United States with his family. It was replete with references of God speaking to him, so I understood he would relate well to that language.

The Outpouring, Full-Time Ministry, and the Call to the Nations

Alastair arrived in the States and I made an appointment to meet with him. With clear and definite divine intervention, we had sold our house and bought one near the school—this was without being hired or even known by Alastair, as I was being moved by supernatural faith. In fact, when I shared this extraordinary series of events with my longtime friend Rabbi Berman (the rabbi who had reached out to me when I was a new believer), he said to me, "Why does it seem as if God is your next-door neighbor?" It was a season of miracles.

When I met with Alastair, I proceeded to tell him how God told me to quit my job and go teach there, making sure I used a lot of "God language" in our meeting, just as he did in his testimony in the school magazine. Only later did I find out that he personally hated talk like that. It was much too spiritual sounding for him. He was more of a down-to-earth, practical wisdom kind of guy. As for his testimony that was printed in the magazine, someone else had written it for him. He was too busy moving with his family to America, so someone who knew his story told it as they thought he would, but not, in reality, the way he would have told it at all. Years later, we laughed about this. But at the moment, when we met for the first time, despite the off-putting nature of my manner or speech (too much "God talk" for him!), he sensed God's hand on our visit. He said to me, "Right now, we have all the faculty we need, with an Old Testament professor and a New Testament professor. But you will be the next person we hire."

Having sold our house, we moved to our new location, and in October of 1983, I started teaching night classes at the school, one on Proverbs and one on Psalms. This gave me a way to get to know some of the students even before I was employed there, and despite some real financial challenges, Nancy and I made it through that fall and early winter season of 1983. Reading Norman Grubb's classic book on Rees Howells, *Intercessor*, also helped my faith, as the Lord met us just in time over and again.

Then there was a sudden and unexpected development. The Old Testament professor, who had moved from Dallas, felt called back to

85

LIVING IN THE LINE OF FIRE

Texas and gave his notice. He was leaving and I would be taking his place, starting in January 1984. Praise God! As for my salary, as a married man with two children living on Long Island, it would be $1,450 per month. Yes, *per month*. We would still need to live by faith. Still, the first time I received a check from the school, I was amazed. I would have *paid money* for the privilege of teaching these students. Now it was my vocation. Incredible!

As for me taking the place of this Old Testament professor, Alastair was waiting for the time to make the announcement, and the students had no idea about the coming transition. Then, because I was in town on a particular Sunday and the school had an afternoon service, I decided to attend. A local pastor named Abe Smith was speaking, and at the end of his message, he had a prophetic word for the Old Testament professor, who was also there in the meeting: "You will be leaving," he said.

Alastair was absolutely shocked. Others did not know about this! Alastair consulted with a few people to be sure that nothing had been said to Abe, then he got up, still stunned, and made the announcement. Yes, the Old Testament professor, named Leonard, was going back to Dallas. And, Alastair said, "It just so happens that Mr. Brown is here today. He will be your next Old Testament professor." The Lord was guiding every step.

As for my time serving under Alastair at CFNI (1983-1987), I grew in wisdom and interpersonal relationships. He was like a detective, spotting things others would miss, with keen discernment. He was also a gifted counselor with lots of insight into human nature. He said to me one day, "I don't doubt your ability with God, I only doubt your ability with people." My zeal needed some bumper guards.

About ten years prior to my calling to CFNI, probably in 1974, I had preached my thirteenth message at a Tuesday night service in my home church. It was a strong word of rebuke and challenge, urging the young people to get out on the streets and share the gospel. The youth responded deeply. But at the end of the message, Brother George got up and prayed, "Lord, temper Your word that went forth tonight." I was not happy.

The Outpouring, Full-Time Ministry, and the Call to the Nations

The next day, I called his house to speak with him, but his wife, Marie, told me he was praying. I called back a few more times, and each time, she said, "He's praying." Finally, she said that he would meet with me that night before our Wednesday night service. As for him praying all day, it was for me.

We met outside, standing on the grass field next to our temporary building on Long Island. I asked him why he prayed that the Lord would temper my message. He said to me, "You're a young whippersnapper. You're wet behind the ears," explaining that I had no right to speak in such a strong manner to the older brothers and sisters, some of whom lived sacrificially so they could donate more money to the gospel.

I said, "But the young people loved it." He affirmed that they would, but, he explained, I needed to speak with a different tone and attitude when addressing the whole congregation. I drank in his words deeply.

Now, in the mid-1980s working under Alastair, there was a different tempering that took place, a growing in wisdom and in the practical out-working of my spirituality. This, too, was an essential part of my spiritual journey. (Nancy would tell you that I still have a way to go!) As for my burden for the outpouring of the Spirit, that first summer, in 1984, as I taught on the tabernacle (not by my preference but in response to a request), we had a mini-outpouring that lasted three weeks. By God's grace, I would carry this wherever I went.

To my surprise, though, just weeks before I started teaching full time at the school, I heard the Lord tell me that my time at CFNI would be limited. I had thought I would teach there for decades. Instead, it was only for four years, from 1983-1987, moving to Maryland with the family to launch a Messianic Jewish Bible institute, then returning once a year to teach until 1991 when the school closed.

For Nancy and our kids, CFNI represented a beautiful season of life without much conflict. It was a place where we had great friends, a great community, and a great ministry environment. To this day, we remain close with a number of the friends we made back then, including the couple who runs our ministry, Gary and Cindy Panepinto, who were our

LIVING IN THE LINE OF FIRE

neighbors in those days and who took some night classes at the school. We've known each other since 1983 and now work together side by side as close friends and colleagues. How wonderful!

We also remain close with some of our former students. They are now dear friends and colleagues, including Ron Cantor, who is a Messianic Jewish leader in Israel, married to his Israeli wife Elana, and Bryan and Michelle McCrea, church planters here in the States. It was Bryan who led Ron to the Lord when they were best friends in high school, and Bryan who asked me to help Ron (then known as Ronnie) as a new believer whose dad had brought him to meet with rabbis in Brooklyn. I was able to coach Ron through those meetings, and that's how we first connected.

During these years, I also began to travel and preach again, traveling by plane to preach for the first time in 1985. Prior to this, I had only been invited to speak at churches within a few hours driving distance, but now the distances were getting greater, meaning it was time to fly. It was also during this season when we met Ari and Shira Sorko-Ram (it was actually during that short outpouring at CFNIBS in the summer of 1984). Shira was the daughter of Gordon and Freda Lindsay, founders of CFNI in Dallas, and Ari had been a decorated athlete as well as a TV and movie actor. (Gordon lived from 1906-1973; Freda succeeded him as the school leader and went to be with the Lord at the age of ninety-five in 2010.)

Ari and Shira were Messianic Jewish pioneers in Israel, and the conversations we had were eye-opening for me in terms of Jewish believers living as Jews. They remain dear friends to this day (they are in their 80s as I write). Their daughter Shani graduated from our school in Pensacola, where she met her husband Kobi (then Jim) Ferguson. Kobi and Shani inherited the leadership of Ari and Shira's ministry, Maoz, and they are like family to us.

Ari and Shira invited us to minister in Israel in 1986, which was also the first year that Nancy and I traveled outside America to speak, first to Vancouver in the summer of 1986 and then to Israel in December. The

The Outpouring, Full-Time Ministry, and the Call to the Nations

next year, through connections forged through the school, I traveled to England to speak, then Nancy and I went together to Italy. The nations were now calling. As of this writing, I have flown overseas to minister on almost 180 trips, with more than 210 trips total outside the USA when including Canada and Mexico. (Yes, that's a lot of time in the air and a lot of time on ground in the nations!)

Earlier in our marriage, I had no desire to travel, very content to stay home and study. On the plane to California on our honeymoon, I remember reading a book by the Semitic scholar James Barr titled, *Comparative Philology and the Text of the Old Testament*. Surely, I could read this and my other books at home! But when traveling back with Nancy from meetings in Tulsa, Oklahoma, on July 29, 1984, during the entire flight back to New York, we saw a circular rainbow outside our window with the reflection of our plane inside it. I sensed that I would be traveling a lot and that God would protect me as I flew, journaling, "Angels watching over me?"

By God's grace, I have now been to India 30 times (normally 40-45 hours of travel each way), Italy 28 times, Israel 18 times, England 18 times, Germany 15 times, South Korea 13 times, Holland 8 times, Singapore 5 times, the Philippines 4 times, Finland 4 times, Australia 4 times, Scotland twice, Sweden twice, Peru twice, Wales twice, Hungary twice, along with one trip each to China, Japan, Spain, Portugal, Poland, Nigeria, Kenya, Malaysia, Latvia, Japan, Hong Kong, Faroe Islands, and the Czech Republic. Closer to home, I have been to Canada more than two dozen times, Mexico 10 times, and Jamaica once. What a glorious privilege and honor it has been!

There is nothing like seeing the Spirit dramatically touch lives in a totally foreign setting that suddenly becomes home to you. Beautiful Jesus! It is worth every hour traveled and every moment of jet lag and the few risks and dangers we have endured.

Later in the book, I'll share some of my adventures in the nations. But before I do, there's one more important piece to the puzzle that ties back to the outpouring and my time at CFNI.

LIVING IN THE LINE OF FIRE

CHANGING MY THESIS TOPIC

During the outpouring in Community Bible Church in November 1982, I realized that I needed to reassess some of my theology. Were my beliefs based on the Word, or were they reactionary? Did I learn these things from God or from other people? I wanted to embrace what the Spirit was doing, but I knew the Word was my guide. Yet what was I to do when someone testified to being healed, as happened quite a few times during the outpouring, but their theology seemed to be wrong? I had believed that "by His stripes we were healed" in Isaiah 53 and 1 Peter 2 referred only to spiritual healing. Yet people in our church were using that verse to explain how they were physically healed.

I said to myself, "They have the wrong theology but they are getting results. I have the right theology but I'm not getting results. How does this work?" I also asked myself why most of the evangelists with powerful healing ministries taught that healing was in the atonement, a position I had not previously embraced. This forced me to reevaluate my views on divine healing. What did God's Word really say?

Prior to putting my doctoral dissertation on hold, which I did after laying my scholarship at the Lord's feet in October 1982, I had started compiling data for my thesis, titled, "Abbreviated Verbal Idioms in the Old Testament: A Comparative Semitic Approach." (I know! It sounds exciting.) But in the months after the outpouring, I questioned the eternal value of the subject, seeking God in fasting and prayer. After about nine months, while on my knees one day prayerfully reviewing the usage of the root r-p-' with a concordance to the Hebrew Bible open before me, a major light went on: this root did not primarily mean "to heal," but "to restore," with "healing" being a sub-meaning under the larger heading of "restoration." This helped me to understand the semantic range of this same root when used in South Semitic languages such as Arabic and Ethiopic. It also helped me to gain a broader understanding of the meaning of healing in the Bible. I was on to something.

I asked Professor Levine if I could switch dissertation topics, and he accepted my proposal. The final title was: "I Am the Lord Your Healer: A

90

The Outpouring, Full-Time Ministry, and the Call to the Nations

Philological Study of the Root *RP'* in the Hebrew Bible and the Ancient Near East." I completed the work in 1985 and received my Ph.D. in Near Eastern Languages and Literatures. Ten years later, after doing an exhaustive sweep of the Bible on the subject of healing, I published a 450-page monograph for Zondervan titled *Israel's Divine Healer*, part of the series *Studies in Old Testament Biblical Theology*.[4] It consisted of 80,000 words of text and 85,000 words of endnotes, with about 20 percent of the content derived directly from my doctoral thesis. I've told readers that if they struggle with insomnia, reading the endnotes will put them to sleep.

Subsequently, I wrote the entry on *r-p-'* for the two largest theological dictionaries, one being used more by critical, liberal scholars and the other being used more by evangelical, faith-based scholars. As a result, wherever you turn to study healing in the Old Testament, you find my writings—and this from the person who had previously opposed divine healing and said that God was more of a Smiter than a Healer! The Lord has a sense of humor, doesn't He?

CHALLENGED BY GIANTS IN THE FAITH

When I started teaching at CFNI in 1983, I was given a box of books and mini-books written by the founder Gordon Lindsay, who had been a prolific author. One of those books was Lindsay's biography of John Alexander Dowie (1847-1907), a powerful healing pioneer who fell into serious deception in his later years. It was a cautionary tale filled with valuable lessons. There was also Lindsay's compilation of some of the sermons of John G. Lake (1870-1935), one of which was called "Spiritual Hunger." Lake had been a missionary to South Africa and a healing pioneer, and I was deeply moved by the Spirit's work through him and the intensity of his hunger for a greater demonstration of God in his life. I, too, longed for that! That's why that sermon resonated so deeply within me. Spiritual hunger has been a major theme in my preaching and ministry over the decades. There is more!

I also read the sermons of Smith Wigglesworth and biographies about his life, which also impacted me deeply. Where was the God of

LIVING IN THE LINE OF FIRE

Wigglesworth and Lake? What was stopping me and others from seeing the Lord's power set the captive free? The Lord actually had to remind me, using Pastor Frank in the process, not to focus so much on healing, since my call was more to bring a prophetic wake-up call than to be a healing evangelist. Still, I saw some powerful manifestations of the Spirit during those days, including a number of dramatic deliverances.

In one case, during a few days of fasting and intensive prayer around 1984-1985, I had picked up a hitchhiker, and the Lord revealed his life to me as we talked. He was shaken. A few days later, while driving in a different direction at a different time of the day, I picked him up again. We were both shaken. What were the odds of this happening?

He agreed to come to a church service, and the night before he was to attend, the Lord showed me that he was bound by a number of demons. That next morning, as the worship team played and sang, I called up those needing prayer. He responded, and I commanded each of those specific demons to leave him in Jesus's name—but saying the words so quietly that he could not hear anything due to the volume of the music and singing. The moment I whispered the name "Jesus," so quietly that he could not have possibly heard it, blood gushed out of the side of his mouth and he fell to the ground, shaking. (I would estimate it was about a communion cup worth of blood, or in worldly terms, a shot glass full.) The whole ride home, he kept saying, "What happened to me? I feel twenty pounds lighter."

In another incident during that same period of time, a couple whose child went to the same Christian school our daughters attended told me that they had a three-year-old daughter who had been completely mute for a year, and the doctors had no idea why. She had been a very talkative girl at the age of two, but one day while her mother looked away for a moment, the little girl had walked down the stairs into the pool in their backyard, going in over her head. Although in a panic, she had no idea what to do and just stood there under the water until her mother saw what was happening and pulled her out. From that moment on, she had

The Outpouring, Full-Time Ministry, and the Call to the Nations

not said a word. I told them, "A spirit of fear got hold of her. Jesus will set her free."

I invited them to come to a service at Pastor Frank's where a guest minister was speaking, then I called them up for prayer at the conclusion of the service to stand in proxy for their daughter. The moment I got near them, they were hit by the power of God and fell to the ground as I commanded the spirit of fear to leave their daughter. When they got home, the little girl was talking up a storm—and remember, she had no idea what had happened at the church. Who can deny the Spirit's work?

It was also during those years at CFNI when I learned that some of those from the local community attending my night classes had given me the nickname, "Knock 'em down Brown." So many people I prayed for were slain in the Spirit, often falling flat on their faces when I touched them, that I became known for this. I found this ironic too, since I had taught against this very thing during my skeptical years. To this day, it's a nickname my non-charismatic critics like to throw at me in mockery. It's a mockery I will take gladly.

CHAPTER 6

THE REFINER'S FIRE, RAVENHILL, AND WILKERSON

In 1987, we moved to Maryland to work with Dan Juster and his leadership team at Beth Messiah congregation in Rockville, Maryland. Dan was a pioneer Messianic Jewish theologian, and Beth Messiah was a flagship congregation in the movement. I maintain a special friendship with Dan and almost all of those colleagues from Maryland to this day. My role was to raise up the ministry school, which was first known as Messiah Yeshiva and Graduate School of Theology but subsequently changed to Messiah Biblical Institute and Graduate School of Theology, and I would travel out from there. As for my spiritual hunger and deep thirst for revival, that remained unchanged.

A large conference was scheduled for Jerusalem in May 1988 during the Feast of Shavuot (Pentecost, or Weeks). We anticipated that it would be the largest gathering of Jewish believers in Israel since the first century, and many other Christians would join the celebration as well. The meetings would last for three days, and it was clear to me who the three keynote speakers would be for each night: one from Israel, and one each from the two major Messianic Jewish organizations in America—the Union of Messianic Jewish Congregations (UMJC) to which Beth Messiah belonged, and the Messianic Jewish Alliance of America (MJAA).

To my surprise, I was asked to take one of the night meetings, and immediately I felt the Lord call me to do a twenty-one-day water fast, the longest I had ever done. As I fasted and prayed, I knew that the fire

LIVING IN THE LINE OF FIRE

was going to fall. We were going to have a visitation in Jerusalem during Shavuot!

Immediately after the fast, I attended a leadership meeting where everyone received a personal prophecy, and when I returned home, I felt the Lord speak a strong word to me. It was April 27, 1988, and the essence of the word stated that God wanted prophets who know His heart not just His voice, His ways not just His words, His pain not just His power. These were the kind of prophets He was looking for. I journaled these words that day:

> "But where are the Elijah's of *God?*" says the God of Elijah. "Where are *My* men? Where are the *intercessors* who *hear* and speak?" says the Lord, "the prophets who moan and weep? Everybody is running," says the Lord, "everybody is running— but I have not sent them all. Everybody has a message," says the Lord, "everybody has their pet. But *I* have a burden," says the Lord, "and *I* have a word. And *My* word pulls down powers of darkness, and *My* word consumes; *My* word is full of My life, and *My* word heals. MY Word," says the Lord.

While I encourage you to test this word for yourself against the Scriptures, I can say with certainty that it reflects my frame of mind at that time, with a burning heart and a broken spirit.

As I focused on the meetings in Israel, the Lord gave me a strong repentance message (which was typical for my preaching), calling out weaknesses and flesh in our Messianic Jewish movement. And I felt the Lord show me what was going to happen that night as people responded to the altar call and the Spirit would touch many dramatically. Something powerful was going to take place! As for those who were planning to attend the conference in Jerusalem, there was great anticipation and hunger.

When the moment came to travel from the States to Israel in May 1988, the flights were packed with believers. This alone felt like a real spiritual happening. But as the conference unfolded, I was grieved over

The Refiner's Fire, Ravenhill, and Wilkerson

what seemed to be a lack of emphasis on encountering the Spirit. After all, this was Shavuot/Pentecost! But it seemed that, rather than focusing on a Holy Spirit outpouring, there was more emphasis placed on the importance of Jewish believers from outside of Israel emigrating to Israel. (It is called "making aliyah," with *aliyah* being the Hebrew word for ascent, since you go "up" to the Land.)

With my burden becoming more intense, on the day I was scheduled to preach, I spent virtually the entire time on my knees in prayer, asking Him to visit us that night. I also wrestled with how much I should say about expectations for the evening. Should I tell the people what was going to happen after my message? "No," I thought to myself, "I shouldn't. That could put suggestions in their mind. On the other hand, if I told them what to expect, this could raise their faith." Wisdom and experience told me to say nothing, but I was so eager to see God break through, I decided to announce what would take place.

I preached with passion and conviction, saying to the crowd—more than 1,500 people—that if we would come together in hunger before the Lord, He would visit us in specific ways, which I then listed. What I didn't realize was just how deep the divisions were between the UMJC and the MJAA, and those divisions came to light that night. Plus, some of the MJAA leaders were not exactly rooting for me, having heard some slanderous reports about me. (I write this with a smile, as we have been friends and coworkers for decades now.)

Thankfully the Lord met us, and more than 700 people stayed until 3:00 a.m. seeking the Lord. Subsequently, Ari and Shira Sorko-Ram, those Messianic Jewish, Israel pioneers, told me that it was the greatest outpouring in the modern history of Israel, and others told me they could sense a distinct change in the spiritual atmosphere in the days following. But others did not see it that way at all, with some accusing me of being a false prophet. In their view, what I predicted did *not* come to pass. I even remember Nancy, along with Dan and his wife Patty, looking at me with questions in their eyes as we walked back to the hotel. Did things really happen as I said they would?

LIVING IN THE LINE OF FIRE

The next six months led to much earnest seeking of the Lord. What actually happened that night? Why did I override my wisdom? Did the fire really fall? I prayed for many days, humbling myself before Him and, as my custom was, staying up very late seeking His face. I needed to hear from heaven!

Over the months, several things became clear to me. First, I overrode my wisdom because I was so desperate to see God move. Second, while it could be argued that the specific things I spoke of did come to pass, and although I had qualified things with an "if," I clearly overhyped the moment, leading people to accuse me of prophesying falsely. Third, the fire definitely fell—on me! This was the greatest result of my twenty-one-day fast. I was being refined and purged.

THE HOLY PURGING GOES DEEP

Since I had started preaching, I also loved to travel and speak. I also loved to give words to people as the Spirit directed. Now, in the months following that meeting in Jerusalem in May 1988, I dreaded going to speak. I wanted to hide instead! As for hearing from the Spirit and giving a word, I wanted the Lord to use someone else. I wanted to hide rather than preach or prophesy.

On September 8, 1988, I wrote this journal entry:

> Reflecting on the supernatural purging which I have been experiencing for some weeks and months now (but especially these last days!), I must record some of my feelings.
>
> *God is absolutely killing my flesh.* I am incredibly conscious of my *total inability* to do anything on my own. In fact, I have little or no desire to *do* anything in any public way. And I am amazed at my poor and immature use of my tongue (Ps. 141:3!). But I also realize how the flesh hates to be crucified and how it runs from God's guillotine. What a frightful thing it is to take up our cross and follow Jesus!

I am dying to all care of what man says or thinks of me. What kind of folly it is to even consider what flesh and blood have to say! And who gives any of us the right to tell God what is right or wrong? *I also realize just how deeply a man-pleasing and/or man-fearing spirit has affected me for years*, both in terms of private confrontation, and even in terms of being accepted in my preaching ministry. God help me and deliver me.

God is searching my heart. For the first time, I am experiencing a deep probing of motives. Why do I want to lay hands on the sick? So I can be seen as anointed? Why do I want to witness? To deliver my soul, or to save the lost? What do I think when I pray or preach in public? Am I really dead to pride?

I am humbled and almost humiliated by the lives of those who have gone before me. Why *can't* I live like Wigglesworth, Finney, or Lake? Do I *really* want to be totally dominated by God? And do I *really* believe that it is the anointing alone (and not Mike Brown or his ways) that brings revival?

I am convinced that the Church of America is asleep and deceived. We are like the church of Sardis, "the perfect model of an inoffensive Christianity," with a reputation for being alive and yet dead. Where is our passion for souls? Where is our conviction of sin (and with that, our power to convict of sin)? How can we be burdened for the lost when we don't truly believe that they *are* lost?

Oh God! I must continue to pass through your fires, until You have completed Your present pruning work on me. God! I must come out a totally different person. You must really remake me in Jesus's image. I cannot tolerate anything less. I am not hungry. I am starving. Hear my heart and catch me up and visit me. For Your glory. And for Your glory alone.

LIVING IN THE LINE OF FIRE

Then this, on October 27, 1988:

> While re-reading the life of Dowie for my Giants course, I see
> and hear clearly a strong word for me: *Remember John Alexan-
> der Dowie*, and never forget how much I believed I was God's
> man for the hour in Israel, as if the salvation of the nation was
> resting on the "Elijah call" on my life. Yes, I'm anointed; yes,
> I'm called. But I'm only one of an *innumerable* company of
> believers called to the pull of the task.

To be clear, as I said in the last chapter in another context, I never
thought for a moment that I was Elijah—God forbid! (To this day, critics
accuse me of prophesying that literal fire would fall during that meeting.
I smile at this and wish them well.) Yet what I recognized when I journaled those words on October 27 was not so much that I over-exalted my
own importance but that I downplayed the importance of others. Their
messages were not important or timely. Only mine was. How shameful
and how full of pride.

That's why the lessons I learned in 1988 have stayed with me for life:
NO ONE is "the man" or "the woman" for the generation. There are NO
superstars, only servants. ALL OF US are needed and NO ONE is irre-
placeable. I live with this reality every day of my life.

AND THEN FOR THE SURPRISES

Because of the controversy following my Jerusalem message, with the praises
as loud as the criticisms, I wrote a letter to all the Messianic Jewish leaders
who attended, saying that I stood by the substance of my sermon (which I
still do), and that while the specific things I had predicted had come to pass,
the way I set things up absolutely led to confusion. For that I apologized.
Some were appreciative, but others felt the apology did not go far enough.
As for the divisions between the UMJC and MJAA, they only deepened.

About two years later, a brother reached out to me. He was the one
who had previously spread a slanderous report about me to the MJAA

The Refiner's Fire, Ravenhill, and Wilkerson

leaders. The Lord had moved deeply in his life, and he wanted to ask my forgiveness for the damage he had done. Of course, I forgave him from the heart. He then told me that, although he seemed to be the least likely person to do this, he felt he had a word for me. If I would humble myself and write a deeper repentance letter to these Messianic Jewish leaders, it would undo the damage he had done.

As I prayed about this, the Lord confirmed it to me. Shortly after that, while praying and listening to my message from 1988, I wept, realizing how proud I sounded at the beginning as I mentioned my twenty-one-day fast and sharing how I had spent that entire day on my knees in prayer. At the time, I wanted to convey how seriously I was taking the moment. But listening two-and-a-half years later, although no one had accused me of pride, the Spirit convicted me deeply.

Then, returning from a glorious ministry trip to South Korea and feeling the favor of the Lord, I asked myself, "How can I better serve the brothers and sisters in the Messianic movement who have opposed me?" The answer was to get low—very low. And so, with that revelation of the favor of God on my life, I wrote a follow-up letter regarding my 1988 message—and I repeat, this was two-and-a-half years after the fact.

Over the years, I have found that when we are secure in God's love and calling, we can really humble ourselves and get low. The greatest example comes from Jesus Himself: "Jesus knew that the Father had put all things under his power, and that he had come from God and was returning to God; so he got up from the meal, took off his outer clothing, and wrapped a towel around his waist" (John 13:3–4 NIV). How remarkable.

So on the flight home from Korea, I wrote the letter of apology. The next day, when I reread the letter—now that I was back in a normal frame of mind—I was surprised. Did I *really* want to send this out? But I knew I had to.

I showed it to Dan and the team. How did they feel? They were concerned that it went too far and could even make all of us look bad, but they told me to send it out if I felt it was the right thing to do. So I sent

LIVING IN THE LINE OF FIRE

the letter out to all the Messianic Jewish leaders who had been at the 1988 meeting in Jerusalem. And then the surprises came.

Not only was the letter well-received by these leaders, including those in the MJAA, but it prompted a response from one of their key leaders: He wanted to humble himself and reconcile with the UMJC leaders! In turn, one of the UMJC leaders wrote back, even more humbly. He wanted to reciprocate in kind! This led to a wonderful reconciliation between these two movements. Isn't the Lord amazing? But there's more.

God joined my heart together with that brother who spread a bad report about me and then apologized. We are close friends to this day, and he has often heard from the Lord on my behalf in prayer. We are joined at the hip, and he is a trusted, dear brother.

As for the building in Jerusalem that hosted that eventful gathering in 1988, it too had a surprise ending. *It is now the American Embassy, the history-making location chosen when President Trump made the momentous decision to move our embassy from Tel Aviv to Jerusalem.* As I said, isn't the Lord amazing?

Yet there's more. After ministering at a leaders' meeting in Jerusalem on June 10, 2024, just one day before Shavuot, a respected Israeli pastor stood to his feet and addressed everyone in the meeting. This was my journal entry for the day:

> Then a brother calls for corporate repentance for slandering me 36 years ago when I preached in Jerusalem at Shavuot, saying that the fire most certainly fell, that his wife thought I was a false prophet and asked God not to let me touch her [meaning at the Jerusalem meeting in May 1988], yet immediately after I laid hands on both of them, the fire fell on them. Ari also tells me that everyone knew that the fire fell, and that is when everything changed in the Land and congregations began to grow.

How kind of the Lord to touch many lives in Israel in May 1988 while at the same time highlighting flesh and immaturity in me. The Lord is the ultimate multitasker!

The Refiner's Fire, Ravenhill, and Wilkerson

A LIFE-CHANGING VISITATION IN KENYA

After that season of divine purging in 1988, the Lord continued to sensitize my heart. On January 8, 1989, I journaled, "Reflecting on the last few months of ministry, I feel that all my spiritual 'achievements' have only brought me to a new level of mediocrity. God, what can I do? God, what *must* I do to really get into Your realm? The answer: 'Get intense. Seek My face. PRAY.'"

Then this on January 20, 1989:

What an unusual place I've been in these last few days! First, I have been experiencing a deep feeling of sadness because of the suffering of the human race. *The reality of it all seems literally unbearable.* How can we have a true faith without a strong degree of suffering in our lives? And then, more than ever before, I am overwhelmed by a *total* feeling of spiritual-ministry inadequacy. My heart is this: Unless God *radically* changes me, I cannot go on. But revelations come today: Yes, all this is God's work in my life to prepare me for the glory and to sensitize my heart [as pointed out by a dear friend of our family] but, *I must do spiritual battle against lying spirits that have been specially appointed to destroy me and which are fueled by judgmental and negative attitudes* (hyper-shepherding!). I must believe all of God's promises to me, discard the lies and their influence, and go after God with the old reckless abandon. AND GOD WILL BE WITH ME.

And then this, on January 28, 1989:

During an intense, desperately hungry and deeply fervent prayer meeting, I am so clearly gripped with God's call on my life (to the Church): to bring the reality of God's judgment day and call God's people to repentance. Yes! *Wake up* the sleeping Church. Things are supposed to be different. Let the

LIVING IN THE LINE OF FIRE

consequences be what they may be (loss of popularity, no tape sales because of altar calls, etc.), I *must* be a true vessel of *revival* (and that means, "Be holy!").

A few months earlier, I made plans with Ari Sorko-Ram and Sid Roth (whom I also got to know in 1984, the same year I met Ari) to attend one of Reinhard Bonnke's gospel rallies in Africa in February 1989. (Bonnke lived from 1940-2019.) Surely *there*, in Africa, with this powerful healing evangelist ministering, we would see open miracles in front of our eyes. The brokenness and desperation I was feeling in the weeks before this were part of the Spirit's preparation of my heart.

We arrived in Mombasa, Kenya, February 1989, where we were expected by Bonnke's team and given seats on the platform with other leaders, most of them local pastors. But we were told that there was a lot of resistance from the Muslim population there, resulting in much smaller crowds than usual. This was before Bonnke preached to crowds of several million in Nigeria, but they had already seen an explosion in Kenya with crowds of more than 200,000. This first night, there were about 10,000 in attendance, and I was on the edge of my seat.

When Bonnke stood up to preach, he made a special announcement, wanting the crowd to know that there was a special section up front for the MVPs. I said to myself, "I really respect him, but I don't like this 'MVP' thing." He then said, "The blind and the lame, you are Bonnke's MVPs. You will see and you will walk!" Instantly I began to cry. This man had seen it over and again. God's power is real!

Then at the end of his message, after giving an altar call for the lost, he told those who were blind to put their hands on their eyes and for others to put their hands on sick parts of their body. I looked intently at those standing or sitting right in front of me in the MVP section, focusing on one particular blind man. But after prayer, nothing happened. Immediately, I felt a wave of unbelief sweep over me: "None of this real. You came all the way to Africa to see miracles under Bonnke's ministry, but the whole thing is a sham." And then, moments later the thought hit, "There is no God!"

The Refiner's Fire, Ravenhill, and Wilkerson

Those thoughts left as quickly as they came, but as I talked with Bonnke's team, they said to me, "We haven't seen the breakthrough yet. In the last city, we saw sixteen blind eyes open. It just hasn't broken open yet here." Bonnke, for his part, went deeper in his preaching, calling for repentance and confession and, where goods had been stolen, for restitution. God was moving, people were getting saved, demons were manifesting and were then driven out, and some sick people were being healed, but not on the level I was expecting.

Still, I knew there was something visible and powerful that was going to take place, and I knew exactly when it would happen. Saturday night, the second to last day of the gospel crusade, would be the time. This was when Bonnke would pray for the baptism of the Spirit, and thousands of people would be slain in the Spirit as an unseen wave swept through the crowd. I had seen it on videos, and it was powerful.

And so, after Bonnke preached on Saturday night and gave an altar call for the lost, the moment came. Bonnke prayed for the Spirit to fall on those gathered—by now, a crowd of about 30,000—and I could feel the Spirit move in. It was tangible. And I could hear a roar from the crowd as thousands began to speak in tongues for the first time. But no one moved, not even slightly, and not a single person fell. What in the world happened?

We went back to the hotel, where I shared a room with Ari, trying to process the events of the night and then falling asleep. But I was awakened at 1:00 a.m., going into the bathroom where I could turn on the light and read and pray. I brought with me a book on revival by Winkie Pratney; and there, alone in that little bathroom, and then later lying in bed silently in the dark while Ari slept, I was visited by the Spirit from 1:00 until 4:00 a.m. This is what I journaled early that morning on February 5, 1989:

> After 5000+ are baptized in the Spirit (but no outward "wave"), and again, no visible miracles, I'm awoken at 1:00 and read about [George] Whitefield (Pratney, *Revival*, 105f.), then *I see it*!! "Focus on My power to call people to repent. *I* will take care

LIVING IN THE LINE OF FIRE

of the miracles. (Remember. You are a prophet, not a healer.) When people die I can give them a new body. I cannot give them a new heart."

In our zeal to recover the power of God to heal, we have over-focused on *outward manifestations*. Wouldn't I be thrilled beyond measure to preach to crowds like last night (in Israel and the U.S.) with similar results? Then in Nairobi (2-6), I see how God can use one man to shake a nation. *Incredible.* [I'll explain the Nairobi reference in a moment.]

This was another turning point in my life. How vividly I remember the sacred presence of God that came over me as I lay in bed, repeating over and again what the Lord was saying to me so I could write down every word in the morning.

You see, by the late 1980s, although I always preached a strong repentance message—really, since my very first sermons—I had also developed a reputation for "power" ministry, including a few miraculous healings, although I never had a strong healing ministry. And so, after I would preach, it became my habit to call up those needing a dramatic breakthrough, meaning those who had tried everything and could not get free, and as I laid hands on them, the Lord would powerfully touch them. But in doing so, I had strayed from my primary calling to wake up the sleeping Church, which included extended altar calls when people would get on their knees or faces and seek the Lord. Now, altar calls like this were largely a thing of the past. I was busy laying hands on people.

The Lord showed me clearly in that early morning visitation in my hotel room in Kenya that I would have rather seen five people healed in the Bonnke meetings than 5,000 people saved. This is why He said to me, "When people die I can give them a new body. I cannot give them a new heart." It's also why He said to me on February 10, "Preach to people's hearts, not their bodies."

As for the Winkie Pratney book, he had cited the writings of Arnold Dallimore, author of a two-volume biography of Whitefield (1714-1770),

The Refiner's Fire, Ravenhill, and Wilkerson

one of the greatest preachers of any era. In it, Dallimore referenced the signs and wonders that followed Whitefield's ministry—the radical conversions and transformed lives. That needed to be my goal!

Still, out of curiosity, I asked Bonnke's team that night (Sunday, which was the final night of the meetings), "What happened to the wave when thousands of people are slain in the Spirit?" His administrator said, "Recently, Reinhard asked the Lord to stop it. Originally, it was a supernatural sign for him, but he didn't need it anymore. Plus, it was hard for him to watch thousands of people falling on each other. He didn't tell anyone about asking the Lord to stop the wave, but the next time when he prayed for the baptism of the Spirit, no one fell. Then he told us what he had prayed." Both the coming of the wave and stopping of the wave were from the Lord.

The next day, on February 6, as we traveled back by way of Nairobi, I was stunned to hear story after story, from gas stations to rental car offices to the place where we grabbed a meal to the airport, about people who had been touched by Bonnke's ministry, with some sharing similar accounts: "I knew someone in my village who was crippled and came back from the Bonnke meeting walking, and I gave my life to Jesus." This moved me deeply. God had used His servant to shake the nation.

Years later, when Reinhard and I became friends, I told him that we had been in the meetings in Mombasa in 1989. "Mombasa!" he exclaimed, shaking his head. He told me that out of all the meetings he had conducted in Africa, those were among the very worst in terms of outward signs and wonders. That's why the Lord sent me there. He had a different lesson to teach me.

After my trip to Kenya, for the next seven years until the Lord called me to Brownsville, I did very little laying hands on people. But when I did pray for them, not a single person fell. Not one! So much for the power of suggestion and my "Knock 'em down Brown" reputation. But when I did lay hands on people, most commonly when they were already on their knees at the altar, the moment I touched them, they would often begin to weep. The Spirit was doing a new thing.

LIVING IN THE LINE OF FIRE

Once I got to Brownsville in May 1996, the Lord said to me, "Everything is in order here," meaning that priority was given to the call to repentance and salvation, with extended time every night at the altar where people could get right with God. It was only after that when we laid hands on everyone, and the moment I started praying for the people there in Brownsville, the Spirit's power was released dramatically. In the years that followed, I would literally see people fly though the air as if a bomb had gone off. And when they stood up, sometimes an hour later or more, they were transformed.

Since then, when I do lay hands on people, sometimes the Lord opens that spigot again and the power of God falls visibly, but most of the time it does not. Either way, the emphasis of my message remains the same, never forgetting what happened in Kenya in that hotel room. And it was during that time of holy visitation the morning of February 5, 1989, that I also journaled these words, the last in my entry for that day: "While reflecting on issues of personal holiness, God says: 'If you ever touch another woman, I'll kill you.'" This was a sober warning.

THE RELEASE TO WRITE AND THE RAVENHILL CONNECTION

On July 14, 1989, while away at a prayer retreat, God moved on me to write. This had happened to me before over the years, but as I shared earlier, the anointing would seem to lift after the first page of fiery writing. Not this time. It continued to pour out of me for several days and showed no signs of abating. I had written a short book in 1985 to answer questions about healing and the goodness of God posed by Robin, my sister-in-law, when she was attending a Word of Faith Bible school. The book was titled *Compassionate Father or Consuming Fire: Who Is the God of the Old Testament*, but it was a teaching book, not a revival book. (We released an updated and revised edition of the book in 2021.)[5]

This new book was different. It was focused on revival and it flowed like a river as I wrote, with plays on words and burning quotes. It was an

The Refiner's Fire, Ravenhill, and Wilkerson

expression of the intense hunger that had burned in me since the out-pouring. At last! But who would write the foreword to the book?

As I knelt before the Lord during that prayer retreat, I asked myself a question: Which leader today do I most relate to? With whose message do I most resonate? It was Leonard Ravenhill! Instantly I knew that he would write the foreword, even though he hadn't the slightest clue who I was. But I knew it. (As often happens, once my rational mind kicked in, I asked myself, "Is he still alive?" My spirit said he was.)

I got home and shared with Nancy that God had moved on me to write, and she was excited as she read those opening pages. (As you'll learn later in the book, she doesn't get excited about much that I do, so this was significant.) A holy fountain that had been stopped up for more than seventeen years had found its release.

A colleague referred me to a potential publisher, Destiny Image, and I set up a meeting with the president, Don Nori, a big, bearded, bear of a man with a soft heart for the Lord. He was excited to hear about a book on repentance and revival. I told him, "Leonard Ravenhill will write the foreword." Now he was really pumped. I called Sid Roth and told him about the book, also letting him know the exciting news about Ravenhill. He was excited too, making plans to have me on his radio show to promote the book.

Nancy said to me, "Did God tell you Ravenhill is going to write the foreword?" I replied, "No, but He doesn't have to. It's all over me!" She said, "Maybe you should just keep your mouth shut for now?" She was right.

The book was finished in three weeks' time, but I had no access to Leonard Ravenhill. Then, while attending some meetings in Kansas City in mid-August and staying at the home of a family there, I heard them reference their pastor David Ravenhill, Leonard's son. I was shocked. "You mean the son of *the* Leonard Ravenhill?" That was him!

The next night, on August 16, I visited David Ravenhill's church and heard him preach for the first time. Afterward, I asked him what his father was doing and he told me he had been physically rejuvenated

LIVING IN THE LINE OF FIRE

recently and was traveling again. (He was eighty-two at the time.) I asked for his father's address, writing to Leonard Ravenhill when I got home and sending him a copy of the manuscript. But I didn't ask him to write the foreword, wanting the Lord to make it happen. Instead, I told him I had the joy of hearing his son David speak and would be honored to receive his comments and criticisms of my manuscript.

I waited a few days and decided to follow up, but I didn't have his phone number. I said to myself, "I bet someone like him has a listed phone number." Sure enough, he did, so I got his number and was about to call. Immediately, I checked myself: "You're in the flesh. You're not trusting God." I replied to myself, "Yes, that's true, but I'm so sure this whole thing is from the Lord that even if I'm in the flesh it won't get in the way."

I dialed his number, and the man himself picked up the phone. I asked him if he had received the manuscript, and he said somewhat gruffly, "Yes, I got your letter, but the package had been opened and the manuscript was missing." Then he said, "If you send it, I'll read it," and he hung up.

Now I was stoked! God *was* in this, and that's why someone opened the package and removed the manuscript. How utterly bizarre!

So I overnighted the manuscript to him, and two days later, meaning, the day after he received it, when I came into our ministry office early in the morning on September 8, the secretary said to me, "There's a Raven Hill calling collect." Now *he* was calling *me*!

He told me that he received the book and read it in one day—something he never does—then telling me that the chapters needed to be broken down into tracts that could be distributed individually. And then, to my astonishment, he said, "If this book would be read at Wednesday night church services, two chapters a time, it could shake the nation." And then this: "And I'll write the introduction." Oh my!

This was not just a confirmation on the book, *The End of the American Gospel Enterprise,* released in December of that very same year, 1989.[6] This was not just a confirmation that I heard from the Lord about Ravenhill. It was ultimately a confirmation of the word that God had

110

The Refiner's Fire, Ravenhill, and Wilkerson

spoken to me in the spring of 1983. I *would* be part of a revival that would touch the world!

I asked him, "Could I come down and spend a day with you?" He laughed and said, "Oh no, I have twenty-five to thirty guests a week, and I give them a half-hour each. But if you come down, I'll give you an hour." (He lived in Lindale, Texas.) I was in awe, grateful beyond words.

Two weeks later, on September 22, he called me again. His heart was in a specially tender place, and he said to me, "I want you to come down and spend a few days with me. I don't know much more time I have here, but I want to pour into you everything God has given me." When we got off the phone, I fell to my knees, absolutely overwhelmed. Oh. My. God.

One week later, on September 30, 1989, I made the first of many trips to see him, staying with him and his devout wife, Martha, in their little home. When he and I knelt alone in prayer on that first trip, I wept uncontrollably. This was sacred ground! To this day, I have never met anyone who prayed the way Leonard Ravenhill did. The brokenness, the passion, the burden, the fire, the eloquence, the penetration, the intimacy. This was the key to his ministry, resulting in meetings so intense that sometimes, he could not even finish his message because the people would begin to run to the altar or fall on their faces, weeping in repentance and conviction. I saw this with my own eyes at a meeting in Anaheim in January 1990 with about 4,500 people present.

At the end of our three days together, he said to me, "I have only asked this of a handful of people, but would you be my friend?" *Your friend? Me?* This was a staggering thought. He was eighty-two. I was thirty-four. He was Leonard Ravenhill. I was me.

I said to him, "But I can't call you Len." He said, "Call me Brother Len." And that's who he became to me for the next five years until his homegoing in 1994 at the age of eighty-seven. Over those years, not only did he pray for me several times a day, but he poured fuel on my fire, confirming the things I had preached and believed for years and deepening

LIVING IN THE LINE OF FIRE

my convictions, also introducing me to many Christian leaders of the past, including Catherine Booth of Salvation Army fame.

Well do I remember being at Brother Len's home after his set time of private afternoon prayer, which he adhered to no matter who was in the house. He would come out of his bedroom staggered, with tears in his eyes saying, "Mike, I'm so ashamed for Jesus! The Bride is naked and she doesn't know it!" Each time, it was as if he had never seen it before. That's how intense the burden was.

As for him writing the foreword to my book, it really was a miracle. That's because he had no secretarial help other than what Martha could provide, and every time I visited his house, I saw that the pile of letters and large envelopes on his desk grew higher and higher, much of it many months old, if not even years old. There was no way he could read everything that was sent to him, yet he read my manuscript from beginning to end the same day he received it.

As for my own writing, the floodgates remained open. I wrote *How Saved Are We?* in 1990, *Whatever Happened to the Power of God: Is the Charismatic Church Slain in the Spirit or Down for the Count?* in 1991, *Our Hands Are Stained with Blood: The Tragic Story of the Church and the Jewish People* in 1992, and *It's Time to Rock the Boat: A Call to God's People to Rise Up and Preach a Confrontational Gospel* in 1993.[7] With each new book, I would send a case to Brother Len, who would then distribute those books to leaders he knew.

When *Our Hands Are Stained with Blood* came out in 1992, Brother Len gave a copy to a missionary-evangelist named Steve Hill who had just returned from several years on the field and was living nearby with his wife, Jeri, in a house provided by David Wilkerson. Steve read my book and reached out to me to endorse something he had written, and that's how God connected us. It was through that connection that God called me to serve as a leader in the Brownsville Revival in 1996, a revival which the Lord ignited through Steve. We both felt deeply that Ravenhill's prayers played a key role in ushering in that mighty move of the Spirit. I am eternally indebted to Brother Len!

112

The Refiner's Fire, Ravenhill, and Wilkerson

TIMES SQUARE CHURCH AND DAVID WILKERSON

In 1990, I received a call from a Jewish believer in New York City named Chuck Cohen. He was a good friend of Don Wilkerson, and Don, along with Bob Phillips and Don's brother David, led Times Square Church in New York City. Chuck wanted to connect me with Don and the church. Shortly after this, Brother Len sent a copy of *How Saved Are We?* to David, and I was told subsequently that David read the book in one sitting.

Then in the summer of 1991, I was speaking at Christ for the Nations on Long Island, marking my last messages there before the school closed. That Friday afternoon, after my last session there, I had an appointment to meet with David Wilkerson for the first time (he was known as Pastor Dave or Brother Dave), but I received a call from his administrative assistant. He was going to be busy that afternoon, but could I preach that night instead? This was amazing and totally unexpected.

When I arrived before the service, Brother Dave said to me, "Preach whatever the Lord gives you, but we could really use help on Israel." And so I preached on God's purposes for Israel from Romans chapters 9 through 11. That was the first of between forty and fifty times that I preached at Times Square Church; and every time I spoke there, I felt as if I was standing on holy ground. It was a sacred privilege to stand behind that pulpit.

Over the years, I became closer to Don than David, primarily because Don was more of a people person than David. And as much as David was a deeply compassionate man, I never felt totally relaxed sitting with him, even when it was just the two of us having dinner at a restaurant. I used to describe it as fellowshipping with a razor blade. He would look at me with those piercing eyes and gently say, "How are you doing, Mike?" I wanted to say, "Brother Dave, I'm clean! Really, I am!" As for his preaching, the moment he would share the burden of his heart, something exploded inside me too. That is how I felt too!

The Lord also used David Wilkerson in a significant way in my life, especially in one pivotal moment in 1992. Several weeks earlier, I received a call

113

LIVING IN THE LINE OF FIRE

from Patty Juster, the wife of Messianic Jewish leader Dan Juster, under whom I served in Maryland. She and Dan sensed that something was off in my message. She couldn't quite explain how, other than it was too hard in some ways. But rather than taking to heart what she said and going to the Lord in prayer, I defended myself, telling her that the Lord was using my books and my meetings in powerful ways. She said, "The books are different." This got my attention, since those early books were quite intense. If those were *not* too hard, how was my preaching too hard? Unfortunately, I responded pridefully and dismissed Dan and Patty's concerns.

Not long after that, David's assistant called me, saying he wanted to speak with me. This had never happened before. David and I would talk face to face when I was there, but his assistant would call to set up my preaching schedule for the coming months. Now he wanted to talk with me by phone. This got Nancy's attention too. It was David Wilkerson on the phone.

David and I talked for one full hour. He explained to me that he saw a similarity in our callings and that the Lord had taught him something he wanted to share with me. He had detected something wrong when we had talked recently, telling me that the other pastors at Times Square wouldn't sense it but he did, because of our similar callings. He proceeded to explain to me the very thing that Patty was trying to communicate, but this time I got it. After all, this was David Wilkerson talking to me!

He told me that Don and Bob Phillips had seen these things in him and that the Lord had spoken Proverbs 17:15 to him after he preached one night, leading to his own life-changing encounter with God. The verse says, "Acquitting the guilty and condemning the innocent—the Lord detests them both." He said to me, "You can go around with a big stick preaching to small crowds, or you can reach thousands. It all depends on how you respond to what I'm telling you."

I asked him, "When did the Lord teach you this lesson in your own life?" He said, "About a year-and-a-half ago." I said to myself, "He's sixty-one," meaning he learned this when he was about sixty, "and I'm thirty-seven." If I can learn this now, I'll be way ahead of the curve.

114

The Refiner's Fire, Ravenhill, and Wilkerson

What had happened in the months prior to our conversation is that I had become so grieved by all the carnality and compromise in the Church that I began looking for things to correct rather than waiting for the Lord to share His burden with me. Recognizing this wrong tendency, as if I was God's policeman and it was up to me to sniff out all the error, I had thought to myself, "I need to do a fresh study of grace." I recognized that I had been getting a bad attitude and ministering out of some level of personal frustration. Now, David Wilkerson was telling me that very thing! That's why, as Nancy came into my study while he and I talked, trying to get a sense of what he was saying, I wrote out one word for her: grace.

When I got off the phone, we sat on the floor and I began to cry. She said, "Why are you crying?" I replied, "Because the Lord loves me enough to correct me," thinking immediately of Proverbs 3:11–12 (NIV): "My son, do not despise the Lord's discipline, and do not resent his rebuke, because the Lord disciplines those he loves, as a father the son he delights in." I felt special!

Immediately, I thought of young preachers with big ministries who seemed to strut, as if they had bypassed the cross. The Lord was not going to let that happen to me. In fact, David Wilkerson's phone call to me was the result of a specific prayer Dan and Patty prayed. They had said to the Lord, "Mike won't listen to us, but he'll listen to Leonard Ravenhill or David Wilkerson, so have one of them call him." He did! Ironically, the thing that got David Wilkerson's attention was a misunderstanding of something I said to him in a private conversation. But that was the trigger the Lord used.

Brother Dave said to me on the phone that he would spend a day with me to share more, but when I overnighted him a long letter, articulating my understanding of what he was saying, he knew I had received and grasped what he shared. Still, to be sure the message hit home, he cancelled the next five times I was scheduled to preach there, all during that the following month, which would have been the most times I had spoken there at any one time. This stung, first because I so loved to preach there, and second, because it was also a financial blow to our ministry.

LIVING IN THE LINE OF FIRE

But I was glad. God wanted me to learn this lesson well. I needed to feel the sting.

In the years that followed, through March 1995, I was one of three "swing pastors" who would come in regularly and preach, so called because we would swing in, preach, and swing out. In 1994, I preached there seventeen times, the most of any year, and all those years, the services were marked by the deepest worship and the most joy-filled praise I had consistently experienced before Brownsville (other than in my first years in the Lord).

One day (I can't recall exactly when), I realized that there were twenty-four years between Ravenhill and Wilkerson and then twenty-four years between Wilkerson and me. Spiritually speaking, I feel as if there are centuries between both of them and me—or in lineal measurement, hundreds of miles between us. I feel quite superficial and out of my league compared to these men of God. Yet I hope that some of what they deposited in me can be passed on to the generations to come.

CHAPTER 7

REVIVAL!

It is tempting for me to change the course of this book and spend the next 100 pages talking about the Brownsville Revival. The visitation was that glorious, the spiritual experience that sacred, the memories that extraordinary. How does one really describe a true revival? How can you put the visitation into words? Perhaps that will be the subject of another book one day, even though, in reality, only eternity will be able to offer the full scope of what the Lord did during those years. So, while I'll do my best to paint a picture of what the revival was like, I can only provide the tiniest glimpse. And even with that, I'll do so largely through the lens of my own experience.

As is the case with all true revivals, the accounts sometimes sound exaggerated, if not totally fabricated. But I report these things either as an eyewitness or as someone who spoke to an eyewitness. I can vouch for everything I write.

At the height of the revival, which lasted from June 18, 1995, until roughly 2000, the lines would form outside the beginning at 6:00 a.m., with the doors opening at 6:00 p.m. and the service starting at 7:00 p.m. and lasting until midnight or later, four nights a week. This was in addition to the Tuesday night prayer meeting, which was also packed. And the crowds stood outside rain or shine in the sometimes fickle Florida weather.

Before the church established the 6:00 a.m. starting time for the lines, people would leave the night service well past midnight, get a meal in one of the few restaurants open late in Pensacola, then come back with

117

LIVING IN THE LINE OF FIRE

their sleeping bags and camp out in the parking lot starting at 2:00 or 3:00 a.m. But because it was not feasible for the church to have a security guard outside at those times, the church made the rule that you could not start to line up before 6:00 a.m., at which point there would be security outside. Can you imagine having to make a rule that the lines can only begin to form outside your church building thirteen hours before service time?

Visitors flocked to the revival from more than 150 nations, with a cumulative attendance of at least two million people (I've heard estimates of three million or higher), and with at least 300,00 different people responding to the altar calls, including many thousands of first-time converts. Pastors would bring their congregations to attend the revival, thinking that their people needed a fresh touch from God. Instead, they would sometimes be the first ones to run to the altar in repentance. Afterward, they would say, "I felt like I got saved all over again!" Reverend Alex Buchanan from England sent this note to us after attending the revival:

> I have prayed for revival for 51 years, 5 months, and fifteen days. I have led and raised up revival prayer movements through most of these years. At last I have seen it—at Brownsville. I felt like Simeon who saw God's salvation after many years, and then asked if he could depart in peace!! You can see how encouraged I was while with you.

Students touched in the revival would go back to their schools, only to be hit by the power of God during class, sometimes shaking and falling to the floor, unable to explain what was happening to them. They would be rushed to the nurse's office, who couldn't find anything wrong. Then the student would get out one word, "Brownsville." The school officials began to piece together what was happening, calling the church angrily, asking to speak with the youth pastor, Richard Crisco, who had a good relationship with all the local campuses.

Revival!

But as the weeks went by, the attitude of these teachers and school administrators changed dramatically, as these students were transformed by the Spirit, some of them going from last to first in their classes or from troublemakers to respected young Christian leaders. This was confirmed to me by Jim May, Superintendent of Schools in Escambia County during our meeting in October 1997. He told me he was an eyewitness to the impact the revival had on the schools, having served as principal at one of them in the previous years.

Dr. Charles Woolwine, who was vice principal of Niceville High School, where hundreds of students were transformed through the revival, sent this testimony:

> I have been saved 40 years. I have been in the district for 20 years and at this school for 9 years. I have never seen a move of God in schools like what we have since the [Brownsville] Revival began. Kids tell me, "I got saved, my attention deficit is gone, I can study. I've been released from getting up every morning hating my uncle for some abuse that occurred when I was younger. I've been released from drugs." One girl said she used to not want to live, she was controlled by drugs, depressed, and it's all gone.

As for the stories that sounded apocryphal but were true, here's a famous example. Early in the revival, two Playboy bunnies had flown in from Chicago for a photo shoot on one of the Pensacola beaches, but bad weather cancelled the shoot. With a free night on their hands, they hired a taxi, asking where the action was in Pensacola. The taxi driver brought them to the revival! Yes, the hot spot in the city was a church.

Deciding to check things out for themselves in a lighthearted way—hey, why not?—they ended up responding to the altar call in deep repentance, weeping and trembling. This got the attention of Pastor Kilpatrick, who asked them what was going on. They explained that they not been living the best lives, saying that they felt God was shaking the hell out of them.

119

LIVING IN THE LINE OF FIRE

An older sister in the church befriended them, giving them Bibles. A few weeks later they called her and said, "We can't live like this anymore." At least one of them moved to Pensacola and became a solid Christian woman. Again, I have eyewitness confirmation for this account.

Two pastors from New Jersey told me what happened to them when they visited Brownsville. They came along with three other pastors from their church, and they went to every meeting for a week, enjoying the services and getting prayer at the end of each night. But they left somewhat disappointed. They were expecting more. Now they were ready to fly home.

At that time, the Pensacola airport was a tiny regional airport with one little terminal and six gates. That was it. Over the years, it has expanded— but not much. Today it has ten gates! In fact, the airport was so small that, if there was a mechanical problem with a plane, you had to wait for the next flight to arrive from Atlanta. The mechanic would be on board. As for flight options, they were limited: Delta, by way of Atlanta (by far, the most common route) or Cincinnati; US Airways, by way of Charlotte; Northwest, by way of Memphis; and Continental, by way of Houston. That was it. There was even a joke that if you died in Pensacola, you went to heaven by way of Atlanta.

These five men were getting on the plane for their short flight to Atlanta, after which they would fly to New Jersey, when they noticed that they were all sitting separately. What happened? They had booked the tickets to all be in a row. Now, each of them was seated separately from the others on the plane.

When the flight took off, the lead pastor was absolutely shocked as the Spirit fell upon him out of the blue and he began to weep in the presence of God. This lasted the entire flight to Atlanta. He couldn't wait to get off the plane and tell the other brothers what happened, only to learn that *the same thing happened to all five of them simultaneously*. How extraordinary.

They quickly realized that this was the plan of God, as He wanted to touch them separately and individually, not in the midst of the crowds

Revival!

and not in any way that they could attribute to emotionalism or the power of suggestion. When they went to the service at their churches that night, the Holy Spirit fell powerfully, and from that point on, they had been experiencing a steady move of the Spirit for the past two years at the time I went to speak for them.

Here's another extraordinary account. A woman was driving by the Brownsville church building without a thought of God on her mind. Suddenly, she felt the presence of God in her car, becoming overwhelmed with conviction and weeping in repentance—right in her car as she was driving. She cried out to the Lord for mercy and was born again at that moment, sharing her testimony when she became a member of the church.

For me, stories like these last two were the most wonderful to hear, as they were clear indications of God moving sovereignly outside of human control or human effort. And we heard countless stories like this over the years, with the Spirit falling on people as they drove back to their homes or returned to their hotels, or from pastors who didn't consciously experience anything at the revival but then saw an outpouring at their church the very first service when they got home. This is what revival is all about. *God comes down in sovereign power.*

While teaching at the ministry school that I led in Pensacola, I came up with an extended definition of revival: "Revival is a season of unusual divine visitation resulting in deep repentance, supernatural renewal, and sweeping reformation in the Church, along with the radical conversion of sinners in the world, often producing moral, social, and even economic change in the local or national communities." But everything comes down to those first eight words: *Revival is a season of unusual divine visitation.*

HOW I INTERSECTED WITH BROWNSVILLE

From the time of the outpouring at Community Bible Church in 1982-1983 until God called me to serve as a leader in the Brownsville Revival in May 1996, the hunger in my heart for revival never abated. Wherever I would go to preach, normally doing two-three days of meetings in a

LIVING IN THE LINE OF FIRE

location, I would often wonder: "Will this be the place where the Spirit falls and revival begins?"

That hunger only intensified after the fall of two leading televangelists in 1987 and 1988 as I began to realize that the church of America, in particular the charismatic church of which was I a part, was in desperate need of awakening. I also noticed a shift in my preaching in 1989. Prior to this, the Spirit would give me a specific word for each congregation where I ministered, often with prophetic significance for that local body. In fact, I would tell the pastor, "Aside from knowing the size of your congregation, I don't want to know anything else." This way, I could hear more clearly from heaven without any preconceived ideas.

But beginning in 1989, when I wrote *The End of the American Gospel Enterprise*, it became much more common for me to preach on similar, national themes as I traveled. Everything revolved around repentance and revival, which became the dominant themes of my books. As I wrote in *The End of the American Gospel Enterprise*,

> Something horrible has taken place. *The Church has backslidden without even knowing it.* Like Sardis, we have become the "perfect model of inoffensive Christianity" (G. B. Caird), "having a reputation of being alive, yet being dead" (Rev. 3:1). Like Sardis, we have so come to terms with our pagan environment that we provoke almost no opposition and make virtually no impact. And like Sardis, situated high on a mountain rock, we have felt safe and secure in this world.[8]

The urgency continued in *How Saved Are We?* in 1990:

> The American Church at the end of the twentieth century is experiencing a crisis. For years we have preached a cheap gospel and peddled a soft Savior. We have taught salvation without self-denial and the crown without the cross. We have catered to the unsaved and compromised with the world. Now we are paying the price.

Revival!

Our "instant salvation" message has dishonored God and deluded men. Our faulty seeds have produced a flaky harvest. What a pitiful crop we are reaping![9]

Then this in *Whatever Happened to the Power of God* in 1991:

While the American Church celebrates, our beloved country sinks into lower and lower depths. We are not only killing unborn babies, but we have begun to kill helpless adults—actually starving them to death! It is claimed that some of them are in a "persistent vegetative state." *I believe it is the Church that is in a persistent vegetative state.* Will nothing awake us from our stupor?[10]

And this in *It's Time to Rock the Boat* in 1993:

Is it time for a new kind of radical army to arise, just as fiery and dedicated to winning souls at any cost as were the original Salvation Army workers? And could it be that some of us will be called on to lay down our lives for the truth *in this generation, right here in America*? May God give us grace to stand firm.[11]

The stakes were getting higher and the burden growing deeper. It really was revival or we die.

HOW LONG, LORD?

In 1993, while still living in Maryland and commuting regularly to New York City to preach at Times Square Church, I heard reports of a fresh outpouring through the ministry of a South African preacher named Rodney Howard-Browne, characterized by "holy laughter." I had seen this phenomenon just one time, back in 1983, and I had a fascinating experience with this while preaching in 1984 (I'll tell that story later in

123

LIVING IN THE LINE OF FIRE

the book), but this was something on an entirely different scale. Was it really from the Lord?

Nancy and I attended some of Rodney's meetings in 1993, wanting to see for ourselves. And while some very strange things took place, there was no denying that people were being touched powerfully, with some repenting deeply and many being wonderfully refreshed. Still, I knew that God had shown me something different, something that was more repentance-based and holiness-focused. So while I rejoiced at what the Spirit was doing, I continued to long for the spiritual outpouring He had promised me.

To be clear, this is *not* to make a comparison between Brownsville and the Rodney Howard-Browne meetings. This is just to speak of my own journey and calling. As I journaled on Christmas, December 25, 1993: "Oh, how I want to raise my voice like a trumpet! God may be pouring out holy laughter on many of His people, but He has not called me to be a primary carrier! I must blow the trumpet. I must sound the alarm. I must awaken and stir sleeping, selfish, complacent believers. I must see the Fire!"

I then heard reports about what God was doing in Toronto through Randy Clark, beginning in early 1994 after he had received prayer from Rodney. I rejoiced over these reports too, although I never made it to Toronto during the years of the Toronto Blessing. But I also began to wonder. "Wasn't I supposed to be on the front lines of the next revival? Isn't that what the Lord had showed me? Why, then, am I on the outside looking in?"

I rebuked myself saying, "Maybe you exaggerated what the Lord said to you in the spring of 1983. After all, you've written books that have helped prepare the way for revival. You've preached messages that have deepened hunger for revival. And you've had countless altar calls where God's people cried out for revival. What makes think you get to have the whole pie? You've had your piece. The revival will come through others." Perhaps that was the case after all. And so I said to myself that I should be content with the role I had been able to play. Maybe the other things I had envisioned and dreamed about were the thoughts of my own mind.

Revival!

To be sure, I did participate in some very powerful meetings during this time, including services in England in 1994, ministering to about 120 leaders at the invitation of apostolic leader Derek Brown. (The connection with Derek is a story in itself which I'll recount in Chapter 12.) As I preached on conviction of sin to these men of God at a retreat venue named Pilgrim Hall, with everyone packed in a small room for the main services, a spirit of repentance fell in our midst, leading to deep, agonized sobbing and weeping. A few weeks later, a number of churches related to Derek all experienced a visitation during their Sunday morning services, totally without human coordination. It was a sovereign outpouring, and it lasted for many months.

Reflecting on this afterward, I knew that the Lord used me to help dig deeper wells to receive that outpouring of holy rain, thereby preparing the way for the Spirit to come. But I also knew I had not brought the outpouring with me, since I had not been carrying it. Still, beginning in 1994, I began to preach on keys to moving from "the blessing" (as they referred to that season of visitation in the UK) to revival, explaining that there were two ditches on either side of the road to revival. On one side was the ditch of traditional religion, which said, "We never did it like this before!" On the other side was the ditch of superficial sensationalism or manifestation mania that focused entirely on the outward responses to the Spirit. How easy it was to fall into either one of these ditches! Instead, we needed to keep our eyes on Jesus, welcome the Spirit, and focus on holiness and harvest, preaching repentance to the Church and to the world.[12]

It was during this time when the Lord stirred me to write *From Holy Laughter to Holy Fire: America on the End of Revival*, but due to a miscommunication with Don Nori the CEO of Destiny Image, who had published my previous five books, I agreed to release the book with Huntington House. (The company is now defunct.) But as we got into the editing process, Huntington House wanted me to shorten the content, because of which I had to remove a couple of chapters. I wasn't happy about it, but it was their decision.

LIVING IN THE LINE OF FIRE

More importantly, they did *not* want the word "revival" in the title, much to my consternation. They were convinced that revival was not a hot topic and was not about to be a hot topic, despite my strong arguments to the contrary. The whole premise of the book was that spiritual renewal was already astir and that revival was about to break out in our midst, but while they liked the manuscript, they rejected my pleas.

At that point, I wanted to back out of the agreement, which I was entitled to do, but I didn't want to delay the publication process at that last stage, so I agreed to the title *High Voltage Christianity: Sparking the Spirit in the Church*. The publishers would not even agree to putting the word "revival" in the subtitle, as I had proposed, *Sparking the Spirit of Revival in the Church*. That's how convinced they were that revival was not a hot topic.

The book came out in March 1995, ending with these words:

> Once, while preaching near Buffalo, I visited Niagara Falls together with Jennifer, our older daughter. As we walked along the bank towards the Falls, there was a clear, strong tide pulling the waters along. The thought struck me: "That is the state of a growing church. It is progressing and moving forward. But that is not revival."
>
> Then we got nearer to the Falls. The flowing stream had turned into raging rapids! The water was capped with white waves, and the tide was almost violent in its pull. Again the thought came to mind: "That is was most of us today call revival. It's a great increase over the normal state of things, much more is happening, and it looks really exciting. But it's still not revival!"
>
> Then we came to the Falls. They were absolutely awesome! I had seen them as a little boy, but the reality was so much more powerful than the memory. They were not just grand and impressive. They were staggering!
>
> But I wasn't content just to see the Falls. I wanted to experience them. So Jennifer and I joined a group of other interested

Revival!

tourists, rented out some big, yellow rain coats, left our shoes in a locker, and went down to the rocks at the base of the Falls. The closer we got, the more overwhelming it became.

Torrents of water—so much water!—crashed like thunder. In a moment we were soaked. The wind—where did it all come from?—blew so hard it actually took our breath away. We were no longer spectators. We were participants, caught up in the pounding, swirling, churning, flooding display of natural glory. There, in a face to face encounter with the raw power of God, with the majesty of the Creator exploding all around me, I could only raise my hands and praise Him who lives for ever and ever. I was swallowed up in the Falls.

That is a picture of revival. Are you ready?[13]

I *knew* that something was about to break. That's why the book ended with the words, "Are you ready?" Three months later, on Father's Day, June 18, 1995, the Spirit fell at the Brownsville Assembly of God in Pensacola, Florida. The visitation had come!

As for sales of *High Voltage Christianity*, they were meager, and once the Lord called me to Pensacola, we bought all remaining copies from the publisher at a big discount (thankfully, the first printing had been fairly small) and I bought back to the rights to the book, adding the chapter "The Prophets of the Thirteenth Year," which I wrote around the time of my first visit to the revival in May 1996. We released it through Destiny Image with the title, *From Holy Laughter to Holy Fire: America on the End of Revival*, including the other chapters I had to omit, and within months, it sold ten times more copies than the previous edition. The time had come!

HEARING ABOUT BROWNSVILLE

It's important to remember that the Brownsville Revival, also known early on as the Pensacola Outpouring, began shortly before the internet explosion, meaning that word about the revival did not spread overnight.

LIVING IN THE LINE OF FIRE

And even though Steve Hill and I had become friends through our connection with Leonard Ravenhill, talking by phone and exchanging books, we had yet not met face to face. In the months leading up to Brownsville, Steve called to tell me that he was functioning under a new and powerful anointing, seeing more powerful results than he had ever seen. He was really excited, even more than normal. But it was probably because of the intensity of the revival that he didn't call to give me an update.

Still, as I began to hear reports about the meetings and learned that Steve was the one God used to ignite the outpouring, I said to myself, "This could be the revival, God, I've been waiting for." I said this because I knew Steve was a strong repentance preacher and a burning evangelist who always went for the lost. So I rejoiced, glad to hear these reports, even if I myself was not involved. The important thing was that the revival was happening.

In October 1995, I read an article about Brownsville written for *Charisma Magazine* by Lee Grady, and one thing in particular got my interest. Steve had been asked why he cancelled all his meetings world-wide once the Spirit fell. He replied, "The opportunity of a lifetime must be seized during the lifetime of the opportunity."

That sounded like Ravenhill to me, but I had never heard Brother Len say those words. Steve subsequently told me that, shortly before Len had a stroke and fell into a coma in September 1994, he turned to Steve and spoke those words, which Steve immediately wrote down.

A few years earlier, when Steve had returned from powerful meetings in Latin America, he said to Len, "I felt like revival was about to break out." Len replied, "Then why are you here? Why didn't you stay there?" Steve took those words to heart, and when the Spirit fell in Brownsville, he told his assistant, who was waiting for him in Russia where he was scheduled to minister, "I'll get there, but we have to push the meetings back." He and Pastor Kilpatrick had agreed to go another night, then another, until they thought, "This might be a really long revival—maybe lasting for several weeks!" Little did they know those days and weeks

Revival!

would turn into more than five years. Eventually, Steve told his assistant, "Come home. I won't be going to Russia."

On my end, I didn't get around to calling Steve until January 19, 1996. He said to me on the phone, "Mike, I happened to be at the right place at the right time. You need to come down for a few days. You'll love what God is doing. And I need to get your books out here. You're the closest thing to Ravenhill alive today." (That was his assessment, not mine.) I journaled: "the divine connection is made (that I felt strongly about for some time)...."

Steve continued, "We have a condo on the beach. You can come down, rest, write, and attend a few services." That sounded like paradise! But because of the intensity of my own traveling schedule, I was not able to get down there until late May of 1996. I would be returning from ministry in England (again with Derek Brown) on Monday night, May 27, then flying to Pensacola on Thursday, May 30. Our older daughter, Jen, would be coming along for the trip.

I got home as scheduled on May 27, but, after falling asleep, quite zonked, we got a jarring call from a local hospital. This was my journal entry:

JEN WAS IN AN ACCIDENT. SHE'S BLEEDING HEAVILY FROM THE HEAD AND HER KNEE HURTS, BUT SHE'S ALRIGHT. We spent the night (from 1:30 until 6:30) at the hospital, Nancy by Jen's bedside and me, queasy and ready to collapse, sleeping in the van. No doubt, satan tried to take Jen out (a head-on collision around a blind curve), but grace prevailed. Thank You, Father, for our Jen, stitched up and all. Now, what about Pensacola?

By God's amazing grace, Jen had no serious injuries, even after smashing the windshield with her head, but she couldn't travel with me. So I flew down alone, arriving Thursday afternoon, excited but with a heavy heart. I also had a bad headache because of lack of sleep. None of that,

LIVING IN THE LINE OF FIRE

however, got in the way of encountering the Lord that night—for me, a sacred, historic night.

Steve had arranged for a special parking space for me behind the building (little did I know what a commodity that would be until I arrived), also telling me he wanted me to sit on the platform with him and Pastor Kilpatrick. So, I had a bird's eye view of everything that was happening, with Steve giving me commentary along the way. This was my journal entry for May 30, 1996:

> What can I say? This is the real thing. God is here. From my jumping for joy (splitting headache and all), to my uncontrollable weeping because of the reality of God's presence and the evidence on the faces of the young people, to my call to Nancy whose watching of the Mercy Seat video again made her also to know that this is it. Let it explode, Lord, and let me explode with Your holy fire.

At last, after thirteen years of crying out and seeking and longing and praying and fasting, *this was it*. At last! (Even now, I write this with tears welling up in my eyes.) I had called Nancy from my car after the meeting, somewhere between 1:00-2:00 a.m., Eastern Time, and I started to say the words, "This is the real thing." But I couldn't finish talking. I was too overcome. To my amazement, she finished what I was going to say, telling me, "I know."

She had been watching a video from the revival that we had received from Sid Roth, featuring the Ward sisters, Alyson and Elizabeth, sharing their testimonies, with Charity James singing "Mercy Seat" for the altar call. And although the video cut out partway through, leaving only the audio, Nancy knew that this was real, even though we were 1,000 miles apart. I was stunned.

One day later, on May 31, 1996, I journaled this, focusing on the confluence of the revival and my calling:

130

Revival!

(The following was received with urgency and intensity.) Being in Pensacola, knowing that my books helped fuel and feed the fire in many here (including, above all, Steve Hill), being convinced (in the words of the song, "The Spirit of the Sovereign Lord") that this *is* the beginning of the day and the hour that I have longed for, I feel overwhelmingly that this is also the hour for "the prophets of the thirteenth year" [meaning, prophetic voices to help take the revival deeper and guard against pitfalls]. Am I dreaming, or is the call to write the commentary on Jeremiah [which I had just received from Zondervan publishing] and the connection to the Pensacola outpouring... confirmation of the fact that *now* is the time for my burden to be delivered?

It was truly a time of destiny, and my life, along with the lives of millions of others touched by the revival, has never been the same. Six months earlier on January 1, 1996, I had written:

Seeking God in prayer past midnight and then reading some of the Wesley's sermons, that intense desire begins to rise in me once more: Oh for the voice of a trumpet! Oh for the blast from heaven! Oh, for the platform to preach searing, shaking, sobering, soaked and soaking words to the people of God here in the USA. I *must* more fully enter my call (this year—may it be!). (*Prophetic* revivalist as opposed to evangelistic revivalist.) Father, open up America to me, and make me ready.

At last the time had come!

The condo where I was staying that first week was about thirty minutes from the church building, and I would literally sob as I drove to the meetings each night while listening to a cassette tape with worship from the revival. It was sometimes hard to see because of the intensity of the

LIVING IN THE LINE OF FIRE

flow of tears, like trying to look through the windshield during a heavy rainstorm without using the windshield wipers.

Two things had converged at once. First, there was the glorious presence of God that revival brings. It is almost unimaginably wonderful. Second, there was my own sense of calling and destiny with the releasing of promises in my own life that tied in directly to revival. The combination of the two was overwhelming.

TIME TO JOIN THE TEAM

That first service in Brownsville on Thursday, May 30, when Steve began to lay hands on all who wanted prayer, along with Pastor Kilpatrick and others on the prayer team, I asked him to pray for me. He laid hands on me, and I fell to my back, where I lay there, communing with the Lord and asking Him to take me deeper into His holiness. But after a few minutes, Steve came back over to me and said, "Come on, get up! You need to help us pray for the people." I was enlisted, that very first night—and every night I was there in the years that followed.

Later during that first week, I met a pastor from Australia who was attending the meetings. He said, "Why don't you do anything in the day?" I had no idea that there were no day sessions of any kind—not for teaching or equipping or anything else—and immediately, God laid something on my heart. Why not hold day sessions for leaders on Fridays, since there were normally several hundred leaders there each week, and day sessions for the general public on Saturdays? I suggested this to Steve, who was really excited, asking me to share it with John Kilpatrick. John said to me, "Would you do that for us?" You better believe I would!

On June 3, 1996, I journaled this: "What is next for Pensacola? Entrench—dig deeper and deeper! Equip—prepare God's people for action! Expand—bigger facilities and more workers! Export—send the fire around the world!" A plan of action was emerging, and I faxed all this to John Kilpatrick.

Then, on June 15, the eve of the one-year anniversary of the revival, when I was back home in Maryland, I wrote this down: "Is God saying,

Revival!

'*Pitch your tent* in Brownsville'—meaning investing myself in more sub-stantial training of workers and leaders from that base, raising up almost overnight a serious, equipping school? (The picture is that of makeshift, semi-permanent facilities erected at a refugee camp or at the site of a nat-ural disaster.)" Now God was speaking to me about a full-blown ministry school.

During that first trip to Pensacola, after getting the vision of doing day sessions, I had called Nancy, telling her I might need to come down monthly to teach at the revival. She said to me, "Once a month is not going to be enough." She was ahead of me again. Now I was asking a big-ger question: Are we supposed to relocate there?

At that time, no one knew how long the revival would last, so the idea of moving to Pensacola sounded fairly radical. But then again, this was the very thing I had been dreaming about and praying for all these years. How could we *not* do it? When revival comes, you must seize the moment.

We had been part of Beth Messiah Congregation from 1987-1993, as I led Messiah Biblical Institute and Graduate School of Theology. But after that season had come to an end, we moved on from Beth Messiah amica-bly, yet without a clear congregational home. I had wanted to move back to New York, making Times Square Church our home church with the vision of raising up a school for David Wilkerson. But he never replied to my suggestion, which indicated to me that God had not spoken that to him. Nancy also never felt right about us making that move, but we were somewhat homeless, especially after March 1995, when things changed at Times Square Church after a temporary separation between some of the leaders. Now I wasn't preaching there either.

Now, in 1996, there was nothing stopping us from making the move to Florida, and I could continue to travel and write while based there. As for raising up a school, I had mixed feelings. On the one hand, I was hesitant. I had led a school for six years and knew the responsibilities involved. It was nice to be free from those. Plus, with the grueling sched-ule of the revival, involving four night services per week, each of which

133

LIVING IN THE LINE OF FIRE

averaged five to six hours, plus day sessions, plus traveling, plus writing, how I could oversee and teach at a school as well? On the other hand, this really was the opportunity of a lifetime, one that had to be seized during the lifetime of the opportunity. It was also in keeping with an internal vision I had for years that I would help raise up a school that would send out thousands of radicals to the nations. This could be that school!

We launched Brownsville Revival School of Ministry (BRSM) in January 1997 with 120 full-time students. Two years later, we had more than 1,000 full-time students. Two years after that, we had sent out grads as missionaries to more than twenty nations, with a peak student body of almost 1,200. And God met us in those classes!

During the first semester in 1997, I was waiting for the students to arrive at the classroom where I was ready to teach. It was the second class of the day, but the students never showed up. (We met Tuesday to Friday from noon to 4:30 PM, due to the late nights of the revival, with two, two-hour classes each day.) The professor teaching the first class walked into my classroom white as a ghost. "Dr. Brown," he said to me, "I think you should see what's happening, since it's your class time."

He had been teaching on the tabernacle, explaining how God's presence was localized there. One of the students asked, "Isn't that similar to what's happening here in Pensacola?" The professor responded, but his tongue was heavy and it was hard for him to get all of the words out. When he looked up again from his notes, he saw a distinct mist in the room. He asked the students if they saw it, and several affirmed they did. Everything then fell completely silent. It was as if the cloud of God's glory had come into the room, leading to extended prayer and praise, which is why the students never made it to my class. When I walked in to see what was happening, some students were on their faces, others standing and worshiping, others running around the room. God was in our midst.

One of our grads penned this account about his time at BRSM:

Revival!

I used to meet with a brother for prayer before our Bible school classes, and I recall pulling up to the school property in March of '98, where the students' morning prayer meeting was moved upon by the Lord in a profound way. When I pulled into the parking lot, students were prostrate all over the campus, laying in the grass or on the sidewalks, groaning with hunger for God, and asking Him for mercy on behalf of our nation. Strong men were broken before the Lord, trembling and weeping in prayer, and everywhere in these times the hearts of God's people seemed fixed on His throne. You were directed heavenward merely by being there. I felt as if I had stepped out of my car and into another world, where the earth was permeated with God Himself! O, that every community of saints would be marked with this kind of reality, for the glory of Christ![14]

This is a picture of revival. This is what happens when God visits. This is why so many who were touched in the revival have never been the same.

When we sent out student teams on mission trips, the fire of God fell in the nations too. One of the first trips was to Nigeria, led by longtime Long Island friend, John Cava, who became our first missions director. When the team arrived in a village to preach the gospel, a demonized man who did not speak English started to run around, shouting (in English), "Oh no! The fire people are here!" Even the demons were aware.

Other good friends from Long Island would visit Brownsville, saying to me, "Mike, you told us this was going to happen!" I had shared with them years earlier the promise the Lord had given me that I would serve in a revival that would touch the world, and now they were eyewitnesses to this glorious, historic outpouring, one which charismatic church historian Vinson Synan described as "the longest running local church revival in American history."

Looking back, it's clear that God used Rodney Howard-Browne as a forerunner, helping to spark many revival fires around the country and beyond. And, without a doubt, there has been massive, worldwide fruit

LIVING IN THE LINE OF FIRE

from the Toronto Outpouring. But Brownsville was the place of my destiny, the place where the Lord's particular calling on my life could be fulfilled, the place where I could serve most effectively. How can I possibly express my gratitude to the Lord?

SOME REVIVAL VIGNETTES FROM MY JOURNAL

On August 24, 1996, we held our first day session for pastors, doing it on a Saturday as our first trial run. The session was scheduled to start mid-afternoon so the leaders could attend the teaching, get a quick meal, then come back for the night service. But something unexpected happened as I taught on signs of a backslidden heart, ending with a teaching on the burden of the Lord. I journaled:

> ...get ready for the day session, good attendance, powerful first session, then *intense* second hour speaking on God's burden, and the wailing, weeping, sobbing, and convulsing is overwhelming. We finish travailing for the youth in particular... then the powerful night service: It erupts with prayer for the youth (what do you know?)....

That first day session was a scene to behold, as these pastors and leaders were overwhelmed by conviction, rushing to the altar of the youth chapel, where we held the meeting and which was used for overflow at night, absolutely broken before the Lord. It was beyond intense. And it happened so easily, without the least pressure or coercion. The fire was burning bright.

The problem was that the ushers had to clear the building to get ready for the night service, but these leaders were on their faces weeping and convulsing before God. What a holy crisis! That's why, after that first meeting, we switched the time to 11:00 a.m. daily. We needed to leave room for the Spirit.

Are you getting a picture of what life was like in the midst of revival? Can you feel the intensity?

136

Revival!

The following are some additional journal entries from the revival, taken from nights that were especially memorable:

> **October 12, 1996**: Sneezing a lot in the morning, then a powerful time of challenging ministry—in spite of the sniffles—to the biggest crowd yet (basically filling the downstairs of the sanctuary), lunch with my friends from Aldershot (with many tears), back to the condo (but no rest), and then—who could have expected it?—the Spirit *falls* on the large crowd of young people on the platform, the weeping and intercession set in, and the glory comes down. *Nothing less than a historic night in the annals of revival.* Powerful prayer ministry, I'm totally on the verge of collapse, as I have been through most of the night. To the condo, warmed up pizza, then collapse into bed after beginning to prepare my message.

LET IT BE WRITTEN IN THE ANNALS OF REVIVAL HISTORY: GOD CAME TO BROWNSVILLE TONIGHT.[15]

> **January 31, 1997**: I want to share my heart honestly with you, holding nothing back. I want to make myself totally vulnerable. The fact is, I *must*.
>
> I have just come from the beautiful presence of the Lord, from a night of glorious baptismal testimonies and incredible stories of wonderfully changed lives, a night of sovereign visitation, a night of deep, sweeping repentance, of radical encounters with the living God, of public acts of repentance—from young people throwing their drugs and needles into the garbage to old people discarding their cigarettes—a night of weeping under conviction and rejoicing in newfound freedom, a night when the Spirit fell upon the children in a side room until their intercession and wailing permeated the sanctuary, a night when Jesus was exalted in the midst of His Church. Yes, I have come

LIVING IN THE LINE OF FIRE

from the holy presence of the Lord in the Brownsville Revival on January 31, 1997. The Spirit moved, the tears flowed, the Lord touched, the demons fled. This is what happens when revival is in the land!

At the end of the night, amidst shouts of joy and victory, amidst the sound of the newly redeemed enjoying their first moments free from captivity, I turned to my dear friend, Evangelist Steve Hill and said, "We don't have to quote from the history books about revival. It's here! We're seeing it before our eyes."

Who can describe a night like this? Who can describe what it is like to be so caught up with God that heaven is virtually here and you can almost sense the sound of the Judge knocking at the door? What can you say when young men come to the platform and begin to throw away their earrings, and another wants counsel because he doesn't know how to remove his *eyebrow* ring, and another tosses out his condoms, while another throws his knife into the trash? What can you say?

What can you say when a thousand people respond to the altar call and stay there for two hours getting right with God? What can you say when the prayers you have prayed for your nation, prayers for the real thing, for genuine visitation, for bona fide outpouring—not hype, not sensationalism, not a superficial show, but an awakening of historic proportions— when those prayers are being answered before your eyes and you know that you know that your country will be *shaken?* What can you say?

What can you say when all you want is Jesus, when pleasing Him is your total delight, when you just have to tell everyone about God's great salvation, when sin's sweetest temptation is utterly repulsive to you, when you just can't find the words to express to the Lord how utterly wonderful He is, how He really is your all in all? What can you say at a sacred time like this?

138

Revival!

It is too precious to fully describe, too intimate to wholly communicate with mere human speech.[16]

There were also entries like these as I traveled out from Pensacola to the nations:

March 25, 1997, Sydney, Australia: Oh what a day! Oh what a day! OH WHAT A DAY! Have I ever seen a heavier single day of ministry? THREE intense and incredible meetings, from the searing conviction of the morning session issuing in mass repentance and brokenness, to the powerful afternoon teaching, ending with hundreds and hundreds powerfully *hit* by the Spirit, to the phenomenal, packed night meeting, ending with massive spiritual hunger and outcry for revival, heaven-shaking prayer, and a shout of victory that virtually knocks me off my feet. What a day! ...Lord, it's time! How awesome this revival is! How awesome it is about to become.... THE FLOOD TIDE IS RISING!

December 12, 1997, Upsala: Reports have now come in about the young people being overwhelmed by the Lord last night, and many gathered for early morning prayer as well as asked if they could pray from 3:00-6:00 p.m. after school today! The final morning session is wonderfully practical, then *heavy* as I pray for all the Bible School students (400)—staggering a little because of the anointing and exhaustion, ...then a great talk with the university students, then share with the high school kids and show a video, then collapse in the room, then back for a final Jabotinsky Project dinner and brief word—but I am *totally* wiped out, having spoken 14 times in 3 days.

This was also a theme that emerged from my first months of involvement in Brownsville: *being totally exhausted and wiped out.* Journal entries

LIVING IN THE LINE OF FIRE

like these could be multiplied by the hundreds. These are all taken from the same month:

> **April 4, 1997**: The biggest attendance yet, the baptisms are wonderful, some good testimonies from local pastors, a strong word from Steve, powerful prayer time (I'm wiped out!!!), then Denny's with Nancy, Meg, and Daniel G. To bed about 2:00. Tonight I am literally shaking in bed at the end of the day, *shaking out of tiredness*, just about *crying* because I am so totally spent. Renew me, Father!

> **April 5, 1997**: A great, utterly wiped-out day. It's almost comical to be so tired. But, thank God, we're fruitful! An excellent, challenging day session...a brief nap, and then a wonderful night, with an unexpectedly massive and deeply broken altar call (including the Chicago teenage miracle—145 in all!) and *intensely* powerful prayer time (although I am literally staggering out of exhaustion). Home to advance the clocks an hour (!), chat with Nancy, and collapse into bed shortly before 2:00 (new time). Revival is heavy!!!

> **April 24, 1997**: ...I'm on the verge of collapse praying for people at the end. Quick stop at Whataburger, then I really struggle falling asleep. Help, Lord!

Be assured that I was not alone in being so exhausted. This happened to all of the leaders on different levels. Yet we were also supernaturally sustained by the presence of God, by the hunger of the people, and by the extraordinary fruit we were seeing. How could we hold back? People had traveled from around the world. Others had been standing in line for twelve hours. Were we going to tell them that we were too tired to minister to them? And when we *knew* that they would be dramatically touched as we ministered to them, who could think of taking a night off?

140

Revival!

Another factor that added to the intensity of the revival was the constant wave of attacks from critics, both inside and outside the Church. As Arthur Wallis wrote: "If we find a revival that is not spoken against, we had better look again to ensure that it is a revival."[17] That's why I said for many years, "You can have controversy without revival, but you cannot have revival without controversy."

I had referenced this in *The End of the American Gospel Enterprise* in 1989, also devoting several chapters to the subject in *From Holy Laughter to Holy Fire*, meaning, before I arrived in Brownsville. If you know revival is coming, you also know that criticism is coming. During the revival, in order to help pastors and believers who were confused by all the criticism, I wrote the book, *Let No One Deceive You: Confronting the Critics of Revival*,[18] subsequently releasing a revised and updated edition titled, *The Revival Answer Book: Rightly Discerning Contemporary Revival Movements*.[19]

We also came under blistering, largely ridiculous attacks from the local newspaper, the *Pensacola News Journal*. Prior to their series of hostile articles, they had written dozens of favorable articles, and after the series of attacks, their tone became fairer and more balanced. But for a season, we were dealing with this onslaught too, including perhaps the most absurd claim of all, namely, that several of the leaders had *planned* the revival, allegedly duping the millions who were touched by it. Common sense tells you that if you could so easily "plan" a revival that would draw people from around the world, we would be "planning" one in almost every church in the nation.

Added to all this was the unusually intense demonic attack that we experienced in those days. Looking back years later, Richard Crisco said to me, "You would battle through hellish oppression all day, just to get to the night service, but then it was all worth it."

I personally found this hard to describe, almost like I was hearing demonic chatter in my ears, feeling bothered and battered by it, having to press through this oppressive cloud. Or as John Kilpatrick said to me, "The divine glory was the greatest I have ever experienced. The demonic

LIVING IN THE LINE OF FIRE

oppression was the worst I ever experienced." It was a battle, but that comes with the turf. And as I think back to those days, as exhausting as they were and as intense as they were, what I remember most vividly, 100 times over, is how extraordinary the presence of God was in our midst. It was, at last, a dream come true.

In the years since the revival, I have sat with longtime friends who had been there or with BRSM grads, and we have exchanged sacred memories. Within minutes, we are all crying, sometimes even weeping, as we recall the splendor of the Lord and sometimes even feel that divine presence again. And while we do not look back nostalgically, since we know that this outpouring was for a time and a season, producing glorious fruit that remains to this day, we have been marked by the revival for life.

CHAPTER 8

REVOLUTION RISING

In the midst of the Brownsville Revival, it was easy to dream big dreams. After all, night after night we were witnessing God move in exceptional power and we were hearing testimonies that seemed too extraordinary to be true—but they *were* true. We were especially stirred by the stories we heard from students, as dozens of kids would come on the platform together, talking about their friends being saved and the Spirit falling right in their school. Sometimes as many as fifty or sixty students from the same school would testify together. The feeling was electric. No wonder Steve Hill used to say, "One of these days we're going to get a call from a school saying, 'The Spirit has fallen on all 2,500 students!'" Why not?

That was one of the most exciting things about the revival: seeing God move outside the walls of the church building. That's what really thrilled our souls. Perhaps in this way the revival could impact the surrounding culture? Could the outpouring become an awakening? As I said, it was easy to dream dreams.

It is true that, just like Toronto, Brownsville attracted visitors from around the world and they, in turn, returned home ablaze for God. This meant that rather than primarily seeing local ripples from the revival, there would be more scattered, worldwide ripples. At the same time, all of us as leaders in the revival were deeply burdened by the condition of America, and we longed to see the Church of America rise up in purity and power, impacting the nation through the gospel. Why not now?

As for the ministry school, the students remained ablaze, with no sign of the intensity letting up, even in the year 2000 as the revival was

143

LIVING IN THE LINE OF FIRE

lessening in intensity. And as faculty and school leaders, our lives were deeply bound up with the lives of the students. We had become a large family, and we cared for them as spiritual parents care for their spiritual kids. In fact, this was one of the most significant things that happened to me during our time in Pensacola.

MY HEART FOR THE STUDENTS

Prior to launching BRSM, I had served as an adjunct professor at Valley Forge Christian College, New York Extension School, from 1983-1985, teaching classes in Old Testament and Hebrew to older Korean students training for ministry. But we had almost no interaction outside of those class times. I commuted to Manhattan, ministered to the students, and returned home.

From 1983-1987, I taught at CFNI on Long Island, and because we lived near the school and most of the students lived on campus, we spent a lot more time together, with students coming over to our house and with me playing sports with them. (In most cases, I was barely ten years older than them, so there was not that much distance between us.) Yet as much as I loved pouring into the students, I did my outside ministry on my own—that is, unless you ran alongside me and got close to me. In that case, I would gladly pour into you. Otherwise, I was running my own race.

It was the same thing leading Messiah Biblical Institute and Graduate School of Theology in Maryland from 1987-1993. It was a delight and a joy, but my outside ministry was quite independent; meaning, I was not one to take student teams with me when I traveled. As for my style of ministry, I was absolutely *not* pastoral, in stark contrast with Eitan (then Andrew) Shishkoff, part of the Beth Messiah leadership team in Maryland. The word *pastor* oozes out of every fiber of his being. (Eitan has served in Israel since the early 1990s.)

Not surprisingly, Eitan and I would have some friendly clashes as fellow leaders in our days at Beth Messiah. He would give a hopeful report about his latest meeting with a discontented couple who was always

144

Revolution Rising

complaining about the congregation. "We had a good meeting," he would say, "and I can see their hearts getting softer." I would reply, "You've been meeting with them for two years already, and it's a waste of time. You'll waste another year, and then they'll leave angrily. Best to bless them and send them on their way now." I was even appointed by the leaders to bring a periodic "membership drive" message at Beth Messiah, meaning, driving out all those who didn't belong as members. "Compassionate" was not my middle name.

When it came time to launch BRSM, I was assured by the Brownsville leadership that I would be free of pastor responsibility and that they would provide pastoral oversight for the students. My job would be to assemble the faculty, create the curriculum, lead the way spiritually, and oversee the administration. This I was happy to do; as for pastoral care, that was not for me.

The first semester was wonderful, starting in January 1997 with 120 hungry and eager students. Teaching them was an absolute delight. But given the intensity of both the revival schedule and my itinerant ministry, I had very little extra time for the students.

That summer, as applications began to pour in and I realized that we would grow dramatically, something began to happen in my heart. "Who will look out for these students?" I wondered. "What can we do to offer them more spiritual care?"

From the first semester to the second semester, we grew from 120 to 600, and the opening chapel service to start the fall classes was explosive. We were amazed to see the sudden and dramatic growth. Look what the Lord has done! But again, due to the intensity of life during revival, we had very few social events for the students, and "campus life" was basically going to school, going to revival services, doing local outreach, and, if needed, going to work.

We did, however, have one volleyball game each semester. The faculty would play alongside the students, and we would divide into teams, with each team representing a nation. And because we were in the midst of revival, everything was super spiritual, so we would intercede for the

LIVING IN THE LINE OF FIRE

nations represented by each team before we played. We couldn't just have fun and games. We needed to pray too!

In keeping with my New York style, I was aggressive in a fun way, trash-talking with the opposing team and trying to intimidate the referees, since they were students as well. So we played, we had a blast, and that was that. I couldn't even tell you the names of almost all the students on my team.

Some days later, I received a heartfelt letter from one of the students. She told me that she grew up without a father, but that day, playing volleyball with me, for the first time in her life, she felt like she had a father. I was shocked, even though I was aware of just how fatherless this generation was. Still, I thought, "I can't believe she felt like she had a father just by playing volleyball with me one time." It made an impression on me.

A few days later, I was walking down the hallway in our administrative building when I came up to the director of our IT department, a married man in his early thirties. As I walked by him and put my hand on his shoulder, a thought came to me: "Leave your hand there a few more seconds." I did so, then walked away. A few days later I got a long email from him, explaining that his father was addicted to pornography and, consequently, he grew up feeling like he didn't have a father. But when I kept my hand on his shoulder for those extra seconds, for the first time in his life, he felt like he had a father. Again, I was amazed.

At the same time, something very profound was happening in my heart. I felt a deep, fatherly responsibility for the students. My life became bound up with their well-being, and wherever I went, I wanted to have students with me. This was something I had never experienced before.

Of course, I didn't go around announcing my new sense of fatherly responsibility to the student body, but I started getting cards and notes from students, even from students older than me, telling me how they felt like they had a spiritual father looking out for them. Some of the cards and notes began with, "Dear Dad."

This feeling of sacred responsibility spread to the entire faculty as well. Our hearts were deeply united with the student body, not in any type of

Revolution Rising

cult-like or controlling sense. Rather, it was a holy burden given by the Lord. Our lives were joined together, just like a shepherd with his flock.

Paul used language like this when writing to the Thessalonians, saying, "Just as a nursing mother cares for her children, so we cared for you. Because we loved you so much, we were delighted to share with you not only the gospel of God but our lives as well" (1 Thessalonians 2:7b–8 NIV). We could relate to these sentiments, as well as these: "For what is our hope, our joy, or the crown in which we will glory in the presence of our Lord Jesus when he comes? Is it not you? Indeed, you are our glory and joy" (1 Thessalonians 2:19–20 NIV).

It got to the point where I could not say the word "students" without breaking down and crying. I would be speaking to several hundred pastors at a leader's gathering, and at the end of the meeting they would ask me questions about the revival. One of them would say, "Dr. Brown, how are things going at the school?" I would start to answer but then was unable to speak, starting to cry instead. That's how deeply my heart was knit with theirs.

During this season, I traveled to Israel and was sitting in a van with my longtime friend Eitan Shishkoff. He asked, "So Mike, what's the biggest burden on your heart these days?" I looked at him and said, "The students," instantly breaking down in tears. I remember him looking at me in the strangest way as if he was wondering, "What alien entity took over the body of Mike Brown?" That's how deep the transformation was, and to this day there is a very special bond between many of the grads and the other faculty and me. God joined our hearts together in those sacred days; and even though, to this moment, no one would mistake me for being a pastor, God did put the heart of a spiritual father in me, and that heart has never left.

In our attic, we have large boxes of extraordinarily touching cards and letters sent to me by our students and grads. That's why, late in 2000, when it became possible that I might lose the school, the very thought of it was absolutely devastating to me, along with the rest of the faculty. These were our kids!

147

LIVING IN THE LINE OF FIRE

While in India on March 8, 2000, working with my dear friend Yesupadam, I journaled this:

> After the message this afternoon, as the altar is filled with praying—and weeping—men, I feel the weight once again of the reality that it is very possible that some will die as martyrs because of my message. This is utterly serious. After the night service, Yesupadam tells the students that I'm not the same man I was three years ago. *That man* was an individual, he says; *this man* is a father, a man of tears and compassion. Thank You, Jesus! He also says that my preaching is different: So much power is coming out of me that it's hard for him even to stand at some points. More, Lord!

REVOLUTION

It was against this backdrop, sometime in 1999, that the Lord began to drop the theme of revolution into my heart, not in terms of rebellion or hatred or anger or violence—God forbid!—but in terms of a transformed Church having a revolutionary impact on the culture. We would overcome evil with good, hatred with love, lies with truth, and the power of the flesh with the power of the Spirit. We were called to shake the nation.

And then something happened while watching a documentary on June 29, 1999, one of those revelatory moments where you see something you never saw before, and once you see it, you cannot unsee it. I was hit between the eyes with a stark reality, and now my course was set.

I had been participating in an Awake America event with the Brownsville team in New Jersey, and after the lengthy and powerful Tuesday night service June 29, I went back to my hotel room and decided to unwind a bit, putting on the TV, which I normally didn't do. Immediately, I was engrossed in a documentary titled "God Fights Back," which I happened to turn to just as the program began. I was drawn in instantly. The documentary outlined the rise of religious fundamentalism

Revolution Rising

worldwide beginning in the late 1970s, focusing first on Ayatollah Khomeini in Iran and then looking at the Moral Majority in America as well as some major televangelists.

The first thing that struck me was the difference in dedication. The Iranian Muslims were willing to die for their cause, and no price was too high for them to pay. In contrast, our TV-oriented, feel-good religion felt like satire. It was actually embarrassing to watch. One faith seemed passionate and burning; the other faith (our faith!) seemed cartoonish and tepid.

But it is what came next that rocked my world. The previous night, before Steve Hill preached the main message at the Awake America event with about 8,000-10,000 in attendance, I gave a brief exhortation, saying, "The gays have come out of the closet, and this group and that group have come out of the closet. It's time for us as believers to come out of the closet," meaning, let's stand up boldly and unashamedly for our faith and let's take the message of Jesus outside the walls of our church buildings.

Now, as I watched "God Fights Back," I was stunned to see footage from August 1980, almost twenty years earlier than our large rally in New Jersey, as evangelist James Robison preached to about 15,000 Christians in a large convention center before presidential candidate Ronald Reagan came out to speak. James said with fire in his voice, "I'm sick and tired of hearing about all of the radicals, and the perverts, and the liberals, and the leftists, and the communists coming out of the closet. It's time for God's people to come out of the closet, out of the churches, and change America." I was floored. Absolutely floored.

It's true that, in that context, James was calling for Christian political involvement and I was calling for evangelism (although he absolutely believed in the priority of evangelism, without a doubt). And Jerry Falwell had spoken earlier in that same meeting, saying that we had a threefold obligation as believers: first, to get people saved; second, to get them baptized; and third, to get them registered to vote. So, again, the thrust of the meetings was different, and now, in 1999, we were in the midst

LIVING IN THE LINE OF FIRE

of a revival. But the similarity between the two venues, with thousands of Christians in attendance, both in a super-charged atmosphere, and the almost identical wording of our messages was striking. Here I was, twenty years later saying the exact same things James said—almost verbatim—except now, things were much worse in our society in every way. And so, despite the Reagan presidency, despite the moral majority, despite our increased political and cultural involvement, America was in serious moral decline. Put succinctly, our plan was not working! *We needed a revolution—and that meant starting with us.* Something dramatic needed to change.

In the months that followed, I began to study the concept of societal and cultural revolution. Why and how did societies change? What sparked revolutionary movements? I wasn't trying to copy the methods of the world; I was trying to understand. And as I looked back at the counterculture revolution of the '60s, I realized that it was much more ideologically driven than I understood back then, since I was too young to appreciate fully the moral and cultural issues at hand and far too interested in pleasure-seeking and feeding the flesh. Now, looking back, I saw the major issues that rocked the nation much more clearly.

We needed another counterculture revolution, one that would push back against the godlessness of the era, one that would recover some of the moral ground that was taken out from under our feet in aftermath of the '60s, one that would flow out of the current outpouring. And just as God spoke to me in 1983 about serving in a revival that would impact the world, He began to speak to me that, as surely as there was a civil rights movement in America, there would be a gospel-based moral and cultural revolution. By His grace, I would be in the thick of it. This was a promise! *The Lord was calling me to speak to—and impact—the nation, not just the Church.*

I journaled this on June 15, 2000: "[Pastor] Larry Hill tells me in my office today (with tears in his eyes) that he remembers a conversation we had in our home in St. James [on Long Island] about 15 years ago where I told him that God had spoken to me that I would be involved in a revival

Revolution Rising

one day that would have worldwide implications. Father, You are SO faithful! And what does this imply re: the coming revolution???"

BURNING WITH REVOLUTIONARY FIRE

The reality of being involved in a gospel-based moral and cultural revolution, just as surely as I was involved in a world-impacting revival, became etched in the innermost part of my being. I have lived with this sense of divinely appointed, revolutionary destiny ever since. Sometimes the call is all consuming: REVOLUTION!

These journal entries reflect this ever-intensifying burden:

October 7, 1999: My heart is flaming for revolution! Watching the *God Fights Back* video [for the second time] tonight, I see again how only a radical, passionate, "by life or by death" movement can shake a nation. And I feel called to help ignite such a movement! But it is while watching some excerpts from the *History of Rock and Roll* that my heart really begins to burst. How I hate white collar religion! How I hate commercialism! How I hate Christianity within four walls! How I hate faith without fire, profession without passion, belief without burden. How I resonate with the total "putting oneself into a thing" mentality the way the godless rock stars did—and the way Keith Green did as he sang and played. (I think that's one of the reasons I find a certain spiritual expression at times only on the drums. I give myself to the worship.)

My heart beats for a [Keith Green] Last Days Ministries kind of atmosphere and emphasis, and it is only through the school that I see the possibility of fulfilling this dream. But how do I break out of the system??? How do I develop a total "go for it" community? How do I raise up an army? I know it's happening in part, but it's still only in part. How do I go for more?

God, if You would only cause my materials to take off in the outside marketplace, then I could concentrate on the matters

LIVING IN THE LINE OF FIRE

at hand without concern. And if you could only show me the way to break with the mold, to be biblically radical, to go for it. Father!!!! Show me the way. And may the messages you have given me—as my heart has almost exploded so many times with Your word while writing—get to millions. If Khomeini's words could spark a satanic revolution that remains to this day, why can't my words, birthed by You, spark a holy revolution??? Anoint my heart, anoint my mind, anoint my life, anoint my words. Fire! Fire!! Fire!!!

February 9, 2000: Father, something within me is stirring. Is it really possible to shake a nation? Will You really give me a national voice? Will a burning pen ignite the masses? Am I dreaming, or is it time? Something is going on! (3:24 AM)

December 14, 2000: How interesting. In years past, I read books about revival and radical service, because that was part of my calling and destiny. I read books about (rabbinic) schools making a generational impact, because that was part of my calling and destiny. These days, I'm reading books about Martin Luther King Jr., Khomeini, Malcolm X, and the Founding Fathers, because....

Years earlier, on April 1, 1994, I journaled: "I want to get hold of God in a way I never have before! I want to be separated to Him! I want to live the life of a holy radical, a revivalist, a spiritual revolutionary, totally caught up with my Master. Why not? What hinders?" Now, in the midst of the revival and with a school of almost 1,200 students from thirty-four nations, that vision seemed closer than ever. It was time for a holy revolution!

This shift in my thinking is reflected dramatically in my journal entries, which indicated that from 1983 until June 15, 1999, the words "revolution" or "revolutionary" occurred only one time, in that April 1, 1994

152

Revolution Rising

entry which I just cited. Then from June 16, 1999 on, when I preached a message at Brownsville titled, "Let the Revolution Begin," the word "revolution" occurs hundreds of times in my journal. In fact, just as I used headings in my journal like "Jewish Ministry" or "Scholarship" to organize content, there was now a new heading: "The Revolution." A seismic shift had taken place.

Today, our ministry emphasizes three R's: *Revival* in the Church; a gospel-based, moral and cultural *Revolution* in society; and the *Redemption* of Israel. And all three are related. It is only a healthy, revived Church that can ignite a cultural revolution, and it is only a healthy, revived Church that can provoke Israel to jealousy. I live and breathe these three R's every day of my life.

It also became clear to me that the call to revolution was a powerful way of framing the message of the gospel. After all, Jesus didn't come into the world to start a lovely, Sunday morning, home and garden religion. He came to announce the arrival of the Kingdom of God, and He prayed revolutionary prayers, such as, "Your Kingdom come, Your will be done," which requires the displacing of all earthly and satanic kingdoms. He called us to live radical, counterculture lifestyles, blessing those who cursed us and overcoming evil with good. And, in keeping with the mindset of revolutionary leaders through the centuries, He called us to leave everything and follow Him, inviting us to change the world together under His authority. (This is known as the Great Commission!) *In short, Jesus came to earth to launch God's revolution.*

You see, for the revolutionary—speaking here in secular, worldly terms—life as it is, is not worth living, but the cause is worth dying for. That's why revolutionaries are willing to make such radical commitments, often to the point of extreme violence, being driven by the spirit of the world, the flesh, and the devil.

We operate by an entirely different spirit—the Holy Spirit—fighting with spiritual weapons and following the example of Jesus, laying down our lives rather than taking the lives of others. And while we do not love our own lives, we do love life itself. We are not like the Islamic terrorists

153

LIVING IN THE LINE OF FIRE

who say, "You love life. We love death." But we do maintain that same revolutionary commitment, leaving everything for the cause of the gospel, putting our bodies on the line in obedience to Him, and bringing the values of the age to come into this current age. That is revolutionary, and the first ones to catch the revolution vision were our students at BRSM.

They had already embraced the message of following Jesus by life or by death, based on a prayer of dedication I would sometimes lead them in together, based on Paul's words in Philippians: "I eagerly expect and hope that I will in no way be ashamed, but will have sufficient courage so that now as always Christ will be exalted in my body, whether by life or by death. For to me, to live is Christ and to die is gain" (Philippians 1:20–21 NIV). For us, this was Gospel 101, the starting point in following the Master, and with that mindset, our students were ready to go anywhere in the world to make Him known, regardless of cost or consequence. That's why I wasn't surprised to see, "By Life or by Death" become the motto of the school, with students making bumper stickers for their cars with that simple proclamation. This happened within the first year of our existence.

But something electric went through the student body in 1999 and 2000 as the revolution theme developed in me and our faculty. As Daniel Kolenda, who took over Reinhard Bonnke's ministry Christ for All Nations, explained to me when we talked on March 27, 2024, the revolution message gave them a fresh vision of going for it, of breaking the mold, of risking their lives for the gospel, of being part of a very real, world-changing movement. "And," he said to me, "when you wrote the *Revolution!* book"—which I'll talk about shortly—"it gave us a manifesto."

This entry from February 2, 2000, captures the spirit of the hour:

> Sleep in, then the awesome, historic day at BRSM, as (in casual dress), we explode with praise and prayer in chapel, then march around the campus (in faith!), and then I lead the revolutionary charge across the field. What an army! What a moment! Breakthroughs! ....

Revolution Rising

Revolution! Something really happened in the Spirit today as we marched, prayed, shouted, and proclaimed. Yes! The roar (surrounded by students at the end in the field) was almost deafening, staggering. Wow! And John Cava really receives some words (as the Spirit falls dramatically in waves of glory, cancelling his Doctrinal Foundations class).

The burning coals of revival were producing revolutionary flames—thousands of them.

But as this message was being formed in me, I realized that it could easily be misunderstood, which is why I always clarified what I meant when speaking on the theme, constantly repeating that mantra of, "Overcoming evil with good, overcoming hatred with love, overcoming the power of the flesh with the power of the Spirit." This was especially important when bringing our student body into the revolutionary mindset since: 1) young people can be rebellious by nature; 2) as Americans, we tend to be very independent; and, 3) once FIRE School of Ministry began, we were mindful of the fact that it was birthed out of a split (as I'll explain in the next chapter), because of which we were careful to cultivate humility and honor rather than pride and rebellion. Thankfully, the students embraced the message in a very healthy way, first at BRSM in 1999, then at FIRE thereafter.

As I write these words today, our army of grads is producing incredible fruit for the Lord in America and around the globe. To use our rallying cry for the past twenty-five years, "On with it!" (or for short, "OWI!"), meaning, "On with the revolution!"

THE MIRACULOUS WRITING AND DISTRIBUTION OF REVOLUTION!

Over a six-week period from the end of 1999 to the beginning of 2000, I was moved by the Spirit to write *Revolution! The Call to Holy War*. I had polled our student body on a subtitle for the book, presenting options like, "A Counterculture Manifesto," but they showed no interest in those

155

LIVING IN THE LINE OF FIRE

options. When I suggested "The Call to Holy War," the students exploded with enthusiasm. I got identical results while polling the first-year and second-year classes at separate times in separate venues.

As for the "Holy War" subtitle, it was in the spirit of John Bunyan's seventeenth century book *Holy War*, which spoke clearly of a spiritual battle. My book was also written before the 9/11 terror attacks which brought the concept of violent, Islamic holy war to the fore. That's why, in the updated and revised edition published in 2020, we changed the subtitle to, "An Urgent Call for a Holy Uprising."

Still, readers of the 2000 edition of *Revolution!* would have no confusion about the message, with two whole chapters devoted to principles of non-violent resistance. One chapter is even titled, "Take Up Your Cross, Put Down Your Sword." That was (and is) the essence of the holy war we are fighting. I truly felt the wind at my back as I wrote.

This intense anointing to write is something very sacred to me, as I often feel carried and almost compelled to write when the Spirit is on me, not in an oppressive, demonic way (as Nietzsche described about his own experience) but in a glorious, life-giving, even thrilling way, as I can't write the words quickly enough. That's how powerfully the ideas come pouring into my heart and mind; and sometimes, as I write, I can't wait to see what's coming next, feeling more like the reader than the writer. It's a wonderful journey of discovery and creativity as I am *moved* by the Lord to write.

I write at my desk and while sitting up in bed. I write at the airport while waiting to board the plane, then the moment I'm on the plane, then as soon as we take off and I'm allowed to take out my laptop again. I write during three-minute breaks during the radio show. I write in hotels. Sometimes when stirred during a worship service, I'll write down notes on my phone. When I'm moved like this, I literally write all the time, sometimes as a passenger in a car while the driver focuses on getting us to our destination. Writing consumes me!

There are even times when my brain feels bionic, as happened when I was working on my commentary on Jeremiah. My goal was to write one chapter of commentary per month, but even at that pace, I was behind schedule for the publisher. Then toward the end of 2003 when school was out of session, I was not traveling and could get extra rest. Nancy had gone away for a few days to help our older daughter Jen with the birth of her first child, Connor, so my schedule was unusually free. And the Lord moved on me to write in an extraordinary way! I was able to finish ten chapters of commentary in just twenty-four days—meaning, *ten month's work in twenty-four days*, and with some of the best content found anywhere in the commentary.

I distinctly remember having dinner at a Chinese buffet when suddenly, it was as if all of Jeremiah was before me, and I grabbed a paper napkin, asked a waiter for a pen, and began writing down furiously all the insights I was receiving. My journal entry for December 6, 2003, reads, "I'm flipping out with joyful amazement after the Lord has now enabled me to complete *two* solid chapters of Jeremiah (16–17) in just *six* days—with almost 7,000 words of commentary writing in the process! What a great God I serve!"

Then this on December 10: "What can I say, Lord? A chapter in one day? [This means *one month's work in one day*.] You're wonderful! And You have made me for such a life as this: Memorizing 20 verses a day at the age of 18; getting immersed in languages in college and grad school; writing whole books in a matter of weeks, and massive apologetic sections in a matter of days.... You've designed me for high speed usage at Your will, and I for one love the ride. OWI!"

Then this on December 24: "What can I say, Lord? Ten chapters of holy commentary writing in twenty-four days. All things are possible with You! And what an experience it has been for me to live with Jeremiah through these weeks. Use this writing for Your glory, Father!"

And finally, this on December 31: "All glory and praise and honor to my Savior and Friend, Jesus, enabling me to do one year's work in one blessed month—chapters 16–27 of Jeremiah. Yes!"

I can remember that awe-filled sense of exhilaration even now as I write. In fact, there are some chapters in this book that I wrote in a single

LIVING IN THE LINE OF FIRE

day, with almost all of the book written within one month—all while doing two daily radio shows, teaching at several different schools, traveling and preaching, and working on a major academic project (plus helping Nancy in the garden). How I love to be used by the Lord!

In saying all this, though, I am not claiming divine inspiration in some biblical way (perish the thought!) or suggesting some kind of infallibility (that would be as arrogant as it is nonsensical). Rather, just as musicians and artists and inventors can testify to a certain inspiration, I can too. In fact, while there is nothing like encountering God together with others as His beautiful presence fills the meeting place, the most powerful personal anointing I experience comes when I am gripped to write. How I love to ride that wave! Readers will often comment that they feel it too when they read, having a hard time putting the book down. As I was stirred to write, they are stirred to read.

When writing *The Real Kosher Jesus* in 2012, I remember feeling as if I was going on a divine adventure from chapter to chapter, not knowing what insights the Lord would give me next. I could hardly wait! From the day I started writing that book, which was borne out of travail in prayer, to the day it was published, was *ten weeks*. In the world of publishing and writing, that is almost inconceivable.

I also got flooded with ideas while working on *Authentic Fire* in 2013, writing 300 pages in three weeks and with contributions from colleagues amounting to another 150 pages. From the day I started writing that book to the day it was published was just *seven weeks*. Normally, from the time you submit a finished manuscript to a publisher until the time the book is released is nine months to a year, and it can sometimes take years to finish a manuscript. You can imagine, then, how exhilarating, not to mention how intense, these writings experiences have been.

A similar thing happened to me while writing *Jezebel's War with America*, which was published in 2019. I wrote 70 percent of the book in a six-day period, going to bed at 2:00 a.m. after hours of writing, only to jump out of bed and write another chapter, finally falling asleep at 4:30 a.m. I could not hold it in.

Revolution Rising

When writing *Revolution!*, we were still in the midst of the intensity of the revival schedule, so getting the book done in six weeks was also quite remarkable. I remember one night in particular around Christmas of 1999 when I went into my school office to write. A few hours later, it's as if I "woke up" to see that I had written an entire chapter. I was so consumed with what I was writing that I wasn't even conscious of my surroundings. It was as if I had daydreamed while driving, thinking it was only for a few minutes, only to realize I had been driving all day and night.

Once again, I was stunned. But why did the Lord want me to write the book so quickly? For what purpose? What was so urgent? Then I realized: the annual Christian booksellers conference was coming in June 2000. I would reach out to one of my publishers, we would get the book out quickly, and we would introduce the revolution theme at the conference, just as we had focused on the revival theme with a publisher at a previous conference.

So I called my friends at Regal Books and shared the vision with them, and they were excited about the revolution theme and the book itself. "But," they said, "there's no way we could get the book out in time for the conference. Plus, all the slots are already taken." They continued, "But if you can get a clean manuscript to us by March 1, we can get it out September 1."

I thought to myself, "What's so special about September 1? Why not October 1 or November 1? Why did I write the book so quickly and with such a feeling of urgency to get it out on September 1?" It felt as if I had raced to the airport at breakneck speed only to arrive there four hours early. Why?

Then one of them said, "Isn't there that big youth event in DC on September 2?" I said to them, "That's it! We're supposed to give away copies of the book at that event. That's the reason for the urgency."

I had heard some friends talking about The CallDC, scheduled for September 2, 2000, and a colleague of mine, Bob Weiner, a man of supernatural faith, had mentioned that he was speaking at youth rallies around

LIVING IN THE LINE OF FIRE

the country that were leading up to The Call. He had contacted me previously, asking me to donate 1,000 copies of my book *Go and Sin No More: A Call to Holiness* to give away at these rallies. (In the end, he was able to purchase them at our cost.) I thought to myself, "That's what we'll do. We'll give away 1,000 copies of *Revolution!* at The Call."

But my thoughts about giving away copies of the book at The Call also tied in with a prophetic word Bob had given me seven years earlier, in 1993. To share the background, Jonathan Bernis had called ten Messianic Jewish leaders together for three days of prayer and fasting in 1993, and Bob Weiner and I were among those who participated. During our time of praying and ministering to the Lord, we also ministered to each other, and Bob had a word over me, saying that he saw within me a seed of a book that would have an *Uncle Tom's Cabin* effect on the nation, and the word resonated with something deep within me.

Now, in 2000, I called Bob and reminded him of the prophecy, saying, "That book may still be thirty years down the road, but this is the closest I've come to it so far and I want to give away copies at The CallDC."

In my mind, the book of which Bob had prophesied was also for the secular world, not primarily for the Church alone; but I knew that *Revolution!*, while written for the Church, was to have an impact on the culture too. That's why I couched things as I did. Could this be *that* book? Bob replied with gusto, "Let's print 100,000 books to give away at The Call. And let's see if we can get the books published for 80 cents to a dollar per book."

I said, "Bob, it's a 300-page book and will sell for $13.00, which is a very good price. If we could get copies for $4.00 per book, that would be amazing." But he was not deterred. He felt something from the Lord.

As for the event itself, the principle organizers, Che Ahn and Lou Engle, were told that the biggest crowd they could expect would be about 50,000 people, seeing that they only had nine months to mobilize from the time they first caught the vision to organize the massive gathering. Why on earth would we print 100,000 books if only 50,000 people

Revolution Rising

would be there? And where would we get the money? At that point, we actually owed our publishers about $12,000.

I reached out to Regal again, and they were very excited as I told them about the vision of printing and giving away 100,000 books at The Call. (Looking back at all this, it does seem utterly audacious. But the Lord was in it!) Now they had to figure out the cost. (I said nothing to them about Bob's impossible talk about getting the books for 80 cents to a dollar each.)

To my shock, they called a few days later and said, "We're bypassing the middle man and taking no profit, and we can print the books for 80 cents per copy." Seriously! "Then you'll have to pay for shipping," which turned out to be well over $10,000. There were a lot of books to ship! In fact, it took two eighteen-wheelers to deliver the books to DC.

But where would we get the funds, well over $90,000? Plus, I didn't even have a role at The Call. Would the organizers even want the books? I called Che, and he was very excited about the plan, actually feeling that there was something to this revolution message that tied in with The Call. He invited me to speak to about two dozen leaders who were helping organize the event when they met in DC on June 21. As for raising the funds, I had planned to write to every pastor I knew, sharing the vision and encouraging them to get behind it, which I did. The result? Just *two* pastors responded, with gifts totaling about $400. We were still short more than $90,000!

Still, before I had written the letters to these pastors or started any fundraising efforts, I journaled this on May 7, 2000:

> I feel a sense of ownership in terms of getting the *Revolution!* book into the hands of the young people at the CallDC in September, feeling strongly that the Lord is saying to me, "Tell Gospel Light [meaning, Regal Books] it's a go. Guarantee 100,000 books. You can raise the money!" I also believe it's probable that the Lord wants me to speak there (with an army of students along for the ride?) The Spirit is on me! It's possible

LIVING IN THE LINE OF FIRE

that Bob Weiner may also raise some funds for the book's distribution, but it's also possible that his main role in all this was to getting into my head the concept of mass-printing 100,000 copies at less than a dollar each. It will happen!

The gift of faith was in operation!

When I spoke to The CallDC leaders on June 21, they too embraced the message of revolution, leading to a change in schedule where I was given a keynote, thirty-minute slot to speak on the theme. Praise God! I also shared the vision of giving away the 100,000 books, saying that it would be just $80,000 for the printing. A fairly young man named Eric (who led a mission's ministry and whom I had never met before) asked me, "How are you going to get the money?" I said, "I'll be writing to pastors and the funds will come in." He thanked me for the answer but then told me his heart was burning as I talked about the books.

After the meeting, he came up to me and said, "I'll give the $80,000." Oh my! This was the Lord! It was only some years later that I learned that he didn't have the money either but felt that God was telling him to do it. And God Himself came through!

THE JOURNEY TO THE CALLDC

I told the leadership team at BRSM, "We're going to The CallDC as a student body. Let's rent buses for the trip." One of my key leaders asked, "Dr. Brown, is this really the Lord, or are you just excited?" I said, "We're going to DC together."

He looked into the cost and he came back to me with another team leader, both of whom were very responsible financially. They said, "We could rent ten buses, which will accommodate 550 students, roughly half the student body, but we would have to put down a non-refundable, $10,000 deposit." (Bear in mind that we were on a very tight budget, so we did not have $1,000 to waste, let alone $10,000.) I said, "We're going to DC together. Do it."

Revolution Rising

So we booked the buses by faith, realizing that when the students returned from summer break, along with all the new students coming in for the first time, we would have only one week before The Call. That did not give us much time to recruit them for the trip, let alone figure out how they could pay for their transportation. But something else was fueling my fire.

Some months earlier, I had watched a documentary titled "A Force More Powerful," focusing on the power of non-violent resistance and featuring leaders such as Mahatma Gandhi and Martin Luther King Jr. It was deeply moving and inspirational. But it also felt personal, and as I watched the footage of Gandhi marching through India, beginning with a small group of followers which became a massive throng, I saw myself in the movie. I was now leading this throng—not because I had delusions of grandeur or was comparing myself to Gandhi or King (not for a moment), but because of this sense of holy calling in the Lord. I had a mission, and it involved rallying an army to stand. In subsequent years, when I watched the video with our students, many of them had the similar experience of feeling as if the video was about them.

In the section about Dr. King, there was footage of freedom riders, both black and white, riding buses together to protest segregation. That image stuck in my mind as well. We would ride buses to DC for the revolutionary cause of Jesus.

And there was an incredibly powerful clip of Dr. King preaching in a church in Selma, Alabama, on March 8, 1965, responding to those who thought that the strategy of non-violent resistance was too provocative and costly, arguing it was best not to be so confrontational. With the building packed with people and a crowd standing outside listening on loud speakers, he addressed these concerns, saying:

> Deep down in our non-violent creed is the conviction that there are some things so dear, some things so precious, and some things so eternally true that they are worth dying for. ... and if a man happens to be thirty-six years old as I happen to be

163

LIVING IN THE LINE OF FIRE

and some great truth stands before the door of his life—some great opportunity to stand up for that which is right—he's afraid his home will get bombed or he's afraid he will lose his job or he's afraid that he will get shot or beat down by State Troopers; he may go on and live until he's 80 but he's just as dead at 36 as he would be at 80 and the cessation of breathing in his life is merely the belated announcement of an earlier death of the spirit.

A man dies when he refuses to stand up for that which is right; a man dies when he refuses to stand up for justice; a man dies when he refuses to take a stand for that which is true. So we're gonna stand up right here amid horses; we're gonna stand up right here in Alabama amid billy clubs; we're gonna stand up right here in Alabama amid police dogs if they have them; we're gonna stand up amid tear gas; we're gonna stand up amid anything that they can muster up, letting the world know that we are determined to be free![20]

Those words exploded inside me when I heard them. Yes! That was gospel truth! As Jesus Himself said, "If anyone would come after me, let him deny himself and take up his cross and follow me. For whoever would save his life will lose it, but whoever loses his life for my sake and the gospel's will save it" (Mark 8:34–35 ESV). And as I saw those freedom riders on the buses rallying against segregation, I saw our students riding buses to DC. I simply had to share the vision with them.

"*WE* ARE GOING TO DC."

As the incoming students arrived, a handful registered for The Call, but that was it. So at our chapel service the first day of classes, I shared the exciting news about the 100,000 *Revolution!* books, telling the students we'd be going to DC together. A few more registered. Just a trickle. The next day at chapel (as we started our new semester with a chapel service each day for the first week), Larry Tomczak gave a great announcement

Revolution Rising

about The Call, and a few more registered. At this point, we had several dozen, but that was all.

Then it hit me. I needed the students to feel what I was feeling, so I played Dr. King's speech—the one I just quoted—and then shared an insight that I had learned from my Indian friend Yesupadam in 1993 during my first trip there. He had asked me to do most of the preaching, because of which another leader traveling with me felt slighted, since he had to sit and listen to me preach more than he got to preach. Yesupadam pointed him to Acts 2:14, speaking of the day of Pentecost. It says, "Then Peter stood up with the Eleven, raised his voice and addressed the crowd."

Yesupadam said to my colleague, "When Peter stood, they all stood. When he spoke, they were all speaking. In fact, the one speaking has the easier job, since when he is speaking, we are all praying and crying." What an insight!

So during the chapel service, I played the clip from Dr. King's speech and said to the students, "I'm not going to DC. *We* are going to DC. I'm not standing to preach. *We are all standing.*" In fact, in my mind's eye, I saw an army of students standing behind me as I preached. It was clear as day.

Once again, the feeling was electric, as hundreds of students signed up for the trip. They swarmed to register! In the end, including faculty and some other guests, we brought 780 people with us on seventeen buses for the twenty-two-hour trip (each way), representing the largest group attending The Call from anywhere in America. The only problem was that we needed $30,000 to pay for the students who could not afford the trip. We received an offering the next day at chapel and all the funds came in!

This journal entry from August 29, 2000, captures the atmosphere on the campus at this very time:

How can I describe how I feel, driving up to the BRSM property with "By life or by death" written on the marquis; wearing the new BRSM tee-shirt with the same message on the front

LIVING IN THE LINE OF FIRE

and the *Revolution!* logo on the back; clutching [an advance copy of] my *Revolution!* book in my hand; watching the revolutionary video with the students—with tears and pain and that overwhelming sense of destiny; then talking with them about what's coming. What can I say? It's as real as if we were going off to war. As one student's note today said, "We too are here to lay our lives down for this revolutionary cause."

Nancy and I had to fly up one day early for the event, and we were stunned at the sight at the Mall in DC, where The Call would take place. As far as the eye could see, there were boxes of books marked "Revolution." It truly felt unreal.

I then received a call from Che. He asked, "At the end of your message, could you ask three of your students to close in prayer, three students who are really passionate?"

"Absolutely," I replied. This was easily done. Then he called me back with a change of plans. He said, "I'd like you to have 100 students standing behind you as you preach." This is exactly what I had seen in my mind's eye days earlier. I wasn't standing. *We* were standing.

But I wanted him to tell me how to do it. I didn't want to suggest anything to him. I said, "So, you want them to come out after I preach?" He said, "No. I want them standing behind you the entire time you preach." I said, "There will be instruments behind me when I speak. You want them behind the instruments?" He answered, "No. I want them directly behind you." To say it again, this is *exactly* what I had seen in my spirit. We were not dreaming!

That's a message I would often convey to the students during a chapel service or revival service, as I looked out at hundreds of them, full of zeal and devotion and faith and vision. I would say to them, "Look in my eyes! We are not dreaming." Now, at The CallDC, as our buses began to pull up for the event and as tens of thousands of participants thronged the Mall—more than 300,000 in all, according to some estimates—we knew we were not dreaming. We were making history together.

166

Revolution Rising

And so we stood together as one (with all the students wearing school tee-shirts featuring the *Revolution!* book cover and 100 of the students behind me) as I proclaimed, "Let the White House know, let the media know, let Hollywood know, we are here to start a Jesus revolution." We were not dreaming. It was happening. On with the revolution!

Looking back almost twenty-five years later, and having discussed all this with Lou Engle, it is clear to us that something dramatic *did* take place that day and that God heard our prayers and took note of our fasting. It's also clear that, more than anything, it was a day of planting hundreds of thousands of seeds, as many of the young people who were there that day are making a powerful impact today, both in the States and abroad.

As for the *Revolution!* book, because of the size of the crowd, Che told people to take one book per family, so *we gave away* that day more than 70,000 books, equaling about one million dollars retail. The Lord knows how to get a message out!

But I was not only preaching on this revolution theme at our school and at The Call. Beginning in 1999 and then into 2000, I had been sharing the revolution theme in the Brownsville Revival services as well, and as we moved into the fall of 2000, it seemed that our path for the next years was becoming clear. The revival, as we knew it, was coming to an end. But the church itself, the Brownsville Assembly of God, was healthy and strong, having almost doubled in numbers during the revival years and with a strong cell-group structure in place. As for the ministry school, it was ablaze. It was time for us to move into this next exciting, even revolutionary phase together—and then we hit a massive roadblock.

CHAPTER 9

THE PAINFUL BIRTH OF FIRE

The Brownsville Revival confirmed things that I had believed for years: if you lift up Jesus and preach repentance in the power of the Spirit, people will come. As Leonard Ravenhill often said to me, "You don't have to advertise a fire." Or, in the statement attributed to John Wesley when asked how he drew the crowds, "I set myself on fire and the people come to watch me burn." People came from far and wide to watch the holy fires!

As the years of revival wore on, though, and as I continued to overcommit, which had become a lifetime pattern, weariness began to set in, also cutting into my private time with the Lord. And even though I taught on the dangers of overwork during revival, somehow, I didn't apply the same rules to myself. As I explained in my 2024 book *Seize the Moment: How to Fuel the Fires of Revival*:

> In 1998, I preached or taught 274 times, flying more than 140,000 miles over the course of nine ministry trips outside the USA and twenty-two ministry trips within the States, some of which included serving as a visiting professor at two different seminaries. This was in addition to serving as the (very involved) president of the Brownsville Revival School of Ministry (which doubled in size in 1998, growing from 500 students to more than 1,000), directing ICN Ministries [the name then for my personal, traveling ministry], writing two books (with a combined length of more than 550 pages), doing a good

LIVING IN THE LINE OF FIRE

number of radio and TV interviews, and dealing with some libel issues with the local press. And while all this was going on, my wonderful wife Nancy, who worked with the students and pastoral staff at our school, was involved with overseeing the building of our house and helping to make arrangements for our younger daughter's wedding in early 1999. Yes, it was quite a busy year!

But here's the punch line: *In addition to this schedule,* I actively participated in approximately 200 services in the revival, services that lasted about five hours nightly, and services in which all of us poured ourselves out in prayer for the crowds that attended. Not only so, but my commitment to the school and the revival meant that all of my stateside ministry trips were for no more than *two* days, while virtually all of my *overseas* trips were for no more than *three* days. This meant that I would teach my regular day session at the revival on a Saturday afternoon, then fly to places as far away as New Zealand or Australia, speak there between four and seven times, and be back home by late Wednesday night! (On one occasion my round trip travel time was 60 hours; my time in the country was 48 hours.)[21]

Eventually, this took a toll, especially when our relationships got tested toward the end of the revival.

Before God called me to serve in Pensacola, John Kilpatrick, Steve Hill, and Lindell Cooley were the three main leaders in the revival, so they had been in the trenches together day and night for the first eleven months. John also had a previous relational history with both Lindell and Steve. Once I got involved, our hearts quickly became joined together, as we had a deep sense of shared life, experiencing the glory of the Lord night after night, ministering to others to the point of exhaustion, being attacked by the critics, and then traveling out as a team several times a year to do Awake America events in different convention centers. Yet in all my years there, the four of us only spent one day together outside of

170

The Painful Birth of FIRE

services, driving to New Orleans just to hang out. The revival schedule didn't allow for much more.

We were also totally different personalities with very different callings, and if not for the revival, it is highly unlikely we would have been on the same ministry team. I'm a New Yorker, and a New York Jew at that. (There's a saying that you can take the New Yorker out of New York, but you can't take the New York out of the New Yorker. That certainly applies to me, as well as to Nancy.) Living in Pensacola meant daily culture shock for me the entire time I was there. I'm sure it was culture shock for those dealing with me too! As for John, Steve, and Lindell, they were all Southerners. That alone made for an interesting mix, although we had no real conflicts over our cultural differences.

John was (and is) a very strong pastoral leader, a tremendous "buck stops with me" person, someone who makes you feel secure. And he is very much at home in the senior pastor role, leading with authority. It was great to have him as the captain of the ship (we were all happy it was him and not us!). I gladly recognized his leadership role, although the model I was more at home with was the pastor being the chief among equals on a team of elders. Steve, who went to be with the Lord in 2014, was a fiery evangelist, full of passion, full of intensity, very high strung and also a lot of fun. During the revival, his eyes were always bloodshot and his voice raspy. He lived on the edge. Lindell, who has been pastoring for the past twenty years as well as doing worship, is much more laid back and happy to get along with everybody. We were always amazed to see how he would flow with the Spirit and bring us into a powerful encounter with God.

I felt very close to these brothers, especially John and Steve, since I sat with them every night on the platform and we would lay hands on the crowds as Lindell led in worship late into the night. But in terms of real-life relationships, of sitting and talking for hours, of getting to know each other's spouses and families in a deep and significant way, that did not happen in the midst of our very intense schedules. Satan, the enemy of our souls, was certainly well aware of this, planning on ways to divide

LIVING IN THE LINE OF FIRE

Pastor Kilpatrick and me as the revival fires waned in 2000, especially after Steve moved on in June of that year when he felt his time at the revival had come to an end.

THE SPLIT

Although BRSM was independently incorporated, our school board consisted of leaders from the church. At one point, both Steve and John told me independently that we needed a board of internationally respected Christian leaders, which mirrored my thinking as well. But because I don't focus on issues of bylaws and boards and governmental structure, I never acted on that. At the same time, having these church-based leaders serving on the school board meant that we would be sensitive to potential conflicts between our school and the Assemblies of God (AOG), to which the Brownsville church belonged.

About half of our students came from AOG backgrounds, meaning that if they were to be ordained and sent out to the mission field, it would be through their regional AOG leadership. (Individual AOG churches do not ordain and send.) But since many of the students had formed relationships with the school faculty, they wanted to be ordained and sent out through the school, even if they came from AOG backgrounds. Understandably, this created some tension.

We had already established a missions sending organization called Brownsville International to help us cover grads on the mission field who looked to us for oversight. But when it came to ordination, we wanted to avoid any further conflict with the AOG, seeking to funnel the students outside of BRSM to be ordained. Still, many of the students wanted to be ordained by us, since they had forged deep relationships with the school leadership, and we felt a responsibility to cover them as well.

With the blessing of the school board, we set up F.I.R.E., which stood for "Fellowship for International Revival and Evangelism," an acronym that two of our leaders, John Cava, our missions director, and Steve Alt, one of our faculty members, came up with independently. We smiled at what seemed like a divine coincidence.

172

The Painful Birth of FIRE

But several things began to muddy the waters, and I present this in a factual way without attributing blame in either direction. I believe all parties were trying to do what was best before the Lord and that we all fell short on some level.

The first factor was monetary. Our school needed to purchase the fifty-acre campus we had been renting. It was owned by Liberty Church, which previously had a large school as well. But the campus had been largely abandoned for years when we began to use it.

We needed three million dollars for the purchase, but because we were only in our third year of existence, we didn't have sufficient history to secure a bank loan. Pastor Kilpatrick took his own initiative and was able to secure a loan from the AOG, and that's how we bought the property. But by the year 2000, as the revival was starting to wane, with smaller crowds and less intense visitation of the Spirit, and with the school emerging as a key part of the lasting of the revival, the AOG felt it would be best if the president of the school was ordained by their organization as well. But they could not require me to do so; it was merely their desire.

This only heightened the tension, as more of the students sent to the school by their AOG pastors now wanted to be ordained by F.I.R.E., while others wanted to be covered on the mission field by Brownsville International rather than by the AOG missions' arm. That's why Thomas Trask, the General Superintendent of the AOG, suggested to me at a meeting together with Pastor Kilpatrick on September 5, 2000 (just a few days after The CallDC), that it would make things much easier for everyone if I was ordained by the AOG. I told him, respectfully, that for a number of reasons, I could not do this, but John said, to my surprise, "Mike, I think it's a good idea. You should do it."

In the weeks that followed, Pastor Kilpatrick became convinced this would be the best course of action, making his feelings very clear to me. But when I could not comply in conscience before the Lord—not out of disrespect for the AOG, which I appreciate and honor to this day, but because of my own particular calling and convictions—trust broke down

LIVING IN THE LINE OF FIRE

between John and me and the enemy got in. In his mind, the only way I could continue to lead the school was to submit to his directive, but this I could not do. Yet to abandon the school and the students was utterly unthinkable.

I shared with the faculty what was going on, and all of us on all sides, both the church and the school, tried to find a way forward, without success. And so, on December 17, 2000, I was dismissed from BRSM because of alleged "irreconcilable differences in the implementation of the vision." To say that this was traumatic would be a massive understatement. Our world, as leaders and faculty at BRSM, was turned totally upside down, first as the board meeting dragged on for hours, then as we met together as faculty into the early hours of the morning.

The school board had known that as leaders in the school, we were committed to the student body, so on that fateful December 17 meeting, they offered me a small severance pay if I would resign and start a new school fifty miles away for those students who wanted to go with us. BRSM would remain on the campus which it officially owned (and into which we had invested as much as one million dollars for upkeep and renovation) and those students wanting to stay there would remain on the campus. I explained that we would gladly relocate in May after classes ended, but it wasn't feasible to make the move in the middle of a school year, given student work schedules and the difficulty of a two-hour roundtrip for classes each day, since the students lived near the current campus.

In the end, I was dismissed with the understanding that the faculty that stayed with me would start a new school (really, the continuation of BRSM under a new name) somewhere in the local area, while BRSM would remain on the current campus. We even planned to have booths at each of our locations during registration, letting students know their options, since all this took place over Christmas break and many would be trying to sort things out upon their return. Unfortunately, for a number of reasons, this never happened—and for the students it was like living through a very public, painful, messy divorce. There was now a split

174

The Painful Birth of FIRE

between the church and the school, and it was all being played out in a very public way on the internet and in Christian media.

But to repeat: I believe all parties, from the school board to the AOG and from our faculty to John Kilpatrick and I, were trying to do the right thing before the Lord. In the moment, though, it was an agonizing and chaotic time for everyone, with emotions running high. We felt deeply wronged and cast out, torn away from the school we built from scratch, the victim of denominational politics and personal feuds. As we met with our school staff the next day, there was weeping and shock. How could this have happened? And why? There had been no hint to them that anything was wrong. From the Brownsville perspective, the leaders must have felt betrayed and undermined, scorned by the very people for whom they provided a home. This is what happens in church and ministry splits: both sides feel like victims, and both sides believe God is clearly "with us" rather than "with them."

Still, as much as I felt that way in my own heart, I knew the Lord wanted us to honor John Kilpatrick and Brownsville, and I gave clear directives to our team not to speak disparagingly of the church or the AOG. We would bless and honor, not curse. Even while lying in bed at night talking to Nancy in the privacy of our home, if I said anything about John or the AOG leadership, I would say, "Lord, You know I honor them and want them blessed." She would say to me, "Honey, it's just the two of us talking." But that was the stance I wanted to take. Even my private journal entries reflect that same sentiment.

I was upset and hurt (as John was as well, undoubtedly), and our faculty, which became our new leadership team, was really beaten up, feeling discarded without a thought on their behalf. But I knew the posture I had to take before the Lord, not just personally, but for the sake of our students, and our team acted with integrity and honor.

On the practical side, after being exhausted from years of revival and now suffering the trauma of the split, we had to incorporate as a new school and find office buildings and a campus in *less than three weeks*. That's all the time we had from my firing until the next semester would

175

LIVING IN THE LINE OF FIRE

start. And we literally had nothing to our name, not even a pencil. Talk about being under the gun. Still, we had the sense that the Lord was going before us, and there was a certain excitement as well. What miracle will the next day hold? Let us make a revolutionary commitment to follow Jesus together!

This deep sense of solidarity from the students and grads greatly encouraged me, especially as my personal email address was leaked to them shortly after I was fired. I received as many as 150 emails a day, many with the same theme: "Dear Dad, thanks for not letting us down." Without us saying it publicly, the students and grads intuitively understood that we felt an obligation to them, hence the difficult decisions we made. This was particularly true for our missionaries on the field, since if the school had become an AOG school, we would have had to dissolve Brownsville International, and rather than us covering our grads around the world, they would have had to transition to a new organization and to leaders with whom they had no relationship. In conscience, as spiritual fathers, we could not agree to this.

As for the BRSM faculty, all our full-time professors, save one, decided to move on with me, with no guarantee of salary. Most of the staff wanted to move on with us as well, also with no guaranteed income. As for the one faculty member who felt to stay back, joined by one of our grads who served as our administrator, the separation between us was extremely difficult for all of us because the three of us had been so close. Emotions ran high here too. Thankfully, for many years now, we have been fully reconciled and remain dear friends and coworkers. I cherish both of these brothers. But in the moment, it was very trying for all of us, and our personal interactions became very strained. As for the reconciliation with Pastor Kilpatrick, that's a beautiful story in itself, which I'll share shortly. But in the days and weeks immediately following the split, our team and our student body were in the midst of a very intense battle. There was not a moment to breathe.

About 10 percent of the students did not return because of the split, something that pained us deeply. They were hurt, and we felt that was

The Painful Birth of FIRE

on us, as much as we were trying to look out for them. Of those who did return, we ended up with about 60 percent, roughly 500 students. Miraculously, two church buildings opened up to us, having read about the split in the local press. Both were virtually all Black congregations, one of them called New Dimensions and the other New Hope. (Yes, it was a new beginning for us!)

New Dimensions met in a former movie theatre, and the leaders had been praying for a White harvest. Here we came! We would hold our classes there as well as our Thursday night services, plus a late afternoon Sunday service, since at this point, we had become a functioning church for the students and grads and their families. The other congregation, New Hope, had a smaller facility, which we used for our administrative offices. The Lord had provided for us! It really was miraculous.

To our surprise, God also provided for BRSM, raising up the faculty and leadership to care for the 400+ students who remained there. Could it be that God was with both of us? That seemed impossible. That's why, the night that Pastor Kilpatrick and I reconciled, we said to each other, "You must have been surprised that God was with us and blessed us!" We smiled and acknowledged that yes, in fact, we were surprised. I'm so glad that the Lord is infinitely bigger than we are.

As for the name of the new school, that was easy. F.I.R.E. already existed as a church on paper, through which we ordained and sent out our grads. The school, then, could officially function under that organization, which is how we received immediate state approval to operate. We hadn't planned out any of this in advance, but Dr. Josh Peters, then the co-director of our missions department before becoming the senior director, was very good with bylaws and structures, and he realized we could immediately begin to function legally as a school under a church. From our perspective, the Lord had gone ahead of us, preparing the way. We were now FIRE School of Ministry and FIRE Church, with the school faculty becoming the leadership team for both entities. As for Brownsville International, it became FIRE International.

LIVING IN THE LINE OF FIRE

Giving honor to our FIRE team members, they included Scott Volk, a Jewish believer whom Nancy and I met in 1993, a man I call "everybody's best friend." He relocated to Pensacola in 1997 to become my assistant, and we traveled the world together, logging about one million miles on Delta during our seven years in Pensacola. He quickly emerged as our lead pastor and oversaw FIRE Church for years. We are close friends to this day. Bob Gladstone combined academic brilliance with a deeply spiritual perspective and was a key faculty member and FIRE team leader for years before launching a house church network in North Carolina.

John Cava, our missions director, whom I previously mentioned, also remained a core part of our team, traveling the world today doing mission's work, a cherished friend as well. Steve Alt made the move with us too, having moved to Pensacola in 1997 even before I had agreed to hire him, as he felt called to teach at BRSM. He became a real father to our student body and he teaches today for Daniel Kolenda's ministry school in Orlando, where I also teach regularly and we get to intersect. Other faculty who stood with us sacrificially during this season included Keith Collins, one of our grads who carries a strong revival anointing and who remains a close friend as well.

We were also joined by S. J. Hill whom we dubbed "Father Love" because of the message of the Father's heart that he so powerfully brought to the students, and Bert Farias, who had served on the mission field with his wife, Carolyn, before returning to the States and joining our team. They continue strong in ministry as I write these words. Larry Tomczak, a wonderful soul-winner and encourager, was also part of our team, but since he lived in Atlanta and commuted to teach, he was not as involved in the new school. I am blessed to call all these men my friends.

When the Lord called us to relocate to North Carolina in 2003, Scott, Bob, Josh, John (Cava), Steve, and later Keith made the move with us. About 200 people moved in all—after all, we were revolutionaries at heart, committed to the gospel by life or by death. Those moving with us included most of our students (our school was much smaller by then), our staff, and some of our congregation. FIRE Church continues to pursue

178

the Lord earnestly, located in Concord, which is north of Charlotte, and led by Chris Williams, a grad from BRSM after the split.

In the fall of 2024, FIRE International held its twenty-fifth annual missions conference in support of our workers worldwide. This was also the year that Josh turned seventy-five. What a journey it has been! As for FIRE School of Ministry, in 2020, after twenty-three years of full-time classes and a diminishing student body, we transitioned into an online-only program. But I've gotten way ahead of the story. For now, we need to return to the year 2001, one of the most difficult years that Nancy and I lived through, as we were still living in Pensacola in the aftermath of the split.

FOUND UNCONSCIOUS ON THE SIDE OF THE ROAD

Although the Lord sustained our team and the work, these were very difficult times, as we were sometimes without funds to pay our leadership team and staff. The leaders said, "When FIRE has the money, it can reimburse us, but we'll just trust the Lord for now." The staff said, "Dr. Brown, we're committed to the ministry, and if we have to get outside jobs to cover our expenses, we'll do it." These were real heroes, every one of them.

But the split was a daily reality, as in some cases, students who were roommates now attended two different schools, and there was a feeling of tension locally. That's one reason we really wanted to relocate, thereby relieving some of the tension, but at that time, the Lord had not called us to do so. As for reconciling with John Kilpatrick, the two of us could not find a path forward, and we were both carrying wounds from the split.

FIRE had also taken a giant step back from the glory of the revival days and from enjoying our large campus. We were now guests in the buildings of others, although they were very gracious hosts. As for my new office, it was a tiny shell compared to my large, presidential office on our old campus, which featured wall to wall, floor to ceiling bookcases. One day, after I had been kneeling in prayer next to a couch in the room adjacent to my new FIRE office, I got a call from Nancy. It just so happened that she wanted to mention something to me: "Honey," she said, "you don't want

179

LIVING IN THE LINE OF FIRE

to kneel by that couch." She told me that the building's former custodian used to live there and his dog often urinated on the carpet. Despite the best efforts of our cleaning team, Nancy said, they couldn't get all the urine out. This was our new reality. I was literally kneeling on it.

As for Nancy and me, we had been building a new house when the split took place, planning to get settled here for the years to come. But our builder got in over his head and was unable to complete the project within our budget. In the end, we lost everything we had, including more than $200,000 in equity from the sale of our houses over the previous twenty years, and we were now totally under the gun to find a way to finish building the house. The bills were mounting and the pressure increasing. By the time we moved to North Carolina in 2003, we had lost the house, we had lost our assets, and we were $150,000 in debt. Nancy, who managed our personal finances, would not even buy a stick of gum. Severe austerity was the rule of the hour.

Looking back, it's hard to recall how intense life was, since the Lord miraculously turned things around in a fairly short period of time. But for those of you who have lived under severe financial pressure or experienced foreclosure or bankruptcy or been harassed by calls from debt collectors, you can relate. I am grateful that the Lord brought us into a wide and spacious place.

And 2001 was also a deeply traumatic year for Nancy personally. She had been battling a serious back condition, and things got to the point where the pain was so severe that it took her forty-five minutes to get out bed in the morning, using two walking sticks. On two occasions after we moved into our new house, which was still being finished, I found her flat on her face unable to move. I had to find a way to get a pain pill in her mouth with water, waiting for it to take effect, before I would try to help her up.

Then there were the personal losses. Nancy's half-brother Douglas (born to Bruce and his second wife), who was married with two young children, was killed in the 9/11 terrorist attack, and roughly one year later, Nancy and Doug's father, Bruce, passed away after a battle with

180

The Painful Birth of FIRE

Alzheimer's. Doug and Nancy had been in increasing contact in the months before his sudden and unexpected death, and it was agonizing to realize that he just happened to be in one of the Twin Towers that day to give a business presentation. On any other day, he would have been elsewhere.

Yet as traumatic as the split was, as hellish as the financial pressure was, as debilitating as Nancy's back pain was, and as painful as these personal losses were, the greatest pressure that she and I experienced was demonic. It felt like there was an all-out satanic plot to take us out. The battering was intense. At the same time, God's refining fire was at work again in my own life, and I became aware of all kinds of ugly flesh that needed to be crucified. So much in me needed to die and to change radically and deeply. And I mean radically. The Lord was bringing me to the end of myself and into a period of deep repentance and purging. This was not a time to strut. This was a time to lay on my face and weep.[22] And then, I almost died. Literally.

I had come down with flu-like symptoms the last week of January 2002 and Nancy said to me, "Just take the week off. You need to rest." I agreed, asking the team to cover my classes for me. But the students prayed for me as if I was dying, since I had never missed a single class or service, sick or not.

By the first Sunday of February, which was also Super Bowl Sunday, I felt good enough to attend our late afternoon service, wanting to be there to introduce an Australian colleague named Jeff Beacham who had moved to New Jersey and would be speaking for us. Driving home, I decided to get a chocolate milkshake at McDonald's, knowing it would be bad for my throat in the long run but wanting to soothe it in the short run. (Needless to say, this was before I started eating healthily in 2014!) But when I saw that McDonald's was featuring a chicken parmesan sandwich, I decided to get that as well. Still, being in a hurry, as I always was, I ordered it to go and ate as I was driving home on the interstate.

This was my journal entry for February 3, 2003:

LIVING IN THE LINE OF FIRE

THE DAY I ALMOST DIE. How can I ever forget this? Still sick in the day, try to pray and rest, then to the evening service for Jeff Beacham. I decide to get a MacDonald's chicken parmesan sandwich on the way home, then driving up 110 at 9:23, I take a bite too big...and almost choke to death. God! The fear, the panic, the sense of possible judgment, the questions about FIRE (What will happen?), the sense that I must get home for Nancy and that I can't die—but I can't breathe! I pull the Jeep over to the side of the road, getting outside in a panic, pounding my chest but hardly able to cough anything up, punching the Jeep in frustration, motioning frantically to get someone to stop, thinking about calling 911 but it's too late...and I cry out, "God save me," and pass out, coming to with a man standing by my side as I sit in the Jeep facing out, with food on the ground and on the window, the result of what one colleague would call the "miracle Heimlich"—God! The ambulance arrives and gives me the briefest of checkups, I call a totally stunned Nancy and barely make it home, staggering in the door to Nancy's terror [as I looked like death warmed over]. God!!! What was this?

"IRON MAN IS DEAD"

This was, by far, the most terrifying experience of my life, one in which the Lord literally saved me from death. Not many hours earlier, Carolyn Farias, the wife of our faculty member Bert and a powerful intercessor, had contacted some of the other women on her prayer team, telling them, "There's a death assignment against Dr. Brown," meaning, the enemy was going to try to take me out. God heard their prayers!

When I came to that night after losing consciousness, I was sitting sideways in my Jeep with my legs out the door, which is the position I was in when I passed out. I then looked down and saw the food that had been lodged in my throat now lying on the ground. I had coughed it up

The Painful Birth of FIRE

after I had passed out, because of which my colleague referred to it as the "miracle Heimlich." What mercy! The man who had pulled over to see if I was okay said to me, "I didn't do the Heimlich on you because I saw you were breathing." That's when I looked down and saw the coughed-up food on the ground. It was a miracle Heimlich indeed!

But because I had been going through a divine purging in the previous days and weeks, rather than having a sense of faith and authority in the midst of this choking attack, I felt terror more than anything. How could this be happening? And is this how it all ends?

A friend of our family, a woman who had made some generous donations to our ministry in the past, had written a letter to me some weeks earlier. It was quite hard, correcting me on a number of fronts, but because I was going through such an intense time with the Lord already, Nancy didn't show it to me at once. After I almost choked to death, she reread the letter, realizing how relevant it was for me, and I called our friend on the phone. She said, "Mike, Iron Man is dead."

Now I understood what she was saying. Although the Lord set me free from drugs totally and completely, and in that sense being "Iron Man" and "Drug Bear" was a thing of the past, I still had the Iron Man mentality. I can do more than everyone else. I can work harder. I can take on more. That is my identity! *In a very real sense, that identity almost killed me.*

That's why I took six languages at the same time in college. That's why, in addition to all my graduate school studies, I rewrote three doctoral dissertations, hired by the university to help several students whose English was not that good. (One was Korean, one Israeli, and one American.)

That's why, when traveling overseas, I would tell the organizers, "Don't worry about the schedule. I can sleep on the flight home." I often lived to regret those words, doing as many as twenty-five meetings in a single week, jet lag and all. In that same spirit, upon arrival overseas, even after traveling as much as forty-five hours, I would go straight from the airport to the first meeting to preach.

183

LIVING IN THE LINE OF FIRE

That's why during the revival, I would travel back from as far away as Australia, arriving home at 9:00 or 10:00 p.m. and going directly to the revival service (rather than to bed!), ready to pray for the crowds at the end of the night. I wanted to set an example for the students.

That's why my journal entry for July 23, 1999, simply stated: "...20 flights in 21 days..." and why twenty journal entries from September 28, 1996 until December 13, 1999 use the phrases "on the verge of collapse" and "totally exhausted."

That's why we recorded one TV episode a day for our "Think It Thru" series on the INSP network, which required me memorizing a new script for six straight days, with the TV crew telling me that the normal pace, which was still challenging to keep, would be one show *per week*, not one show *per day*, let alone for six straight days.

That's also why I never took a rest day on either side of an international trip, at one point during the revival going six weeks without a single day when I wasn't teaching or preaching or ministering in a revival service or traveling. So much for Sabbath rest.

And that's why I would constantly put myself under pressure to finish writing deadlines, always thinking to myself, "I can do this," thriving as I took on more and somehow absorbing the additional assignments without skipping a beat.

To be sure, I was deeply aware that I was sustained by God's grace and could do nothing on my own. But I intentionally overbooked myself, enjoying the challenge of the moment. I did this with the help of the Lord, but it's as if I said, "**I** can do all through Christ who strengthens" (Philippians 4:13), with a massive "**I**" and a very small "Christ." Now, everything had to change, with a very tiny "I" and an absolutely massive "**Christ**." Iron Man was dead!

It was only then, in early 2002 and in deepening form after getting wonderful input from some godly counselors, that I began to take hold of the principle of "strength out of weakness." It has truly been life-changing, and toward the end of the book, I'll share about this in greater depth.

The Painful Birth of FIRE

THE JOY OF RECONCILIATION

Thankfully, after the traumatic choking event, 2002 turned into a much better year than 2001, but still, there was no reconciliation between John Kilpatrick and me. He was willing to meet as long we didn't discuss issues. The last thing he wanted to do was get into an extended argument or debate. For my part, I saw no purpose in meeting if we weren't going to discuss the issues.

Then, something unexpected happened. I was returning from India by way of Paris, France, on December 9, 2002, with my flight from Mumbai leaving a few hours past midnight. I got on the flight very tired with a bad headache, but I could barely sleep the entire flight, about nine hours long. My head was pounding. I was exhausted, but no matter what I tried, I could not fall asleep for more than a few minutes at a time. This went on for nine miserable hours, one of the worst flights of my life, too tired to read or write or even watch a clean movie, hour after endless hour.

I had an extended layover in Paris, so I went to the Business Lounge and began to look at my emails, with more than fifty in my Inbox that I had not seen while in India. They were filled with bad news, one thing after another. Finally, I got to one of the last emails, which was actually one of the first ones that had been sent, since I was reading from top to bottom (meaning from the most recent to the earliest). It was an email from Nancy saying, "Call me as soon as you get this." This meant some seriously bad news.

We talked by phone as she shared a litany of problems that had arisen, from interpersonal issues with leaders to financial issues and more, apologizing for dumping all this on me in the middle of my trip home. To our mutual surprise, when she was done sharing all the news, I said to her, "I'm feeling encouraged." She responded, "Encouraged?" It was totally counterintuitive.

I got on the flight home, still exhausted and with a bad headache, but as soon as I got settled on the plane, the Spirit fell on me and I was energized. God was speaking to me! First, He told me not to be so self-righteous regarding the events surrounding the split. I was far from Mr.

185

LIVING IN THE LINE OF FIRE

Perfect. Second, He said to me, "Meet with John Kilpatrick. I will bless that too. ...Humble yourself and I will work. I am in *both* Brownsville and FIRE. Be a true son and share My joy and desire for both."

That was it! In a moment, everything changed. Everything! I knew what I had do to, and I was ready to do it. Still, I wanted to be sure, and I said to myself, "I'll go to sleep first, and if this is really from the Lord, I'll journal it when I wake up." But the Spirit was on me so strongly I could not sleep, so I took out my laptop, wrote down what the Lord had said to me, and promptly fell into a deep sleep.

When I woke up, I drafted a letter to Pastor Kilpatrick, telling him I didn't want to win an argument or prove a point. I was happy to meet and not bring up any issues, but for the sake of the Body of Christ, we needed to reconcile.

When I arrived home, I shared all this with Nancy, telling her, "I may never get to address areas where you were wronged." She told me not to worry about it at all. I shared the same thing with the FIRE leadership team. They too replied, "Mike, do what the Lord told you to do and don't worry about us."

I emailed the letter to John on a Thursday afternoon. His son John Michael received my letter and called his dad to read it to him while John was driving with his wife, Brenda. When John heard the contents of the letter, he said to Brenda, "The dam just broke."

He immediately called me to ask when we could meet, and I suggested after our FIRE Church service that night. We agreed to meet at his home office, which was in a barn next to his house. It was a rainy night, but when I arrived, he was waiting for me on the porch. I hurried over to meet him, and he hugged me saying, "Mike, it's all over." This too brings tears to my eyes! As David said, "Behold, how good and pleasant it is when brothers dwell in unity!" (Psalm 133:1 ESV).

We hung out together for hours, sharing our own perspectives and, interestingly enough, bringing up all kinds of difficult issues. But it was not in a combative way. Instead, it was all done with love and joy, as two men who truly cared about each other and honored each other in the

The Painful Birth of FIRE

Lord were now friends again, sharing how we had each perceived the events of the split. At one point he said to me, "Mike, if we weren't so exhausted, I don't think the devil could have gotten between us." I totally agreed with him, since our relationship before the split had been good, and I always honored his authority as the senior leader. Reconciliation is so beautiful!

In the days that followed, John met privately with Nancy and me to reach out graciously to her as well, and then we had a public service together. I presented him with the opening verses of Isaiah 61 written in Hebrew and framed. He pronounced special blessings over Nancy and me, symbolically cutting off bad things that had been said about us. All of us were now free! Not long after that, the Lord called our team to leave Pensacola and move to North Carolina, which we did in the late summer and fall of 2003. We have lived here, right outside of Charlotte, ever since, and this is where my radio studio is located. How I got on radio and got called into the culture wars is the subject of the next chapter, a chapter that takes up the revolution theme once again.

But before I transition from the birth of FIRE, I want to underscore that in the midst of the pain and trauma and upheaval of the split, there *was* a sense of exhilaration. Somehow, FIRE made it. Somehow, funds came through. Somehow, we stayed together. We even drew closer because of our joint commitment to a higher cause, and to this day, there's a sense of closeness we enjoy—FIRE leaders and grads around the world—because of this shared experience.

As for miracles of provision, my journal entries say it all. First, from December 31, 2000, our last day on our beloved BRSM campus, with the ministry totally bereft of funds, and nothing certain about where we would meet as a school or church:

> **December 31, 2000:** The last day of the millennium is my last day on the BRSM campus (for now?). I kneel down in my office—almost ready to break into tears—but then I say to the Lord, "It's worth it," simply saying "Goodbye" as I leave alone.

LIVING IN THE LINE OF FIRE

Then, after being bothered by some disturbing emails in the afternoon [which already presented a revisionist history of the split] the Jeep (packed to the gills with office stuff) begins to malfunction as Nancy and I drive [it actually died on the side of the road], my world is closing in on me every second, but I feel sure that it's a sign of coming wideness. It must be! Then—God You are so amazing!—Scottie [meaning, Scott Volk] calls with the news: $160,000 (yes, I said $160,000!) is coming to ICN via Bill F. OWI!!! Yes!!!!!!!!!!!!!!!!!!!!! ...We end the old millennium singing, worshiping, praying, and laughing—most of the new school staff and faculty—which is quite a testimony, in light of the present straits. What will the new millennium hold? Revolution!!!!!!!!!!!!! I'm ready, Father, despite the cost.

Talk about God saying to us, "I'm with you!" As for the donation from Bill F., that was the one and only time we received a gift from him, and to this day, it is the largest single donation our ministry has received.

There were also those times when I knew, by faith, that a breakthrough was coming. Look at these entries, from the evening of July 11 to the morning of July 12:

> **July 11, 2002**: My word to Gary [Panepinto] via email at 11:13 p.m.: "God has really been moving on me/us today, and I can say with total confidence and without any natural evidence at all: BREAKTHROUGHS ARE COMING! FINANCES ARE COMING! RELEASE IS COMING!! I KNOW IT."

> **July 12, 2002**: Ha! Ha! Yes! Janine [our secretary] calls with the news that there's mail from Kate with a check for $30,000 for ICN. Ha! Plus, today—not yesterday—FIRE also received $9,000 from some regular supporters. Devil you're coming down!! What encouragement for the flock to see the beginning of the breakthroughs!

The Painful Birth of FIRE

On one occasion while we still lived in Pensacola, the school needed $50,000 to pay our staff and all the bills that were due. Our backs were against the wall, as we simply didn't have the funds. So we called for a day of prayer and fasting, without mentioning any of the needs to the student body. At one point in the afternoon prayer meeting, I led us in prayer for provision, proclaiming God's faithfulness. The next day, we receive a check for almost $49,000. It was overnighted to us by regular supporters who had been giving more than $8,000 per month, but they had not given anything in six months. Somehow, they thought all our needs were met, and they just put the money aside in a separate account. The day we fasted and prayed, they felt the Lord tell them we needed the money, so they overnighted the check to us.

It was challenging to live like this, but as I said, it was also exhilarating. On with the revolution!

CHAPTER 10

THE CULTURE WARS, RADIO, AND MY CALLING TO BE A VOICE

On January 31, 1991, after months of urging from Nancy as well as encouragement from other ministry colleagues, I wrote a letter to Giant Food, the largest grocery chain where we lived in Maryland. I commended their fine chain of stores for cleanliness, service, product selection, and competitive prices. In particular, I thanked the vice president for her consumer's rights ads that had been airing on the radio. But we, too, had something to air, and it was not a radio ad. It was a serious grievance that many of our friends and coworkers shared—must we be exposed to sexual smut at every single check-out counter? They already had a candy-free checkout aisle in deference to the wishes of some parents. Why not a smut-free aisle?

Enclosed with my letter was one day's representative sampling of magazine and tabloid cover lines (these are just a few of the examples we listed): Sensual Treats to Enjoy Alone; Diary of an Affair—A Tale of Lust and Betrayal; When Happily Marrieds Are Secretly Unfaithful; My Husband Met Her at Church—Why Even Good Men Stray; Men We Lust For—Men We Marry; Woman Caught in the Grip of Love, Sex, and Alcohol; Oprah Was Pregnant at 14—Her Sizzling Romance with a Married Man; Grand Ole Opry—Sex Scandal; Preacher Caught with Mistress; Mistress Mom Tells All; Romantic Revenge—The Heady Pleasure of Getting Even.[23]

In response to my letter and a call I received from Giant, I was invited to meet with the leadership of Giant Food and with representatives from

LIVING IN THE LINE OF FIRE

Cosmopolitan, since I cited some of the worst headlines from that magazine. But after the meeting, when the Giant senior executives said they would not take action, I decided to go public with the story, contacting the local newspaper, the *Montgomery Journal*, since a free edition of the paper was delivered weekly to every home in the county. The story made the front page (it was dubbed, "Pursuing a Giant Conversion") and then, as the saga continued to unfold, it became known as "Giant vs. the Fanatic." Yes, I was "the Fanatic"!

The story also received major coverage from the *Washington Post* and the *Baltimore Sun*, and I was able to write op-eds for the *Montgomery Journal* as well as a letter to the editor for the *Post*. Our battle with Giant was also picked up nationally by James Dobson's Focus on the Family, and I ended up doing several TV and radio interviews. (I give the full account in my 1993 book, *It's Time to Rock the Boat*, which was written in part as a result of this confrontation.)

We also circulated petitions to churches in the area, asking the believers to join us in calling for Giant to take action, promising that we would take our business to any store that complied with our request. We even had a local mosque reach out to us, asking if they could sign the petition!

Other pastors told me they were glad we addressed the issue, and one of my neighbors commended me for taking a stand, saying that if I ever ran for political office, she and her husband would vote for me. (For the record, I never felt called to run for political office. Not in the slightest.) The story became so well known locally that, when I was having surgery on one of my fingers to repair an old basketball injury, the doctor and nurse started to argue with me about my viewpoints—I mean during the surgery, which only required a local anesthetic—accusing me of calling for censorship. Wild! But overall, I was able to share the gospel with many more people and raise issues of morality in the public square.

In fact, a Jewish professor who was reading the *Montgomery Journal* took exception to the concept of "Messianic Jews," accusing of us being frauds in an op-ed published by the *Journal*. I, in turn, was allowed to write a response, preaching the gospel of Jesus the Jew! This, in turn,

The Culture Wars, Radio, and My Calling to Be a Voice

triggered a larger debate in the paper as to whether a Jew could believe in Jesus and continue to be Jewish. It was a hectic time, but a blessed time.

As I wrote in *It's Time to Rock the Boat*:

> My schedule was turned topsy-turvy. Things were unbelievably hectic. But almost every day, I was able to discuss the miserable moral condition of our nation with news people or with neighbors. "Twenty years ago, did we bombard our children and families with sexual trash *at the grocery stores*?" We were now being held "captive at the counter," as one newspaper put it. What had become of our moral standards?

In the end, though, we never got near our goal of 10,000 petition signatures, underscoring the apathy of many local churches and their fear of rocking the boat or offending their neighbors. I also realized that I was *not* called to be the leader of a Moral Majority type movement, nor did I have the anointing to call for boycotts like the American Family Association has done so effectively over the years. But I *was* called to be a voice. That was clear.

And the gospel *was* designed to confront culture as well as call sinners to repent. As I wrote in *It's Time to Rock the Boat*, "But one crucial lesson was learned. Whenever the people of God, led and equipped by His Spirit, confront sin and unrighteousness in the society, it will always provide a platform for the preaching of the Gospel message. *This book is a biblical challenge to each and every one of us to rise up and preach a confrontational Gospel.* It is a call to rock the boat!"

The revolution message only increased my burden for the Church to impact the society, not by taking over and imposing our values on others but by functioning as salt and light, by winning the lost and making disciples, by preaching repentance, by confronting unrighteousness, by prayer and fasting, by the power of the Spirit, and by using our democratic rights and privileges. Still, to focus on one specific example of my non-involvement in the culture wars for the first thirty-plus years of my

LIVING IN THE LINE OF FIRE

salvation, prior to 2004, the words *homosexual* or *gay* occurred just seven times total in all my journal entries, dating back to 1983. From 2004 on, those words are found multiplied hundreds of times (especially when you add in various LGBTQ acronyms). Something dramatic shifted.

It's the same thing with my books. In my first nineteen books, if you added up every single sentence or paragraph mentioning "homosexuality" or "gay" or the like, I don't believe the content would fill a single page. That was before I wrote *A Queer Thing Happened to America*, which is 700 pages long and includes 1,500 endnotes, before I wrote *Can You Be Gay and Christian?*, before I wrote, *Outlasting the Gay Revolution*, before I wrote hundreds of articles on LGBT issues and people. What brought about the dramatic change? And why does that dramatic change date back to 2004?

GAY PRIDE COMES KNOCKING ON OUR DOOR

In August 2004 while I was ministering in South Korea, some of our FIRE leaders were invited by local Christian activists to share the gospel at the Charlotte Pride event. It took place in the heart of the city in Marshall Park, and my colleagues were there to talk to people individually and offer them gospel tracts. They did so in a loving, non-intimidating way, but still, they were escorted out of the park by the police, some of whom held hands with their same-sex partners. (In reality, the police had no right to force my colleagues out, an issue we raised to local authorities in subsequent years.) Yet while the police ordered my friends out of the park, they did nothing to discourage a tutu-wearing drag queen from gyrating in the presence of little children, some of whom put dollar bills in his waistband. And they did nothing to keep children out of a tent displaying pornographic material.

My colleagues shared all this with me when I returned to the States, telling me how shocked they were by what they witnessed. I was shocked too, also feeling something else that surprised me: "Not in my city!"

You see, prior to moving from Pensacola to greater Charlotte, I had really wanted to go back to the New York area. First, New York City was

194

The Culture Wars, Radio, and My Calling to Be a Voice

a happening place, a world center. What you did there echoed across the nation and beyond. Second, three million Jews lived in greater New York. I wanted to reach my people! Plus, I loved the fast-paced life there. So, I moved to North Carolina with a little reluctance, recognizing that God was calling our team to the area (He spoke it to others on our leadership team, then confirmed it to me), but thinking (or at least hoping) the move might only be temporary. Now Charlotte was "my city"! The Lord was burdening me.

In the months that followed, I began to sense the Lord calling me to help push back the rising tide of homosexual activism, recognizing that, already in 2004, it had become the principal threat to freedom of religion, conscience, and freedom in America. I also realized that without divine intervention, we had already lost the battle for the next generation.

At the same time, while I realized I was called to confrontational ministry and that the revolution message tied in with the culture wars, I still wondered, "Why me? Why call *me* into this particular cultural battle?" After all: 1) my Ph.D. was in Near Eastern Languages and Literatures rather than in counseling or family dynamics or sexuality; 2) I did not come out of homosexuality, so it was not part of my own testimony; 3) I did not have a particular burden to reach out to those who identified as gay or lesbian, even though someone close to our family was ex-gay; and 4) there were already fine ministries and leaders addressing the relevant issues, most prominently James Dobson and Focus on the Family, Chuck Colson (as a prophetic voice), and Tony Perkins and the Family Research Council (from a political perspective), among others. Why was I so needed?

This was in stark contrast with my calling to Jewish ministry, since: 1) my degree helped me immensely in debates about the Hebrew Bible; 2) I'm Jewish; 3) I have been burdened to reach my people since my first days in the Lord; and 4) no one was effectively debating the rabbis and there were no comprehensive responses to the objections of the rabbis and counter-missionaries. Someone had to do something, and by the Lord's design, I fit the bill. In fact, when I would be introduced over the

LIVING IN THE LINE OF FIRE

years as "the world's foremost Messianic Jewish apologist," I would say, "Correct! I'm number one among one." There was no other competition. I would also say, "This is like playing center on the pygmy basketball team. You don't have to be that tall!" All this only underscored the question of, "Lord, why are You calling *me* to confront gay activism?" It didn't seem like a natural fit.

The answer came quickly. It was not just that I had the constitution to tackle controversial issues like this. Rather, this was an issue that no one could avoid. No one would get to sit this one out! LGBTQ+ issues would become the great culture war of our generation, both in the Church and in the world. And so when friends began to ask me, "Mike, why are you spending time on this? It seems like a distraction from your calling," I would reply, "I feel like an umbrella salesman in the desert, with our company building more and more warehouses filled with umbrellas. We're doing this because we know a big storm is coming, and everyone is going to need an umbrella." Metaphorically speaking, for many years now, we have not been able to manufacture umbrellas fast enough.

Today, Americans are used to constant headlines about transgender issues or the latest conflict between LGBTQ+ activists and Christian conservatives, to the point that it seems hard to remember when this was not the case. In reality, when I started raising my voice about these issues, they were hardly in the news every day. (Ironically, while writing this very chapter, the internet was ablaze with headlines about the shocking actions of President Biden, who announced on Good Friday, March 29, 2024, that Sunday, March 31—meaning Easter Sunday!—would be the first annual celebration of "Transgender Day of Visibility."[24] But is anyone surprised?)

By the Spirit (and simple observation), I knew that this major societal transformation was coming, to the point of predicting that same-sex "marriage" would become the law of the land, that LGBTQ+ activists and their allies would win one legal and cultural victory after another, eventually overplaying their hand, and that there would be a pushback—one that we are witnessing in ever-increasing measure, from boycotts

The Culture Wars, Radio, and My Calling to Be a Voice

against Bud Light (led by people like Kid Rock!), to denunciations of biological males competing against biological females (led by people like the tennis great Martina Navratilova, herself a lesbian), to strong vocal opposition to what I have dubbed "transanity" (led by people like *Harry Potter* author J. K. Rowling, herself a long-time gay-lesbian ally, and the famous atheist, Richard Dawkins, along with another famous atheist, Bill Maher). The pushback has begun!

Once again, however, I've gotten ahead of myself. Let me return to another pivotal event in my own life with regard to the revolutionary, culture war calling. It took place on January 17, 2005.

"REACH OUT AND RESIST"

In the previous months, I had been seeking the Lord earnestly, knowing that pushing back against *gay activism* was only part of the big picture. What about God's heart for *the people?* What about seeing the world through their eyes with empathy? We were not simply dealing with an *issue*; it was also a matter of *people*—of people loved by God, created in His image, and for whom Jesus died. What about them? After all, they didn't ask to be gay, and same-sex relationships were as natural for them as heterosexual relationships were for the rest of us. And in their minds, they were fighting for equality and freedom, simply wanting to live and let live. Why couldn't they walk down the street holding hands or have the courts recognize their marriages? How were they hurting anyone else?

I began to read whatever I could from the gay and lesbian perspective, especially personal memoirs and anecdotes, be it from professing "gay Christians" or from pioneer gay activists. I wanted to understand their perspective, not just on same-sex relationships, but on how they perceived Christian conservatives, indeed on how they perceived God Himself. And the Lord began to break my heart for them.

Then, on January 17, 2005, while participating in a pro-life event in Washington, DC, with my friend Lou Engle, standing in front of the Supreme Court in freezing temperatures while engaging in silent prayer

LIVING IN THE LINE OF FIRE

with "LIFE tape" on our mouths (this was red tape with the word "LIFE" written on it), I heard the Spirit say to me, *"Reach out and resist,"* meaning, "Reach out to the people with compassion; resist the agenda with courage." In that one moment and that one phrase, everything came together. This was the commission!

I understood that extreme compassion would be needed because of all the rejection gays had suffered over the years, both from the Church and/or family members and friends. At the same time, I understood that extreme courage would be needed, since the moment you pushed back against gay activism, you would be attacked in the ugliest, most vile ways. Put another way, I began to realize that we need *hearts of compassion and backbones of steel.* (For a full exposition of this, see my October 2024 book, *Hearts of Compassion and Backbones of Steel: How to Discuss Controversial Topics with Love and Kindness.*) [25] Grace and truth must be fused together as one, just as Jesus came into this world full of grace and truth (see John 1:14–18).

In the months and years that followed, I made appointments to meet with gay and lesbian activists, always wanting to hear their hearts. I also made efforts to interact extensively with transgender-identified individuals, especially those claiming to be committed Christians, as well as to read whatever I could that would help deepen my burden for those who identified as LGBTQ+. Sometimes, my heart became so broken that I fell to my knees in prayer weeping, saying, "God, I don't want to hurt people. I just want to help them." The Lord really did change my heart; and the fact that I, the debater, the confronter, the prophetic repentance preacher, have become known for compassion is a testimony to the grace of God. If He could soften my heart, He can soften anyone's heart. He alone gets the credit it—He alone. Trust me on this.

On the local level, in Charlotte, I launched the Coalition of Conscience with the goal of rallying Christian activists (although, in the long run, again, it was clear that my calling was to be a voice more than an activist), and we raised up teams from our ministry school to share the gospel at the annual Pride events. The students would spend several days in

The Culture Wars, Radio, and My Calling to Be a Voice

fasting and prayer before reaching out and were able to impact a number of hurting, seeking individuals. We also handed out thousands of bottles of water and asked attendees if they needed prayer.

I also felt led to hold a five-night lectures series in 2007 on the topic of "Homosexuality, the Church, and Society," making clear in our ads in the *Charlotte Observer*, which the Lord provided for supernaturally, that we would have an open mic for dialogue after each lecture and that no hate speech would be allowed. Little did we know, but the venue that my assistant booked for the lectures, the Booth Playhouse, had been nicknamed "Gay Central" by the locals because of a controversial play that was performed there years earlier. And so the lecture series drew a lot of attention, especially since we timed it to coincide with the annual fundraising event held by the Human Rights Campaign (the HRC), the world's largest LGBTQ+ activist organization. That's why I devoted one lecture to exposing the real agenda of the HRC.

At that time, the HRC's annual budget was about $45 million dollars; ours at the Coalition was about $7,000. Yet the lecture series drew enough attention that it prompted Joe Solmonese, then the leader of the HRC, to call me out by name during their gala fundraising dinner, at which the biggest companies in Charlotte all vied with one another to demonstrate how gay friendly they were. A colleague of mine attending the dinner secretly recorded Solmonese's talk, in which he said:

> So how about this Pastor Michael Brown? [Some jeers] Are all of you familiar with him? For those of you who are not, uh, from out of town, he's a right-wing preacher who's holding a five-day lecture series about homosexuality in response to this event tonight....
>
> And Pastor Brown, if you're here tonight [loud laughs]...do you remember Ted Haggard [hoots and applause]. If you're here tonight, know this: We are not afraid to take you on and take back the conversation about religion and faith in this country [cheers and applause].[26]

LIVING IN THE LINE OF FIRE

I remember getting a call that night from the colleague who recorded this, telling me that Joe Solmonese had called me out personally. At that very moment, I had been working on *A Queer Thing Happened to America*, documenting the varied sexual and gender identities by which college students identified themselves, feeling sick to my stomach because of their lost and confused estate. But when I learned that I had been called out publicly by the leader of the HRC, meaning that our little lecture series hit a nerve, I was instantly supercharged with holy adrenaline. I was now marked by the world's largest gay activist organization. Praise God!

It reminded me of what happened in Acts 19 when seven Jewish men were trying to drive the demons out of a man "in the name of the Jesus whom Paul preaches" (Acts 19:13 NIV). The demon in the man replied, "Jesus I know, and Paul I know about, but who are you?" (Acts 19:15 NIV). In the words of Leonard Ravenhill, I was now "known in hell"— not that Joe Solmonese was a demon or that all gays are Jesus-mocking satanists. Rather, it was that already, our presence was being felt. This was a cause for rejoicing.

I decided to take up his challenge, reaching out to Mr. Solmonese, who then agreed to send his faith representative, Harry Knox, to debate me the following year, when we held a second set of lectures in the same venue.[27] The night of the debate, the building, which seated about 450 people, was packed, equally divided between Christian conservatives and the LGBTQ+ community and their allies, many of whom also professed to be Christians, leading to lots of important dialogue. The culture war calling on my life was being confirmed.

Of course, I have not focused only on LGBTQ+ issues, devoting time and energy to the pro-life cause and confronting the larger agenda of the radical left, as well as calling out sin and hypocrisy in the Church, just as I have done since my earliest repentance-based messages in 1973. The housecleaning starts with us. But I did receive a particular commission from the Lord to help turn the tide of LGBTQ+ activism, because of which I was:

200

The Culture Wars, Radio, and My Calling to Be a Voice

- Branded by the influential Southern Poverty Law Center (the SPLC) as one of the new leaders of the radical right, alongside men like David Duke, former Grand Wizard of the Knights of the Ku Klux Klan, and Malik Zulu Shabbaz, former head of the New Black Panthers, as well as neo-Nazi leaders.[28]
- Blacklisted by GLAAD (the Gay and Lesbian Alliance Against Defamation), who put me on their Commentators Accountability Project in which they called on media outlets not to platform people like me. (I'm still on their list and felt honored to be considered dangerous enough that I was on their initial list of thirty-six conservative commentators.)[29]
- Listed by the HRC for "Exporting Hate" overseas.[30]

It looks like the devil had taken notice of this calling on my life! (As I quickly learned and began to say publicly, "Those who came out of the closet want to put us in the closet.") And while I feel bad for those attacking me, since they are in darkness and needing the Lord, I consider these attacks a badge of honor. In fact, these kinds of attacks make my day.

I also rejoice in the open doors the Lord has set before me, including:

- Addressing congressional leaders and university chancellors in Peru on what happens when you redefine marriage and normalize homosexuality.
- Serving as the host of the powerful, award-winning, American Family Studio documentary *In His Image*.[31]
- Meeting privately with senior government and/or ministry leaders in other countries including Singapore, South Korea, and India, as well as here in the United States, to discuss the relevant issues.
- Doing relevant outreach lectures or debates on college campuses, despite protests, administrative efforts to shut the events down, and the requirement of police protection.
- Teaching the principles of "reach out and resist" in major churches in Hungary, the Philippines, and other nations, as well as throughout America and on major Christian media.

LIVING IN THE LINE OF FIRE

- Delivering seminary lectures on the subject.
- Being in the hot seat on secular TV, including shows such as Phil Donahue, Tyra Banks, and Piers Morgan (on CNN), along with countless radio programs.[32]
- Writing hundreds of relevant op-eds for a wide range of conservative and/or Christian publications.

All this underscores the fact that God can use whomever He chooses to use, despite our many limitations, with me at the top of the list of unlikely candidates.

THE CALLING TO WRITE OP-EDS

Since my earliest days in the Lord, when I would hear myself preaching my sermon in advance, thereby knowing what He wanted me to speak on and how the message would unfold, I have "seen myself" doing things before they happen, almost like reading newspaper headlines in advance. It's not by way of open vision or trance or in a dream. Instead, it's something I'll see in my mind's eye (like thinking back to a memory, except the thing hasn't happened yet). Or when seeing someone else doing something, I have that sense of, "I'm supposed to do that too."

It has nothing to do with ambition or personal desire. To the contrary, it's often something unexpected or even unwanted. Yet I know it's part of my calling.

That's what happened with writing op-ed pieces. I did feel the Lord's grace when I confronted Giant Foods, writing articles and letters to the editor for different news outlets. But that was "one and done," until I started writing some op-eds for the *Charlotte Observer* in response to local gay activism in 2007.

It was around this time, as I was reading an op-ed by a well-known, highly controversial, conservative commentator—the article was posted on a secular website, not a Christian site—that the feeling arose within

The Culture Wars, Radio, and My Calling to Be a Voice

me, "I'm supposed to do that." Some years after that, in 2010, I wrote my first op-ed for a conservative, political website.[33] Then, in 2012, Steve Strang, my Charisma colleague, reached out to me saying that he felt I was supposed write op-ed pieces, and he wanted to publish them.[34] Since then, I have written more than 3,000 op-ed articles, sometimes as many as six per week, and all this in addition to my general book writing, academic writing, daily radio shows, teaching at different schools, and traveling and preaching, both in the States and abroad. This, too, has been a calling from the Lord! (And yes, God has given me grace to do all this even since "Iron Man" died. It's not a burden. It's a joy, a privilege, a sacred calling.)

These articles have been published in venues including *Newsweek*, the *Daily Wire, Human Events, Christian Post, One News Now, Townhall, World Net Daily, Charisma Media, The Stream,* and many others, plus major Jewish outlets such as *The Jerusalem Post, Haaretz,* and the *Times of Israel.* Some of these articles have been shared hundreds of thousands of times, massively multiplying their circulation.

To repeat: this too has been a calling from the Lord, one that is especially gratifying because people will tell me, "You say what I feel." Or, "You articulate my thoughts." Or, "You use your platforms to get out my message." As one man said to me as his wife stood by his side with a smile on her face, "She calls you, 'my voice.'" Praise God! What a privilege and honor!

I've also written three books relating to evangelicals and politics (*Donald Trump Is Not My Savior: An Evangelical Leader Speaks His Mind about the Man He Supports as President;*[35] *Evangelicals at the Crossroads: Will We Pass the Trump Test?*[36] and *The Political Seduction of the Church: How Millions of American Christians Confused Politics with the Gospel*[37]), other books focusing on moral and cultural issues (such as *Jezebel's War with America* and *The Silencing of the Lambs*), along with the aforementioned books addressing LGBTQ+ issues and people, one of which deserves a section of its own.

LIVING IN THE LINE OF FIRE

THE WRITING AND PUBLISHING OF *A QUEER THING HAPPENED TO AMERICA*

Not long after God called me to the front lines of the culture wars in 2004, I felt burdened to write a book that would powerfully illustrate just how much LGBTQ+ activism had already changed the nation. But rather than this book being written in a matter of days or weeks, the process of studying and learning and writing took six years, during which time God continued to sensitize my heart for the people while also increasing my concern for where our nation was heading. The result was *A Queer Thing Happened to America: And What a Long Strange Trip It's Been*, published in 2011.[38]

I felt that this should be a definitive study, one that could even make a national impact, in keeping with Bob Weiner's *Uncle Tom's Cabin* word to me in 1993 (mentioned in Chapter 8). And this book, in contrast with the first eighteen books I had written, did not presuppose a Christian or faith-based audience. It was written for the general reader and, ideally, I wanted a conservative, secular publisher to release it rather than a Christian publisher.

But no publisher I reached out to was willing to touch the book, neither secular nor Christian, even though not one of them said that the book was lacking in accuracy, research, or compassion. Instead, it was simply considered too hot to handle. "We dare not touch this!" was the prevailing sentiment. Christian publishers were also scandalized by the title, even though the gays and lesbians I talked with thought it was a great, clever title. (After all, by this point in time, "queer" had already been mainstreamed for years. Remember the cable TV show, "Queer Eye for the Straight Guy"?) On top of all this, the book was 700 pages long with 1,500 endnotes. How many people would even read it?

One of my Christian publishing colleagues connected me with a literary agent, which marked the first time I officially worked with one. This agent represented some of the best-known Christian authors in the country and had procured major, lucrative contracts for them. Perhaps

The Culture Wars, Radio, and My Calling to Be a Voice

this agent could make a good connection for me, especially since I had no desire to make any money off the book sales, not even taking royalties on any of my books at the time but donating all proceeds to ministry. Yet the agent struck out, with one of his staff members sending me this email: "Most thought the material was too controversial...all felt that the title would need to be changed."

I distinctly remember receiving the email while in a hotel room somewhere in America where I was scheduled to preach. I punched the air with excitement, saying to myself (or perhaps out loud?), "Yes! We nailed it!" Rather than being stung by the rejection, I knew I was right on track. This was confirmation.

In the end, we formed our own publishing house, EqualTime Books, and rather than putting endorsements on the back cover, we billed this as, "The Book the Publishers Were Afraid to Touch." That heading on the back cover was followed by these quotes, but without attribution, since I didn't want to embarrass anyone.

- From a conservative pundit: "Book publishing is a difficult business now, and no media is willing to promote a book that opposes homosexuality.... Economic self-interest is going to make it very tough for a publisher to say yes."
- From a conservative publisher: "There would be a very concrete, though difficult to measure financial penalty to pay for publishing your book.... Practically speaking it could actually destroy the firm...."
- From a bestselling conservative author: "Honestly, there is no NY publisher...who will touch this manuscript."
- From the head of a New York City publicity firm: "Unfortunately [he] spoke with his team and he doesn't have anyone willing to take on Dr. Brown's book."
- From a publishing insider: "I'd be better off burning the money in my fireplace.... The economics of publishing a book like this are bleak."
- From a leading Christian literary agent: "Most thought the material was too controversial...all felt that the title would need to be changed."

LIVING IN THE LINE OF FIRE

Quite to my surprise, my longtime friend Sid Roth expressed a desire to feature the book on his TV show (if you watched *It's Supernatural*, this is *not* the kind of book you'd expect Sid to promote!), helping to pay for the publishing cost with his pre-order. Other ministries did e-blasts for me announcing the book, and I joined with Lou Engle's team in St. Louis for several days of prayer and ministry surrounding the book's release.

In the end, we sold out the first printing of almost 11,000 hardcover books, plus sold thousands of e-books. We are now prayerfully considering an updated, second edition. And while I can't explain this right now, there were some prophetic words about the book being like an *Uncle Tom's Cabin*, including a stunning prophecy from Pastor David Davis on Mount Carmel in Haifa on November 13, 2010. In his prophetic word to me, he referenced the famous quote allegedly spoken by President Abraham Lincoln to Harriet Beecher Stowe, author of *Uncle Tom's Cabin*, when he met her in 1862: "So you're the little woman who wrote the book that made this great war!"[39] Pastor Davis told me that would raise up others with me for this cause, highlighting how the Lord would use the book.

I know this seems completely preposterous, especially since the book came out in 2011 and more than 99 percent of Americans have no clue it was even published. This is hardly comparable to the extraordinary sales of *Uncle Tom's Cabin* and the powerful impact it had on the nation, helping to abolish slavery from our land. Obviously! Still, I believe that this book also represents something larger, like a seed planted in the ground of the promised moral and cultural revolution, a seed that, by God's grace, made an impact on many leaders and believers, also laying the foundation for so much of the work I have done since then. And just as God takes the foolish things of this world—like me!—and uses them to confound the wise, perhaps He can do the same with the eye-opening documentation in this book. At the least, I can point back to the specific predictions made in the book and say as to where LGBTQ+ activism was going and say, "I told you so! Will you listen to me now?"

206

"YOUR VOICE OF MORAL, CULTURAL, AND SPIRITUAL REVOLUTION"

The last major piece in my culture war commission is the Line of Fire radio broadcast, which also connects with something I felt called to much earlier. Fittingly, once the radio show went national, I was introduced daily as "your voice of moral, cultural, and spiritual revolution." Exactly! And it was another radio media executive who came up with those words after listening to a number of shows. It wasn't my idea. (In 2022, we changed the introduction to "your voice for moral sanity and spiritual clarity," which more fully reflected the broader contents of the show.) If ever there were an outlet for being a "voice," it is on radio.

The following are some important journal entries, going back to the first relevant entry dating all the way back to 1993:

July 11, 1993 (Returning from NY, listening to a talk radio show) Lord God, get me on every Christian and secular radio or TV station You want me on. Lord, I feel it is part of Your call. I only want Your plan!

April 10, 1997 In the same way that Voltaire's home ended up being used for distribution of Scripture and Wurmbrand's cell in his Romanian prison is now used to house Bibles, so also the very vehicles used by the critics to attack revival will soon be used to promote revival. Spots on radio shows devoted to denigrating revival will be taken over by God to foster the work.

August 11, 1997, in California: Quite out of the blue, and clearly as opposed to loudly, I hear this after returning to my room at the Fuller guesthouse after dinner with the brothers from Regal: "When the revival is over, you'll be on the air" (meaning radio). Once again, the concept of a large national platform through radio comes to my heart and mind....

LIVING IN THE LINE OF FIRE

June 22, 1999 Something has really been in my gut lately re: being before the media, both in the role of controversialist and confrontationalist...and also in the role of regular radio show host. How and when it will happen is God's business, but I'm as sure as sure can be that I was made for this too. Father! Your will, Your timing, Your impact. Yes!

October 20, 1999 (after praying over all my present ministry activities, I laid out these for the future): Radio; Controversial Media; further development of Israel outreach.

October 13, 2000 (during prayer retreat) ...bring me before the right secular audiences.... It's time, isn't it, Lord? And get me on the air on a regular basis if and when it's Your plan.

February 16, 2001 I am a voice. That is my primary calling. To rally the troops together, to put the vision before them—in writing and speaking—and to lead the battle charge.... Because I am called to be a voice and my authority comes from being a voice, I have that deep sense of destiny that I will be on radio and TV—as a voice, not a personality—talking, impacting, influencing. That will be my place of power! (1 Cor. 4:19-20— words backed with power.)

August 6, 2002 Talking with Sam at WWDJ today [a large Salem radio station in NYC], I get stirred in my heart again (on my own, not as his suggestion) at a thought of having a weekly, live call-in show in NY (late Monday nights?), talking about Jewish objections to Jesus, talking about revival.... Who knows?

January 6, 2003 God, You know that this is not a matter of ambition but one of calling, and so, without fear, I ask You to get me on NYC radio (and television) as often as You desire.

The Culture Wars, Radio, and My Calling to Be a Voice

Give me a voice in the city—a known, familiar voice—first in the believing community, then in the world. And give me wisdom and help to schedule my life accordingly.

March 16, 2003 [My birthday, while in New York City at a branch of FIRE School of Ministry]: Significantly, when the grads and students pray for me at the hotel (specifically, for the dissemination of the messages God has given me in print), Pat Mahoney [a longtime pro-life leader and friend] really prays for a national media platform for me...I believe!

March 27, 2003 [Again, in New York City]: Father, watching news coverage of the war, I feel more convinced than ever that I'm to be an influential voice before the media. But how can it possibly work? With my schedule and commitments, how will this ever pan out? ....

Sometimes, I would listen to conservative talk radio and I would have that same sense of, "I'm supposed to be doing this." Yet I saw no way this could happen, not with all my travel and not with the constant changes in my schedule from day to day. Plus, I had no radio connections and our ministry never had extra money. Yet I would wonder to myself, "How can I free up several hours a day for radio?"

THE LAUNCH

In the late summer or early fall of 2007, one of my publishers hired a publicity firm, called Special Guests, to help book interviews for their authors. The firm was led by Jerry McGlothlin, who had helped book pro-life activist Randall Terry on Oprah years earlier, garnering Terry instant, national attention. Jerry's plan was to have authors write opinion pieces (or short blurbs for press release) in their areas of specialty that related to relevant topics in the news, which would then make it easier to get interviews for these authors. This was a very different strategy

LIVING IN THE LINE OF FIRE

than most publishers normally used. They would simply send out a press release to all the media outlets in their database, announcing that So-and-So, the author of this great new book, was available for interviews, then highlighting the contents of the book. Generally speaking, though, unless you're a well-known author already, you won't get many significant interviews.

Jerry reached out to me, having followed my ministry for years, and I was happy to adapt his strategy, since I always enjoyed doing radio interviews. Very quickly, I became the poster boy for the publisher in terms of taking interviews, finding a way to connect relevant news items with one my books. As a result, Jerry said to me, "Dr. Brown, I really like working with you, and you've done far more interviews than any other author with this publisher. Give me a topic, and I'll pitch it for you for free." I suggested, "Can you be gay and Christian?", and he was on it, soon letting me know that I'd be doing an interview with Stu Epperson on October 15, 2007.

I was actually surprised to hear that Stu had a radio show, since he was a legend in Christian media, being the cofounder of Salem Media with his brother-in-law Ed Atsinger. And I knew he was an older man at that point, probably in his seventies. It turned out the interview was with his son, Stu Jr., who headed up his own, small radio network called Truth. Like his late dad, who went to be with the Lord in 2023, Stu Jr. stands about 6 feet 6 inches tall. (Funnily enough, he is known as "Little Stu." His outgoing, multitasking, effervescent personality is as big as he is.)

While ministering in Nashville the day of that interview and not even knowing at that point that there was a Stu Jr., I had a clear sense that Stu—thinking it was the father, not the son—was going to tell me I needed to have my own show. And that is exactly what happened, just as I journaled it that day:

> This is wild. Before being on with Stuart Epperson, I had it in
> my heart to talk with him about getting my message out on

The Culture Wars, Radio, and My Calling to Be a Voice

the radio, but prayed that, if this was from the Lord, he would bring it up—and he does, throughout the show during breaks and then afterwards, wanting me on his show perhaps monthly, even as a guest host, suggesting that FIRE come on his new station in Charlotte, that I do a weekly call-in show on Saturdays, wanting to put my Revolution Now minute across the nation on satellite and more. Some of this, at least, seems to be from heaven, and it's interesting to know that according to Stu, my name has been coming up everywhere these days. Of course, this is 100% meaningless from a human standpoint, but it's in keeping with that unshakable sense that God is calling me to be a major voice in the media in the coming days. Your will alone, Abba! Everything else is *hevel havalim* [Hebrew for "vanity of vanities" from Ecclesiastes 1].

One day later, on October 16, while still in Nashville and ministering for musician, pastor, and prophetic leader Scott MacLeod, I journaled this:

This is really wild. In the middle of a conversation with Scott MacLeod's friend Dale, pastor of the Foursquare New Song Church in Nashville, Dale changes subjects and begins to declare to me that my influence now is only a fraction of what it's about to be, that I'm supposed to be sitting across from Larry King on TV—and becoming a regular presence in the secular media—and that as the insanity of the present American Church becomes apparent, I will arise a voice of sanity. So, how many more times do I need to hear this spoken? ☺ What makes this even more interesting to me is that as I was listening to Dale talk (before he spoke this word to me), I said to myself, "I don't care how big his church is. I have no interest in traveling to speak there. I'm supposed to be on radio and TV!"

LIVING IN THE LINE OF FIRE

Things were becoming crystal clear. And I repeat, none of this appealed to my flesh or fed into wanting to be someone or desiring to be seen or known. It only had to do with divine calling and destiny.

Stu Jr. and I agreed for me to launch a live Saturday broadcast named the Line of Fire (something that came to me after weeks of prayerfully searching and brainstorming for the right name), with the first show scheduled for March 1, 2008. I would broadcast from the Truth studios in Winston Salem, North Carolina, about 75 minutes from my home.

Previously, after my first interview with Stu, I had joined him on the air in the Truth studios for his own broadcast. Now it was my turn to be live, and I expected Stu to be there to coach me through the first show. Not so! Instead, he left me a note, assuring me that I'd do great, and I was then given instructions by the engineer on duty as to how to take live calls on the air. That was it—and I loved it—every minute of it. I was made for this! The only problem was that the hour flew by quickly, and then I had to wait an entire week to do the next show. But I was in my element.

Shortly before I went on radio, Nancy told me that I was supposed to be a "Christian Rush Limbaugh," not in terms of me being a Christian version of Rush, but in terms of having a national radio influence as a believer. (As for Rush's radio abilities, he's in another league entirely.) But she warned me, saying, "This could be very dangerous for you," meaning, I could do a good radio show that could even become very popular, just using my own natural abilities. Instead, she cautioned me, I could not rely on this. I needed to be anointed by the Lord, even for talk radio. I agreed with her totally.

One week after that first broadcast, on March 15, 2008, a respected prophetic leader was ministering with a team at FIRE Church. During the service he said to me, "You have the anointing of Jonathan Edwards [by which I understood him to be saying, "You combine intellect with the Spirit and are a revivalist"]. You are called to start a revolution. You are called to bring cultural reformation." This certainly hit home!

Later, when I told him that Nancy had said that I was supposed to be a Christian Rush Limbaugh, he said, "Yes, you're a Christian Rush

212

The Culture Wars, Radio, and My Calling to Be a Voice

Limbaugh. I received that word for you yesterday." Oh my! I ended the journal entry with these words: "OWI, Abba, for Your glory and for the transformation of this nation!"

Two months later, on May 26, 2008, I ran into Shelly and June Volk at the airport. They had been disciples of Art Katz, a deeply prophetic Jewish believer, and were the parents of Scott Volk, my dear friend and colleague whom I mentioned previously. They had joined me at the radio studio for my last broadcast and they stopped me on my way to my flight. I journaled this:

> Shelly knows that he knows that this is my primary calling and what I have to give myself to, that I could literally impact the nation speaking forth God's Word, that I'm supposed to be the Christian Rush Limbaugh but with an impact that neither Rush nor Hannity have because they are not believers. He is absolutely sure of this! Yes, indeed, Abba. I have been born and brought into the world for such a time and such a purpose as this.

Reading all this, you might be tempted to think, "Who do you think you are? You must really have an exaggerated sense of your own importance." To the contrary, when you realize that you are nothing and He is everything; when you have been through the refiner's time and again and you walk with a limp; when you have a sense of destiny and calling that only deepens when you spend time with the Lord; and when you have already seen Him do impossible things in your life, you realize that *this is all about the purposes of God, not about you.*

I don't mean that the flesh can't enter into our thinking, especially when people recognize you and praise you. What I mean is that, in all the prophetic words I have received over the years regarding my destiny and calling, they only left me in greater awe of the Lord and wanting to make Him known even more. Not once did they get me to think more highly of myself. Many of you reading understand exactly what I mean.

LIVING IN THE LINE OF FIRE

"PUFF GRAHAM"

As the weekly shows continued, I sensed that God was calling me to shift to daily radio and that Stu Jr. would soon ask me to make that shift. A few days later, he called and asked me to do that very thing, and we launched a Monday through Friday evening broadcast that first aired on June 30, 2008. Then, toward the end of that year, I sensed that Stu would be asking me to switch to daytime hours, something I had previously envisioned as well. At the same time, I had felt since my earliest radio-related journal entries that I was supposed to have a show on the Salem Radio network, since it covered all the major cities of the nation. And by then, in 2008, I had already met Stu Sr., and he had given me words of encouragement about being a radio host.

Interestingly, on January 9, 2009, I received a call from both Stu's the same day, without either of them knowing the other was calling me. I journaled: "Stu Jr. calls asking me to switch to afternoons with a vision to get the show on 100 stations, then Stu Sr. calls me wanting to talk with Ed [Atsinger, CEO of Salem and Stu Sr.'s brother-in-law] and me about syndicating me on Salem."

Subsequently, I had a great talk with Stu Sr. and Ed, who made clear they wanted me to be one of their national radio hosts but that I needed more experience first (they were completely right about my need for more experience). Then, on February 9, 2009, not only did I switch to an afternoon slot on Truth, but the Line of Fire went to two hours daily. Everything was unfolding according to the divine plan!

The only problem was that, when I traveled, I had to bring a portable radio unit with me to do a live broadcast, allowing me to connect by Ethernet (meaning, a cabled internet connection) anywhere in the world. But if I was overseas, I would have to broadcast live at all hours of the day or night, doing shows from 12:30-2:30 a.m. while in India (despite jet lag, a ten-and-a-half hour time zone difference, and full ministry days) or from 2:00-4:00 a.m. (or even 3:00-5:00 a.m.) while in countries like Singapore or Malaysia or South Korea (with time zone differences of twelve to thirteen hours).

214

The Culture Wars, Radio, and My Calling to Be a Voice

Eventually, Nancy convinced me that this was not a good idea. Plus, I had experienced more than enough crisis situations overseas where the internet connection failed right before the show—or was only corrected *seconds* before the live show began. This was too stressful! So, I would prerecord shows while traveling overseas, thereby alleviating the pressure and allowing me to focus on the ministry at hand.

As for Salem, after further talks with senior management, we agreed to launch the Line of Fire on some of their biggest national stations—including their New York station, just as I had journaled in March 2003. They would help me fund the show during the first few years, but I needed a large sum of money to guarantee my part of the bargain—and money was the one thing that I did not have.

On January 19, 2011, the breakthrough came, as I journaled in detail that day. The reference to "puff Graham" in the journal entry refers to what happened when media mogul Randolph Hearst learned about Billy Graham's ministry in 1949 before Graham came to national prominence. Hearst liked what Graham was doing and sent out a two-word memo to all his media outlets, "Puff Graham," meaning, speak well of Billy Graham. Overnight, he became a household name, an "instant celebrity."[40]

I was about to get on my knees to pray, planning to say to the Lord, "If You will 'puff me'" (meaning, give me a large national platform), "I will puff You" (meaning, point everyone to Jesus and give Him all the glory). But as I knelt down to pray, I noticed my Kindle digital reader by the bedside, thinking to myself, "I just want to read a little bit more of the *Unbroken* book." This was an incredible book that told the story of Olympic runner Louie Zamperini who survived months afloat in the Pacific after his plane was shot down and then endured brutal treatment as a Japanese prisoner of war. It was a secular, non-fiction book written by bestselling author Laura Hillenbrand, with the subtitle: *A World War II Story of Survival, Resilience, and Redemption*, but thus far in my reading of *Unbroken*, while telling an extraordinary, totally riveting story about Zamperini's miraculous survival during World War II, there was no

LIVING IN THE LINE OF FIRE

redemption in sight, as his life spiraled out of control once he returned to the States. Where was the positive ending?

So while I was about to bring the "puff Graham" story to the Lord in prayer and while still on my knees by the bedside, I got distracted and began reading *Unbroken*, later journaling this:

> This is just incredible. Amazing. Out of this world. God!!! Joe D. had left me a voice mail (at the Salem meetings this week), having finally talked with R. [a wealthy businessman] about getting behind me, and I had been feeling deeply that if I could just get jump-started with some big gifts, I could raise up an army to get behind me—especially through my speaking tour and other means—and "join the revolution," and I had it on my heart to pray now about the whole "puff Graham" thing which I've thought about a lot. Well, on my knees, I decide to read *Unbroken* a bit more, and to my shock—I mean shock!—who walks into the picture but none other than...Billy Graham! And the author proceeds to tell the "puff Graham" story, and then—to my greater shock, although I hoped throughout the book that something dramatic would happen to Louie Zamperini—he gets radically and dramatically saved through Graham's message, leaving me crying, punching the bed, exclaiming repeatedly, "That is the power of the gospel!" JESUS IS LORD! And moved and overwhelmed, I tell the Lord that if He will raise up people to "puff Brown," I will absolutely "puff" Him. This is the Lord!

Soon after that, that businessman (identified as "R" in my journal entry) made a significant donation to the ministry, and on March 14, 2011, which happened to be our thirty-fifth anniversary and the day that *A Queer Thing Happened to America* was published, we went live on Salem for two hours a day. This was just as the Lord had shown me!

We continued with our live daily, call-in broadcast on different stations through 2024, as well as livestreaming on our large Facebook and

The Culture Wars, Radio, and My Calling to Be a Voice

YouTube platforms (once we added the video feed, we dropped from two hours to one hour daily). The podcast is rated in the top 0.5 percent worldwide, and, at times, has reached #1 ranking in the category of "Christianity" in countries including Israel, Pakistan, Saudi Arabia, Bulgaria, Croatia, Kazakhstan, and others.[41] And, beginning in January 2024, we launched a new thirty-minute, prerecorded broadcast—also called the Line of Fire (but as a podcast, called "Courage in the Line of Fire")—designed to "infuse you with faith, truth, and courage, so you can stand strong on the front lines, since all of us today are in the line of fire." It currently airs on more than 200 stations, including significant outlets in major cities, but rather than doing both a pre-recorded daily show and a live daily show, at the end of 2024, we dropped the live talk radio show and switched our live programming to online only, taking advantage of the massive growth of online platforms, adding long-form interviews (without the time constraints of a radio) and special teachings and all kinds of new content. We are stoked with all the possibilities that lie before us!

Over the years, we have received amazing phone calls on the live, talk show, and I have been astounded to see who has been listening, from ultra-Orthodox rabbis to a gay rabbi (who was a regular listener and who later tied in with an amazing story in my life),[42] from Black Hebrew Israelites to White Supremacists, from women weeping over their past abortions to a Christian woman conflicted about working for Planned Parenthood,[43] and from Christians of every stripe to Israelis wanting to know the truth about Yeshua. What a glorious ride it has been so far!

As for our impact, I truly believe that we have barely scratched the surface of our potential and calling, especially in light of some of the aforementioned prophetic words. And although I have done TV programs for the INSP network (a very creative, two-season, on location, Jewish-outreach show called *Think It Thru*), for GOD TV (two seasons of revival-oriented preaching), NRB TV (several seasons of apologetics shows), and METV (Middle East TV, owned by Sid Roth; we recorded two seasons of Jewish outreach programming with captions in Hebrew),

217

LIVING IN THE LINE OF FIRE

I believe my ultimate media calling will be expressed on radio and online, and to this day, I look forward to daily broadcasts like a kid in a candy shop. We shall see what the Lord does in the coming years!

This much is sure: to the extent God gives me a national voice, I will point everyone to Him. He alone must be "puffed" and lifted up, since He alone is worthy. As for each of us, at the end of the day, if we have done our jobs well, we say to Him, "We are unworthy servants; we have only done our duty" (Luke 17:10 NIV). What sacred (and often enjoyable!) duty it is.

CHAPTER 11

TO THE JEW FIRST

The calling to reach my own Jewish people with the gospel, representing the third "R" of our ministry—the redemption of Israel!—is for the me the highest and final calling on my life, since, whoever lives to see all Israel saved (Romans 11:26) will witness the return of the Lord and the resurrection of the righteous. These are high stakes![44] Whatever role I can play in this is an honor and privilege beyond words.

It is also a calling that the Lord brought to my door, which is significant since: 1) not every Jewish believer is called to make this a priority; 2) my heart also burns for the first two R's of our ministry, Revival in the Church and a gospel-based, moral and cultural Revolution in the society; and 3) I love going to the nations! Yet in all this, the call to see my people saved, which also connects with a burden to see the Church feel the pain of the lost sheep of the house of Israel as well as the burden to push back against the ever-rising tide of antisemitism, always burns bright in my heart. It is a given, no matter where I am or what I am doing.

As for the Lord bringing this calling to me, as I mentioned in Chapter 2, it was a matter of sink or swim. It began with my dad bringing me to meet the local rabbi when I was just a few weeks old in the Lord and then that rabbi bringing me to meet other rabbis and Jewish scholars. This forced me to dig deeper in my studies, learn the Hebrew language, and find answers to the powerful objections of these rabbis and counter-missionaries (which is a name some of these rabbis use for themselves, since they consider Jewish believers to be "missionaries"). And along the way, I received numerous, quite supernatural confirmations of this calling, the

219

LIVING IN THE LINE OF FIRE

first ones coming in 1984. This was also the year that, for the first time, I realized from passages like Romans 11 and Isaiah 25–26 that Israel's salvation was directly connected to the resurrection of the righteous, something the Spirit opened up to me in an unlikely setting: a Kenneth Hagin camp meeting in Tulsa, Oklahoma. That's also where I first met Sid Roth.

Although I had strong issues with several aspects of Word of Faith teaching, I had been blessed by some of Hagin's teaching, and it was Word of Faith believers who joined with my sister-in-law Robin in praying me back to my first love. During one of the meetings, I sensed that Brother Hagin was about to prophesy over me, even though I was not sitting in the minister's section, and the very few prophetic words he had delivered in the previous meetings were only to those sitting in that section. (Frankly, I didn't know such a ministerial seating section existed. I was too new at this!)

Yet as I sat with the crowd of thousands while he spoke, I knew he was about to call me out, and I said to the Lord, "Let's do this," raising my hands to Him. A moment later, Brother Hagin's attention suddenly shifted in my direction and he said, "The man, the young man over there," looking right at me. I stood to my feet. He continued, "The work you're doing is of tremendous—it's of greater importance than what you even know—and through these channels, work will be done that, if it could be told you at the moment, you wouldn't hardly believe it. But you'll be faithful, and it will be consummated."

He asked me, "Did that mean anything to you?" I replied, "One hundred percent," about to explain to him that I knew he was about to call me out of the thousands in attendance. But I wasn't able to get that out, as he went back to teaching and ministering, explaining that sometimes you prophesy something having no idea what it means, but it means something to the person receiving the word.

Once again, I was stunned by the Lord's goodness, especially because, only a few days earlier, I had to humble myself and get very low in order to alleviate a conflict for another leader. Now the Lord was pouring out His gracious favor. But there was something I did not understand. Moments

220

before Hagin spoke that word over me, I was saying to the Lord in my youthful zeal, "I want to shake the whole world for Jesus!" What could be of greater importance than that? What was it that I "wouldn't hardly believe it" if the Lord showed me now?

Later in the same week, on July 25, 1984, Reinhard Bonnke was speaking, and it was the first time I heard this fire-breathing, faith-filled evangelist. What a message! But as he shared the story of God saying to him, "Africa shall be saved," in my own heart, the Spirit began to open various passages in the Bible regarding the significance of Israel's salvation. This was all going on in my mind as I listened intently as Bonnke spoke.

In a moment, scriptures I had known for years suddenly came together with clarity, and the Lord said to me, "Yes, I gave that promise to Bonnke, but how much sure is what is written in My Word, namely, that 'all Israel shall be saved'?" Later that day, I journaled: "Bonnke preaches and I explode—All Israel shall be saved—signs and wonders over Israel." Now I understood the Hagin prophecy: it referred to my role in helping to see Israel saved. This was the work that would be of even greater importance than I could imagine. It was clear!

THE STRACK-BILLERBECK MIRACLE

Prior to this, Robin had mentioned me to Sid Roth, whom she had recently met, thinking I would be a good guest for his radio show. After Hagin prophesied over me, Sid introduced himself to me, leading to the first of many interviews we have done over the years. At that time, I was teaching at Christ for the Nations on Long Island and commuting into New York City to do research for my doctoral dissertation, using the libraries at New York University, where I was studying, and Hebrew Union College and Jewish Institute of Religion, which was a few blocks away. One day, I received a call from Sid, who understood my calling to both the Word and the Spirit. He said to me, "Mike, I'm having a problem. The more I get in the Spirit, the less I feel connected to my Jewish roots. The more I connect to my Jewish roots, the less I get in the Spirit. I believe you're the man to help figure this out!"

LIVING IN THE LINE OF FIRE

I replied, "Sid, these are massive issues which scholars have debated for centuries, including the relationship between Law and grace and faith and works and the Jewish roots of the faith. It would take decades to sort this out."

To be sure, I was interested in these topics, but until that point, I had focused almost all of my attention on learning Hebrew and the related Semitic languages, as well as getting a basic grasp on the massive body of rabbinic literature, known as "the sea of the Talmud," in order to better counter Jewish objections to Jesus and more rightly connect to my people. But I had not focused on what you might call "Messianic Jewish" issues. Was this something the Lord was calling me to do?

There was an expensive, massive, five-volume set of books published in Germany in the 1920s and authored by Herman Strack and Paul Billerbeck, titled, *Kommentar zum Neuen Testament aus Talmud und Midrasch* (*Commentary on the New Testament Based on Talmud and Midrash*). It was the most comprehensive compilation of rabbinic literature relative to the New Testament, even if some of its methodology was flawed. I had really wanted to get it, but it was way out of my price range.

So I did something I have rarely done over the years, namely, put out a fleece before the Lord. I prayed, "God, if You're really calling me into these studies, give me a set of Strack-Billerbeck" (which was how scholars referred to the work). Not long after that, while doing doctoral research at the Hebrew Union College library, the librarian, named Phil Miller, who seemed to know everything about every book in the library and about every author, pulled me aside.

It turns out I owned a book he needed for his own doctoral studies. It was a slender but expensive volume that was now out of print and hard to find, written by a French scholar named Georges Vajda and titled, *Deux commentaires karaïtes sur l'Ecclésiaste* (*Two Karaite Commentaries on Ecclesiastes*). As for the subject matter, it was quite specialized, focusing on two commentaries on Ecclesiastes written over 1,000 years ago by two Karaite Jewish scholars. (Karaites are Jews who follow the written Torah but reject rabbinic tradition.) As for the commentaries, they were written

222

in Judeo-Arabic, which is Arabic written in Hebrew characters, and I had purchased the book for a paper I had done in a class in Judeo-Arabic taught by a visiting professor from the Hebrew University in Jerusalem, the legendary Semitic scholar Joshua Blau. Now that the class was over, I had no use for the book.

Phil said to me, "Mike, I called Eisenbrauns [the name of a major used book dealer], and I was informed that they sold the only copy they had of that book to someone named Michael Brown. Well, I need that book! So, I'll make a deal with you. I have an old set of Strack-Billerbeck here in the library that needs to be re-bound, so I have to order a new set to replace it. I'll trade you the whole set for that one book."

I couldn't believe my ears. We had never once discussed Strack-Billerbeck and I didn't even know that set of books was in that library. It was a deal! Yes! To this day, those old volumes sit behind me in my home study as a holy reminder. It was the first specific, supernatural confirmation of the divine mandate to reach my people with the good news of Yeshua.

ANSWERING JEWISH OBJECTIONS TO JESUS

It was sometime in the early 1980s when I began to sense a calling to provide answers to my people's objections to Jesus, as if this, too, was part of my destiny, even conducting some debates with Rabbi Berman in his own synagogue, at his invitation. I had already seen as a new believer challenged by the rabbis that there was a massive void in this area, as other, new Jewish believers were having their faith destroyed by learned rabbis. Someone needed to fill that void, and I sensed a calling to do that.

After years of intensive interaction with rabbis and counter-missionaries, I wrote the five-volume series, *Answering Jewish Objections to Jesus*, published from 2000-2010,[45] with some of the volumes subsequently translated into Hebrew, Russian, Spanish, and Portuguese. I was deeply humbled to read the endorsement to volume 3, which was published in 2003, by Dr. Barry R. Leventhal, then academic dean and professor, Southern Evangelical Seminary: "Michael Brown has established himself

LIVING IN THE LINE OF FIRE

as the foremost messianic apologist in the world. This volume deals with that most vital and controversial area of messianic prophecy objections: Is Jesus really the promised Messiah? All three volumes exhibit Dr. Brown's unique contributions to Jewish missions: biblical accuracy, Jewish sensitivity, and personal compassion." This is exactly what I felt destined to do, and it was coming to pass, just as the Lord planned it. What an amazing God!

By the Lord's grace, I have also been able to provide other apologetic resources for the Body, including *The Real Kosher Jesus: Revealing the Mysteries of the Hidden Messiah*,[46] and *Resurrection: Investigating a Rabbi From Brooklyn, a Preacher From Galilee, and an Event That Changed the World*,[47] along with full-length video courses and specialized outreach videos, not to mention our Real Messiah, outreach website (RealMessiah.com).

It has also been my privilege to conduct more public debates with rabbis than any man on the planet, including almost twenty debates with my good friend Rabbi Shmuley Boteach, known as "America's most famous rabbi." One of these debates was conducted at Oxford University, and I also delivered an outreach lecture at the International School at the Hebrew University in Jerusalem, as well as outreach lectures at Yale and Columbia University and USC. And remember: I'm the former idiot who used to huff diesel gas to get high, who broke into a doctor's office and shot adrenaline, and who used to see how much LSD I could ingest without losing my mind. How the Lord loves to use unqualified vessels like me!

THE FIRST SIGN IN SOUTH KOREA

Prior to traveling to Korea for the first time in 1990, I taught Korean Christians who were training for ministry at a school in New York City, also preaching at some Korean church services. I was blown away by their spiritual devotion, especially their focus and intensity in prayer, something they were famous for worldwide. In fact, a megachurch pastor in Korea once said to me, "For decades, I have led the 6:00 a.m. prayer

To the Jew First

meeting at our church every morning. I also lead the early morning prayer at 4:30 a.m. every morning." In the Korean church, 6:00 a.m. is late morning prayer!

My first trip to South Korea was in 1990, and my translator and I arrived late because of a delayed flight, meaning we had limited time to rest on Saturday night before I had to preach on Sunday morning. To make matters worse, our hosts awakened us extra early, since this was my only opportunity to visit Dr. Cho's church and worship with the multiplied thousands who gathered there. (Actually, hundreds of thousands worshiped there over the course of the day, including their satellite churches). We also had to leave extra early because of traffic. (Yes, traffic was heavy even on Sunday morning in Seoul.) I was even more tired now, but the day was just beginning. Then, after taking in the service at Cho's church, we had a long drive back to the church where I had to speak, and I had to concentrate all my mental energy to stay focused on the message. I was tired!

Over lunch, one of the leaders said to me, "Reverend Brown, what are you discerning?" I said to them, "I'm too tired to discern! I'll start discerning tomorrow." I just wanted to sleep!

We were staying a nice apartment on the outskirts of Seoul, and when we returned from ministry and lunch on Sunday afternoon, I went straight to my bedroom and crashed. A few hours later, my translator tried to wake me up: "Dr. Brown, we should go eat before the restaurants close." I asked him for another hour, then another. Finally, he said, "We have to go now."

I dragged myself out of bed and he asked, "Where would you like to eat?" This was in my unhealthy eating days, when I also hated to try to new foods. But earlier in the day I had seen one sign on a restaurant written in English rather than Korean. It said, "Pizza." I said to him, "Let's go there."

We walked over to the pizzeria—or whatever they call a pizza place in Korean!—but they were closing their doors when we arrived. We were too late after all. My translator talked to the man who was closing the

LIVING IN THE LINE OF FIRE

doors, then came back to me surprised. He said, "Normally, they don't do this, but the man was very nice and told me there's another pizzeria a few blocks away." It was very hard to find, and we never would have known about it unless we arrived late at the other place and were given specific directions.

When we entered this pizza place, there were only two other people there, but they were not Korean. As we sat waiting for our food, I was shocked. These were Israelis, speaking Hebrew! I asked them in Hebrew, "What are you doing here?" They replied nonchalantly in typical Israeli fashion, "Eating pizza." I asked in Hebrew, "Are there many Israelis here?" They said no, there were very few. And yet here we were, less than twenty-four hours after arriving in Seoul, and my translator and I ran into two Israelis in a pizzeria on the outskirts of Seoul. What were the odds of that?

Immediately I sensed the Lord say, "Yes, I have raised up the Korean church to bless Korea and to bless the nations. But I have also raised up the Korean church to pray for the salvation of Israel." I sat there stunned. In the days that followed, I surveyed multiple hundreds of Koreans. Not one of them had ever met an Israeli in their country. I repeat: what were the odds of me meeting two Israelis in an out of the way location on the outskirts of Seoul within twenty-four hours of my arriving there for the first time? For the skeptics who say, "That was just a coincidence," then keep reading. This is just the beginning.

Later that same week, I did some teaching on Israel at the request of the Korean leaders, and at the end of one of my sessions, a Korean couple came up to me speaking fluent Hebrew, much better than my poor, modern Hebrew. They had served for some years in Israel and had a great heart for my people. In the months that followed, some of these Korean believers formed a prayer group that focused on Israel and the Jewish people. I'll share more about that shortly.

To the Jew First

THE SECOND SIGN IN KOREA

The second trip took place just a few months later, as I was asked to return on fairly short notice for a special, annual prayer meeting that lasted for three-and-a-half days, ushering in the year 1991. About 1,800 believers would be shut up in a gymnasium, spending the entire time fasting and praying and then sleeping in sleeping bags on the floor. It was quite spartan. I would be staying in a nearby hotel, but my room was so tiny that there was barely enough space to stand, let alone walk around.

I fasted the entire time as well, speaking at different hours of the day and night and commuting back and forth between the hotel and the gymnasium. The spiritual atmosphere, as you could imagine, was intense. There was prayer and then preaching. Prayer and then worship. Teaching, and then prayer—hour after hour, with the emphasis being squarely placed on prayer.

The last night, we began to intercede for Israel, and then, in response to a burden I was feeling, we singled out Russian Jews and Jews from New York City, crying out to God for their salvation. The next day, I was flying home from Kimpo International Airport on Korean Air. Almost all the passengers were Korean, and many of them were reading Bibles as they sat waiting to get on the plane. I was amazed to see how rapidly the Christian faith had spread through the nation in recent years. Then, to my shock, I noticed an ultra-Orthodox Jewish man in the same gate area. What in the world was this bearded, ultra-Orthodox Jew doing in Seoul? What did he even eat in Korea? I don't imagine there's a lot of Kosher food there!

I went over to talk with him, asking him a somewhat difficult Hebrew and rabbinic question, just to start a conversation and to indicate my interest. We talked for a while before boarding and then, during a one-hour layover in Anchorage, Alaska, we continued our discussion, which became fairly intense.

He said to me, "Go ahead. Do it the easy way"—in other words, don't bother keeping all the commandments. Take the easy "Christian" way. I said to him, "It's not always so easy. In fact, I spent the last three-and-a-half

LIVING IN THE LINE OF FIRE

days fasting and praying with Korean Christians here, and we were praying for people just like you." Then I asked him (although I already knew the answer), "Where are you from?" He said, "New York." But of course!

On subsequent trips, I surveyed hundreds more Koreans, asking them if they had ever seen an Orthodox Jew in their country. Not one of them had. Now, I was two for two on my trips to Korea. What would happen next?

THE THIRD SIGN IN KOREA

The third trip, which was in 1991, was again super intense, with day and night ministry, as with all my trips there. But with one only day of ministry left, I had not met an Israeli or an Orthodox Jew on the trip—just like tens of millions of other Koreans over the course of their entire lives. To be sure, one significant thing connected to Israel had already happened. I had joined together with an Israel prayer group that had been formed after my first visit in 1990. It was a small group, perhaps ten to twelve people, but the depth of heartfelt prayer was indescribable. I remember these precious believers literally scratching the carpet with their fingernails, as if they were trying to grab hold of the floor as they lay on their faces weeping, interceding for the lost sheep of the house of Israel.

I had brought with me the manuscript of my book *Our Hands Are Stained with Blood*, which documents the horrors of antisemitism in church history, but we did not yet have a publisher. I put the manuscript in the middle of the prayer circle as they lifted their voices to God and wept. I heard the Spirit say, "It is only tears of intercession that can wipe away the stains of blood."

After the prayer meeting, a young Malaysian woman told me that she had come to faith when revival hit her village some years earlier, something quite special in this Muslim nation. Then she said, "We don't know much about the Jews. We just know we love them!" How beautiful!

But that was just the beginning. My translator and I were staying at the Bando Youth Hostel, something my translator found very offensive. He said to me repeatedly, "Dr. Brown, why they put us here? You are

228

To the Jew First

important speaker. This is tiny hotel. I know the general manager of the Shilla Hotel, where President Bush stayed. I get 75 percent discount. Why they put us here?"

I said to him, "Maybe because it's closer to the meetings?" But he would have none of it.

He was a brilliant man, Korean born but now a university professor in the States, and he had planned to return home the day before me. He told me I would have different translator for the Sunday morning service, which was my final meeting of the trip. But he changed his mind and decided to stay the extra day. Then, to my surprise, he called my hotel room early Sunday morning shouting over the phone, "Dr. Brown! I just met an Israelite on the elevator! And he think he knows you!"

An Israelite? What? Did he mean Moses or Elijah? I said to him, "You mean an Israeli?" He said, "Yes, and he studied in Israel with a Dr. Brown. Maybe that's you? Here's his room number."

I called the room, and this Israeli man was quite happy to meet me, although I was not the "Dr. Brown" he was thinking of. I shared the gospel with him and told him about the great love these Korean Christians had for Israel.

But something was bothering him, and he looked very downcast. He said, "I work for a very rich company based in Japan, and wherever I travel, I stay at only the finest hotels. Why did they put me here in the Bando Youth Hostel? The CEO of the company dropped me off here himself!"

I said to him, "It's all because of me!" This made my sharing of the gospel even more powerful. The Lord had set it up! This was now three trips to Korea with three, supernatural Israeli-Jewish encounters. The odds of this are beyond astronomical. (On a pragmatic note, Nancy asked me, "Why didn't the Lord put both of you in a nice hotel?" That was a fair question, but the fact that this all happened in this little youth hostel really got our attention.)

I then went to preach at the Sunday morning service, and when I returned to the hotel, I found the Israeli man in the lobby. He was

229

LIVING IN THE LINE OF FIRE

looking very happy, standing there with his luggage, about to be moved to another hotel. He explained to me that the CEO contacted him to say there had been a mistake and they were moving him to the right hotel. *The Lord had him there just for that one day.* I introduced him to the Korean Christians who were dropping me off, telling them this was the Israeli I mentioned. With radiant faces they said, "We love Israel! We love the Jews!" I doubt this Israeli man had ever been greeted overseas like this before. Once again, I was stunned.

THE FOURTH SIGN IN KOREA

For the next trip, though, which was in 1992, I joked with the Koreans saying, "I don't need to meet an Israeli there, since we're bringing one." I was referring to Reuven Doron, an Israeli believer then living in Iowa. The Koreans were hosting a three-day conference on Israel where I would be speaking, along with my Messianic Jewish colleague Dan Juster, and Reuven. Shortly before the conference, I was asked if I could come in a couple of days earlier. One of the Korean leaders we worked with, Han Si Kim, had rented the Olympic stadium in Seoul for five nights of meetings, with two of the most famous pastors in the nation speaking each night. I was asked to share one of those evenings, calling on the Korean church to pray for Israel and bless Israel. What an honor!

At the stadium event, I read from Genesis 12 in Hebrew God's promise that those who blessed Abraham's seed would be blessed, thinking to myself, "I bet this is the first time the Hebrew Bible has been read over the loudspeakers in this stadium!" (On a side note, as you could guess, the monitor in the stadium was absolutely massive, allowing everyone to see the faces of the speakers as if they were only a few feet away. Unfortunately, I had just gotten over chicken pox—at the age of thirty-seven—and I had red pockmarks all over my face. You bet they were quite visible on the giant screen which I was told was seventy-five feet in size!)

When it came time for the three-day conference, two of the organizers said to me, "We are very excited that Korea is about to open an embassy

To the Jew First

in Tel Aviv. In turn, Israel will be opening an embassy in Seoul, and while the ambassador has not yet arrived, the *charges d'affaires* is here. We have invited him to come to the conference."

I said to them, "He'll never come to a church conference." They replied, "Dr. Brown, we are praying." I thought to myself, "I guess he's coming!"

Still, even though I had confidence in the power of their prayers, I was stunned to get the news that he would actually be attending the last night. Hundreds of us had been fasting that final day of the conference, and the faces of the believers in the audience were just radiant. And everything was planned for the arrival of the Israeli *charges d'affaires*. Reuven would meet him at the door, speaking to him in Hebrew—the last thing he would have expected—then the worship team would turn to him and sing in Hebrew (they had learned two beautiful songs that were fitting), then I would give him *Our Hands Are Stained with Blood*. The book had been published since that prayer meeting in 1991, and I had brought a copy with me to honor those who had prayed. Now, I inscribed it in Hebrew for the Israeli *charges d'affaires*.

Reuven greeted him at the door then came up to join us on the platform. And as he watched the Koreans sing in Hebrew, their faces aglow, he said to Reuven with tears in his eyes, "This is the most moving, incredible thing I have ever seen."

Afterward, he greeted the people, speaking in English with a translator, explaining that the Israelis were actually very nice people (since in most places he had traveled, there was often hostility toward Israelis). Then, Han Si Kim came to the pulpit to pray for Israel, speaking in Korean with an English translator so the words could be understood. To this day, I do not remember hearing a more passionate prayer for Israel. Once again, I was stunned. What a night!

The *charges d'affaires* then left, I preached on how I knew Israel would be saved, first using the Word, then sharing my experiences. Then I called for everyone to come to the altar in prayer for Israel. I got off the platform and joined them, but the presence of the Spirit was so great that I fell to my knees, unable to stand. Yet the presence was still too strong, so I fell

231

LIVING IN THE LINE OF FIRE

on my face. That's when I heard the Lord say, "I'm going to save Israel." In other words, this was His work, not ours. He would use us, but He had to work in His sovereign ways. Four trips to Korea. Four supernatural encounters with Israelis or Orthodox Jews. Yet there is more.

THE FIFTH SIGN IN KOREA

Right before my fifth trip to Korea, which was in 1993, Nancy and I were introduced to an ultra-Orthodox Jewish teenager in New York City. (He told us he was eighteen, but at the time he was only seventeen. We'll call him Yaakov.) He had previously peeked in the door of Sid Roth's Messianic congregation that used to meet in Brooklyn, and Sid wondered if he was just spying things out or was sincere, since it was beyond highly unusual for an ultra-Orthodox Jew, someone who lived in a very closed community, to show any interest in a Messianic Jewish congregation. Not a chance.

It turned out Yaakov was sincere, and after meeting with Nancy and me one time, he said, "I want to move to Maryland and study in your school, but we have to meet my parents and family and tell them." What an absolute shock this was going to be to them! He might as well have said to them, "I'm going to become a Nazi." That's the way they would have viewed him saying he wanted to follow Jesus.

Yaakov's whole story will be told one day, but here, I can only tell you that Nancy and I met together in Manhattan with Yaakov and his family, and it was a horrific, traumatic meeting. He was one of ten kids, and two of his brothers were there, along with his father, who was pleading with me not to interact with his son and other family members. As the night wore on, one of the brothers said to me, "There's a really big rabbi in Brooklyn, Avigdor Miller. He knows the New Testament inside out. Let Yaakov meet with him tomorrow morning, and if he still wants to go with you, he can go. Here's my number."

I called the number the next day, only to learn I had been duped. There was no such number. Yaakov's own brothers had kidnapped him! (Again, what happened to him during this time needs to be told one day, but I'll

232

To the Jew First

let Yaakov tell the story at the appropriate time.) Nancy and I went to the police to report that we believed there had been foul play, but they said there was nothing they could do based on our scanty information, and they were obviously right. We returned to Maryland with heavy hearts, then I flew to Korea.

One service, I preached a message on Israel from Romans 9-11, culminating in Paul's promise in 11:26 that, "All Israel shall be saved," asking the Koreans to proclaim those words with me in Korean: "Israel shall be saved!" But as I said the words "Israel shall be saved" out loud in English, I heard the Spirit saying in my inner ear, "Yaakov will be saved!" I knew he would make it! Still, there were no encounters with Israelis or Orthodox Jews while in Korea, the first time in all these trips, and I left to travel back slightly surprised.

I flew home by way of Detroit and I was walking through the Detroit airport toward my gate when, to my astonishment, there was an ultra-Orthodox Jew standing there with his black hat, black coat, and long beard. I didn't see that regularly in my travels. But there was something more. I knew this man! He had been in my house once in Maryland—and he was also a secret believer in Yeshua, making him the only ultra-Orthodox Jew I knew on the entire planet who believed in Jesus. This was unreal! Out of more than six billion people in the world and out of fourteen million Jews, and to my knowledge, this was the one and only person of his kind that I knew. Yet here he was at the gate in Detroit, even though he lived in Jerusalem. Incredible! This was God confirming to me that Yaakov, himself an ultra-Orthodox Jew, would be saved as well. Five trips to Korea out of five!

Sadly, Yaakov suffered much over the years, being kidnapped a second time when he expressed his faith again and broke away, then brought to Israel against his well, beaten, and drugged. But when we would talk, even if he expressed no interest in Yeshua. I would tell him, "You're going to make it. I know it."

Twenty-five years later, in 2018, he called to let me know that he had committed his life to Jesus. Yes! He has been on fire ever since, working

LIVING IN THE LINE OF FIRE

secretly to win more of his people to the Lord. What a faithful God we serve! He hears the cries of our heart! He finishes what He starts! Israel shall be saved!

I have now been to Korea thirteen times and in all my trips since 1993, I have never once met an Israeli or Orthodox Jew there. Not once. These were special, supernatural signs, always reminding me that the salvation of Israel requires the prayers of the nations. Will you join in prayer too?

THE AGONIZING SIGN IN KANSAS CITY, 1991

In 1986, the Lord took me through a heart-wrenching spiritual experience of intercession in order to help me to feel His heart. It was a Saturday night, and I was scheduled to preach the next morning in a local church, but I sensed that something was terribly wrong in the pastor's life. (It turned out that this was an accurate perception, as he committed adultery just a few months later.) While praying, a sense of dread came over me, as if something very bad was going to happen to him. Then, things shifted in my mind: something bad was going to happen to someone in his family, to one of his daughters. She was going to die! Then things shifted again: instead of something happening to one of his daughters, something was going to happen to one of my daughters. This was because I had interposed myself between him and judgment through my intercession.

This all felt very real, even though I kept hoping to myself that it was just some kind of prophetic lesson God wanted to teach me. But I couldn't shake the feeling, finally waking up Nancy in the middle of the night and telling her someone in our house was going to die. (Can you imagine your spouse waking you up at 2:00 or 3:00 a.m. with news like this?) We went into another room and began to pray together, and I fell to my face sobbing for my daughter. Then, suddenly, the burden lifted. The Lord spoke to me that He had wanted me to pray for that church as if it was my own daughter dying, because that's how He felt. It was simply a prophetic experience, a lesson in intercession, which, as I said, I

To the Jew First

had hoped was the case the whole time. But I had to get to that place of agonizing prayer before I understood the lesson.

Fast-forward to March 1991 when I was speaking in Kansas City at an Israel conference with Dan Juster and Reuven Doron, both of whom I mentioned previously. Reuven and his wife, Mary Lou, brought their little baby Rachel with them, just six weeks old, and I remember Reuven referencing her in first two messages, speaking of how she was a type and sign of Israel. He was very clear in making this point.

After his second message, which was at a night service, I returned to the home of David Ravenhill, Leonard's son, where I was staying. (He was pastoring in Kansas City during those years.) Because I had to speak in the morning, I wanted to go to sleep earlier than usual, since I'm normally a very late night person, but I couldn't sleep. The Lord was stirring me to write out notes for the morning message on the theme, "A Baptism of Tears for Israel." This was unusual, since I normally didn't preach with notes unless there was something critically important the Lord wanted me to say.

I got out of bed, took out a pad of paper, and began to write out some key themes for the message. Then came the struggle: I felt God telling me I needed to tell that story from 1986 where I was brought to the place of agonizing intercession as if my own daughter was going to die just to learn to pray with a divine burden, learning to share God's pain. I said to the Lord, "I can't do this. That story is too intimate, and I don't know the people at this conference." (There were about 1,000 in attendance.) But you can't argue with God. I knew He was calling me to do this, and I was to end the message with the story, saying to the people, "God wants you to pray for Israel as if it was your own child dying, because that's how He feels."

The next morning, as David drove me to the service, he saw I was quite serious, and after the first minute of small talk, neither of us said a word. I was deeply sober and gripped. When we arrived at the church building, something didn't feel right, but I had no idea why. The pastor sat down next to me and said, "Mike, I can't stay here. Something crazy happened. Early this morning, Reuven and Mary Lou's baby died."

235

LIVING IN THE LINE OF FIRE

No! This couldn't be true. Rachel died, suddenly, and without any sickness or any kind of warning? Really? The pastor said to me, "Do you want me to make the announcement, or will you do it?" I replied with tears, "No, I'll make the announcement. I know exactly when I'm to do it."

With one of the heaviest burdens of my life, I preached the message on the need for a baptism of tears for Israel, also calling out so much of the superficiality in our charismatic circles. Then I closed the message with the story of that night of intercession for my daughter, saying with a broken heart to the people that God wanted us to pray for Israel as if it was His own child dying, because that's how He felt. Then I said, "I have a tragic announcement to make. Reuven and Mary Lou's baby died this morning. Please pray for them, and please pray for Israel," and that was it. Instantly, the building was filled with wails and sobs and agonized cries, both for the grieving mom and dad and for Israel.

I cannot explain this to you theologically, especially since I believe in the goodness of God and His healing grace. I can only recount what happened, point to chapters like Ezekiel 24, where the Lord took the prophet's wife as a prophetic sign to the nation, and leave the explanation to Him. What I can say for sure is that we were all marked indelibly by the Lord that day, understanding His pain for the lost sheep of the house of Israel in the most real, vivid, staggering terms. If only the whole Body could receive this burden! As for Reuven and Mary Lou, God ministered graciously to them in the midst of this tragic loss, and they are strong in the Lord today.

TWO MORE DIVINE CONFIRMATIONS

When we lived in Maryland (1987-1996), I became a friendly with a Jewish Seventh Day Adventist named Clifford Goldstein, and we would often have lively debates and discussions as we challenged one another about doctrinal differences. At one point, he was doing graduate studies at Johns Hopkins University, so I agreed to help him with his biblical Hebrew, and he would come to my house where we would read and study

To the Jew First

together. One afternoon, before he came over, I prayed one of those very rare "fleece" prayers (similar to the Strack-Billerbeck prayer, mentioned previously).

We had been discussing a scriptural issue and I thought there might be something to his argument. Now I know without a doubt that we determine doctrine by what is written in the Word, not by our experiences, so I was fully aware that the prayer I was praying was quite secondary in terms of determining truth. Still, I said, "Lord, if there's anything to his argument that I should consider scripturally, then when he comes over today, have him ask if we can study ancient Palestinian Hebrew texts without vowels instead of our normal biblical Hebrew studies." What a totally random prayer!

Bear in mind that the subject of Palestinian Hebrew texts without vowels had never once come up in a conversation between us—not a single time; nothing even close to it—so I was amazed to hear his request when he walked into my study that day: "Hey Mike, can we study ancient Palestinian Hebrew texts without vowels today?" How wild!

Well, I told you *that* story to tell you *this* story. In 2018, quite out of the blue, I felt the Lord stirring my heart to write a Jewish outreach book comparing Yeshua (Jesus) to an influential twentieth-century rabbi named Menachem Mendel Schneerson (1902-1994), known as the Lubavitcher Rebbe and still hailed as the Messiah by many of his followers. One of those two influential rabbis, Yeshua, rose from the dead, to the complete shock of His disciples; the other, Rabbi Schneerson did not, even though many of his disciples were sure it was going to happen.

This is my journal entry from August 7, 2018:

> Living God! Miracle-working God!!! This is beyond amazing! This is the voice of the Lord!! ...So, last night and then very heavily this morning, I'm flooded with an idea for a new book, based on the controversy about the Lubavitcher Rebbe rising from the dead and being the Messiah, something like: *The Resurrection of the Messiah: A Jewish-Christian Perspective*; or, *The*

237

LIVING IN THE LINE OF FIRE

Resurrection of Jesus: A Messianic Jewish Approach. And I'm pumped and blessed in my spirit, also feeling that this is some of the answer to the cry from the depths of my heart. Then, right before radio, I see a voicemail from Clifford Goldstein [whom I had also thought of out of the blue yesterday after not talking to him for years]: He's thinking about writing a book on this exact same subject, needing some book references from me (the very same books I was going to look for as soon as I unpack my books). Is this unreal or not? I will write this, and the Lord will use it!

Once again, Clifford was used to bring an unusual confirmation in my life, putting more fuel into my fire for the writing of this unique book. (If I'm correct, we had talked by phone one other time in the previous twenty-five years.) The book was released in 2020 with the title, *Resurrection: Investigating a Rabbi From Brooklyn, a Preacher From Galilee, and an Event That Changed the World*, and we are working on getting it translated into Hebrew, where I'm confident God will use to it to touch ultra-Orthodox Jewish readers, especially the followers of Rabbi Schneerson.[48]

The last confirmation took place on February 2, 2020, when I received a text on WhatsApp from one of my grads, who has become a spiritual son, Kobi Ferguson. In the text was a short, grainy video featuring me on a TV screen, preaching the gospel. What made the video so significant was that this TV screen was in the Ben Gurion airport in Tel Aviv. I was preaching Yeshua on every monitor in the airport! With the video was this message from Kobi: "Well what a shock to be in the Ben Gurion airport and see a familiar face on the TV! OWI!!!!" (OWI is our code for "on with it," meaning, "on with the revolution.")

Kobi had been working with friends of mine at GOD TV, Ward Simpson, a BRSM grad from Pensacola, and the CEO of the network, and Ron Cantor, a CFNI grad from Long Island who headed up the Israel branch of GOD TV. They had received permission to launch the first-ever, all Hebrew, gospel-preaching channel in Israel on the most-watched

238

To the Jew First

cable network, but it was going to be a very big project requiring a lot of work. He was sitting at the airport the day he texted me before flying to the States, thinking about how hard it would be to get all the work done. He asked himself, "Will anyone really see our show?"

Kobi's text explained what happened next: "And I kid you not, I look up and see you!!! It's quite [a] top 10 profound moment Doc! You can't make this stuff up! It's METV [Middle East TV], they have the sound off but the timing was just so divine!" Oh my! Sounds like the Lord once again, this time confirming to both of us that our message about the Messiah will reach our people in Israel, in Hebrew.

But why on earth was METV, which is owned by Sid Roth, airing on the monitors in the Ben Gurion airport? I believe this is what happened. In order to draw non-believing Israeli viewers to METV, where the gospel is clearly preached, Sid purchases the rights to air the Super Bowl every year. METV also features some old secular programming from the States (like the classic cowboy shows, which are popular in Israel), as well as gospel-based shows. The day Kobi texted me was Super Bowl Sunday, and my assumption is that they were airing the game through the airport but forgot to change channels, leaving me on the screen preaching Yeshua as Messiah. Extraordinary!

As for Shelanu TV, it is doing really well, but in a digital, online platform rather than on cable TV in Israel because of lots of opposition to the network launching. And even though GOD TV had the contractual rights to broadcast, they didn't want to get into a battle with the country they love, opting to go online instead—with excellent results so far. But there was a bonus to the opposition to the TV show: it launched Ron Cantor and Shelanu TV into the Israeli headlines. Ron was able to share his testimony on numerous secular platforms, and it even gave me a platform to weigh in on the situation in writing in major Jewish publications, proclaiming Yeshua as our Messiah and King. What a God we serve!

239

LIVING IN THE LINE OF FIRE

HOSTILE REJECTIONS, WARM RECEPTIONS

It has been my privilege to suffer rejection for the sake of the Messiah over the decades, but overall, it has been minimal. For example, in the early 1980s, an Orthodox Jew, furious with me for being a believer, threw my Hebrew Bible down the aisle of the Long Island Railroad before spitting in my face as we sat next to each other traveling to New York City. I remember feeling a distinct love after he spat on me, telling him that I could see how much he cared for me as a Jew, which was why he was so upset. I affirmed my love for him as well. He then threatened to strangle me with his own hands if he ever saw me talking to another Jewish person about Jesus, then got off the train.

When I lived in Maryland (1987-1993), I paid to be part of a daily study program, conducted by phone, where you could call in and listen to a prerecorded lesson of a rabbi teaching on the particular page of the Talmud being learned that day. I called in when I could and listened along, trying to get a better understanding of this massive text which is so sacred to traditional Jews. One night, I called one of the toll-free numbers, but it wasn't working. I tried the next, then the next, then the next. All of them were out of service.

What happened was that word got out that I had joined this paid study service, and since they could not stop me from calling, they contacted every other person in the program, giving them new phone numbers to call, then cancelling the other numbers simply to exclude me. In their eyes, I was guilty of a double sin, not just believing in Jesus but maintaining my Jewishness as well.

More than twenty years later, I had another interesting encounter with my own Jewish community when my precious mom died in 2016 at the age of ninety-four. After she passed away, I was told by the local funeral director where we lived in North Carolina (and where we had brought my mom the last few years of her life) that there might be a problem with my mom's funeral. My sister had requested that a rabbi preside at the small graveside service at the Jewish cemetery in New Jersey where she would be buried next to my beloved dad, who passed away in 1977 at the

240

To the Jew First

age of sixty-three. What could be the problem? According to the funeral director, since this was going to be a Jewish ceremony at a Jewish cemetery for my mother—and I was a well-known Messianic Jewish leader and "missionary"—this could be an issue.

A day or two later, I received a call from a rabbi, saying he would be happy to do my mother's ceremony. Then he told me the story: He had received a call from the cemetery, asking him if he would have a problem doing the service for the mother of Dr. Michael Brown. He didn't understand their question. Why would there be a problem? They repeated, "This is for the mother of *Dr. Michael Brown.*" He then understood what the issue was—apparently, I have become somewhat notorious in some of the larger Jewish world—assuring them he was fine doing the ceremony, since he did "interfaith" services too.

Then, the most surprising part of the story. The rabbi told me that he listened regularly to my radio show on the Salem network in New York City! And when he missed a show, he would catch it on podcast. How remarkable!

When we got off the phone, I sensed there was still more to the story, searching online for information about this rabbi. Sure enough, there *was* more to the story. He was a pioneer gay rabbi! We have stayed in touch over the years in the midst of very different approaches to life and faith, seeking to love our neighbor as ourselves. Welcome to my world![49]

I have also had the extraordinary joy of being warmly welcomed by Christians around the world, not just as a fellow believer but in particular as a *Jewish believer*, even though in God's sight, we are all totally equal. If I had the space, I could tell you amazing stories from Kenya and Finland and Sweden and Mexico and Germany, but two stories from my first trip to India in 1993 will have to suffice. We were in a rural village in Andhra Pradesh, far from the nearest city, getting ready to minister to the believers there when one of the leaders said to me in English, "We have been praying for the Jewish people for decades now, and we celebrate the feasts of Israel!" Yet again, I was shocked by what I heard. How did they get this burden? Who taught them? It was something that God dropped in their hearts through the Word.

241

LIVING IN THE LINE OF FIRE

Later in the trip, our team of five was scheduled to have lunch at the home of an Indian couple. The husband worked for the government, and he and his wife were committed Christians. We learned that his wife had not slept all night, staying up to prepare a special feast because, for the first time, she would have Jews in her home for a meal! (Three out of our five team members were Jewish believers.) Her husband greeted me at the door, saying proudly, "You are the second Jew to enter my home. The first was Jesus Christ!"

I have told rabbis and counter-missionaries whom I have befriended over the years that I wish I could take them around the world to meet some of these precious believers, since so much church history has been stained with antisemitism. Around the world, I have experienced the exact opposite of this, encountering extraordinary love, honor and grace, specifically because of my Jewish heritage.

A BROKEN HEART FOR MY PEOPLE

As with every chapter in this book, there's so much more I could share. But before we move on, there's one last story I must tell. I pray the Lord will touch you as you read!

In the mid-1980s while teaching at Christ for the Nations, I took out the *Siddur*, the Jewish prayer book, and began to read some of the prayers. Normally, when studying rabbinic texts, I had focused on legal and expository texts, not prayers, so this was different from my normal custom. But as I read the words, my heart broke, seeing the beauty and passion of the prayers of my people. Immediately I was struck with the thought that no people is so near and yet so far, not thinking of secular, non-religious Jews, but of those who are deeply devoted. My heart was deeply torn.

In the decades since, I have become friends with some ultra-Orthodox rabbis, men whose lifestyles put many believers to shame. And yet despite their devotion and zeal and commitment, I know they are missing out on that intimacy with God that can only come through Jesus. This has

To the Jew First

often burdened me deeply in prayer. And that leads to my final story here.

It was October 1988 in Cleveland, Ohio. Some of the Messianic believers there rented a former synagogue which seated over a thousand people for three nights of meetings featuring the Messianic Jewish worship group, Israel's Hope (led by Paul Wilbur, and joined by Marc Chopinsky and Renee Bloch) and me. The first meeting was October 20 and we had an open forum, and I gave a hearing to ultra-Orthodox Jews who were there. Things were heating up. When the meeting ended, some of the men surrounded me, asking me questions and challenging my knowledge of the Hebrew Bible and rabbinic literature. Yes, Jewish ministry is quite unique! I ended up having a long conversation with one of the local rabbis as we stood outside the building in the cold night until my feet like they were frozen.

The next night was Friday night, which was the Sabbath, so none of the religious Jews attended. But on Saturday night, October 22, once it got dark and Sabbath had ended, they showed up at the meeting again. At the end of the meeting, I gave an altar call, then laid hands on some of those who needed prayer, with a number of them falling to the ground under the Spirit's power.

As for the religious Jews who were there, some of them came up to watch, trying to understand what was causing the people to fall. It was quite an interesting scene! Israel's Hope then came up again to lead worship, and I went outside to talk to these Jewish men who were now lighting candles and saying post-Sabbath prayers in front of the building. There were a couple of police cars outside, and I told some of the officers not to worry about the candles. It was just part of a religious ritual. Then some of the Jewish men starting dancing in a circle, and one of their colleagues said to me, "These are your people, not the people inside. Dance with us!"

I was more than glad to comply, and as we held hands and danced in a circle and sang and chanted, they would challenge me with questions, which I was able to answer effectively. Again, it was quite a scene. But

243

LIVING IN THE LINE OF FIRE

as we kept dancing, rather than getting tired, I felt supernaturally invigorated, despite preaching and ministering already. I said to those who began to drop out of the circle, "Where's your zeal for God? Dance to Him!"

Eventually, the circle broke up, and some of the men stood on the street, raising their hands to heaven and shouting loudly, "God! We want Moshiach (meaning Messiah)! Send the Moshiach now!" I stood right next to them, shouting as loudly as I could, "God, show them that Yeshua is Moshiach!" They in turn shouted heavenward, "No, not that Moshiach! The real Moshiach!"

It was as intense and it was surreal, almost a made-for-Hollywood moment contrasting our two faiths side by side. On a certain level, being able to cry out side by side with these sincere men—my own people—pleading with God to reveal Yeshua to them was somewhat exhilarating. But when Nancy and I got back to the hotel room, I broke down weeping because of the painful reality of the moment. No people is so near and yet so far.

Please do not stop praying for the salvation of my people Israel! Your prayers can literally make the difference between life and death.

CHAPTER 12

ADVENTURES IN THE SPIRIT

It has been my extraordinary joy and privilege to preach the gospel around the world, flying overseas roughly 180 times as of this writing, which means spending a good number of years in flight and in the nations. There is nothing like it! There is nothing like seeing the Lord move in a culture and setting that is so foreign, from the dress to the language to the music to the foods to the sounds and even to the smells, only to find yourself totally at home with your brothers and sisters as you weep together in His presence or as you celebrate His goodness with hugs and tears. It is worth all the travel and the jet lag and the expense and the wear and tear on your body. Absolutely!

I have also had countless amazing experiences while ministering here in the United States, some of which I shared in the previous chapters and some of which I'll share here as well. I'll do my best to give you a picture of what that feels like in this chapter, which is really a series of vignettes in no particular chronological order.

First, some journal entries from my times in the nations, which could be multiplied hundreds of times over. And note that, in some cases, where I speak of believers falling to the ground, overcome by the Spirit, I do so because this was not the norm for them and I had never seen it happen like this in their country before.

June 24, 1996 (Italy) Amazing. Last night, just before reading from Acts 2:2—suddenly—the wind starts gusting, so strongly,

LIVING IN THE LINE OF FIRE

in fact, that the ushers had to close the large, church windows. Tonight, after preaching on Zech 10:1 (it's time for revival! it's time for rain!—in real harmony with [my translator's] earlier sharing), and with a huge, hungry altar response, after much prayer for rain, suddenly, there is *heavy* downpour. Awesome! And then the sinners come to be saved—in tears, some with lines of mascara running down their cheeks. The Lord is at work!

February 26, 1997 (India) Pretty good night's sleep (a few mosquito-caused interruptions and some uncomfortable heat), then up about 7:30 to pray and get ready for the day. And what a day it is. The brokenhearted prayer for revival after my morning session is the most intense I have ever seen in India.... [At night], I preach on "It's Time for Rain," the altar is packed with praying people, and then as I lay hands on the believers, the river flows in India! Some weep, others stagger, and five or six Indian saints are laid out on the ground, lying motionless for good periods of time. The Lord is touching His people. Revival is near!

Who can describe the scene? As I speak on our need for revival, Krupa kneels on the ground crying and praying, others begin to cry, and soon, as we pray, everyone is on their knees or faces (in the dirt!), many weep and groan, Krupa rolls in the dirt, a mother clutches her baby in her arms with tears streaming down in her cheeks, John can barely lead in prayer as he breaks down, Yesupadam falls on the ground clutching his dear fellow-workers and his son as they weep together.... The Lord will hear their cry! It's time for revival in the land! Then Brother R's mother, a zealous believer for 17 years, tells me that she has been dissatisfied with her walk with the Lord all these years, never feeling intimate with Jesus. Today, He spoke to her

Adventures in the Spirit

directly, telling her of her need for revival, and beginning to touch her life. And the first two Indians (women) fall to the ground from their knees under the power. A sign of more to come? Yes!

December 6, 1999 (Sicily) Wow! Awesome! Jesus! As I write these words—1:00 a.m. in Catania—I can hear the cries and prayers and worship of believers in the hallway of the hotel after an incredible meeting tonight in the (still more than half-empty) sports arena. And today after lunch in the restaurant, Victor called Charles over to the tables and he began to lead in worship. No one moved, and at the end, three waiters prayed to receive the Lord. Wow! Revival is getting closer!

September 29, 2000 (Essen, Germany, Guga Hall, where the Beatles performed in 1966) What a day! The breakthrough comes! My message on daring to dream brings about a spiritual explosion, as thousands flood the altar, Walter Heidenreich leads the cry (telling me he has waited for this moment for years), and Jobst leads the crowds in a "Revolution" chant. Yes! The leaders are touched beyond words. Mission accomplished! Catch up on some emails (in a back room behind the front desk of the hotel, due to problems with internet connections in the rooms), then back to the meeting hall to pray with the intercessors during the night meeting—and it explodes! Wow! What intensity and fervor. The Spirit is on me too! Back to the hotel to pack and get ready for a very early flight.

This entry reflects back on April 3-12, 1998, where due to a scheduling error in the midst of the Brownsville Revival, I flew to Australia, ministered for two days, returned to the States to teach at our school and minister in the revival for two days, then flew to London to minister day and night for another two days:

LIVING IN THE LINE OF FIRE

April 13, 2000 How God's grace has carried me these past nine days! Just think: I left for Australia sick and worn out, and I return from an almost ridiculous schedule *healthier* and *more vibrant* than when I left! Not only so, the impact of the meetings—especially here in London—has been extraordinary, with the Kensington Temple folks saying that this weekend was *the most impacting time they have ever had in the history of the church*! Jesus, You're awesome! And You really do answer the prayers of Your saints. (I *knew* the prayers of the student body for me were heard.)

Can you sense the reality of the spiritual atmosphere as you read these words? Can you feel it?

This short entry speaks to the intensity of my overseas schedule, this one journaled while traveling back from Italy to the States on December 19, 1993: "Feeling free! Although this was absolutely the most tiring ministry experience of my life (37 meetings in all; 9 different locations; 5 different cities, ending with a 10:00 a.m. to 11:00 p.m. marathon in Genoa), and although I was feeling quite drained and in need of fresh fire, I really am refreshed and feeling right with God within. The Lord is pleased!"

THE NIGHT OF VISITATION IN THE CZECH REPUBLIC

In August 1996, I took my second overseas trip since being involved in the Brownsville Revival, and I was carrying the fire of revival with me. But the trip had some bumps. First, my luggage did not arrive for three days, and the leadership retreat where I was speaking, with about 120 pastors and wives, was held three hours outside of Prague on the campus of a Bible college in a rural area. That meant that, after a couple of days without a change of clothes, sharing a cramped dorm room with the national leader who coordinated the retreat, I had to make do with some ill-fitting replacement items bought at a local shop. That's also when I

Adventures in the Spirit

learned that, by and large, Europeans used deodorants but not anti-per-spirants. So yes, I was hot and sweaty.

The morning of August 29, 1996, when I preached about sexual purity, I was stunned to hear the confessions of sin breaking out among these leaders, not just from the men but also from women who were into porn or who had been unfaithful. They were weeping and crying out under deep conviction, something I had seen before, but not so freely among pastors and leaders.

It reminded me of a sacred meeting in Korea in the early 1990s where we squeezed as many people as possible into a fairly small room, with everyone sitting on the floor as I ministered on the Lord coming as a refiner's fire from Malachi 3, one of my life texts. (I distinctly recall the massive pile of shoes outside the room, in keeping with Korean custom, with my shoes much bigger than the rest.) When the message ended, there was deep conviction in the room, and I knew that some people there needed to make open confession to get relief for their souls, something that is not so easily done in an Asian culture that puts a high emphasis on "saving face."

Suddenly, one man began to cry out, "You think I am a good man. I am not a good man! I have committed adultery!" Can you imagine how deeply the sword of the Spirit had cut his soul in order for him to speak out? Now, in August 1996, one leader after another was confessing sin and asking for forgiveness. I thought to myself, "We're going to have a visitation tonight. Repentance has prepared the way." This is my journal entry from that day and night:

> **August 29, 1996** (Czech Republic, leadership retreat) Up at 6:30 (not too tired, but really hungry!), then study and pray. By the time of the meeting I'm really tired (and ready to have a regular meal again), but the Lord speaks deeply, first about relinquishing our "control," then, more deeply and quite plainly, about sexual sin. The resulting (numerous) confessions are genuine and heartfelt. Oh to walk in deeper purity! More

249

LIVING IN THE LINE OF FIRE

bread and butter for lunch, meet with M., the school director here at Harvest, nap, brief meeting with a Romanian sister on staff, a piece of bread and some odd-tasting cucumbers, then finish praying for the evening meeting. And then—suddenly He comes! The atmosphere is ripe, the preaching is passionate (spiritual hunger), and then the glory comes down for three hours! Never in my life have I been in an international service like this. First the wails, cries, and travail for revival here, then we divide into small prayer groups, the intense burden explodes again (with some outbursts of victory and joy too), then I go through the group and lay hands on everyone, and it makes Brownsville look tame! Then the spontaneous, wordless worship breaks out for another hour or so, with dancing, leaping, and clapping, followed by more anointed laying on of hands. You are awesome Lord!

The next morning, we were stunned to hear this follow-up report. Because there were limited dorm rooms on the campus, some of the couples brought small tents with them, which they set up a few hundred yards from the main buildings, sleeping there with their kids. The night of the outpouring, the wife of one of the leaders was in their tent, reading bedtime stories to their two boys. Suddenly, one of them said, "Did you hear the thunder?" But the "thunder" continued without interruption. The brother answered, "That's not thunder. That's the sound of planes!" Then, after a little while, one of them concluded, "No, that's the sound of drunken people!" Shades of Acts 2 and Pentecost, when some of the devout Jews in Jerusalem mistook the outpouring of the Spirit for people being drunk.

What really astounded us, though, was how the boys heard anything, since we were inside a building, there was very little amplification (if any), with none at all for the people as a whole, and we were at a substantial distance from the tent. The Lord had announced His visit, and as He touched His people, their cries of rejoicing and victory were heard.

250

Adventures in the Spirit

INDIA, 1993

In the last chapter, I mentioned our first trip to India, which was in 1993. It was remarkable in many ways, especially because it was our first time in that country. Nancy and I had no idea that so much of India was quite rural, imagining big cities like Calcutta rather than 600,000 villages, some located in dense jungles. We traveled there with three of our friends from Maryland, having met Brother Yesupadam the previous year when he came unannounced to meet me. Today, he is one of my closest friends in the world, a man whom I consider to be the truest Christian I know. But back then, I just knew that this little Indian, born an untouchable and once stoned for preaching the gospel, had a tremendous passion for the Lord, for the lost, and for revival.

We flew into Delhi, where he met us at the international airport and escorted us over to the national airport, where we spent the night sleeping on the floor and the chairs. Given his background and the cost of hotels, sleeping on the airport floor was the logical choice. We waited through the day for our flight to leave for Hyderabad, which it finally did, after many delays, at which time we then took a train for fourteen hours into his home city, Visakhapatnam. It's only a two-hour flight from Hyderabad, but in those days, the flights did not run every day, hence the long train ride.

When Nancy and I woke up on the train early the next morning, we were stunned to see the surrounding countryside. We felt as if we had gone back in time to prehistoric days. I remember thinking to myself jokingly, "I wouldn't be surprised to see a dinosaur soon." Then, as we drove from the airport to Yesupadam's ministry base (which, at that point, was basically a couple of houses where they cared for orphans), we were stunned again with all the animals on the road—from pigs to cows to water buffalo. We had arrived in a different world.

It was then time to drive to Paderu, a largely unreached tribal region about four hours up a mountainous road. We were driven in three white cars which looked as if they had come out of a movie from the 1940s or '50s in America, and every hour or so, the drivers had to pull over and

251

LIVING IN THE LINE OF FIRE

put water in the batteries. The ride itself was quite dangerous, and before we embarked on the journey, our driver stopped his car, went into a little booth with a Hindu idol, prayed for a few minutes, and then came out with the red dot (marking spiritual devotion) on his forehead.

I asked Yesupadam's daughter, Suneeta, what the driver was doing. She said, "He's praying because it's a dangerous road." I replied, "Tell him to concentrate on driving. I'll do the praying."

Toward the end of the drive, we stopped again for the drivers to put water in the batteries, and once more, Nancy and I were stunned as we saw monkeys in the trees right next to us. We really were heading into the jungle! When we arrived, we were told not to go out of our rooms at night since there was a man-eating tiger on the loose. I kid you not.

Because of our delayed flight, we arrived at the first meeting while it was in progress. It was a rainy night, and there were about 300 people in attendance. But what got our attention was the music. It was *Hindu* music! Nancy and I looked at each other with disappointment, thinking, "I'm sure Yesupadam means well, but you can't use demonic music like this, even to reach the lost." In reality, it was just normal Indian music, with great gospel lyrics at that, but we had only heard these sounds in the context of Hinduism. So much for our great discernment. (This was a rare "miss" for Nancy.)

It was now time for my first sermon in India, and I launched an attack against idolatry, something which was incredibly overt, wherever you turned, replete with temples and statues everywhere. I pointed to the one true God alone and then gave an altar call, but there was virtually no response. Not what I expected! Afterward, Yesupadam told me graciously, "We prefer to speak here about the beauty of Jesus more than the ugliness of idols." I appreciated his words, but still felt the first night was the time to make a statement, especially when I learned that the loudspeakers reached into thousands of unreached villages through the mountains.

The next night, I preached on Jesus setting the captives free, even quoting verses such as Isaiah 61:1 in Hebrew and then translating into

Adventures in the Spirit

English. There was a great response from the crowd, which was much bigger the second night because the rain had stopped, and we sensed a breakthrough spiritually.

The next day our team of five, along with Yesupadam and some of his team, were going to walk up the side of a mountain, then down on the other side, where we would share the gospel with an unreached village and where we would most likely be the first white faces they had ever seen. (This happened regularly on those early trips where we had time to travel to these outlying places. Crowds would form around us for minutes at a time—as long as twenty or thirty minutes if we stayed in one place— just staring with curiosity and wonder. Some of the children screamed and ran when they saw Nancy because of her red hair and freckles.)

We stopped to rest on the top of the mountain, where we could see where bears or tigers had relieved themselves. These were big animals. Then, as we stood there in the middle of nowhere, a tribal man came walking up the mountain with his demonized daughter. She had a look of terror in her eyes, her arms were bloodied from where she had been tied up but broken free, and she had a small hole on her neck where the witch doctor had tried to drive out the demon. Her father had just returned from the government base in the main town, but the doctor could not help his daughter either.

We began to pray for her, coming against these demonic forces in Jesus's name until finally, after about ninety minutes, she was delivered, asking the Lord to save and forgive her. (Aside from the prayers we prayed, everything was done with the help of a translator, since they spoke no English.) When we finished ministering to her, we looked up, and to our astonishment, there was a small crowd of tribal men standing on one side with a group of tribal women standing on the other side. Why they were there at that moment, we did not know, but we preached the gospel to them in the simplest terms we could, and all of them said they wanted to renounce their idols and follow Jesus.

Now it was Yesupadam who was stunned, having done ministry in this area in previous years but never seeing fruit like this. He was convinced

LIVING IN THE LINE OF FIRE

that something had broken open spiritually the night before when we proclaimed liberty to the captives, and this was the firstfruits. I remember thinking to myself, "Not long ago, I was giving an outreach lecture at Yale and delivering a scholarly paper at Harvard. I'm in a different universe now!"

Some weeks after we arrived home, we received a letter from Yesupadam. We had been in India from late February to mid-March, and every April, they sent the students from their intensive one-year ministry school into the unreached villages of Paderu, even though it could be very dangerous to preach. The male students would go for three weeks while the female students stayed back and prayed and fasted.

Yesupadam was thrilled to tell us that, for the first time, they saw supernatural breakthroughs in the villages marked by signs and wonders and many glorious conversions. Something really did break as the Word of God was proclaimed over loudspeakers to these terribly impoverished, very lost people sitting in their huts (if they even had a roof over their heads) and we drove the demon out of that girl. Today, Yesupadam has informed me that *every single village in Paderu has a church that was planted by their ministry*, likely numbering as many as 6,000 at this point.

On a sober note, over the years, some of these pastors have been martyred. In fact, while in India on December 5, 2019, I journaled this: "I also learn today from Brother N. about two of their pastors who were killed in Paderu while trying to build church buildings." Their reward has gone before them!

One last highlight from that first trip in 1993. For the last four days of the trip, we were going to be ministering in Yesupadam's home city Vishakhapatnam. However, he decided to hold the meetings in a different location than normal, one that was more outlying and in an industrial area. The last night, one of my colleagues preached a short message, and then I preached the longer message, pouring out my heart on spiritual hunger and revival. Then, suddenly, the power went out. The lights were still on, but there was no sound as we preached.

Adventures in the Spirit

There were about 5,000 people present and I turned to Yesupadam and saying, "We should call the people to come forward and pray." He had sensed the same thing, and so we began to shout at the top of our lungs, calling everyone to come forward and cry out to God for revival. Some of his team then went out through the crowd as well, shouting as loudly as they could, inviting the people to come forward.

Then, something electric happened. People began running to the altar and seeking the face of God as if their lives depended on it, with the intense prayer continuing for about forty-five minutes. (Afterward, Yesupadam told me it was the greatest joint prayer meeting for revival he had seen in his city.) And then, as soon as the prayer time was over, the power came back on, and we closed out the meeting.

But something else had gotten my attention while we were praying with the large crowd of people at the altar. I was looking out at the end of the large field where the meeting was being held, and I saw a steady line of buses and trucks stopping at the gate by the roadside, which was the only place to enter or leave. It was getting late, so I assumed the buses and trucks were picking up passengers, since it was common for people to climb on the back of trucks and hitch a ride. The next day, I asked Yesupadam about it.

He said to me, "Brother! They weren't stopping to pick people up. Instead, as they drove by the field they saw people burning! They stopped to see what was going on." Talk about the fire of the Spirit! These passersby literally saw people burning as they prayed for revival at the altar, and word got out into the community. All of us were stunned at the report.

"SUDDENLY" HAPPENS TWICE IN FALERNA, ITALY

In May of 1998 I made my twelfth trip to Italy, the first being in 1987, and in the height of the Brownsville Revival. By this time, I had a strong relationship with many of the leaders there, especially those on the missions team Cristo e la Risposta (Christ Is the Answer). They had been living in Italy for about twenty-five years at that point, traveling around the

LIVING IN THE LINE OF FIRE

country with a large tent, preaching on the street and then having tent meetings at night, almost every week of the year. In keeping with their mobile lifestyles, they lived in tents or small trailers themselves, even for a period of decades. They really lived in light of eternity.

I was traveling with Scott Volk, my assistant at that time, along with some of our ministry school students. When we arrived in Rome, I asked him what time we left for our next flight, assuming we were flying to Sicily, which was most common, or to Milan or Naples. To my surprise, he told me we were going to a place called Falerna. I told him, "But I don't know anyone there."

It turns out the Christ Is the Answer team set up our three-day conference in this location so it would be completely neutral. About 100 pastors were coming from all over the country, which was a significant turnout at the time, along with perhaps 2,000 believers. The meetings would be held under the tent morning and evening, with a leaders-only meeting in the afternoon at the hotel.

The first morning was powerful, but I ran late in preaching and ministering. The missionary leaders told me, "Mike, you can't do this again. You see, all of us will be eating at the hotel where they have lunch scheduled for us at a specific time. With this many people, we have to be on schedule." All clear!

That afternoon we had our first pastors' meeting, set aside for teaching and then Q&A, but it felt very sterile, both naturally and spiritually. The room where we met seemed more suited for a UN press conference then for a gospel meeting, with cold, marble floor and furnishings and lots of mics across the desk in front. I sat next to my translator, Paul Schafer, a Canadian who has now lived in Italy more than fifty years, working side by side with Clark Slone from the United States, who led Christ Is the Answer. To my disappointment, though, the leaders' questions seemed to focus on the unusual manifestations. "Brother Mike, what about all the shaking?" (Or, the falling, or the weeping, or whatever they had heard about.) At night, the Lord moved powerfully, and I sensed that a breakthrough was near.

256

Adventures in the Spirit

The next morning I preached from Acts 2, saying that when God visits, it is often more than we expect and different from what we expect, noting that He comes "suddenly" (see Acts 2:2). And remembering the instructions from the day before, I finished the message way ahead of schedule so there would be no problems with the lunch schedule at the hotel. I just wanted to lay hands on the pastor who sat on the platform as I spoke, intently focused on the message, before I dismissed the meeting.

The pastor stood to his feet, I put one hand on his stomach and one on his back, saying one word, as was my custom (due to laying hands on many hundreds of people every week): "Fire!" At that moment, it's as if he was hit with a bomb. He exploded to the floor on his face (I don't know how else to describe it), and at that precise moment, a group of teenagers from the Christ Is the Answer Team began crying out with groaning and intercession. Instantly! They were all the way in the back of the large tent, but it was if the spiritual explosion hit them too. The previous year, my missions colleague John Cava brought a team of BRSM students to Italy and ministered under the tent, and many of the teens were powerfully touched then. Now, it was a fresh visitation on their lives.

I called all the pastors to come forward, which they did immediately, laying hands on each one of them. Boom! Boom! They were hit by the power of God, falling on their faces, on their sides, on their backs, weeping and sobbing and shaking. I had never seen anything like this in Italy, where the Pentecostals debated among themselves whether being slain in the Spirit was of God or the devil, and where I had laid hands on thousands of people there over the years and only seen a handful (at most) fall under the Spirit's power. This was a holy outpouring!

It was about thirty minutes into this move of the Spirit when it hit me: "What you preached about in your message just happened! God came suddenly with more than you expected and different from what you expected." We went to lunch stunned, with the missionary leaders and the Italian pastors telling me they had never seen this happen in Italy their entire lives. Unfortunately, this just triggered more questions during the afternoon leaders meeting, despite me doing my best to tell these

LIVING IN THE LINE OF FIRE

brothers that the manifestations were not our big focus in Pensacola. The focus was on Jesus changing lives.

Then, it happened again. I can never forget it! The pastors had been asking me questions such as, "Brother Mike, do the people bark like dogs in the meetings in Pensacola?" (I told him no, dogs bark like dogs on the streets, but the people do not bark like dogs in the meetings.) And, "Brother Mike, have you ever experienced holy laughter?" (No, I explained, but I've seen it happen to others—a story I'll share later in this chapter.)

I then explained that none of that mattered to us in Brownsville saying, "This is what matters to us," sharing an incredible, recent account of Friday night baptisms in the revival, where a fairly young girl, then her older sister, then the oldest sister, then the mother, then the father, were all baptized. The cumulative effect was overwhelming that Friday night, with each baptismal testimony becoming more intense than the last until almost the whole congregation in the revival service was crying by the time the father testified and was immersed.

With tears I shared this story, with my translator, Paul, breaking down as he translated into Italian. And then—suddenly!—it happened again, but this time even more unexpectedly than in the morning. It was totally out of the blue! In an instant, these men began to weep and sob and cry out in prayer, some of them hugging one another as tears streamed down their faces. Clark leaned over and said to me, "Mike, do you see those two pastors hugging? We couldn't even get them in the same room together to pray for the services, that's how divided they were." Once again, the Lord had surprised us all.

This is my journal entry for the day:

> **May 19, 1998** A historic day for Italy! ...after ministering on God's sudden movings in the morning, suddenly He comes, with everything breaking when I pray for just one pastor on the platform. Wow! The Spirit falls, the young people go wild in prayer, and the power comes down on the pastors I pray for.

Adventures in the Spirit

Then, after extended teaching and Q & A, I break down crying talking about my experience in the revival these last two years, Paul breaks down translating, and the Spirit falls in our midst, once again, suddenly, leading to an unprecedented time of pastors praying one for another. Then—fighting off exhaustion through the day—the tent is packed at night, many more enter into worship, I preach on fire, and the Spirit falls intensely on many, laid out all over the tent. To the hotel wiped out, with only a plate of pasta for food for the second straight day, but absolutely blessed to be used in this historic event.

Amazing! Glorious! After all these years coming to Italy, I finally get to bring the fire in the deeper sense of the word, and we participate in a day that, no doubt, will be remembered for years to come as the time when God broke forth in revival power in many lives in Italy. Jesus!

But the trip was not without some obstacles, which leads into my account for the final day of meetings. It began on the flight over. Scott had put down a metal seat rest without knowing that my brand-new laptop was underneath it. This left a visible gouge in my prized possession. Little did I know that would be a foretaste of the next few days, during which I cut or bruised myself in five different parts of my body, accidentally bumping into things to the point of bleeding from my arms and legs in several different spots. (When is the last time you smashed into different things five separate times in a few days to the point of bleeding from the bruises and wounds?) And every day of the trip, right until the last meeting the third night, I was sick with a different sickness, from bad allergic reactions to fever to severe headaches to the runs, shifting from one to the other each day. Not fun!

This was from my journal entry our first day there (a Sunday, which was a rest day): "I have a strange and strong allergic reaction to an apple— with burning mouth, tearing eyes, and other symptoms.... Back at the hotel, feeling very sick and tired...."

LIVING IN THE LINE OF FIRE

The first day of meetings:

> **May 18, 1998** Boy, do I feel terrible! Jet lag is heavy, I have real cold-allergy symptoms, the dust-filled tent only exaggerates things, I stubbed my toe badly last night [to the point that it is bleeding]. ...and I have to minister three times today at a key national conference. Still, I know the Lord will give totally sufficient grace, and—yes—He moves powerfully, beginning with the morning word and then prayer time, the afternoon teaching, Q & A session is fairly tame, and then the night meeting almost explodes with incredible worship, and the message really hits home. Something's happening—in spite of my sickness, weakness, severe headache, and a stubbed toe, a banged head (on concrete!), and a strange bleeding wound on my leg. It looks like a battle!

The second day of meetings: "I feel a little better (the headache is gone, but I do feel feverish)...." Then, the third day:

> **May 20, 1998** Wake up with back and stomach pain...the Spirit falls in the morning, but I've got the runs (embarrassingly humbling!) and really battle during the service (a brief word, prayer for the CITA team, and then it gets intense), brief rest, very practical leadership teaching in the afternoon, and the Spirit falls *again* in corporate prayer time for revival in Italy, then I'm on the verge of collapse, meeting with individuals to answer questions, 30 minute nap, and the final service is glorious—heavy worship, the young people are *gripped*, a strong word on holiness and harvest, and the Spirit falls *powerfully* as I pray for the pastors. Glorious! And then, like never before in my life, I am totally mobbed trying to leave and am barely pulled to safety by Nikola the cop. Wow!!! Late pizza, pack, and get ready for the early flight, awed.

Adventures in the Spirit

By God's grace, I have become part of modern church history by being involved in the revival, and by heading up the school. But I honestly believe that now, through these national meetings in Italy, I have been involved in church history in Italy. Fan the flames, Lord! And what a battle it has been: Terrible tiredness, oppression, and bad allergies and headaches the first day, fever and weakness the second day, and back and stomach pain, the runs the last day! (The dust-filled tent didn't help much either!) 2 Cor 12:9? Whatever the cause, it was worth it!!!

The day after I got home, Nancy had to be rushed to the emergency room, ultimately having to stay in the hospital. She had been diagnosed with a non-cancerous nodule in her thyroid, but the nodule burst, leaking into her neck, which swelled up grotesquely to almost twice the normal size, hence rushing her to the hospital. It was a terrifying sight, and the doctors were concerned the swelling could affect her breathing. The surgeon was prepared to remove her thyroid, something Nancy did *not* want to happen, yet it seemed unavoidable, and the doctor assured us that this had to be done, especially now that the thyroid was infected. But he couldn't operate immediately because of the infection, sending her home to wait until it passed. During that time the Lord told her He would take care of things. And He did! She was completely healed without a problem to this day. Talk about a series of highs and lows!

HEARING THE VOICE OF GOD AND FEELING HIS TOUCH

The following are four brief accounts that testify to the beauty of the Spirit's leading and one that illustrates the tangibility of His presence. I often tell the Lord, "I'm just a dumb sheep. It's up to You to communicate in a way that I can hear and understand."

The first took place on a Saturday night in the early-to-mid 1990s. It was before I made daily journal entries on my computer, so I don't have the exact date, but I do remember the details well. A friend of mine, Jeff

LIVING IN THE LINE OF FIRE

Rogers, pastored an all-Black congregation, but because they were so small at that time, they didn't have their own place for services, meeting instead on Saturday night in a small Pentecostal church building. (Some years later, a synagogue opened their doors to Jeff's flock, where they met for years. That's an amazing story in itself.)

I didn't know it, but Jeff called his congregation to fast the entire day, wanting the Spirit to move through me—and He did, releasing specific words for individuals there after I preached. The people were touched dramatically, and in my experience, this was the clearest I had ever heard God speaking to me, which was evident from the way Jeff's people responded to the words, one woman screaming out, another weeping, another man visibly touched.

But there was a young man on the front row who was not moved at all. Instead, he looked around the little room mockingly, with a big, smirking smile on his face. I said in my heart, "Lord, that's not right. Your Spirit is working and Your power is evident yet he's mocking."

At that moment, something unique happened to me that has never happened since. I said to myself, "The Spirit is here, and the Spirit knows all things. I'm going to open my mind to the mind of the Spirit."

Then I turned in the direction of the young man without singling him out completely, not wanting to embarrass him publicly. I said, "You're a pickpocket. In fact, you're such a good pickpocket that on the way to the meeting tonight, you picked someone's pocket, and before the service, you were boasting about it to one of the people here. God wants you to know He knows who you are." Immediately, the smirk left his face.

The next day Jeff called to ask me about that word. Who was it for? What had the Lord shown me? I gave him the details, and he told what I said was 100 percent accurate. Jeff remarked, "Needless to say, he came into the building mocking but left with a very different attitude."

Would anyone claim that this was a matter of chance or a lucky guess, with less than thirty people present in the meeting? I think not! How good is the Lord!

Adventures in the Spirit

The second instance also took place when we lived in Maryland. I was trying to work out my international travel schedule for 1994, with meetings planned for Finland and Italy, but we were having communication problems between phone and fax, and I was a little frustrated. While praying about this on a Sunday night, I sensed the Lord assuring me that things would fall into place the next day, meaning that we would hear from both countries. Then I heard the Lord quietly say, "And you'll hear from England."

I had only ministered there once before, in 1987, and I had no active connections in the country at that point. But I noted what the Lord had said.

The next day, my secretary called to tell me, "Mike, we got a call from Italy and a fax from Finland. We also got a call from a leader in England who wants to talk with you." What do you know!

I told her I would talk with him, and we set up the call for later that day. It was with a leader named Derek Brown—no relation to me; yes, Brown is quite a common name!—and he oversaw a network of churches in the UK and abroad. He invited me to come and preach at a leaders retreat to about 100 men (I told the story about this retreat in Chapter 7), as well as in his home church and some others. I said to him, "I don't know anything about you, but the Lord told me I'd be getting a call from England today, so I'll come." He replied, "I don't anything about you either, but the Lord told me to invite you." That began a wonderful, decades-long relationship with Derek, marked by some powerful meetings in the UK along with Derek being a key friend during some critical times in my life, including the split after the revival.

But there's more to the story. Derek worked with a Scottish pastor named Douglas, a big, young man with bright red hair and a bright red beard. Douglas had come to the States and while there, preached in a church on Long Island, a church I had ministered in several times over the years. After Douglas preached, the pastor said to him, "We have our own bookstore, and we probably have some books here that you can't get in Scotland. Take any book that you want." Douglas then surveyed all

LIVING IN THE LINE OF FIRE

the books, and took just one: my 1991 book *Whatever Happened to the Power of God: Is the Charismatic Church Slain in the Spirit or Down for the Count?*

Sometime later, Derek happened to be speaking at Douglas's church in Scotland and was sitting in his study with him. Derek was looking at the bookcase when he noticed *Whatever Happened to the Power of God*, telling Douglas, "I'm taking that book." When he got home, he read the book, and God said to him, "Have him preach for you," even though he knew nothing else about me. What an amazing Lord we serve!

The third example took place in the spring of 1983 after the outpouring had ended in my home church and God had been gripping me in deep travail. One day, quite out of the blue as I communed with the Lord, I found myself on my face in agony of spirit under a tremendous burden from the Lord, groaning in intercession. What in the world was going on? Because it was so intense, I said, "Lord, what was I praying for? Instantly I heard in my inner ear, "Muslim strongholds in South Africa."

I thought to myself, "That's crazy! Why on earth would God grip me in New York to pray for this, especially with such intensity? Plus, the Muslim strongholds in Africa are in the north, in countries like Egypt and Sudan." This made no sense to me at all, but because the experience was so powerful and the word in my ears so distinct, I stored it away.

The next year, in July of 1984, while attending a conference in Tulsa, Oklahoma, I heard Reinhard Bonnke preach for the first time. I was stunned to hear him recount the story of extraordinary meetings his team held in Johannesburg, South Africa, the previous year, where the Lord held back the rain during the rainy season after their massive tent, which sat 34,000 people, had been destroyed. But the greatest miracle of all, Bonnke said, was the salvation of thousands of Muslims. And these meetings took place just weeks, if not days, after the Lord gripped me in prayer in 1983. Muslim strongholds in South Africa indeed!

I sensed that I must have been one of many intercessors the Spirit called on during that time to help the work go forward and to overcome the many extreme obstacles that Bonnke and his team had to face, as he explained in his message. How I love the Spirit's leading!

264

Adventures in the Spirit

The last example is a longtime favorite, taking place in the mid-1980s when I taught at Christ for the Nations. There was a young couple from Virginia, Bryan and Michelle, who were engaged. Nancy and I knew them first as singles, then they got together and were going to be married, and we had become fairly close to them.

After one of the classes, I told Michelle I had a word for her, prophesying to her about the blessing that would be on their marriage and on their children. I finished giving her the word, we both paused for a moment, and then I said to her, "The Lord says yes, they'll be children from your own womb." She nodded and walked away, without saying a word. "What was that about?" I wondered. Of course they would be the children of her own womb. Obviously! What other children would they be?

A few months later, Bryan and Michelle came over to our house, wanting to share something with us. The day before I had given her that word, they had gotten into an argument. He wanted to have kids as soon they were married, but she did not, saying that all the pastors' kids she knew were brats. Her plan was to wait until they were older and then adopt children.

So when I gave her that prophecy about her children being blessed, she asked the Lord in her heart, "God, are You talking about children from my own womb or adopted kids?" I then said to her (without the slightest clue why), "The Lord says yes, they'll be children from your own womb." Today, Bryan and Michelle are successful church planters and dear friends, with five grown children and a whole bunch of grandkids. I smile at the goodness of the Lord as I share this, especially knowing that I don't hear the Lord's voice particularly well. He just knows how to get the message across to a dumb sheep like me.

THE LORD HAD MY BACK

As to God's tangible presence, on May 24, 2007, I arrived at FIRE School of Ministry to teach my 11:00 a.m. class, but the students were lying on their faces all over the building, absorbed in prayer. It looked like a battlefield. What had happened? I journaled this:

LIVING IN THE LINE OF FIRE

A sacred day at FIRE! I drive up to school with "Consecrate your-selves, for the Lord is about to do wonders among you" on my mind, ready to tell the students that another wave is coming our way (and it turns out that 6 kids were filled with the Spirit last night at youth), and I arrive to find the whole student body pray-ing and in the Spirit all over the building, which continues past 12:30, having started before 8:00 this morning. Wonderful Jesus!

It turns out some students came in at 6:00 a.m. to pray, with the rest arriving at chapel at 8:00 a.m., when they too joined in prayer, and the chapel service became a prayer meeting. The same thing happened with the next two classes, as the professors came in to teach, unnoticed by the praying students, now joining them in prayer. When I arrived, it was obvious that the only thing to do was pray as well, and I got on my face, seeking the Lord.

After about thirty minutes, I said to myself, "I would love it if the stu-dents would come and pray over me." Soon after, without me saying a word, the students had swarmed around me, laying their hands on my back and shoulders as they prayed fervently, finally leaving one by one. I was blessed and stirred!

But one student kept his or her hand on my back, praying silently, so I thought, "I won't move until they move." Yet they never moved. Finally I realized, "This is not a student! They obviously laid a blanket over my back while I was lying on the floor (in keeping with a custom in some charismatic churches where, if you fall to the ground in prayer, they throw a towel or blanket over you for modesty). No wonder they had not moved in minutes. It wasn't a person, it was a blanket!

So I reached over to pull the blanket off my back, but there was no blanket—and no student. It was the hand of God! As I got up to go to my car, His message to me was clear, "I'm covering your back!" In other words, I've got you covered. I've got your back.

Eight days later, the "new smile" intervention took place (described in the last chapter of the book, giving me ten new teeth). Three weeks

266

Adventures in the Spirit

after that, while doing an all-day TV shoot with the INSP network in New York City, God had my back in a personal and practical way that was clearly providential. At that moment, I remembered His word to me from the previous month! He had my back indeed.

GOD MANIFESTS HIS GIFTS AS HE WILL

In 1983, Nancy and I were in a meeting where Jim Spillman spoke at the just opened Christ for the Nations campus, where God would soon call me to teach. Jim was a former Baptist pastor and educator and has been a staunch cessationist, meaning that he strongly opposed the charismatic movement, once calling Kathryn Kuhlman a witch from his own pulpit. As the Lord would have it, he was miraculously healed under her ministry and became a very free-spirited charismatic. As he was preaching in that 1983 meeting, he pointed to a woman in the front row and said, "The joy of the Lord is on you!" Immediately, she began to convulse in laughter, not stopping for at least thirty minutes. It was the first time I had seen "holy laughter."

About one year later, I was speaking at a Messianic congregation in Florida, and as was my custom, I had preached a very strong word, calling for a response and then laying hands on those who needed a breakthrough. And while we would sometimes end a service with singing and rejoicing and dancing, it was only after much repentance and even weeping. Laughter was not what you would expect in one of my meetings, nor was it on my mind at all.

There was a woman in the prayer line who was very pregnant, about to give birth any day. She and her husband had a Messianic Jewish TV show, so I knew who she was. I was about to pray for her when the thought hit me, "Lord, why don't You ever use me in holy laughter?" It was completely out of the blue, beyond totally random, making no sense at all in light of my ministry calling and the nature of my messages. Laughter? Hardly!

The pregnant woman said to me, "I'm forty-two years old. Please pray that the delivery will go smoothly and that the baby will be healthy." I

LIVING IN THE LINE OF FIRE

replied, "I'm not going to pray, because the delivery *will* go smoothly and the baby *will* be healthy." I just knew it.

To my shock, she began to convulse with laughter, rocking back and forth, to the point that the ushers got a stool for her to sit on. She continued to laugh and rock, and the ushers, sensing that the Spirit was on her, began to bring her people who were depressed and struggling, and as she rocked back and forth, she slapped her hands on them, and they were being touched and delivered. I stood there marveling, yet again, stunned.

The Lord said to me, "I can use you like that if I want to. But it's not Your calling." What an incredible lesson!

A few years later, she called me with a Hebrew question for a book she was writing. I asked her, "Whatever happened with the delivery and your baby?" She said, "Well, I continued laughing the rest of that day, woke up the next morning laughing, went to the beauty parlor to get my hair done, still laughing, then realized I was in labor. They rushed me to the hospital, where I continued laughing through a *pain-free, thirty-minute delivery*, giving birth to a healthy boy."

I was speechless. What an amazing God! This was far and away the most extreme, supernatural story about holy laughter I have heard in my life, and it was simply the Lord's way of saying, "These are My gifts and My Spirit, and I move as I want to move, when I want to and how I want to." All clear, Lord! Years later, I met that boy, then about twenty years old, and I told my side of the story of his birth.

To say it again, what an amazing God we serve! In fact, as I write these words and as more stories come flooding to mind, my own faith is being stirred to hear the Lord more clearly in the days ahead. "Speak, Lord! Your servant is listening."

CHAPTER 13

CALLED TO BE A LIGHTNING ROD

"Michael Brown, the Phd scholar who swallows false teaching like tic tacs. Either the cognitive dissonance displayed by Brown is evidence of dementia, or it is intentional. Those are the only two options."

"Mr. Brown is a professional LIAR for his tribe. Mr. Brown is a born LIAR!!!"

"Shut up diaper boy brown."

"Dr. Michael Brown. Guardian of the False Teachers."

"dr brown subversive wizard."

"Michael Brown is a pagan polytheist deceiver and a disgrace."

"U ...must be smoking crack. Spreading these lies u a devil . . . ."

"I look at Dr. Brown and feel disgusted by his face, knowing he is a messianic missionary."

"Your [sic] an idiot. I hope you die slow from prancreotic [sic] cancer."

"Calling out for an assassin please."

This is just the tiniest sampling of countless thousands of hateful comments that have come my way over the years—meaning the tiniest sampling of the comments that I happened to see and archive, which in turn represent the tiniest fraction of the hate that comes my way. But these comments, which are often too sick to repeat and yet could fill many books, do not discourage me in the least, Instead, they are badges of honor, tokens of obedience, signs that we're on target and doing our job. I rejoice in being maligned for the Lord!

Being a lightning rod is my assignment, my calling, my lane, and it is for this purpose I was brought into the world—to tackle controversies,

269

LIVING IN THE LINE OF FIRE

to confront error, to challenge the darkness. In that sense, my spirit says, "Bring it on!" I am literally *energized* by the attacks to the point that I file the worst of them away for my encouragement. (You should see the file!)

Of course, in some ways, getting rejected for the gospel and for the truth is painful. First, I want the lost people who are rejecting me to know the Lord. It saddens me that they don't. If it is fellow believers attacking me, I want to be a blessing in their lives. Now I can't. That hurts me too, but for them, not for me. Second, as human beings rejection can sting. But when the rejection is for the Lord and His work, it's a sacred privilege and can even be a joy. To be treated like Jesus was treated, even in the most microscopic way, is an honor. Truly![50]

JESUS WAS CALLED TO CONTROVERSY AND SO ARE WE

When Jesus was being dedicated in the Temple as a baby, Simeon spoke these words over Him to his mother Miriam (Mary): "This child is destined to cause the *falling and rising* of many in Israel, and to be *a sign that will be spoken against*, so that *the thoughts of many hearts will be revealed*. And a sword will pierce your own soul too" (Luke 2:34–35 NIV, my emphasis). Notice these three important points.

First, Yeshua, the Messiah of Israel and the King of the Jews, was appointed for the falling and rising of many in Israel—not the rising and falling, but the falling and rising. First, there would be rejection; only later would there be acceptance.

Second, He Himself would be a sign that was spoken against. This applies to us as His followers as well, as He said, "The student is not above the teacher, nor a servant above his master. It is enough for students to be like their teachers, and servants like their masters. If the head of the house has been called Beelzebul, how much more the members of his household!" (Matthew 10:24–25 NIV).

Third, through the life and ministry of Jesus, the thoughts of many hearts would be revealed. That's because He functioned as a refiner's fire (see Malachi 3:1–5), bringing impurities to the surface and revealing what was hidden deep within human hearts. A religious leader might

Called to Be a Lightning Rod

look good from the outside, but Jesus saw the corruption within. And when His light shone in the hidden places, the darkness was revealed.

That's why He said,

> I have come to bring fire on the earth, and how I wish it were already kindled! But I have a baptism to undergo, and what constraint I am under until it is completed! Do you think I came to bring peace on earth? No, I tell you, but division. From now on there will be five in one family divided against each other, three against two and two against three. They will be divided, father against son and son against father, mother against daughter and daughter against mother, mother-in-law against daughter-in-law and daughter-in-law against mother-in-law (Luke 12:49–53 NIV).

Many times, reading these words, especially about bringing fire on the earth and being under divine constraint because of a holy baptism, my own heart burns with holy fire and I feel that divine constraint. It is my calling. It is my destiny. It is my privilege.

That's one reason I believe God has corrected me so often, humbled me so often, put me through the fire so often, and broken me so often. It's so I wouldn't think too highly of myself (I can thank Nancy for that too!), that I would not imagine myself to be God's Hatchet Man, but instead would seek to be redemptive, something that my dear friend of the last decade, James Robison, has drilled into me time and again. (Often, as I am writing an article, I hear his wonderful Texas voice in my ears, saying, "Be redemptive, Michael.") At the same time, I want to be a threat to the kingdom of darkness. In that sense, I want to be dangerous.

DANGEROUS!

About twenty-five years ago, I discovered a Jewish website devoted to countering the "missionaries," meaning Jewish believers in Jesus who were active in sharing their faith. As I scrolled through the site, I found thread

LIVING IN THE LINE OF FIRE

after thread devoted to attacking me. I was the main target! A surge of joy flooded through me, as for a moment, in the most minute way, I was being treated the way Yeshua was treated. I was bearing insult for Him! On the tiniest level, I could relate to what the apostles felt after being flogged for preaching Jesus. They "left the Sanhedrin, rejoicing because they had been counted worthy of suffering disgrace for the Name" (Acts 5:41 NIV). What a privilege to suffer disgrace for that Name!

I felt the same thing when different gay activists or radical leftist groups put me on their hit lists. They made my day! That's because they weren't rejecting me because of foolish behavior on my part or because I was a hypocrite or because I was a mean-spirited, nasty person. They were rejecting me because of Jesus. They were rejecting me because of the sacred convictions He put in my heart. It was all *for* Him and *because* of Him. Praise God! That's why I journaled on May 24, 2012: "...get the amazing news from K. that I'm on the SPLC [Southern Poverty Law Center] list of 30 new activist leaders of the radical right—and I am pumped. OWI!"[51]

That's why, when a colleague or staff member sends me the latest video or website or article or book or meme attacking me, I feel the pleasure of the Lord. These are badges of honor, encouragements to remind me I'm on the right path, signs that we're making an impact. They actually encourage me! As Peter wrote, "If you are insulted because of the name of Christ, you are blessed, for the Spirit of glory and of God rests on you" (1 Peter 4:14 NIV).

And that's why, when my former producer Matt sent me a link to two well-known Christian leaders attacking me on a national radio show, telling me I really needed to listen to this, rather than taking offense, I took it as a confirmation on my calling. This was my journal entry from January 18, 2018:

> Teach advanced apologetics from 8:30-6:30 today [in New York City], with a break for radio, and all is well. A fine class and a fine time together! Some writing at night, but not pushing hard, then learn that [T.F.] and [P.J.] branded me "dangerous."

Called to Be a Lightning Rod

Yes! Yes! Yes! I am "Dangerous Dr. Brown"—as branded by [T.F.] and [P.J.], just not as they meant it. This is the very thing I've been praying about, as recently as November 15, 2017, laying out potential contents for a book called, *The Gospel Is Dangerous* on the 16th. Ha! Oh, Lord, make me more dangerous than I could ever imagine, a walking, talking, living threat to the devil himself! And when [T.] says that I'm on too many radio stations, I take this as a further promise of divine expansion. So be it, Lord! May I SHOUT Your name across the entire globe. DANGEROUS DR. BROWN.... And Father, bless my brothers [meaning, those who attacked me] with Your grace and goodness, that they may fulfill Your purpose and calling on their lives. Boy, do I feel the Spirit on this![52]

This is what I had prayed on November 15, 2017, as referenced in my journal entry:

[God] reminds me that He has given me a great platform, but I'm not burning bright enough. I must be more incendiary and I feel deeply that I need to write a burning, red-hot screed. Words on fire that are dangerous to the devil! This is the key to everything: greater fire in my life to make me more dangerous to the devil and the world. Then holy promotion will come. The Spirit will not back something that is not dangerous to darkness.

One day later, I wrote this by hand in red on my tablet rather than typing it into my computer. **"Without a doubt, God has given me a voice and a platform, but I am *not* nearly incendiary enough. Why? Because I am not close enough to the Fire! I must burn more brightly! Oh for fresh fire! No revolution without fire!"**

To say it again, it is for this purpose God has brought me into the world. It is in my spiritual mind. It is my sacred calling. I am made for

273

LIVING IN THE LINE OF FIRE

it. That's why we made a special video in response to the attacks from these two brothers, branding me "Dangerous Dr. Brown," even using a clip from their show to introduce my show for a few days.[53] They meant it one way; God spoke it to me in another way!

HE GIVES US GRACE TO RUN OUR RACE

In the most famous line from the classic movie *Chariots of Fire*, Eric Liddell is asked by his sister why he plans to run in the Olympics before going on the mission field. Why not go straight to the field now that he has been accepted by the mission society? He replies, "I believe God made me for a purpose, but he also made me fast. And when I run I feel His pleasure." That is true for us as we yield to the calling and purpose of God. We find fulfillment in doing His will, with the wind at our backs, even in times of hellish, demonic, oppressive resistance. In the midst of the slog and fog, we sense the favor of God. We have come into the Kingdom for such a time as this, and He will give us the grace to do what He has called us to do.

As the aged John Wesley wrote to William Wilberforce shortly before his death in 1791, encouraging Wilberforce's efforts to eradicate slavery and the slave trade,

> Unless the divine power has raised you up to be as Athanasius against the world [Athanasius stood his ground for the truth against what seemed like a tidal wave of opposition], I see not how you can go through your glorious enterprise, in opposing that execrable villainy, which is the scandal of religion, of England, and of human nature. Unless God raise you up for this very thing, you will be worn out by the opposition of men and devils. But, "if God be for you, who can be against you?" Are all of them together stronger than God? O "be not weary in well doing!" Go on, in the name of God and in the power of His might, till even the American slavery (the vilest that ever saw the sun) shall vanish away before it.[54]

Called to Be a Lightning Rod

That really says it all, straight from the Word: if God be for you, who can be against you? (See Romans 8:31.)

In my case, among other things, God made me for controversy. He made me a debater. He called me to confront error. He wired me to endure insult. He built me for conflict. And just as the pastor has grace to counsel (whereas counseling wears me out) and the CPA has grace to balance books (an absolute drudgery for me) and the nurse has grace to clean wounds (I would probably faint), and the homeschooling mom has grace to spin five plates at once (I would quit in less than a day), I have grace to be in the line of fire.

As Jesus said to all of us, but also to each of us individually, "For my yoke is easy to bear, and my load is not hard to carry" (Matthew 11:30 NET). That means that the yoke He makes for us and the burden He calls us to carry suits us just right. It may be challenging. It may stretch us. It may bring us to the end of ourselves. But if we really walk with Him and yield our will to His, not only will He give us the grace to do His will, but we will *thrive* while doing it, as if to say, "Lord, I am made for this!"

To be sure, there are times when the constant attacks can be wearying, when I say to myself, "Can I just have one moment without controversy?" And there are times when I feel defiled by the constant stream of hatred and invective coming my way. But for the vast majority of the time, especially if I am spending quality time with the Lord, I embrace this as part of my calling, finding God's grace and affirmation there. The more the attacks come, I say, "Go ahead, bring it on. Make my day."

Of course, I appreciate the kind words too, and we get plenty of them. But what fuels my fire is the attack. The uglier it is, the more I know we're on target. As someone said, when you throw a rock at a pack of dogs, the one that yelps is the one that got hit.

That being said, I despise controversy for controversy's sake. I have no desire to stir up a fight just to get clicks or likes online. And wherever possible, I'm a peacemaker, not a troublemaker, doing my best to have behind the scenes, gracious conversations with cult leaders and schismatic believers and left-wing activists. Not only so, but if I can minister

LIVING IN THE LINE OF FIRE

to someone else by getting low, I'm happy to do it. If using me as a door-mat will get that person through the door, that's fine with me. I want to overcome evil with good, always remembering these biblical principles: "A gentle answer turns away wrath, but a harsh word stirs up anger," and, "Through patience a ruler can be persuaded, and a gentle tongue can break a bone" (Proverbs 15:1; 25:15 NIV). Where I have fallen short and been contentious or argumentative or unloving or impatient, I truly regret it. It dishonors the Lord and hurts others. I always want to step higher.

That's why, when I pray for my critics (meaning critics within the Body), I pray the same prayer for both of us, "Father, to the extent we are doing Your will, confirm it and back us. To the extent we are in error, show us, and help us make the necessary changes. Reveal our blind spots and lead us into greater intimacy with You and a deeper understanding of Your truth." I will not join the devil in being an accuser of the brethren (Revelation 12:10). At the same time, when it comes to standing for the truth, if you challenge me, I will push back twice as hard, and rather than running from controversy and conflict, I run to it.

OBEDIENCE MORE THAN COURAGE

People have often said to me, "Dr. Brown, I admire your courage," and again, I appreciate the kind words. I also know that one of my callings is to impart courage. But for me, doing these difficult things is not a matter of courage. It is a matter of obedience. If I'm sure the Lord is sending me with a message, then my concern is not for my own safety or the negative fallout from the message. My only concern is delivering that message accurately and in a way that honors the Lord.

Plus, the Lord never promised us a bed of roses, and almost every book in the New Testament speaks of persecution and opposition and hardship for the faith. As John Stam challenged his graduating class at Moody Bible Institute in 1932 before leaving for the mission field in China where he married his wife, Betty,

Called to Be a Lightning Rod

Shall we beat a retreat, and turn back from our high calling in
Christ Jesus; or dare we advance at God's command in face of
the impossible? Let us remind ourselves that the Great Commission was never qualified by clauses calling for advance only
if funds were plentiful and no hardship or self-denial involved.
On the contrary, we are told to expect tribulation and even persecution, but with it victory in Christ.

That to me is Gospel 101, the most basic of the basics. That to me
is normal discipleship, not heroic service. That to me is the lived experience of tens of millions of our brothers and sisters around the world.
Why should *we* flinch or cower or hesitate? (I should mention here that
John and Betty Stam were martyred in China in 1934, just two years after
he preached this message. John himself was beheaded.) In the words of
John "Praying" Hyde, "I know but one word...Obedience! I know how
a soldier will obey an order...even to death. I cannot expect to look Jesus
Christ in the face and obey Him less than a soldier his commander." Once
you understand your marching orders, obedience becomes the only issue
and thoughts of your own welfare can even disappear.

I experienced this in 1995 while preaching side by side with Yesupadam
in a radical Hindu village in India called Karamchedu. The first night, he
initially held our team back, not knowing if it would be safe for us to
minister. But that's why the Lord sent us there, and so Yesupadam gave
me the green light to preach. Prior to the service, we had both been urged
by the local believers not to say a word about idolatry since the villagers
were fervent idol worshipers, or to mention murder since they had participated in a massacre about a decade earlier,[55] or to speak of adultery
since many of the men were adulterous. We told them we understood,
and of course, we were concerned about their own safety, but we had to
do what God called us to do.

To my surprise, that first night, the Lord gave me a message from the
Ten Commandments (of all texts!), declaring everyone guilty in God's
sight and then preaching the riches of His grace through the cross. (This

LIVING IN THE LINE OF FIRE

reminds me of the first message I preached in a Baptist church. It was called, "Paul Was Not a Baptist"—but the whole point was that he wasn't a Pentecostal or a Presbyterian or Catholic; Paul didn't fit our mode; we had to fit his.) After the message, Yesupadam sent his people to mingle and listen and monitor things. Thankfully, there was no backlash and there were no threats.

But the next night, the crowd erupted in anger when the worship leader shared how he used to worship the snake god. Now, he said, if a snake comes into his room, he kills it without fear. What the worship leader didn't know was that the snake god was the favorite god of the villagers! They thought he was trying to provoke them and immediately, they started shouting, with some pressing toward the stage. His coworkers had to cover him up using women's saris (think of wrapping someone in several capes), smuggling him out of the village (quite literally). With tensions rising, Yesupadam and I immediately went to the platform and began to preach. Still, I had no sense of fear at all, even as the Hindu radicals came on the stage, some of them with knives and razor blades hidden in their hands, taking the microphones from us. The only concern was getting the message to them, which we could not. Personal safety was not the issue.

It was in that same spirit I confronted a group of Black Hebrew Israelites in New York City in the early 1990s. I was walking down a busy Manhattan street with a younger colleague of mine, who was also a Jewish believer in Jesus, before doing an outreach talk that night. As we walked the streets, I was struck by these men, seeing them for the first time. Their outfits looked like a cross between biblical times and Star Trek, with large men holding clubs standing at the foot of their platform. They were thundering their hateful rhetoric through a loud PA system with a small crowd hanging on their every word. I knew that they taught that the White man was the manifestation of satan and that today's Jews were not really Jews, so I asked the main speaker, "Then why did Hitler try to kill us?" He gave a lame answer, but because he had the mic and wouldn't engage, I walked away.

Called to Be a Lightning Rod

A few steps later, I heard the Lord say to me, "You're not done yet." I immediately turned around, with Ron at my side, and started shouting loudly to the crowd, "These men are deceiving you! Jesus preached a religion of love, but they're preaching a religion of hate! And one day, as Blacks and Jews, we're going to be at the bottom of the barrel and we're going to need each other." Then I approached the platform, and as the guards approached me menacingly, I told them that I loved them.

Unfortunately, I failed to read the crowd—I was the only White man, along with Ron—and they began to shout, "Death to the White man! Death to America!" As we walked away, Ron said to me with a smile, "That may not have been the wisest thing to do, but I appreciate your courage." Again, though, courage didn't enter into my mind (nor did I actually think they would get physically violent with me). It was simply a matter of obeying the Lord.

It was in that same spirit that we did those week-long lectures series on "Homosexuality, the Church, and Society" in 2007 and 2008 at the very moment when these subjects were completely taboo to most Christian leaders. They ran from the controversy; God called me to run to it.

That's why, in 2018, I accepted an invitation to speak at the "Christ at the Checkpoint" biannual conference in Bethlehem, a conference where I had previously been called out as being anti-Zionistic and even antisemitic. Many Messianic Jewish colleagues urged me not to go, saying that speakers like me were just being used to further their purposes (they would invite one pro-Israel speaker to each event). Some believers even posted editorials criticizing me for going.

Naturally, I gave consideration to their concerns, not wanting to be arrogant. But in the end, I knew the Lord wanted me there, and I went, not with anger or hostility, but with humility and with tears. And as I brought a loving rebuke to those attending, I began the message by reading Proverbs 27:6 in English, Hebrew, and Arabic: "Wounds from a friend can be trusted, but an enemy multiplies kisses."[56]

Was it a difficult message to deliver? Absolutely, one of the hardest of my life. But it was not because I was afraid to deliver it or concerned

LIVING IN THE LINE OF FIRE

about the consequences. (And again, no one there was going to harm me physically. These were fellow believers.) Instead, the message was difficult to deliver because I cared for the people, because I didn't want to hurt them, because I truly wanted them to receive my exhortations, and because I knew that Israel had mistreated them at times as well. But it took no courage to bring the word. I had my assignment, and I felt the Spirit's grace on me.

In the same way, when Yesupadam and I ministered to the city of Vijayawada in 1994, which is the home of the most worshiped deity in the state of Andhra, the goddess Kanaka Durga, the Lord led me to call for a public confrontation on the second night, inviting all her worshipers and priests to attend. Again, without any sense of fear, I preached on, "Who Is the Real God, Yahweh or Kanaka Durga?" and the Lord moved mightily.[57] Afterward, Yesupadam, who has risked his life for the gospel over and again, told me he was too terrified to translate my final challenge, softening the words just a little. As the preacher, I had more grace than the translator!

You might say, "But aren't you concerned with what happens to the local believers once you leave?" I am very concerned and never do anything to knowingly endanger them. But my only responsibility is to obey my Master, and what He says, I must do. He knows best. As Amos wrote, "Surely the Sovereign LORD does nothing without revealing his plan to his servants the prophets. The lion has roared—who will not fear? The Sovereign LORD has spoken—who can but prophesy?" (Amos 3:7–8 NIV). Many of us, whether prophets or not, can relate to those words: "God Almighty has spoken! Who can but prophesy?"

A DIVINE INSIGHT ABOUT BEING A LIGHTNING ROD

All that being said, there was one time in my life when I complained to the Lord about a difficult, messy task I had taken on, telling Him on two occasions that I wasn't happy with the assignment, which we'll call "the R. D. assignment." What made it worse was that I never heard Him tell me directly to take on this particular ministry task. Instead, after

Called to Be a Lightning Rod

different leaders appealed to me, Nancy said to me, "You should do it. You're always talking about the problems in the Church. Now you can help fix it." But without that sense of divine calling, I was struggling.

The R. D. assignment called for me to oversee a team who would evaluate serious charges brought against another leader when he refused to repent after being confronted. And even though none of us had any spiritual authority in his life, as elders in the Body, we knew our combined voices would carry weight. But it was ugly. And dirty. And messy.

His supporters rallied around him, sending us prophecies that we would die before our time because we were touching God's anointed. Others posted slanderous videos about us on their social media pages, accusing us in vile ways. And because an investigation was taking place at that time, led by a former policeman who was interviewing alleged victims, we could not say a word publicly to set the record straight.

Then, something happened. I was in India once again with Yesupadam getting ready to speak to a few hundred of his workers, but before the message, he called everyone to pray. I had no idea what they were praying about, as the service was taking place in Telugu, but I got on my knees with everyone else and began to pray. Very quickly, the Lord started dealing with me about that difficult situation I was involved in, since it was heavily on my mind at that time. This was what I journaled later that day. Some of it may sound odd at first, but it will make sense when I open up the Scriptures:

> **December 5, 2019** As I ask the Lord about my involvement in the [T. D.] situation during a time of powerful prayer in the morning service with the leaders in India, He says to me, "Who else could I have asked?"—and realize immediately that very few would have the constitution to take all the abuse and lies that swirl around this case, and immediately, I have peace. He also says this, "I need someone to bear My reproach"—which I suddenly understand to mean that as He is being reproached, He needs one of His children to serve as the earthly target—and

LIVING IN THE LINE OF FIRE

with that, I see that the dirtier I get so to say, meaning, the more false accusations and dishonor that comes my way in obedience to the Lord, the better job I am doing. What a revelation! And how this further colors my understanding of what happens to us as we are persecuted for righteousness. I am honored!

In a moment of time, everything changed. First, I understood that it was an honor to be called to this task. By God's grace, I had some level of stature in the charismatic world, and He had made me for situations like this. Some of my colleagues who are far more pastoral than I am, far more caring, far more compassionate, far more patient, far more gentle, would not be able to take the heat. I should be blessed rather than resentful. (And, to say it again, I could collapse under the load that they carry. We each have grace for our own specific calling.)

Second, just as the Lord sends someone to share the gospel when He wants to save a sinner and just as He moves on someone to pray when He wants to move, working with us rather than apart from us, when people want to attack Him, they need an earthly target. We are that target! As Paul wrote, with reference to Jesus, "For even Christ did not please himself but, as it is written [in Psalm 69:9]: 'The insults of those who insult you have fallen on me.'" (Romans 15:3 NIV) Do you see that? In the same way, the insults of those who insult the Lord now fall on us. What a sacred privilege! The arrows of hatred and malice and mockery that are directed at God hit us!

This truth really rocked my world, and immediately my mind went to this text from the pen of Paul: "Now I rejoice in what I am suffering for you, and I fill up in my flesh what is still lacking in regard to Christ's afflictions, for the sake of his body, which is the church" (Colossians 1:24 NIV).

What, exactly, did he mean? He was *not* teaching that anything was lacking in what Jesus did on the cross. God forbid! Paul would be the last person on the planet to suggest that. Instead, in keeping with ancient Jewish thought, there was a certain amount of suffering associated with

282

the advent of the Messiah, and that suffering had to be filled up before He would establish His Kingdom. The persecution Paul—and all of us—endure for Him helps fill that suffering up, thereby hastening His return.

When I ministered these truths to the leaders there, most of whom had been physically attacked for preaching in the past, the effect was electric. They got it too. Their suffering became more sacred, even more purposeful. With every blow they endured, with every insult, with every slap, not only did they have the honor of suffering for His name (something they already understood), but they were also hastening the redemption. Oh, what a truth!

But there was one more insight that was especially relevant for me, and that had to do with the calling to be a lightning rod, a concept I also knew from Numbers 8, where the Israelites laid their hands on the Levites, who then served as a wave offering for the people (Numbers 8:10–11), making atonement for them. As the Lord said, "From among all the Israelites, I have given the Levites as gifts to Aaron and his sons to do the work at the tent of meeting on behalf of the Israelites and to make atonement for them so that no plague will strike the Israelites when they go near the sanctuary" (Numbers 8:19 NIV). As explained by the Jewish biblical scholar Jacob Milgrom, this verse "would then imply that the Levites are ransom for Israel, a lightning rod to attract God's wrath upon themselves whenever an Israelite encroached among the sancta [i.e., the holy place]."[58]

Now I understood! Just as the refiner's fire brings impurities to the service, which is why the repentance is often so deep in times of revival, so also the lightning rod attracts the lightning. The more lightning it attracts, the better!

Suddenly, it became crystal clear to me. The messier things got as I dealt with this difficult ministry assignment, the uglier the attacks, the viler the accusations, the better. All the junk was coming to the surface. I was effectively attracting the lightning. I was doing my divinely appointed job! It was like cleaning out an infected wound, with all the puss and disease oozing out. (I know it's a gross picture, but it's what came to mind.)

LIVING IN THE LINE OF FIRE

From that moment on, no matter how messy things got, I did not have the slightest regret I had accepted this assignment. And to this day, when things get crazy after a debate, or there's a rabid response to one of my writings or messages or radio shows, I'm reminded of this calling: I'm attracting the lightning! The sickly state of the Body (or the society) is being revealed! I feel honored rather than sullied, as much as I hurt for our lack of unity and grieve for the confusion others are suffering.

Oh to be a holy, undefiled, Christlike lightning rod! Oh to step higher into this sacred calling! Oh to be truly dangerous to the dominion of darkness! That is the cry of my heart. And the less there is of the obnoxious Michael Brown, the contentious Michael Brown, the carnal Michael Brown, the argumentative Michael Brown, the immature Michael Brown, the better. Continue to refine and purify me, Lord!

WELCOME TO MY WORLD!

Allow me, then, to take you into my world and share some of the reproach I have been honored to carry for my Master. (For the sake of decency, though, I won't post the vilest comments.)

FROM MY OWN JEWISH COMMUNITY

- The man is a pariah and soul murdering liar who we MUST not only pay attention to, but to also exhaust ALL EFFORTS to stop this deceiving trickster. Have you never heard the phrase, "keep you friends close and your enemies closer?" We keep a close eye on this man because he is the leading cause of Jewish spiritual deaths.
- DR BROWN IS NOT A JEW
- You do not deserve the time. I'm sure I can show you the truth but you are a lost case as it says if you sin and cause others to sin you do not get the divine help to return to Hashem [God]. As you stick your head deeper in garbage you go further away from the truth. Worse than being sick is being sick and thinking that you are healthy.

Called to Be a Lightning Rod

- Mr Brown ur a hoax deceiver.
- honey you do what you do !!!! STOP SAYING YOU ARE JEWISH !!!! STOP !!! YOU CAN BELIEVE IN JESUS IN MAO IN SANTA CLAUS MESSIANIC WHAT ??? YOU PRETEND TO BE STUPID LIKE THAT ??? IM ASHAMED YOU ARE A MORON LISTEN YOU NEVER HAD TO HIDE THAT YOU ARE A JEW !!!!! SHUT UP YOU MAKE US SICK HOW THE HECK ITS ABOUT JESUS ???? OMG CANT LISTEN ... GO BECOME CHRISTIAN ..BOO THEY PAT YOU !!! YOU GO [EXPLETIVE] YOURSELF WHAT KIND JEW ARE YOU ?????? PEOPLE LIKE YOU KNOW [EXPLETIVE] SAY [EXPLETIVE] THINK [EXPLETIVE] YOU ARE A FLAMING IDIOT LEAVE US ALONE !!!!BE ANYTHING YOU WANT TO BE BUT YOU ARE NOT A JEW ....GET OFF THIS IDIOT

FROM ANTISEMITES

- Jew worshiping Dr. Brown. Dr Brown is an ignorant man and has not enough information to defend his position. Stop worshipping Jews. He is a foolish man.
- You are leading the flock to Hell Dr. Michael Brown so we know that Jews are allowed to lie about their ancestry etc. . . . Hell awaits you and the Lake of Fire.
- Mr Brown, who controls the media? Who controls Congress? Why do we have a majority of people in our government who have dual citizenship? Who controls Hollywood? Who controls what we can and cannot say about Israel with the antisemitic trick? Who are the banksters? Who created Israel? And no God, would never create a racist, cruel occupation of ethnic cleansers. So why, should we not be concerned? We aren't blind to the Zionist agenda, and Zionists are not friends to Christians. Shame on you Brown. Dr Brown is laughing at Christians who have legitimate concern. His hubris is nauseating. He is a Zionist gatekeeper. Beware of his koolaid. Mikeal Brown. The Zionist gate keeper. Beware of his lies.

285

LIVING IN THE LINE OF FIRE

- This guy is a mossad funded psyop to convince evangelicals that they should be bestest goys [Gentiles for Zionists].
- Michael just admit that you're a fake Christian and nothing but a subversive Jew.

FROM LGBTQ+ ACTIVISTS AND THEIR ALLIES

- Michael Brown is such a fatuous jerk. Same sex marriage will not "ruin" America nor bring down the wrath of a non-existent Biblical bronze age god on us any more than allowing blacks and women to vote, blacks and whites to serve together in the military or to marry each other did. Brown is noting but a ridiculous chicken little hysterically screaming "The sky is falling" constantly.
- Crackpot rightwing neo Nazi using the Bible to spread hatred.
- You are quite possibly one of the stupidest men on the face of Earth. You are no less dangerous than Hitler, and you are a threat to society.
- It is people like this so called "Doctor" are what is wrong with the world. People like him need to be bound and tied by their hands and feet, beaten repeatedly in the head with their book of fairy tales until they are twitching from never [sic] damage and bleeding profusely from their ignorant heads.
- Brown is a committed liar, fundamentalist bigot...and earns a living selling books that demean gay people and gay Christians. And then claims himself to be a victim. He is a hypocrite and fraud. And his followers resemble the members of an obsessive cult.
- The madman fully understands that he only has to create a hostile climate to inflame the most unstable of his thugs and they will eventually provoke the type of confrontation that this pathological monster deeply desires.

FROM BLACK HEBREW ISRAELITES

- This guy is the devil.

Called to Be a Lightning Rod

- Mr. Brown, you and your white, racist, bigots conservatives spews utterly false [expletive].... There is no truth in you or your race of Esau. You were a liar and a murderer in the beginning.
- You are ridiculous. Your specious lies are totally racist and inflammatory [expletive].
- There is NO such thing as a Caucasian Hebrew or Israelite. There is No White Person in the Bible of Prominence. And No amount on White Washing Biblical Images from Black to White can no longer change that.... They are what the Bible call the Synagogue of SATAN.. you are a DEVIL in sheep's clothing.... a VILE Edomite Devil.
- You WHITE COON CHRISTIANS, OR WCC, ARE SOME OF THE MOST RACIST PPL ON EARTH.... God said he hates Caucasians the most. Who said brown is a Dr? Another Caucasian, does everything have to be signed off from a Caucasian? Brown no Dr, is spit.
- Dr. Brown you are definitely not a man of the Lord. Just put your hood on, don't hide! White Devil.
- I'm not seeing PhD intelligence here at all. Dr. Brown (Phony Heathen Dog)?

FROM RADICAL MUSLIMS AND THEIR ALLIES

- Allahu Akbar! [Expletive] Judaic and Christianic law! Your gang will pay the price for your attacks against Islam! Repent openly or else.
- You Dr your date of death is so near! Shut up and get ready for it Old cockroach.
- Dear Dr Brown, you being a "strong CHRISTIAN Evangelical" just wait for the in-evitable Muslim infiltration, and be afraid, be VERY AFRAID. You INFIDEL you Especially a CHRISTIAN one.
- May Allah destroy I$rael and Brown!
- ...the racist DrBrown, a charlatan "Christian" who disseminates anti-Islamic poison on his website.

LIVING IN THE LINE OF FIRE

FROM ANTI-CHARISMATICS

- This is the "gospel" Brown is now defending [with reference to a YouTube video from the Brownsville Revival]. Sorry, that looks a lot like satanism.
- What part of, "be not unevenly yoked together with unbelievers" was optional for you all at Brownsville?
- Brown, repent of all your Charles Finney type emotional manipulation and semi-pelagian errors and learn to preach the true Gospel.
- Dr. Brown, you create mass hysteria and you say that this is from God?
- Brown is a nutjob tare....no eyes to see or ears to hear wt scripture teaches in 1 cor 12,13,14...u say why ? bcz in mt 13 is ur answer....be bereans not nutbags...
- The blood of the false converts that are being produced in the Pentecostal/Charismatic movement is on your hands, sir. You didn't warn the sheep to RUN from wolves. Instead, you affirm the wolves.
- Dr. Brown is inspired by Satan.
- I believe @DrMichaelLBrown is far more dangerous to the true Church than any Muslim Imam.

And how about a closing comment from an atheist? "doctor brown gives new meaning to fundie/mental case, he needs a BRAIN transplant...him an his 'sky god' lol."

Are you getting the picture now, even though these sentiments represent just the tiniest sampling of the hate that comes my way? If so, welcome to my world! And can you understand why, as much as I regret that people are so lost and angry and confused, I copied and pasted these quotes with a smile on my face and with joy in my heart? *I am blessed to be a lightning rod for my Lord!* There's also a side benefit to being attacked and slandered all the time: it can help keep you humble, since you're not just hearing words of praise and affirmation all the time. I smile about that too!

Called to Be a Lightning Rod

May our gracious heavenly Father have mercy on all those who scorn His love, malign His truth, mock His Son, and reject His Spirit. May every curse that has been spoken be turned into a blessing and may everything satan means for evil be turned for good. All for Your glory, Lord!

CHAPTER 14

TIME TO MEET NANCY FOR YOURSELF

Because Nancy has played such a crucial role in my life for the past fifty years, it's only fitting that she gets her own chapter in the book. In fact, while sitting with my longtime friend Steve Alt in Orlando on March 27, he said to a colleague, "Mike would not be the man he is today without Nancy." That is absolutely true!

A few months later, while Yaakov, the ultra-Orthodox Jewish man whose story of salvation I told in Chapter 11, was visiting Nancy and me in North Carolina he said to a colleague who was traveling with him, "Mike wouldn't be Mike without Nancy." He was right! That's why I want to tell her story in this memoir about the first seventy years of my life. But I've also found that people really enjoy hearing stories about Nancy, so here we go! My only concern is that my readers will say, "Dr. Brown, we enjoyed reading your story, but we really want to hear more about Nancy!" That's a risk I'm happy to take.

Nancy is the ultimate truth teller, saying it like it is regardless of the possible consequences. (She absolutely abhors deceit.) When our daughters were teenagers, they would ask her, "Mom, does this outfit make me look fat?" She would reply, "Yes, it does," which would then hurt their feelings. She said to them, "Then don't ask for my opinion. I won't volunteer it if you don't ask for it."

She is also not big on flattery. (Okay. I apologize. That is a *massive* understatement. She doesn't flatter at all, and consequently, her words of praise are worth their weight in gold.) She is not impressed by human beings (especially me!), and her standards and expectations are very high.

291

LIVING IN THE LINE OF FIRE

In fact, when I asked her to describe herself in one word, she responded with, "Perfectionist." What this means in practical terms is that if one thing is glaringly wrong to her, that's what stands out to her—and she has an incredible eye to spot what is wrong. Others may not notice it, but it is shouting aloud to her.

Once while preaching in our home church in North Carolina, I noticed that she was trying to get my attention, looking quite annoyed. Something was wrong, but I had no idea what, and all the while, I was trying to focus on preaching the message. But she kept looking at me and pointing down to the ground, somewhat angrily, almost glaringly. What did it mean? I glanced down at my pants (thankfully, my zipper was properly zipped). I looked down at the floor, but nothing. After the message, I asked her, "What were you trying to tell me?" Somewhat exasperated, she replied, "The cuff of your left pant leg was stuck in the top of your shoe." Because of *that* she could hardly concentrate on a word I said.

In the late 1980s or early '90s, while preaching at Christ for the Nations on Long Island, I saw that Nancy was very disturbed, actually getting up, leaving her seat, and walking out of the main sanctuary a couple of times. What was going on? I was already bothered because of some recent attacks coming against me from some brothers in another state, but now I wondered if she had just received some bad news. Did something happen to a family member or friend? Did she get a bad report about something?

After the sermon, as we walked out together with some dear older friends of ours, I asked her, "What was the matter?" She said to me, "That was the worst sermon I ever heard you preach." I asked the friends, "Was it the worst message you've heard me preach?" They replied, "Well, it wasn't one of your best." With that, I smiled, and we went out to eat. I was actually relieved to hear that the problem was the quality of my message, which obviously was *not* one of my best. I had thought something was seriously wrong with a friend or family member. A bad message was no big deal at all, but it was almost unbearable for Nancy to hear, like someone scratching their nails on a chalkboard.

Time to Meet Nancy for Yourself

It's true, of course, that many husbands would not appreciate her perspective and approach, needing to hear more words of affirmation and encouragement. That's why the Lord gave different wives to them! For me, though, while I don't always appreciate the negativity, I tend to be so super positive and upbeat—to the point of being pollyannish—that it doesn't faze me in the least. (I'll return to the unique mix we have shortly.) In that respect, I'm kind of like a lively rubber ball, bouncing higher the harder I'm thrown down. Boing!

QUALITY CONTROL

In 2009, a leader who worked with the Gallup organization in leadership training had dinner with the lead pastor of our congregation, giving him ten copies of the *Clifton Strengthsfinder* book, one for each of our five leadership couples. Each book contained a one-time code to use for the Strengthsfinder online test, helping individuals identify their top five unique strengths (out of a possible thirty-two strength descriptions). I actually found it quite helpful, as my greatest strength was that of Achiever, which means that I start every day with a fresh slate as if I had not accomplished anything at all previously. This helped me better understand myself.

Once all of us had taken the tests, I had dinner with that Gallup representative, who had trained thousands of leaders and taken them through deep-dive versions of Strengthsfinder. (The test we took resulted in more surface level, summary types of answers; he was highly qualified at digging very deeply into the significance of these answers and had great understanding of both human nature and leadership qualities.) The results of our tests were all coded numerically, but he knew what each number stood for and simply listed all the numbers in columns under each leader, without knowing who was who. These were just lists without names for him.

As he was plotting everything out, he came to one list that got his attention. As he wrote out the numbers, he exclaimed, "That's a very unusual combination!" He then stated emphatically, "That's the one the

LIVING IN THE LINE OF FIRE

team needs to listen to. That's the one who can tell you where the train is going to get off track and who can tell you what is wrong right now." Yes, that was Nancy's list, and that is who she is.

During the Brownsville Revival, we would sometimes have dinner at a restaurant called Bennigan's, which was part of a national chain. One night as we ate there, she said to me, "This place is going to close." I said to her, "Why do you say that?" She replied, "Can't you see? Everything is going downhill." For my part, I didn't see it at all. The next time we went to eat there, to my shock, it had shut down, just as she predicted.

When building our house toward the end of the revival (it was a house Nancy helped design), we ran into some major problems with our builder, because of which we hired a new builder, one of the top builders in Pensacola. He came by the house with one of the city's top architects so they could survey the situation. While walking through one room, Nancy pointed to a wall and said, purely by outward observation, "That's about a quarter of an inch off. It's not even." They assured her that she was wrong, just by looking at it. But to appease her, they took out a tape measure and proceeded to examine the dimensions. To their shock, she was completely accurate. In her mind, it was as plain as day. (I've told friends in the building industry that she would be an incredible general contractor or house inspector, guaranteeing that the work would be done at the highest level. The only problem is that, in the process, she would probably bankrupt the company because of her high levels of quality control.)

When we were building our house in North Carolina (a house she also helped design), she told the builders, who were friends of ours and top builders and solid Christians, that, with the current structural plans, there would be a problem with a leak under a particular part of the roof, causing damage to the wall below. They reviewed it carefully with the architect, assuring her that everything was sound and there would be no problem. Within a year of living in the house, the builders had to rip out much of that wall due to the unforeseen leaks. She can just see things that others don't see.

294

Time to Meet Nancy for Yourself

It's the same sometimes with people. She just knows things, but not in some kind of spooky, hyper-charismatic way. It's self-evident to her, like the nose on her face. (If you ever get to meet her, don't worry! She doesn't go around trying to analyze people or get some kind of prophetic insight. But she can see through people who are disingenuous, so it's best just to be yourself around her.)

Once when I was on the road, I called her to tell her I had met another leader for the first time and had a great lunch with him. He seemed like a terrific guy. That's all I said. She replied, "Nope. Something is wrong with him." It turns out she was absolutely right. Another time, I was helping a longtime friend whose wife had suddenly and unexpectedly left him, moving in with someone else. Nancy knew my friend from a distance but knew nothing about his wife. Nancy had never met her, and she knew literally nothing about the woman. One night, there appeared to be a big breakthrough. We were told the wife was back home, weeping and repenting, wanting to restore the marriage. God had broken through!

I told Nancy the good news and she immediately replied, "Nope. It's not real. She's too unstable." I asked her how in the world she knew this. After all, we had been praying and crying out to the Lord for this very thing, and a very solid woman with lots of experience in deliverance was right there with my friend's wife, giving us the report. Nancy answered, "Can't you see? This won't last. She's not stable." Sadly, once again, she was right. To this day, it baffles her that I couldn't see this as well.

NANCY KNOWS

In the early 1990s, after having an impromptu debate with a counter-missionary rabbi in the home of a new, Russian Messianic Jewish believer, I met an ultra-Orthodox Jewish woman named Joanne. She had driven to the debate with the rabbi and some of his colleagues, and she had questions she wanted to ask me. Years earlier, she had become a believer in Jesus, but her faith wasn't that deep, and she ultimately was pulled away from Jesus through her interaction with an Orthodox Jew, becoming ultra-Orthodox herself.

295

LIVING IN THE LINE OF FIRE

We began to dialogue over the months, talking by phone and then interacting with material I sent her to listen or to read, and the discussion was often very intense theologically and intellectually. Nancy, for her part, never met or talked with Joanne, but she would sometimes be in the room while Joanne and I talked by phone, hearing what I was saying to her.

At that time, Joanne lived with an ultra-Orthodox family in Brooklyn and we lived in Maryland, but I was going to be in Stony Brook, Long Island, teaching at Christ for the Nations, about a 90-minute drive from Brooklyn. She reached out to me, saying, "Mike, you're the only person I can trust right now. I don't know who else to talk to." So we set up an appointment to meet after I spoke one night at the school, even though it was a long drive for her.

I told Nancy about it, and she said, "Don't meet with her." I was completely surprised, having no idea why she would suggest this. After all, Joanne was a very sincere Jewish seeker and I was uniquely qualified to answer her questions. Nancy said, "That's her whole problem. She looks to man too much. She just needs to seek God."

Somehow, without understanding this myself, I knew that Nancy was right, but I had no way of contacting Joanne, meaning that she drove all the way out from Brooklyn, then sat through the whole service and my message. When the meeting was over, to her shock and deep disappointment, I said to her, "I'm sorry, but I can't meet with you." She was confused, but not angry, completely baffled by my response. I said to her, "You just need to seek God." She left saddened and made the long trip home. I felt bad personally, but I knew Nancy well enough to recognize that she saw something important and that her advice was right.

Quite a few months later, I heard from Joanne. She had called to tell me she was now a solid believer, absolutely sure that Yeshua was the Messiah. She said to me, "No more questions, Mike. I'm sure." Thrilled, I asked her, "Joanne, we talked for many hours and I sent you lots of material. Was there anything in particular that brought you back to the Lord?" She

Time to Meet Nancy for Yourself

replied, "Yes, it was when you told me on Long Island that I just needed to seek God. That's what changed everything."

How remarkable. It wasn't my great answers and brilliant interpretations or rock-solid apologetics that changed her life (although she appreciates my work and uses it until today). It wasn't all the hours that we interacted that made Yeshua real to her. It was Nancy's simple insight that she looked to man too much and just needed to seek God. That's what changed everything! Hours and hours of my best efforts, based on years and years of research, did not have the impact of six words from Nancy: "She just needs to seek God." My amazing wife knows how to get to the heart of the matter. Joanne has been strong in the Lord ever since, subsequently serving for more than a decade in Nigeria, educating and caring for the poorest of the poor.

One night, a little more than twenty years ago, I received a phone call from a good friend, an internationally respected Christian leader, telling me about a great opportunity for our ministry. He had invited a number of other top leaders, all of them with international ministries, to join him in Dallas to meet with a Kingdom-minded businessman who had some great ideas which could help us fund our ministries. If I paid my airfare, he would pay for the hotel. I asked him if I could bring a good friend of mine who was a solid Christian leader with vast experience in the financial world, and I was told he could come too. When I called my friend to invite him he was thrilled, saying he would make plans to join me, also asking for the name of the company involved so he could research things.

At the time I received the call from my colleague inviting me to this meeting, Nancy was in bed, watching the news—so, she wasn't praying or listening to worship music or in some spiritual frame of mind; she was just watching the news. I told her about the opportunity, relating to her everything I've shared here. That was it.

She smiled knowingly, nodded her head from side to side, and said, "No, you don't want to do that. It's multi-level marketing." When I asked her how she knew this—after all, this was an invitation from a mature Christian leader, and I only told her what I wrote here, which was almost

297

LIVING IN THE LINE OF FIRE

nothing, since I had no further information—she couldn't explain how. She just knew it. A couple of hours later, the friend who was going to accompany me on the trip called me to say, "Mike, we don't want to do this. It's a multi-level marketing company." By this time in my journey together with Nancy, I was not surprised.

As for how often this happens, it's not really that common—in other words, she's not telling me every week, "This business is going to close," or, "That person can't be trusted." But in the fifty years I have known her, I can't think of a single time when she was 100 percent sure that something was wrong that she was not right. That is no exaggeration.

A colleague once asked me whether he should release a prophetic word to the public or if it would be better to keep it private. I discussed it with him at some length, giving his question prayerful consideration. In the end, while I told him I could see why he would want to release it, I felt now was not the right time to do so. I told Nancy about it, asking for her thoughts. She replied immediately, saying it was "sheer stupidity" to release it publicly. "How could anyone not see this?" she wondered. Why was there a need even to pray about it or discuss it? For her, this was a matter of basic common sense. Once again, she proved right.

Over the years, my rule of thumb is to yield to her common sense approach, barring a clear directive from the Lord to the contrary. It's proven to be a good strategy, especially in day-to-day affairs where her practical wisdom far exceeds mine. In this context, she once described me as being "very smart and very dumb." Even writing this brings a smile to my eyes.

PERFECTIONIST, BUT MUCH MORE

As I mentioned, Nancy is a self-described perfectionist—that's the one word she used to describe herself when I asked—and is actually harder on herself than on anyone else. So, after spending a whole day cooking a special meal for the family and getting rave reviews, she probes deeper, asking everyone what they didn't like and what could be done better. In that same spirit, when we used to hand out surveys to our students in our

Time to Meet Nancy for Yourself

ministry school, asking them questions about each class, each professor, and their overall experience, I always wanted to hear the good, encouraging reports. She wanted to know what disappointed them or fell below their expectations. Her M.O. was, "Tell us what's wrong so we can fix it." For me, I'd rather hear the praise reports!

Naturally, as her soulmate and best friend and life partner, I feel the brunt of her perfectionism, which does not need to be expressed in words. Often, just a picture suffices.

I could be on my way to the airport for a major international trip when I receive a text message from Nancy with no caption or message. It's just a photo of a door that I left ajar or unlocked on the way out. Or I can come back from a drive to the Whole Foods grocery store, which is about twenty minutes from our house, proudly carrying in all the bags containing the long list of items she asked for (sometimes having to add extra items to the list when she calls me with an update when driving, which I then memorize and add to the list). In my mind, I did a great thing, saving her a trip. For Nancy, despite being appreciative, one thing stands out to her: what I got wrong—either leaving something out or buying the wrong brand or the wrong kind of product. And so, as I'm helping to unpack everything after my shopping outing, her first words might be, "I asked you to buy this item, not that one." It's not what's right that gets her eye but what's wrong.

One time I walked into our home scullery (a very large pantry, really like a small kitchen) where I prepare my daily salads and cut up my fruits and make other meals. I saw what looked like arrows on the countertop, but I couldn't figure out what they meant. Then I got the message: the arrows were formed by crumbs that I had left on the countertop. She rearranged them in arrow form to be sure I didn't miss them.

That being said, there *are* times when she lavishes compliments on me, and I can actually think of *two times* when she did this recently—yes, that's *twice*, not once. She wanted me to know that I had brought home really good onions. Yes! Then, one day, after I pulled the weeds out the garden bed which houses the bird feeders (after she had done the harder

299

LIVING IN THE LINE OF FIRE

work of digging most of them up). She said to me, "You did an awesome job!" That is who I am! Now I have something to boast about!

Nancy also seems to know the best way to do things (and you can be sure she has an opinion about them too), often bemoaning a conspicuous flaw in an appliance or app or product that could have been avoided. It is so obvious to her. She once contacted Apple tech support, telling them that something was wrong with some hardware she had purchased. The agent assured her she was wrong, explaining that the product had passed thousands of tests. You can guess what came next when they dug deeper. They gave her the product for free, saying she discovered something they had missed.

While writing this chapter, Nancy went to the dentist for the first time in fifteen years. The hygienist who cleaned her teeth was stunned, telling her that her teeth were amazingly clean, like nothing she had seen before. She even told Nancy she needed to take lessons from her! Nancy explained to me that she knows how to brush and clean her teeth. When she puts her mind to something, she really does it well. (When did the hygienist ever tell *you* that he or she wanted to take tooth brushing lessons from you?)

DEEPLY COMPASSIONATE

But to share all this only tells one part of the story. Nancy is also one of the most compassionate people I have ever met, deeply moved by human suffering. In fact, when people tell me I'm compassionate—which I know is true on a certain level—I'm quite aware that my compassion is a fraction as deep as hers. That's why, many a night, she has literally cried herself to sleep because of the pain and suffering in the world. That is no exaggeration.

Days after two of our dear friends lost their child, I called Nancy just to chat, but she sounded very down. When I said, "What's the matter?" she was quite surprised. Our friends were in deep pain. They had lost their child. How could she not be hurting? This doesn't go away in a day.

300

Time to Meet Nancy for Yourself

One night, while driving home, we passed what looked like a bad accident, with the cars mangled and ambulances caring for the injured (or dead). As is my custom, I prayed a quick prayer for God's merciful intervention and didn't think about it again. After all, I had no idea what actually happened, and the people involved were total strangers to me. Later that night, I could see that Nancy was not herself. When I asked what was troubling her, she replied, "That accident." People's lives were turned upside down in a moment of time, perhaps for the rest of their lives. Families were in turmoil. How could she *not* be burdened?

She is also the ultimate foul-weather friend, and the few times I have dealt with serious sickness, she has been there by my side, unwaveringly. She's done that for others in need with whom she had little contact for years. When they had a need, she was there, quite selflessly. And with her tenacity and focus and compassion, she is the ideal person to have by your side in a time of crisis. Her New York, Jewish personality might not be everyone's cup of tea (neither is mine!), but you know who she is and where she stands, and she is loyal to the core of her being.

Nancy also knows the Lord deeply, with incredible insight into His character and nature. This is the result of countless hundreds of hours she has spent seeking Him in prayer and pouring into His Word. The insights she has gained into who He is, what He does, and what He desires from us have been life-changing for me and others with whom she has shared.

THE LEAD WEIGHT TO MY HELIUM BALLOON

I once received a call during the Line of Fire broadcast from a listener who thought very highly of me. He asked, "Dr. Brown, with all that you have accomplished, how do you stay humble?" I didn't want to make light of his call, since he obviously respected me and was showing me honor. But knowing myself as well as I do—which is the tiniest fraction of how well the Lord knows me—I am *not* in awe of myself. Hardly! Still, as I was beginning to formulate an answer to the caller's question, I saw some texts coming in to my phone from friends and colleagues who were listening, as well as posts from my staff on my radio screen monitor. All

LIVING IN THE LINE OF FIRE

of them said the same thing: Nancy. Exactly! As I have said many a time, she is the lead weight that keeps my helium balloon from flying away, and in this regard, I believe she serves the greatest purpose in my life.

When I had finished the first draft of my doctoral dissertation in 1985 after two years of arduous research and writing and the culmination of more than a decade of intense Semitic language study, I was able to print it on a laser-jet printer at the computer store. In those days, the HP Laser Jet had just come out, costing $3,000 per printer and, in contrast with the other printers of the day, where the printed page looked as if it had been typed on a typewriter, the printed page looked as if it had really been typeset. It felt like I was holding a book in my hands—and it was my dissertation: *I Am the Lord Your Healer: A Philological Study of the Root RP' in the Hebrew Bible and the Ancient Near East*. With pride and joy, I showed it to her, wanting her to see how amazing it looked. She replied, "It's all going to burn." Yes, *that* was her response to my magisterial efforts. It's all going to burn!

She was also quick to point out to me that what she did in this world—beautifying the garden and taking pictures of nature—could continue in the world to come. But of what use was my Semitic acumen? And who, she wondered, would I debate in heaven?

It's not that she didn't believe I was called to scholarship. And she certainly didn't glory in ignorance, being self-taught herself in many subjects over the years. It's that she saw that scholarship had become an idol in my life, contributing to the loss of my first love (as I explained in Chapter 2), and because of that, she reacted against my efforts. It was her internal alarm going off, even though I was sure it was God's path for me. And it *was* God's path, which is why at no point did she ever tell me I shouldn't get my doctorate. It was the direction of my heart which she resisted, knowing that my primary calling was to be a man of the Spirit rather than an academic and seeing that I was losing my intimacy with God for the sake of advanced studies.

This has not been easy for her over the years, as I can be stubborn and argumentative and self-justifying, making it hard for her to hold

Time to Meet Nancy for Yourself

her ground. Yet she can do no other, and in the end, her stubbornness (meaning, the spiritual side of it, not the fleshly side) has been a lifesaver to me.

In the early 1990s, one of my ministry school grads, who had become a family friend, gave some of my books to a well-known, megachurch TV preacher. Our friend told me that this preacher had been devouring my books and that he was even quoting them from the pulpit. At one point, he read some extensive sections from one of my books, holding it up as he preached, and saying, "I didn't know anyone was as hungry for God as I am."

Sometime after that, I was told that he had written a book about living a holy life in this fallen world, and I wondered if he had quoted any of my books in his new book. But before I could get a copy for myself, I received a call from a female pastor. She told me that she had practically memorized my books, and when she got a copy of his book, she was shocked to see how much he had plagiarized my material without acknowledging my books at all. She sent me a copy of his book and when I read it I was shocked and angered. On page after page he had lifted direct quotes from my books, including some plays on words and alliterations and very unique expressions. There was no question whatsoever that he had plagiarized my books in the most blatant form. A court of law would recognize it in a matter of seconds.

Visibly upset, I told Nancy about this. She replied, "Well, it's just pride on your part. You know that he'll sell more books than you, and people will read your words and think that they're his, and he will get credit for it. But any good thing in your books came from God, so you don't deserve credit for it anyway." That is *not* what I wanted to hear, but I knew she was right. It *was* a matter of pride, and I wanted people to know that I wrote those words, not him.

After getting alone and praying this through, dealing with my pride, I said to Nancy, "What he did was still wrong." She responded, "Yes of course, it's wrong." But her first reaction, being who she is, was to recognize and call out my pride.

LIVING IN THE LINE OF FIRE

About five years ago, I came up with a great idea for the beginning of a book, somewhat out of the box for my normal writing. I printed it up for Nancy to review, eagerly awaiting her comments. She returned it with the words, "**Total Fail!**" written in large, red letters across the top. She was obviously not impressed! When I told her I really felt it was a great way to start the book, she made clear to me that, if so, it would have to be changed dramatically. For my part, I was not bothered in the least since: 1) I had asked for her input. 2) She was not trying to insult me but to make the book better. And, 3) I always bounce back!

Another time, back in the late 1990s, I presented the opening chapter of *Go and Sin No More* to her, and she also reacted strongly against it, although not with the words "Total Fail!" She simply told me that in no way was this a good way to start the book. This time, I was completely sure the content was strong, but I realized that her point had substance. I then showed her the second chapter of the book, and she loved it. The problem was not with the material but with the placement. So, Chapter 2 became Chapter 1, and my original Chapter 1 became Chapter 5, "Go and Sin No More: What Does the Bible Say?"

And she is such a wonderful realist. The other day I said to her, "Think of how little we knew when we were first saved and in our first church." She replied, "Think of how little we know now." Indeed!

In 2014, I was on the Piers Morgan show on CNN, part of a three-person panel talking about homosexuality and the Bible.[59] (This was in response to some controversial comments made by Phil Robertson on the wildly popular TV series *Duck Dynasty*.) Thankfully, the show went really well, and within minutes of my appearance, my cell phone lit up with congratulatory texts and emails, all of them telling me what a wonderful job I had done. They were thrilled! But as I drove home with my radio show producer, I said to him with a smile, "We haven't yet heard from the one person who matters."

Seconds later, Nancy called, with one question only: "Who did your makeup?" She actually called a second time, probing me further about the makeup job. In fact, she was so surprised by the way I looked that,

304

Time to Meet Nancy for Yourself

when the faces of the panel came on the TV screen (we were not in the studio with Piers but appeared as talking heads), she said out loud, "Where's Mike?"

In truth, it wasn't the fault of the woman who did the makeup for me that night, a friend of my producer. What happened was that I was filmed sitting in a tiny satellite studio in Charlotte (really, just one small room with a camera and lights). The CNN team asked me to sit in front of the camera to check out the makeup, and they told the woman who was helping me that it was put on too thin. They wanted a second coat! Well, they got what they asked for—again, she was just following instructions—and I have joked since then that, if Hollywood ever decides to produce a remake of the mummy, I have just the look for them.

But I tell this story for one reason only. Nancy didn't see the amazing job I did on the show. She saw the bad makeup. That's what got her attention, and that's what she wanted to talk about after the program.

It's the same when she sees some pictures of me posted on social media by the church or ministry where I was speaking. "You're hunched," she'll say to me, reminding me that I have bad posture, which is not only bad for my back and neck but makes me look older than I am (and certainly much older than I feel). She offered no comment about the great reports posted about the ministry. Just a comment on my slumping neck and shoulders. In fact, in 2023, I had to have a surgical procedure because of a large kidney stone, and I was sitting in bed in my hospital gown before being taken to surgery. "You're hunched," she said again. I thought to myself with a smile, "Really? Now? In a hospital bed right before surgery?"

NOT IMPRESSED

What about the times when I do well and Nancy recognizes the significance of my accomplishment, especially if it would have been very difficult for someone else to do? "You have a gift," she says. "You have nothing to boast about."

305

LIVING IN THE LINE OF FIRE

We once joked that if I came to her and said, "Look at this! I wrote this 300-page book in three weeks" (which I actually did one time), her response would be, "You obviously weren't praying enough if you had so much time to write." That would be my bride. And when I did say to her excitedly one time, "Honey! I was able to write this little book in just eight days," she simply replied again with those words, "You have a gift." Why should she be impressed with that?

In December 2020, I went away for an eight-day prayer retreat, the longest prayer retreat I had done in many years, coming home deeply impacted by the Lord. I told Nancy, "I think I need to do a weekend prayer retreat once a quarter. And on Saturdays when I'm home, unless you need my help outside, I won't leave the bedroom until I break through in prayer." She responded, "You'll never get where you need to go in God unless you do this once a month"—meaning, shut myself in and seek God from Friday night until Sunday night, once a month.

Since May 2021, that has become the norm, meaning that I had to cut back on my traveling ministry schedule, making these prayer times a priority. They really have been life-changing! But I tell the story to underscore that, after fifty years in the Lord (as of December 2020) and more than forty-eight years of preaching and teaching, after serving as a leader in the Brownsville Revival, after pioneering several different ministry schools, after traveling outside the USA more than 200 times, in Nancy's mind, I was nowhere near where I needed to be in God. Unless I did something radical, I would never get there. She is right!

During the Brownsville Revival, I accepted an invitation to preach in what seemed like the middle of nowhere in Canada. My assistant, Scott, had received endless requests from a church and ministry there, and after months of saying no, we finally agreed to come. About 1,000 people were packed in the church building, including overflow rooms, and they came from forty different locations in the region, some traveling a good distance to get there. I also noticed some First Nation people there (Native Canadians), and my heart went out to them, knowing that they, just like

Time to Meet Nancy for Yourself

Native Americans, had suffered much over the years and had many serious struggles to this day.

After a long service of worship, preaching, and altar call, I then laid hands on every person in the building wanting prayer, which was basically everyone. The next day, Scott and I returned to Pensacola, but because of odd travel arrangements, we had to fly west first before making our way to the east and the south. In the end, it took four flights and fourteen hours to get home in what would have been a four-hour direct flight had such a flight existed. And that was that.

About one year later, on the same day, Scott was contacted by two different people from Canada, neither knowing the other was reaching out to him, and they both shared the identical story. The Native Canadians had driven to our meeting from a reserve (what we call a reservation) more than one hour away. They represented two very small churches, the result of a split, meaning that the one small church on the reserve was now two, even smaller churches, and all of them were discouraged.

But something amazing had happened. They went back to the reserve after that meeting we had one year earlier revived in spirit and full of faith, holding a joint meeting shortly after that. The meeting was so powerful that they went another night, then another, then another, finally getting so exhausted that they had to call in other local pastors to help with the services. (One of those pastors verified this story to me firsthand a couple of years after that. He saw this with his own eyes and participated in the meetings himself.)

And then for the miraculous news: after one year of meetings, *1,150 out of the 1,200 people on the reserve had professed in Jesus.* Yes, 1,150 out of 1,200! It was the most outstanding contemporary revival account I had heard in my life and certainly, by far, the most dramatic. (Remember that three independent, unrelated witnesses confirmed this to me.) With great excitement, I shared the miraculous account with Nancy, to which she replied, "And you can't take any credit for it." (Yes, those were her opening words!) She continued, "Just think of all the thousands of people you have prayed for over the years and that never happened."

307

LIVING IN THE LINE OF FIRE

Of course, she was right. I couldn't take any credit for it, as if I myself had done something or it was somehow my miraculous powers that produced this extraordinary harvest. Instead, it was the power of God touching hungry, desperate believers. As Paul wrote, "What, after all, is Apollos? And what is Paul? Only servants, through whom you came to believe—as the Lord has assigned to each his task. I planted the seed, Apollos watered it, but God has been making it grow. So neither the one who plants nor the one who waters is anything, but only God, who makes things grow." (1 Corinthians 3:5–7 NIV) But what other person would respond to my story the way she did? That's what makes her so special.

She has also willingly sacrificed over the years as I have spent so much time on the road, carrying lots of responsibility for our daughters when they were younger (thankfully, I didn't travel much when they were very little) and managing the affairs of the household. And she has not minded being alone at all in the decades since the girls have been out of the house. In fact, we realized during Covid when I was home for five straight months that she actually *needed* time alone, telling me with a smile one day, "Honey, the nations need you!"

But once my travel schedule picked up again and I have asked her if I could take certain ministry invitations that would create hardship for her or cause her real inconvenience, she has said to me in all seriousness, "The world needs you." That has meant everything to me.

That's also why the whole world wants to meet her. You see, after traveling with me overseas in the early years, going three times each to Israel, Italy, and India, Nancy took a real dislike to flying, meaning that people would hear me talk about her without having the chance to meet her for themselves. (When people would ask her if she traveled with me when I preached, she would say, "Why would I want to hear him speak? I know all his stories.") Once while I preaching in South Korea, I referenced her having red hair and blue eyes, but the translator said it backward, telling the people she had blue hair and red eyes. Afterward, my Korean friends said to me, "Everyone here *really* wants to meet her!"

308

Time to Meet Nancy for Yourself

But I can best sum things by saying this. When I told her that I was going to write my autobiography and that the publisher was excited about it, she said to me, "But why? You haven't done anything yet." When I smiled at her response, she replied, "But really. You haven't." Months later, when I told her the title of the book, *Living in the Line of Fire*, she replied with her own smile and said, "I am your line of fire." Then, when I sent her the chapters I had written about her, quite excited to get her response—after all, this was about her!—she only managed to get through a few pages, finding it boring to read. And I repeat, this was about her! That's my bride, and I love her more than anything in this world. Without her, I would be a fraction of who I am in the Lord.

CHAPTER 15

LESSONS LEARNED AND LESSONS STILL BEING LEARNED

In writing this book, my primary goal has been to glorify the Lord by testifying to His goodness and faithfulness. I am a living witness! At the same time, I've done my best to present an honest picture of both the good times and the bad, being candid about some of my own failings as well. In this chapter, I hope to share some of what I've learned while being open and vulnerable about things I'm still trying to learn. Hopefully, as I near seventy (by God's grace, I will have reached seventy the month this book is released), I've gotten a few things right!

Here, first, are some of the major lessons I've learned over the decades.

THE LESSONS LEARNED SO FAR

THE IMPORTANCE OF WALKING IN DIVINE FORGIVENESS.

Some weeks after I came to faith, I was sitting in the kitchen one night, talking with my dad, and he asked me a direct question: "Did you steal that money from me a few months back?"

Not only had I stolen the money—the last of several times I had committed that shameful, ugly act—but I had cut through the screen door in the back of the house to make it look as if someone had broken in. When my father came home and saw the damaged door and the money gone, I told him friends of mine had stolen it. To punish me, my dad said that none of my friends could come over to the house again, but I was sure he knew I did it.

311

LIVING IN THE LINE OF FIRE

Well, I was a believer now, and I couldn't lie to my wonderful dad, but I did. I told him I hadn't stolen the money, and with that I went upstairs to my bedroom and fell to my knees to pray, feeling miserable. Immediately—and I mean immediately!—I was stricken with the Spirit's conviction, and I knew I couldn't lie to my father. So I told the Lord I was sorry for lying and that I would tell my dad the truth. At that moment all conviction left, and I thought to myself, "Well, maybe it was enough to tell the Lord I was sorry. Maybe I don't have to tell my dad." But like a holy dagger, conviction hit me again and I said, "All right, Lord, I'll tell him the truth."

So I went back downstairs where my father was still sitting, and I told him what I had done. And, as remarkable as this sounds, this is how my father responded (and he was not a believer in Jesus in any way at that time). He said to me, "Michael, when I saw the money missing I immediately knew you had stolen it, and I forgave you on the spot. But what hurt me was that you had a need and didn't come to me for help." That was my earthly father!

Can you imagine what it was like to have a father like that? That's one reason I believe that for almost all my years in the Lord I have never doubted my heavenly Father's love and approval. That's also part of the reason I walk in a deep sense of security, why I find it easy to receive forgiveness when I have fallen short, and why walking in grace seems as natural to me as breathing air.[60]

I mentioned in Chapter 4 that I experienced a level of condemnation once I was unable to spend six-seven hours alone with God every day in my early years in the Lord, and that further drove me away from intimacy. Thankfully, this deep assurance of the Father's love has been with me ever since, and it is at the foundation of my life in Him.

GOD GIVES GRACE TO THE HUMBLE.

Because I made so many mistakes as a new believer and had to get low and ask for forgiveness so many times (as I mentioned in Chapter 2; I've had to get low a bunch of times since!), I discovered quickly that God gives

Lessons Learned and Lessons Still Being Learned

grace to the humble—and I love grace! The place of grace is a great place to be; and so while it is true that I can still be stubborn or contentious at times, arguing my point rather than acknowledging my error, once I'm thinking clearly, I find it easy to apologize. Not only it is truthful, but it releases grace.

I like to think of it in terms of an underwater cave where you can breathe. You have to swim down to find it, but once you do, you'll find refreshing and renewal. You'll breathe easier!

NOBODY IS ANYBODY.

When our older daughter Jennifer was a young teenager, she was at a Messianic Jewish conference with me where, in the eyes of many of the attendees, I was some kind of bigshot. She said to me, "Dad, everyone wanted to meet you, but you're just Dad." I said to her, "Exactly, everyone is just mom or dad." She understood the principle immediately. We're all just regular people. The only one who is "amazing" and "incredible" is the Lord.

In reality, then, nobody is really anybody when it comes to the work of God. We are servants, not superstars, and the only name we want to promote is His name. Our goal is to draw attention to Him, not to ourselves, and to the extent people look to us, we point them toward Him. As for anything of eternal good that comes through us, be it a song we sing or a book we write, be it the salvation of a soul or the healing of a Body, it is He who does the work through us. That's why, on that day, people will be worshiping Him, not us.

This has also given me pause for thought regarding the name of one of my popular classes in years past called "Giants of the Faith" in which we studied the lives of people like Smith Wigglesworth and John Lake and John "Praying" Hyde and George Whitefield. Without a doubt, all of them were mightily used by God and, to the best of our knowledge, served the Lord with devotion and fervor. But are there really any spiritual "giants"? Does God Himself look at any of us as "giants"? I think not.

LIVING IN THE LINE OF FIRE

LOOSE LIPS SINK SHIPS.

For decades, I have meditated on verses in Proverbs warning about the dangers of careless speech, of too many words, of destructive talk, often teaching on these subjects as well. And as someone who communicates day and night, there is a filter on my lips. But in 2002, shortly after choking to death and while receiving ministry myself, the Spirit took me back to a painful childhood memory and to then to recent, painful events, and all of them had the same thing in common: sharing something I should not have shared. To be clear, though, it was not that what I shared was sinful or gossip. Not at all. Instead, it was information I should have kept to myself. By speaking prematurely or immaturely, I caused great pain for myself and others.

That moment when I realized all this while receiving ministry and counsel, as these stinging memories came together as one, changed my life. Since then, there's one extra filter over my lips, reminding me again to zip it. There's also the ever-present voice of Nancy in my inner ear saying, "You don't want to say that," even when we're 10,000 miles apart. How I wish I had learned this years earlier.

LIFE IS NOT ALWAYS "ALL OR NOTHING."

One of my former students from Long Island likes to tell the story of the time we were driving together to a meeting in New Jersey in the early 1990s. It was during the winter, and I would turn the temperature dial in my car all the way to the right for maximum heat. Then, when it was too hot, I would turn it all the way to the left. At one point, he turned it to the middle, which was the logical thing to do, producing the desired temperature on a steady basis.

As he recounts, I rebuked him, saying, "No! It's either all the way to the right or all the way to the left!" We've had lots of good laughs over this, but I realized that this was indicative of my personality: I'm totally black or white, in or out. Being in the "middle" seemed like compromise, like being wishy-washy. Being in the middle was not radical!

314

Lessons Learned and Lessons Still Being Learned

Unfortunately, the middle is sometimes the right path, and life is not always lived in all-or-nothing terms. So while I strive to be "all in" in terms of my commitment to the Lord, I realize that life as a whole requires more balance. In the same way, I need to remember that people are not all good or all bad. There is more nuance to our nature!

THE ACHIEVER MENTALITY CAN BE UNHEALTHY.

Over the years, I've taken several leadership or gifting tests, and for the most part, in the end, they told me what I already knew. But in 2009 when I took the Gallup Clifton StrengthsFinder, I learned a lot about myself, with my first value being "achiever." According to Gallup, "People exceptionally talented in the Achiever theme work hard and possess a great deal of stamina. They take immense satisfaction in being busy and productive." That sounds like me!

And then this, which was the eye opener: "Your Achiever theme helps explain your drive. Achiever describes a constant need for attainment. You feel as if each day starts at zero. By the day's end, you must achieve something tangible to feel good about yourself. And by 'every day,' you mean every single day—workdays, weekends, and vacations."[61] What a revelation it was to read those words. That is *exactly* how I think.

It doesn't matter how many books or articles I've written, how many messages I've preached or radio shows I've done or ministry trips I've taken. Instead, "each day starts at zero." That means that unless I've produced something new before going to sleep, almost always meaning producing something new in writing, I feel as if I haven't accomplished anything, no matter how many hours I have spent preaching or teaching or doing my Line of Fire broadcast or meeting with people. The only real exceptions to this mindset would be: 1) if I spent the entire day ministering and we were visited by the Lord in a powerful way, but even then, when I get back to my room, I want to "produce" something new; or 2) if the Lord spoke something very clearly to me that was critical for my life and ministry, in which case I experienced a major breakthrough. But even then, of course, I have to write that down!

LIVING IN THE LINE OF FIRE

Until recently, though, especially with the "Iron Man is dead" word in 2002, I've thrived in the Lord as an achiever, energized by the holy adrenaline of the call and enjoying the intensity of the adventure. And since 2014, when the Lord intervened in my life and helped me transform my lifestyle and diet, I'm virtually never exhausted or feeling burned-out. Still, as I've gotten older, especially after I got Covid at the end of 2022, revealing some issues with my heart from my former days of unhealthy eating, because of which I was hospitalized for a day, the clock of life began ticking more loudly in my ears. (Thankfully, those heart issues were successfully treated, and by God's grace, I am stewarding my body well.) And that's when I started to notice how the achiever mentality could be harmful. That's because I truly believe that my greatest days of service are still ahead (this is *not* a boast; it is a deep hope) and there are still large, unfulfilled promises that remain before me. Yet every day, there's less time to see those promises come to pass, even if I live to be 100 years old (and healthy to the end). No matter how you do the math, there are less years ahead for me on this earth than behind me.

I really sought the Lord about this early in 2024, and overnight, everything changed. First, He helped me to see some of the work I have been able to accomplish, all by His grace, since I normally feel as if I haven't done anything yet. Instead, He wants me to enjoy ministry and life as a respected father in the faith with many sons and daughters who are making an impact for Him around the globe. I'm not starting every day from scratch.

The Lord also gave me this insight, which turned everything on its head: every year I age is a year closer to seeing the Lord! Talk about a change in perspective! So, I still burn and I still travail and I still run hard with passion and fire and fervor and faith and vision—with joy and with spiritual intensity. But I don't chafe. What a relief that has been.

I also realized something very simple which I'm trying to integrate fully (although I still have a long way to go in taking hold of this): if you live in the moment, you don't have to think about the future. In other words, there's no need to calculate how much time you have left and how

Lessons Learned and Lessons Still Being Learned

much work still has to be done. Just focus on "now" and everything else will take care of itself.

WE MUST FIND OUR SECURITY IN HIM.

John tells us that, immediately before Jesus had His last meal with His disciples, and knowing "that the Father had put all things under his power, and that he had come from God and was returning to God" (John 13:3 NIV), He did something extraordinary. What was it? Did He raise His hands to heaven and say, "I Am!" with thunder and lightning confirming His words? Was He transfigured and glorified before His disciples' eyes, as He was on the Mount of Transfiguration? Quite the opposite. John records, "so he got up from the meal, took off his outer clothing, and wrapped a towel around his waist. After that, he poured water into a basin and began to wash his disciples' feet, drying them with the towel that was wrapped around him" (John 13:4–5 NIV).

What? The Lord of glory, the One who came from God and was returning to God, the One with all things under His power, God Himself in human form—that One!—did the work of a lowly slave, washing the feet of His disciples? But that's the whole point. *Because He knew exactly who He was, He could get low*. He could not care at all about what humans thought because He knew what His Father thought. That is so liberating!

In 1986, I was scheduled to bring the keynote message at a famous Bible school at their annual Israel Day celebration. Nancy and I arrived the day before the meeting (I was scheduled to speak the next morning), and we were invited by a friend to visit the rehearsal that night, as the teams prepared to sing Messianic Jewish worship songs with accompanying dance. As we watched the rehearsal, I noticed that the drummer on the worship team was not familiar with Jewish-sounding music and he was putting the accent in the wrong place.

As a drummer myself, I went up to the worship leader, asking if I could show the drummer the right way to play the song. But the worship leader didn't know me from Adam and assumed I was another student (since I was just thirty-one at the time). Looking at me with scorn, he said, "No!"

LIVING IN THE LINE OF FIRE

He then started to walk away and looked back and me and said it once more: "No!" Then, finally, as he was at a distance, he looked back yet again and mouthed, "No!"

I smiled to myself, knowing exactly what happened and why, also realizing that the next time he saw me, I would be sitting on the platform in my three-piece suit, right next to the school president. Sure enough, the next morning, he strode onto the stage with enthusiasm to start the worship and song, only to see me in the special guest speaker's seat, next to his boss, the president. He was mortified, saying to me, "I'm so sorry!" I just smiled.

This, for me, has been a source of strength and security over the decades. Not only do I know the Father's love for me, which is the same for all His children, but I know that, as my life is yielded to Him, He is smiling on my life. He has my back! Sometimes, I have pictured a similar scene on judgment day as my harshest critics come to give account to God, only to find me sitting right next to Him, with them blurting out, "I had no idea you two were so close!"

Of course, this is just an image that comes to my mind to illustrate a truth. As for what will actually happen on that Day, I expect to be on my face, prostrate in His presence, overcome with worship, adoration, and awe.

GOD'S STRENGTH IS MADE PERFECT IN OUR WEAKNESS.

I shared the importance of this theme to me in Chapter 9. Here, I want to point to the relevant verses and explain a little more why this was such a life-changing revelation for me.

If you study 1 and 2 Corinthians, especially in Greek, you'll notice that Paul keeps referring to the theme of "weakness" or being "weak." See 1 Corinthians 1:25,27; 2:3; 4:10; 8:7,9–10; 9:22; 11:30; 12:22; 15:43 and 2 Corinthians 10:10; 11:30; 12:5,9–10; 13:4. It seems that the Corinthians were impressed by outward display, by outward strength, by outward rhetoric, by outward riches, by the superstars, those whom Paul labeled "super-apostles" in 2 Corinthians 11:5 and 12:11 (NIV),

Lessons Learned and Lessons Still Being Learned

elsewhere calling them "false apostles" (2 Corinthians 11:13–15 NIV). In stark contrast, Paul pointed to the "weakness" of the cross and to his own weaknesses.

Then, in an extraordinary passage toward the end of 2 Corinthians 11, after listing all the ways he has suffered for Jesus—the exact *opposite* of the boasts of the false apostles—Paul says, "If I must boast, I will boast of the things that show my weakness." (If you haven't read 2 Corinthians 11 in a while, I strongly encourage you to read it slowly and carefully when you have a chance.) Paul then speaks of himself in the third person, recounting the extraordinary revelations he has received from the Lord, because of which,

> ...in order to keep me from becoming conceited, I was given a thorn in my flesh, a messenger of Satan, to torment me. Three times I pleaded with the Lord to take it away from me. But he said to me, "My grace is sufficient for you, for my power is made perfect in weakness." Therefore I will boast all the more gladly about my weaknesses, so that Christ's power may rest on me. That is why, for Christ's sake, I delight in weaknesses, in insults, in hardships, in persecutions, in difficulties. For when I am weak, then I am strong (2 Corinthians 12:7–10 NIV).

What an incredible revelation! What a life-transforming truth! Are you grasping the significance of this?

I don't believe Paul was referring here to being physically sick, although a similar application could be made. Instead, I believe, along with other scholars, that his thorn was the unusually intense persecution he experienced wherever he went. This is something that really keeps you humble since, rather than crowds praising you after your great message, you're being flogged and thrown into a prison cell. So in verse 10, Paul is saying this: "That is why, for Christ's sake, I delight in weaknesses, namely, in insults, in hardships, in persecutions, in difficulties. For when I am weak, able to put no trust in myself and having to put all my trust in Him, I am strong."

319

LIVING IN THE LINE OF FIRE

As paraphrased in *The Message*, once Paul heard from the Lord that His grace was sufficient for him and His power was made perfect in weakness, "I was glad to let it happen. I quit focusing on the handicap and began appreciating the gift. It was a case of Christ's strength moving in on my weakness. Now I take limitations in stride, and with good cheer, these limitations that cut me down to size—abuse, accidents, opposition, bad breaks. I just let Christ take over! And so the weaker I get, the stronger I become." Yes!

I understood this in part before 2002, but since then, I have understood it much more, often walking up to the platform to speak repeating to myself with each step, "Strength out of weakness, strength out of weakness." I put zero trust in me and total trust in Him. How liberating that is, and how it makes the impossible become possible. After all, if it's all on Him and not on us, why can't He do impossible things through us? Why not?

IT'S GOOD TO WALK WITH A LIMP.

This flows directly out of the last lesson learned. Of course, I enjoy being physically healthy and experiencing the blessing of God in every area of life. Who wouldn't? But I'm careful to walk with a limp rather than to strut. So, on the one hand, I embrace God's call on my life and believe Him for extravagantly impossible things, seeking to walk in the fullness of my stature as a father and elder in the Body. On the other hand, I recognize I am the recipient of massive mercy from Him—meaning both before and after I was saved—understanding that my only boast is in Him. Only He knows how kind and longsuffering He has been with me.

RECOGNIZING WHEN I'M TAKING ON MORE THAN THE LORD'S BURDEN.

Even though Iron Man is dead, my schedule is still quite full. Yet I've learned not to strive or push in my flesh but instead to be quick to recognize when I'm taking on something the Lord has not called me to carry. Time to make an adjustment! John Wesley said, "Though I am always in

Lessons Learned and Lessons Still Being Learned

haste, I am never in a hurry, because I never undertake any more work than I can go through with perfect calmness of spirit." I have not fully mastered this yet, but it's become more and more real to me.

GOD KNOWS HOW TO OPEN IMPOSSIBLE DOORS.

This is something I have seen for more than fifty years, and I could have written a whole chapter (or several chapters) giving example after example. Here are just a few.

In the summer of 2002, I was walking down the streets of Manhattan prior to a major debate when I heard the Lord say, "I want you on secular TV more." When I returned to Pensacola, I received a call from a man named Bobby, saying, "I'm a producer for the Donahue show, and we'd like to have you on as a guest to discuss two questions: Do Jews need Jesus? And who goes to heaven and who goes to hell?" I thought at first it was a prank call, especially with those subjects, but it wasn't, and not long after that call I was back in Manhattan to do a live show with Donahue on August 20, 2002. The Lord Himself set it up through an interesting series of connections, none of which I initiated in the least (or, for that matter even had any idea of). The show went so well that on December 17, 2002, I was invited back for a second show. The Lord opened other doors for me on secular TV as well, all without my initiative.

On July 31, 1998, Suzette Hattingh, formerly Reinhard Bonnke's lead intercessor and for many years now, a powerful evangelist in her own right, prophesied over me, saying that, among other things, I would meet with princes and royalty, which was absolutely the last thing on my mind.

Such a thought had never occurred to me, not a single time. Two weeks later, once again without any initiative on my part, I was in a private meeting in Buckingham Palace with Prince Andrew, getting to share my testimony with him and, with his permission, praying for God's blessings in his life. (Who knew back then the trouble he'd be in today?) This was my journal entry for August 12, 1998: "Amazing! We go to Buckingham Palace and meet for an hour with Prince Andrew, where I get to clearly

LIVING IN THE LINE OF FIRE

share my testimony and lay hands on him and pray for him. Jesus, touch him and transform him!"

Over the years, people have told me that I could never preach in certain circles or minister in certain settings. I was told I had to do things their way, to become someone I was not, to compromise my convictions. I would tell them politely, "I'm sorry, but God has not called me to do this," knowing that if He wanted to open those doors to me, He would make it happen. Time and again, He did.

Not only so, but He has also done the exact opposite for me many times, supernaturally preventing success when it was not His will or plan. I have even warned those who asked me to try something out, such as advertising on their platform—meaning in a way that was godly and Christian and ethical, but perhaps not my normal style—that if the Lord wasn't in it, the results would be worse than anything they had ever seen. That too has happened several times, to the point that they've even run the same ads again for free, but with equally horrific results. I smile and tell them, "It's not your fault. It's just something the Lord does for me." It makes me feel safe and protected.

THEY MUST COME TO YOU; YOU DON'T GO TO THEM.

At the end of Jeremiah 15:19 (NIV), the Lord tells His servant, "Let this people turn to you, but you must not turn to them." This is something He has drilled into me as well, but I need to remind myself of this constantly, as it ties in with the previous lesson about God opening doors. To be clear, on a personal level, when it comes to fixing broken relationships or asking forgiveness, I reach out to people all the time. I will come to them. I will get low. I will try to find common ground.

But when it comes to opening doors for ministry, all too often, when I felt God was calling me to do something, I have sometimes tried to open the door on my own, thinking to myself, "Maybe if I take the initiative here, I can get things going." (Yes, this is despite seeing Him open so many doors on His own.) I have to crucify these desires repeatedly, unless He explicitly leads me to contact someone or knock on a door. They will

322

Lessons Learned and Lessons Still Being Learned

come to me if that's what He desires, and when it happens that way, it is all the more supernatural. And when it comes to the holy convictions He has laid on my heart, that's a non-negotiable. I will lose everything rather than compromise, and Nancy will be right there with me, standing side by side. In that sense as well, this word speaks to me: "Let this people turn to you, but you must not turn to them."

LET OUR NAMES PERISH THAT HIS NAME MAY BE EXALTED!

Once I became part of Beth Messiah Congregation in Maryland in 1987, I dove into Jewish apologetics even more, beginning to compile answers to Jewish objections to Jesus and, after much prayerful thought and study, to write out principles of interpreting Messianic prophecy. I felt the Lord had given me some really good insights, the result of more than twenty years of interaction with my Jewish people. Sid Roth, who had been a founding member of Beth Messiah, told me he was publishing a Messianic Jewish Bible and for the front of the Bible, he wanted to use some of the material I had compiled, along with a few shorter contributions from others. Of course, with joy, I was in.

Some months later, I was on my knees in prayer, reflecting on the words of George Whitefield who had prayed, "Let the name of Whitefield perish that the cause of Christ may live." With all my heart, I cried out, "Lord, let the name of Michael Brown perish that the cause of Christ may live." I wanted all attention and glory to go to Him. While I was praying the phone rang (this was before the days of caller ID, so I had no idea who was calling). Normally, I wouldn't have stopped praying to answer the phone, but I felt the Lord say, "It's okay. Answer the phone." It was Sid.

He said, "Mike, I have good news and bad news. The good news is that the new Messianic Bible came out and it looks beautiful. The bad news is that the names of the other contributors are listed before their work, but your name is missing." It was the Lord! How could I argue with this in light of what I had been praying at that very moment?

A few years later, on August 10, 1998, I was ministering in London but was a little frustrated when a colleague was credited publicly for doing

LIVING IN THE LINE OF FIRE

some very important things that I had done. This was not the first time this had happened, and I felt somewhat bothered by it all. Back at the hotel where I was staying, I went up to my room and sought the Lord in prayer, asking if this had happened so that God could kill more of my flesh. "Why," I asked myself before the Lord, "should this bother me at all? Why should I care about getting the credit I deserve?" I finished praying and came down to the lobby where a longtime friend was sitting, holding the Sid Roth Messianic Bible in his hands. "Mike," my friend said, "have you ever seen this?" Had I seen it? I was the main contributor to it! Once again, this was the Lord.

In the years following, in many different situations, I have seen others get credit for what I have said or done or written, or, when I'm being cited by a scholar for my work, with my last name, which is really quite simple, misspelled or with my work wrongly cited. The amount of times this has occurred is absolutely uncanny. When this happens, I can only smile. It's exactly what I prayed for!

I AM NOT THE CORRECTOR IN CHIEF.

During my theologically proud years before God brought me to repentance in 1982, I delighted in pointing out error and even mocking those I felt were wrong. I knew the Word better than they did. I knew the original languages. I was right—all the time.

Thankfully, the Lord delivered me from that arrogant attitude, and I'm happy to learn from the simplest believer who loves Jesus. At the same time, I'm often burdened by undeniable error, by dangerous doctrines, by things in the Church or culture that need correction. That's where I need to remind myself that, in the words of James Robison to me, I am not the "corrector in chief." If the Lord directs me to write or speak or address things on the air, I will not hesitate. But I'm only a miniscule part of the Body, with limited insight and experience, therefore I need to lead with humility.

As I shared in Chapter 6, this was a major lesson I learned after my controversial message in Israel in 1988, but as the years have gone on and

THE PROMISES OF GOD WILL TEST YOU.

my platform has increased, with more people wanting to know my opinion on an issue, I've had to grasp this principle more deeply. James has played a key role in this, reinforced by Nancy, who is quick to remind me, "I've been trying to tell you that for years."

This, too, could be the subject of a whole message or book, based on Psalm 105:19 (CSB), referring to Joseph as a prisoner in Egypt: "Until the time his prediction came true, the word of the Lord tested him." Or, as rightly explained and rendered in the Amplified version, "Until the time that his word [of prophecy regarding his brothers] came true, the word of the Lord tested *and* refined him."

In other words, as Joseph sat languishing in prison, the very promises that God had previously given him, namely that all his brothers would one day bow down to him, now came back to test him. "Joseph," he would certainly hear in his own mind, "what about those promises? I thought you were going to be some great man, towering over your brothers. What happened?" This is exactly what his brothers said before abandoning him in the countryside (and, ultimately, selling him into slavery): "Come now, let's kill him and throw him into one of these cisterns and say that a ferocious animal devoured him. Then we'll see what comes of his dreams." (Genesis 37:20 NIV) Now his own mind was saying to him, "So much for those dreams!"

At times like this, when the divine promises in your life have been delayed, you go through different phases, thinking, "I never heard God at all"; or, "I did hear God, but I exaggerated"; or, "Yes, God spoke to me, but I didn't pray enough (or, fast enough, or whatever)"; or, "Yes, that was the Lord, but I blew it that one time." But the more time you spend with Him, the more that promise burns afresh in you, challenging you, testing you, refining you. (The Hebrew verb used in Psalm 105:19 means "to refine, to test," and it's the same root found in the phrase "refiner's fire" in Malachi 3:2.)

LIVING IN THE LINE OF FIRE

I've been through this process several times in my life, and each time, after the Lord comes through, I say to myself, "I'll never question the promises again." The only problem is that the next time, you're older, the delay seems longer, and the possibility of fulfillment seems fainter.

Once again, those promises refine and test you!

During a prayer retreat in May 2021, I was wrestling again with unfulfilled promises, wondering if I had really heard the Lord. After all, I was now sixty-six and the vision within me was massive. Was there even time for it come to pass in my lifetime? The Lord said to me, "Where is your faith?" I replied to Him, "But that's the whole problem. If I was sure, I would exercise faith, but I don't want to deceive myself." He asked, "Didn't I do all the other things I promised to do?" With that, I knew there was one choice only: No matter how unlikely the scenario, no matter how impossible the fulfillment of the promises might be, I will believe God. May it be settled forever!

In the Lord's goodness, after reaffirming to me in the early spring of 2023 that He was going to fulfill the promises He made to me twenty-five years earlier, Chris Berglund, a prophetic intercessor and close friend of Lou Engle whom I talked to for the first time earlier that year, sent me this text:

> I wanted to share a dream I had for you, to submit it to you for your consideration.
>
> In this encounter the Lord or angel of the Lord was reading Hebrews 6:11-19 over you. He was answering a question in your heart and I heard a phrase saying, "Abraham [needed] patient endurance for 25 years to obtain the promise." (I do remember that you shared at the meeting that you were saved during the Jesus movement)...However, in this encounter the Lord seemed to be highlighting the past 25 years of promises over your life and saying to you that you shall see them fulfilled. I don't remember all the details but remember Psalm 68 being highlighted and again hearing the Voice saying you (Michael) have Assaulted

Lessons Learned and Lessons Still Being Learned

the bulls or the mountains of Bashan with your words...both spoken and written was my knowing.... I also knew it was by attacking false ideologies and speaking/writing Truth....

What a glorious confirmation! Thank You, Lord! By Your grace, I will live believing and die believing.

SLEEP IS A GIFT.

We had a saying during the revival, "Sleep is for wimps." The harder you pushed, the better! Of course, the intensity of the revival put heavy demands on all of us, but long term, you cannot live without solid sleep. I've learned to recognize that is a gift from God, even a divine promise: "Unless the Lord builds the house, the builders labor in vain. Unless the Lord watches over the city, the guards stand watch in vain. In vain you rise early and stay up late, toiling for food to eat—for he grants sleep to those he loves" (Psalm 127:1–2 NIV).

In years past, "vacation" was a also dirty word to me, since I loved to run hard all the time. It almost felt like compromise if I took some time off. Here, too, my attitude has changed, although I have to do my best to get ahead on all my writing assignments and radio work in order to enjoy the down time. As for the promise in Psalm 127, just cited, the verses that follow shed further light on how God gives sleep to those He loves: "Children [literally, "sons"] are a heritage from the Lord, offspring a reward from him. Like arrows in the hands of a warrior are children born in one's youth" (Psalm 127:3–4 NIV). The point is that, when you have raised up faithful sons, while they work, you can now rest. It is a multigenerational promise.

GOOD THINGS TAKE TIME.

The longer you live, the more you see how true this is, and one of the unexpected blessings of getting older is that you get to see more prayers answered. It has been my incredible, profound joy to see my

LIVING IN THE LINE OF FIRE

longtime best friend Jon (the bass player in our old band), come back to the faith after *more than forty years* away from the Lord. He has been on fire for several years now, sharing the gospel without fear, and conquering what appeared to be terminal cancer—he did this without fear too. When he was hospitalized with cancer in 2022, he was preaching to everyone who came to visit him, chastising them for being concerned or down. When we talked by phone, he almost shouted to me, saying, "Mike, you prayed me back in!" What a faithful God we serve! He heard my cries and saw my tears (and the cries and tears of others).

It has also been my incredible, profound joy to see the ultra-Orthodox Jew we called Yaakov in Chapter 11 surrender to the lordship of Yeshua after a twenty-five year battle from 1993-2018. And in 2024, I was delighted to receive the news that a ninety-six-year-old Jewish man named Mark put his faith in Jesus after many years of prayer from his Christian wife, who was more than thirty years his junior. She told me I was the first Jewish believer he met (back in 2017), making a lasting impact on his life. I hope you're rejoicing too! With good reason the psalmist wrote, "Wait for the Lord; be strong and take heart and wait for the Lord" (Psalm 27:14 NIV). I encourage you with the encouragement I have received from Him—be strong; take heart; and wait, in expectant faith.

There are surely many other lessons learned, but these are the ones that struck me the most when praying over this chapter. Now, for the lessons I'm still learning. This section will be much shorter for the very reason that I'm still working on these.

THE LESSONS I'M STILL LEARNING

IT'S IMPORTANT TO STOP AND SMELL THE ROSES.

Our younger daughter Megan was married the afternoon of Sunday, January 10, 1998, and I attended the service at Brownsville Assembly that morning. As for the wedding itself, I journaled,

Who can describe the feeling of the wedding, walking Meg down in the aisle.... It's actually happening...it's not a dream any longer...the

Lessons Learned and Lessons Still Being Learned

excitement...the "nervous" anticipation...finding the right words as I give her away...sitting with Nancy and [my] Mom, crying at the unity candle lighting.... The only way I can describe it is this: Just as the star-filter on the wedding video turned the candles into so many "X's," so the whole atmosphere glowed with the moment. And how the people loved it, from the ceremony to the reception. Jesus, may this be the pattern of the rest of their lives!

As for the morning message from Pastor Kilpatrick, I journaled this: "An absolutely wonderful Sunday morning (John Kilpatrick is an extraordinary pastor!)," adding this note, which underscored what God was saying to me through the message: "Enjoy life! Enjoy the moment!" Yes, I needed to stop and smell the roses!

That continues to be a challenge for me, since I'm always in motion, always producing, always working with a pressing deadline, always moving on to the next thing before I finish the current one. Somehow, I need to be put all that aside, sit back, and enjoy the view. As Nancy said to me when we talked about this recently, "You can't just stop and smell the roses. You have to *enjoy* smelling the roses."

In 2023, in the midst of a beautiful fall season when the trees on our property looked as if they had been painted, Nancy asked me, "When you sit in your office," which has floor to ceiling windows on the walls in front of me and to my right, "have you noticed the trees?" Frankly, I had not, since I was too focused on my computer screen. But little by little, God is helping me take strides here. Hopefully, I will learn this one to the point that it becomes natural.

BEING IS MORE IMPORTANT THAN DOING.

It's been easier for me to write a whole chapter of a book in one day (as happened with a few chapters in this book) than to meditate quietly for an hour. It's part of my achiever mentality, but it's not ideal. Being *with* God is more important than working *for* Him, and the latter must flow out of the former. These monthly prayer retreats are helping me a lot here too, but I have quite a way to go.

LIVING IN THE LINE OF FIRE

THE SECRET PLACE MUST COME FIRST.

This is a similar lesson, but one that ties in even more directly with the call to put the secret place before the public place, to focus more on ministering to the Lord than to ministering to people. Once again, the latter must flow out of the former.

On June 13, 2010, I was with my longtime friend Gaspar Anastasi, a New Yorker like me but for years pastoring in Florida. He told me that he saw me now as being raised up by God on a national level as a key voice in the revival-reformation movement and as a plumb line for the others involved, asking me if I felt the same. I told him that I did, sharing more details of the burden and vision the Lord had given to me, asking him how he would have me spend my time if he were my "manager." He responded, "Double your time in the presence of God."

How I wish I had taken him up on that word! If I had, I believe I would be much closer to the Lord today, more like Jesus, more full of the Spirit, and more effective. This is similar to what Nancy has urged me to do for years as well. Oh, to get this right and put first things first! By His grace, I am giving myself to this more and more with each passing day.

Jesus set the example after telling a healed man to tell no one about it: "Yet the news about him spread all the more, so that crowds of people came to hear him and to be healed of their sicknesses. *But Jesus often withdrew to lonely places and prayed* (Luke 5:15–16 NIV).

I HAVE TO LEARN TO SAY NO.

I still fall into the trap of wanting to help everyone, especially colleagues. Enough said.

WHEREVER YOU ARE, BE THERE.

When I was in China in 2013, I had a meal with the man known as "Billy Graham's pastor," since Dr. Graham would attend church services there when he was home in North Carolina. I asked this pastor and his wife,

330

Lessons Learned and Lessons Still Being Learned

both of whom were from South Africa, "What made Billy Graham so special? What stood out about him the most?" His wife answered, "He was totally present when he was with you." How that convicted me!

As our older daughter Jen said to me one night over dinner after I had returned from an overseas trip (she was in her teens then), "You're here, but you're not here." She was right, and she had picked up that observation from Nancy. Physically, I was sitting at the table with the family. Mentally, I was in my study, working on a book. Today, with so many more distractions pulling at me, I need to work on this all the more. With the Lord's help and Nancy's prodding, I will!

FINDING THE BALANCE BETWEEN KINDNESS AND SEVERITY.

Paul writes in Romans 11:22 (NIV), "Consider therefore the kindness and sternness of God." This is something I've been reflecting on more in recent months in terms of my own ministry to others, especially to other leaders. On the one hand, I don't want to crush people with my words; on the other hand, I don't want to be a toothless grandfather. When is it time to rebuke, to appeal, to affirm, to correct, to discipline, to encourage? The answer will be found deep in the Word and in intimate fellowship with the Lord.

STILL BELIEVING THE LIE THAT MY SCHEDULE WILL LET UP TOMORROW.

You would think that, after five decades I would have figured this out already, but I'm always thinking, "I'll be able to do this or that or help others with their project or accept this invitation when my schedule lets up soon." Except that it never lets up. I either have to accept the reality that it will never change or else make decisions today that will make room for other things tomorrow.

ASSUMING THAT TOMORROW WILL BE BETTER.

Related to the last lesson I'm still learning is my pollyannish attitude that says, "Today is good but tomorrow will be better," even when there's no

LIVING IN THE LINE OF FIRE

reason for this whatsoever. And as much as it's great to live with so much optimism and positivity, it does allow for some level of self-deception, since you keep doing the same things while expecting different results.

I NEED TO KEEP MY HEAD IN THE CLOUDS.

I have mentioned our dear friends and team members Gary and Cindy Panepinto earlier in the book, and I am blessed beyond words to have Cindy running our ministry and Gary serving as our CFO. For years, I would pray, "God, give me a Gary, and I can change the world," meaning, if I just could separate from the day-to-day operational things that drain me dry and get my head in the clouds (the heavenly clouds, in the presence of God!), He could speak things to me and through me that could impact the world.

The Lord answered that prayer with a double blessing, giving me both Gary and Cindy. What an amazing team they make, and how wonderfully they run our ministry, taking so much of the load and responsibility and burden off of my shoulders, freeing me to do what I'm called to do. I just need to do my part with more focus and less distraction. Oh, to clear away the clutter and meet with Him more deeply!

I MUST LIVE FOR INTIMATE FELLOWSHIP WITH THE LORD MORE THAN MINISTRY BREAKTHROUGHS AND "HAPPENINGS."

While praying a few years back, I asked myself, "What brings me the greatest joy? What brings the most excitement to my spirit?" My first thought was seeing God open new doors or supernaturally expand our ministry reach and impact. These are good things in themselves, since I'm rejoicing in what He is doing. But it's even better to find my highest joys in who the Lord is, even more than in what He is doing.

A discerning reader might say, "I see a pattern here," in terms of my achiever, always doing, always going mindset, and you would be right. These different strands are all connected. That's why, once again, these monthly prayer retreats have been so crucial, helping me get a heavenly

Lessons Learned and Lessons Still Being Learned

perspective and helping me, like Miriam (Mary) in Luke 10, to choose that which is "better" (Luke 10:42).

THE LESSONS I STILL NEED TO LEARN BUT DON'T YET KNOW ABOUT

Obviously, I can't write this part of my story yet, but I'll let you know when I find out! Hopefully, as the Lord extends my life (by His grace), I'll have plenty more lessons to learn. May all of us keep learning and growing until we see Him face to face!

CHAPTER 16

THE BEST IS YET TO COME

When I was ten, I felt like I was ten. It was the same when I was twenty or thirty. But the older I get, it's not that like anymore. Like many of you who are older, I still feel young on the inside. Even now, as I write these words, I feel like a kid in a candy shop, like I'm just getting started, full of energy and vision and vigor. Let's do this!

In my consciousness, in terms of passion and mindset, I feel as if I'm still in my twenties (and I'm so thankful that I can work out with guys in their twenties too, often taking them down). And as these journal entries indicate (from 2011 to 2022; I could fill many pages with similar entries), that revolutionary fire is still burning:

> **July 2, 2011** Over the last couple of days, as I have been unboxing books and putting them back on the shelves, I'm amazed at how many books I'm "rediscovering," and as I do, my heart is burning with passion. I'M NOT CALLED TO MAINTAIN THE STATUS QUO. I *AM* CALLED TO STOKE A REVOLUTION. I *AM* CALLED TO ROCK THE BOAT. And I feel this on an academic level too, as I do desire to respond to wrong teaching and refute and expose it. Oh for an undistracted, uncluttered life! Oh for the discipline to take hold of God and wrestle with the deep questions and separate myself so I can receive the deep answers—and be so transformed that I transform an entire generation. Abba!!! My heart is exploding with this.

LIVING IN THE LINE OF FIRE

June 26, 2020 In my heart of hearts, I know that I know and I cannot shake it. I am called to be a REVOLUTIONARY!! On with it!

April 26, 2022 I am really meeting with the Lord tonight, and the theme of revolution is all over me. It's time! I am called to stoke the fires!! Only this Jesus-based, Spirit-empowered movement can shake the nation!!

But before I look ahead and dream my dreams with you, allow me to look back once again.

What a joy it has been to see our girls grow up, both of them with great husbands and kids. Jen and her husband Jimmy still live in Maryland, where they run a super successful business. When Jen was little and would get her weekly allowance, she used to kiss the dollar bill she received. To this day, she is a great money manager (although she doesn't kiss the bills anymore—at least to my knowledge!), hardworking, and a totally loyal person. Jimmy has grown into a real entrepreneur and responsible business manager, as well as being an incredibly devoted dad and loving husband. He also taught Jen to enjoy fishing (she didn't get that from Nancy or me) and got their two kids into fishing and hunting too.

Their son Connor, who will be twenty-one when this book is published, is currently serving as a fireman just as his dad has done for decades. Connor is one of a kind, someone who stands out in a room and a real hard worker. You cannot miss him! Riley will be eighteen, a horse rider like her mom (who has taken Riley to shows and back and forth to the stable thousands of times), her aunt (Megan) and her grandmother (Nancy). She is a beautiful, sensitive soul with a really kind disposition.

Meg and her husband Ryan live near us in North Carolina and have both been involved in ministry work over the years. Meg was always the sweet obedient daughter while Jen got disciplined all the time (inheriting some of Nancy's stubbornness), and to this day, Meg always puts others first and works tirelessly. I still call her "sweet Meg." She and Ryan met at

The Best Is Yet to Come

BRSM where he led our outreach teams after graduation, even directing FIRE School of Ministry for a season. He is multitalented and has also served as a pastor and written several books, all with a great message on the transforming power of the Father's love. He has also been a super devoted dad.

Meg has done bookkeeping for our ministry forever (not quite, but it feels like that, as she and Jen used to duplicate cassette tapes for our ministry while roller skating in our basement in Maryland and, when the ministry was really small, she basically took care of everything from order fulfillment to paying bills). She has been totally involved with both of the kids in every area of their lives, being their best personal coach.

Their daughter Elianna graduated from Liberty University in 2023 and will be twenty-three before this book is released. She is super responsible, full of creativity, and, like the females in our family, rode horses most of her life and was part of the equestrian team at Liberty. Andrew will be twenty-one, just a few weeks older than Connor, inheriting Nancy's red hair and my pollyannish positivity. He plays college baseball and actually started a ministry outreach at the junior college he previously attended.

There is nothing like watching your kids (and kids-in-law) and grandkids grow and develop and thrive and grow. Great-grandkids should be next!

PUTTING ALL THE PIECES TOGETHER

As you've seen, I've bounced off different walls over the years, from a narrow-minded but deeply devoted spirituality to a place of academic and theological pride, hopefully landing somewhere near the middle. I've also carried many different burdens and callings, ranging from debating rabbis at prestigious universities to sharing the gospel in tribal villages, and from serving as a professor at eight seminaries where, in some cases, I delivered lectures to Ph.D. students, to serving as a revival leader, laying hands on thousands of hungry believers. Often, these different callings created a feeling of tension, as each one vied for my heart and my energy,

LIVING IN THE LINE OF FIRE

and over the decades, especially before I got to Brownsville, I would wrestle with this in prayer, feeling called in so many directions at once.

Many times I laid all this before the Lord, saying, "I can't do all this at the same time. Which one is supposed to be the priority? What area should get the focus?" I even made charts and diagrams using Mind Manager software, breaking things down into categories and sub-categories, trying to get more clarity. One of the charts, "My Calling," contained these major categories: Making Disciples (which included teaching at or leading schools); Revival (which included national and international preaching); Revolution (which included impacting the culture); Jewish Ministry (which included debates as well as producing apologetics materials); Popular Writing (which included books and articles); Scholarship (biblical and Jewish in particular); Media (which included radio and TV, both Christian and secular).

At times, it felt like I was training to be a Sumo wrestler and a pole vaulter all concurrently, or preparing to be a power lifter and a ballet dancer simultaneously. You can't do both at the same time. As I prayed about this—and again, this is something that came up many times over the years—the Lord would affirm to me, "You are called to do them all." I would pray over these different aspects of calling, wanting one of them to "light up" as I prayed over it, but I would feel God's fire burning in each one of them, especially as we have reduced them to the three R's of our ministry: Revival in the Church, moral and cultural Revolution in the society, and the Redemption of Israel. With God's wisdom and empowerment, they all work hand in hand!

As for scholarship, I died to the idea of being a world-class Semitic scholar many years ago, and so scholarship serves as a tool. As for radio and TV, there's no ambition for me to be known, only to make Him known, so media outlets serve that purpose alone. "Expansion" in and of itself is meaningless. Still, for me to be fully thriving, I need to be in services where God's people are encountering His power and presence, I need to be pouring into hungry students, I need to travel to the nations, I need to be writing books and articles, I need to do live broadcasts and

The Best Is Yet to Come

tackle the controversies. And as long as I keep my priorities straight, beginning with time alone with Him, everything falls into place. No longer is there a feeling of spiritual schizophrenia, of feeling torn between callings (which I used to experience years ago). Instead, there is a sense of wholeness and well-being, especially when hitting on all cylinders. So, on with it!

But how do all the visions and goals come to pass in the years I have remaining in my journey? What about the drive inside of me to see God's purposes for my life accomplished while I still have breath without feeling under the pressure of the rapidly ticking clock of life? A few things have helped me here: 1) The preeminent goal—really, *the* goal—of my life is to hear Him say on that day, "Well done, good and faithful servant!" If I make that the goal of each day, all will be well. 2) I understand that, unless I live to see Jesus return (the ultimate dream!), then the work will carry on for generations. So, just as in a relay race each runner hands the baton to the next runner until the last runner takes things home, my dream is to hand the baton to Jesus when He returns. That failing, I will run just as hard and hand the baton off to the next generation. That's one reason I continue to pour into young people. May our legacies outlive us for decades or centuries to come! 3) Toward the beginning of my eight-day prayer retreat in December 2020, in the midst of intense travail, I sensed the Lord saying, "Everything is on schedule. I drew you aside now, not last month or last year." I rest in that word, even as I run with all my might.

THE MANY DIVINE INTERVENTIONS IN MY LIFE

I'm also encouraged by the many times and ways that God has intervened in my life, something that struck me when writing this book, leaving me humbled and awed. What a merciful Father! In the early days, He intervened by saving me from destruction as a teenage drug abuser, and since then, He has intervened many other times, as I've shared many through the course of this book. In 2014, He intervened in answer to Nancy's prayers, the prayers of others, and some of my own prayers, delivering

LIVING IN THE LINE OF FIRE

me from a lifetime of unhealthy eating, helping me to lose 100 pounds in less than eight months (from 275 to 175 pounds; I'm about 177 as I write now), extending the length of my life and improving the quality of my life. I am grateful beyond words, especially after discovering that I would have almost certainly have been dead from a heart-related condition without this lifestyle change, one that calls for super healthy eating, without exception, 24/7. It is a joy! (Nancy and I actually wrote a book about our journey, *Breaking the Stronghold of Food: How We Conquered Food Addictions and Discovered a New Way of Living*.)[62]

The Lord also used a variety of leaders to speak into my life at key times, including each of my first three pastors and the director of the first Bible school where I taught (as I shared earlier in the book). He connected me to men of God like Leonard Ravenhill and David Wilkerson and, more recently, James Robison, all of them making a profound impact in my life. Most recently, he has raised up Michael Ellison, a longtime friend of James and a pioneer leader in Christian media. Michael has graciously and sacrificially poured countless hours into me and my ministry team, helping us in ways that we could never pay for. And he has done this as a gift to us from the Lord. I am indebted to the Lord and His servants!

During our years in Maryland, working with Dan Juster, Paul Wilbur, Asher (who was then Keith) Intrater, and Eitan (who was then Andrew) Shishkoff, God deepened my understanding of the Jewish roots of the faith, and through these brothers, all of whom remain dear friends, enhanced my understanding of covenantal relationships. They have served together over the decades under the name Tikkun, which is short in Hebrew for Tikkun HaOlam, a Jewish term referring to the spiritual restoration of the world.

When I moved to Maryland, that was actually the name of my traveling ministry: "World Restoration" in English and "Tikkun HaOlam" in Hebrew. Not long after I moved to Maryland in 1987 to work with these brothers, Asher said to me with a smile, "We're very covenantal here. What's ours is yours and what's yours is ours, and we like the name

The Best Is Yet to Come

Tikkun." That's how they got the name Tikkun! They took it from me. (Hey, I need to throw a little trivia into my story, right?)

God has even intervened in extremely personal and practical ways, even down to my smile. If you see videos of me prior to 2008, you'll see that my upper teeth were discolored and quite ugly, also highlighting my very pronounced underbite. But God spoke to my old friend Bob Weiner, a living faith dynamo, telling him that I was going to be on TV a lot and needed new teeth. (The old teeth were an eyesore and a distraction up close, especially under glaring TV lights, but never once did I think of fixing them.) I was ministering at a night of worship in Jacksonville, Florida, with Paul Wilbur on June 1, 2007, and journaled this: "Well, this is certainly a surprise! It turns out that Bob Weiner told Messianic leader K. L. that his ministry needed to take care of my smile—since they have a dentist, Stan, who does this in Israel and elsewhere, and they're ready to bless me with new porcelain teeth. Ha! The door to speak to the world via the secular media continues to open."

What had happened was that Bob had been preaching at their congregation near Tulsa when he learned about what Dr. Stan did, saying to him, "You need to give Mike Brown new teeth." That night, before the worship began in Jacksonville, the pastor and Stan came up to me and said, "Bob Weiner says that we need to give you new teeth." In January 2008, I had a new smile. What a gift!

The Lord has also raised up special prayer support for me, also in sovereign ways. Back in 2018, one of my key staff members said to me, "Dr. Brown, there's a lack of prayer support undergirding the ministry." Not long after that, Trent and Amy Pruett stopped by the office, having returned for a short time from the Philippines. Trent had served as my assistant a few years earlier and was an incredible spiritual armor bearer to me, and he and Amy were (and are) doing an amazing work on many fronts in the Philippines.

Quite out of the blue he said, "Dr. Brown, I sense a lack of prayer support for your ministry," telling me that, even while serving in the Philippines, he still felt responsible for me as an armor bearer. He said,

LIVING IN THE LINE OF FIRE

"I think I have the solution." Shortly after that, he connected me with his longtime best friend Rui Porfirio, who, together with his wife Stacy, leads a house of prayer and congregation in McKinney, Texas. Both Trent and Rui had been impacted decades earlier by some of my revival books, and both shared a tremendous burden for the outpouring of the Spirit.

Ever since then, Trent, Rui, and I have been a threefold cord united to see God's purposes for our ministry come to pass. Rui contacts Trent and me once a week, asking for the most pressing prayer needs, then the next morning, the key intercessors at his house of prayer pray for those requests, as does Rui on a daily basis as well. And their prayers are making a difference!

In December 2023, the four of them—Trent and Amy, Rui and Stacy—joined me for my annual trip to India, further deepening our shared burden and vision. This too, is another gracious intervention of the Lord, mobilizing more prayer warriors for the battles ahead. Again I say, on with it! (They are often joined by Trudy Bangs, another experienced intercessor, who helps carry our ministry burdens to the Lord.)

And of course, the Lord continues to use Nancy to intervene in my life with key counsel (and warnings and exhortations!) at the right time, until this day. At the risk of being redundant, I cannot express my gratefulness to her. She continues to hold the standard high.

THE SCHOOL CONNECTIONS

There has been one other highly significant development in recent years that I believe is crucial for what still lies ahead, and it has to do with training and equipping the next generation of ministry students. This was a part of my calling that I thought was phasing out in 2018, as FIRE School of Ministry had become so small that, barring divine intervention, we were going to have to close the doors in another year. I thought to myself, "With rare exception, since 1982, I've been teaching in or leading ministry schools until now. Perhaps this season is coming to a close?"

The Best Is Yet to Come

Then, there was another divine surprise. I journaled this on July 13, 2018:

> Quite out of the blue, and when I was feeling drained...I'm hit with the sense that something is profoundly wrong with me just having a tiny school and dealing with such small numbers (in this aspect of my life and ministry). I'm *hit* by this so forcefully! Something is very wrong! And I write out this question in prayer: Father, where is that *school* connection where I and my team can **train *thousands*** to touch *millions*? *WHERE????* (And as much as I'm looking forward to training the next generation at FIRE School, it doesn't seem right that we go on like this, even with a slight increase in the Fall.) Father!!??

I remember the intensity of the prayer burden I was under that day as I was laying on my face groaning in travail, which is the very place from which so many important things in my life have been birthed. We continued our classes for one more year, after which we put everything online. (You can take these terrific courses from BRSM and FIRE, taught by our gifted faculty, at FireSchoolofMinistry.com.) But what about that "school connection" word?

What did it mean?

In the months that followed that word, right through 2020, I was approached by different colleagues, asking me to help them with a school project. One school would be online only, but with a massive global platform. I said, "I'm in!" We worked together, but it didn't pan out. Another school would be local, with in-person classes. I said, "I'm in!" That didn't pan out either. A third school would combine advanced academics with the power of the Spirit, also online and global. I said, "I'm in!" But that one never got off the ground. What was going on?

I felt like an unmarried man who was waiting to meet the woman he would marry, and the Lord had told him, "You'll meet her this year!"

343

LIVING IN THE LINE OF FIRE

Quite naturally, every time this man would meet a nice, single Christian woman, he would ask himself, "Is this the one?" That's what happened with me and the school connection. I was not teaching anywhere, but that "WHERE????" word was ever in my heart and mind. "Is this the one?" I asked with each new opportunity presented to me? The answer, each time, was no.

Finally, on January 29, 2021, I received a call from Landon Schott, a young pastor who had planted a rapidly growing church in Fort Worth, Texas, and who had reached out to me in 2014 to be a mentor in his life after seeing me on Piers Morgan. Since then, we had become very close, and I have served as an apostolic elder to the church, called Mercy Culture. He was starting a leadership school and wanted my involvement right out of the gate. I said, "I'm in! What would you like me to do?" He said, "I'd like you to come once a month and teach."

Once a month? How could I do it? I was trying to cut back on my schedule, not add to it, not because I was burned-out or tired but because I felt the Lord wanted me to slow down and spend more time with Him. Once a month? I said, "I'll need a studio where I can do my radio broadcasts." He said, "This will be a home away from home for you, and we'll build a studio for you." When I shared all this with Nancy, she was excited about it as well. I was in!

But there was more. In October 2021, while teaching at Christ for the Nations in Dallas, after a hiatus of ten years since being a guest speaker there, I shared with one of the leaders, Pastor Adam McCain, about my "school connection" word and how I would be teaching at Mercy's Culture school. He told me God had spoken to him several months earlier that I was to be involved with the school but he didn't know how to ask me. I asked him, "What if I come here once a month, since I'm already coming to Fort Worth? I just need a studio to broadcast from." He said, "It's a deal!" (That's a rough paraphrase of his response; I remember the other details well.)

I had also made a commitment to Daniel Kolenda, telling him that when he launched his full-time school in Orlando for Christ for All

344

The Best Is Yet to Come

Nations (CfAN), I would come down and teach monthly. I now have the joy of doing that as well, meaning that six to eight months per year, I'm teaching between one and three days each in three different schools, one in Florida and two in Texas. I love every minute of it! In fact, as the school vision with Daniel has developed further, I will be serving as chancellor at the CfAN School of Ministry, scheduled to launch in the fall of this year (2025), replacing the current school there (called Nations College). The calling to help birth ministry schools has come upon me again as I approach seventy!

But there's more. Since November 2022, I've had the joy of teaching one intensive week per year at Randy Clark's Global Awakening Theological Seminary (GATS), which is unique in that most of the students in the seminary have many years of ministry experience, yet they are still growing and pursuing advanced theological degrees. I do my radio shows remotely in the afternoon and then teach and minister all night. So, that makes four schools a year, each with a different flavor and each with something that is very special to me.

But there's more still. In February 2023, I flew to Kona, Hawaii, to teach for the first time at the YWAM base, where more than 600 DTS (Discipleship Training School) students were gathered together, along with hundreds of leaders. I was asked to do a three-day intensive on the Church and the culture wars. When I arrived on the campus, I said to my assistant Brandon, "Oh no. I'm having that feeling again," meaning, that sense of connection, that I'm supposed to be here regularly as well. But all the way in Hawaii? They have now asked me to come in annually, if possible, which has also been a great joy.

But there's even more, this one the most surprising of all. In 2023, I was contacted by a longtime Messianic Jewish colleague living in Israel, Akiva Cohen. He said that he and Dan Juster and some other leaders were launching a new ministry school in Jerusalem, the only full-time, Hebrew speaking, accredited school in the nation with an emphasis on revival and the power of the Spirit along with solid theology and practical training. Would I like to be involved in some foundational way? I

LIVING IN THE LINE OF FIRE

felt a strong witness of the Spirit, immediately saying, "I'm in!" Since then, I have been part of the core leadership team of the Jerusalem Bible Institute (JBI), along with Dan, Akiva, Zvi Randelman (an American Israeli, like Dan and Akiva), and Eli Dorfman (a Russian Israeli). My official title is Director of Spiritual Renewal and Apologetics, and the school launched in November 2024 following an introductory Holy Spirit seminar I taught in Jerusalem in June 2024. How amazing!

We have spent endless hours brainstorming and planning and praying, and all of us involved see this as part of God's sovereign plan for the salvation of Israel, right out of Jerusalem, however small or large our role might be. This is the answer to many decades of prayer offered up to God by His people worldwide. Now is the time! God willing, I'll go to Israel once or twice a year for special seminars and intensives with the students, also connecting by Zoom.

And so, the "school connection" question has been answered many times—from Mercy Culture's Spiritual Leadership School to Christ for the Nations and their international study body, from CfAN's school in Orlando to YWAM in Kona, and from GATS to JBI. The plans of the Lord are amazing! And in all this, I have peace, I am not stressed, there is a beautiful rhythm of life, and Nancy is fine with my schedule. The plans of the Lord continue to blow me away.

In the previous chapter, I quoted John Wesley's dictum, "Though I am always in haste, I am never in a hurry, because I never undertake any more work than I can go through with perfect calmness of spirit." But there is important background to this quote. It was December 10, 1777, and Wesley was seventy-four years old, incredibly busy, always on the move, and pushing hard. His brother Charles was concerned that this might be taking a toll on his health. This is the relevant part of John Wesley's reply, in full: "I have more business than I can well manage, owing to the number of societies which have been lately formed in various parts of England and Ireland. But it is a happy problem; and I am willing to be a slave for the service of poor souls. Though I am always in haste, I am never in a

The Best Is Yet to Come

hurry, because I never undertake any more work than I can go through with perfect calmness of spirit." I can relate!

And remarkably, as I have looked back over the decades, while writing chapter after chapter of this book, I thought of so many more stories to tell, so many lessons to relate, so many accounts to give. What a truly blessed life it has been so far. And yet, there is more. I know it!

WHAT LIES AHEAD?

As I arrive at seventy, my life is full and overflowing, but my soul is at rest. God made me to do daily broadcasts; He made to write books and articles; He made to teach and preach and travel and debate; He made me to be embroiled in controversy. By His grace, I am thriving, and to my knowledge, in excellent health as well. And even though I do not boast about my next breath, let alone about tomorrow, I know that He extended my life until now, changing my lifestyle in 2014.

Interestingly, when I approached fifty years old in 2004 and early 2005, I went through what must have been a mid-life crisis. I was not my normal, full of expectation, full of hope self. Instead, for the first time in my life, I feared that my best years were behind me. After all, before the split at the end of 2000, everything in my life had been on an upward trajectory, from my earliest days of preaching to the outpouring in 1982 followed by my calling to CFNI in 1983, then from Times Square Church in the early 1990s to the revival in 1996. Everything seemed to be on schedule, and I felt sure that the rest of the promises would fall into place as well.

But now in 2004-2005, after the split in 2001, things had stalled, if not gone dramatically in reverse. Our whole organization had to relocate and start afresh, with much smaller numbers. Nancy and I had endured a massive financial crisis, and our whole ministry had been under non-stop monetary pressure. Plus, the divine purging I had gone through in 2002 really stripped away any fleshly self-confidence, leaving me feeling weak and emotionally vulnerable.

LIVING IN THE LINE OF FIRE

Sometimes, praying late at night, I would weep at the thought that the best years of life and ministry were behind me. I would say, "Lord, I'm grateful to You for everything You've done and for everything I have seen and experienced, things that very few others have been privileged to see and experience. But if the best days are in the past, that would be a tragedy." And I would sob.

Looking back, it's hard for me even to relate to how I felt back then. It is utterly foreign! Yet I know it was real. I journaled the pain, and Nancy witnessed my struggles. Still, I can't help but smile as I write about that difficult season twenty years later, now overflowing with life, with vision, with faith, with purpose, and with energy. In my heart of hearts, I know that the best is yet to come. In fact, as I approach seventy years of age, I feel that I must get into the best shape of my life, spiritually, mentally, emotionally, and physically since I'm nearing the *starting line* of the most important part of my race so far. That's really how I feel. I cannot wait to see what the future holds in Him. I am stoked!

To be sure, I have sometimes worn Nancy and my family out with saying that "the best is yet to come," but I have a ready answer: unless you are going to hell, then the best *is* yet to come! Yet even here and now, in this world, in my lifetime, that is my expectation as well. The best is yet to come—and I say these words, not out of rote, not out of my sanguine personality, but out of the inspiration I feel when I meet the Lord and encounter His presence. It's as if He's saying, "You haven't seen anything yet!"

What then are the dreams that burn bright in my heart? What are the goals and priorities my Master and Lord has set before me? (These are all desires and prayers, not boasts, since, to say it again, my next breath in His hands.)

I long to be closer to Him, lost in His presence, absorbed in His Spirit. That is the cry of my heart! That is the most fervent desire, the most passionate plea, the most intense cry within me. Oh, to really know Him! Oh, to really encounter Him! Oh, to really be changed by Him! In the years ahead, may there be more of Him, less of me; more of His work, less

The Best Is Yet to Come

of mine, as if to say, "We've seen what Mike Brown can do. Let's see what God can do!"

I long to see the greatest outpouring in our nation's history, something that will rock America from coast to coast, with a massive harvest of souls and the people of God awakened. May it be! May I serve on the front lines once again, not just in one place of outpouring, but across the land.

I long to see the fullness of that promised moral and cultural revolution, that pushback against the kingdom of darkness, bringing about radical, dramatic, sweeping change. I long for it! May I have the privilege of being a voice of moral sanity and spiritual clarity as the tide rises, helping lead the army into spiritual battle.

I long to see my Jewish people saved! I long to see the Spirit poured out in Israel and in the nations where we are scattered, resulting in the salvation of multitudes of my people, including hundreds of thousands of ultra-Orthodox Jews. Hasten the day, Lord! I can see it!

I long to see the next generations raised up and sent out, equipped, grounded, full of fire and zeal, ready to give their lives for the gospel. That includes my kids and grandkids too! God's best for each of them!

I long to see the glory of God in the nations, to see revival fire overseas, to see the greatest ingathering of souls in history. I want to be there, in the thick of it, as it happens. And I want the schools where I serve to help raise up and send out this holy army. It is time!

I long to glorify Jesus by life or by death, to rock the boat, to live an incendiary life, to be a real threat to the kingdom of darkness, to bring a smile to my Father's face. HOW I LONG FOR THIS!

And I long to do it all with my bride at my side, both of us feeling younger and stronger by the year. He renews our youth like the eagle's![63]

More than anything, I want to see Him face to face! Again I pray, hasten the day! Even so, come Lord Jesus!

May this book serve as a fitting introduction for the years that lie ahead, and may the sequel be far more exciting, far more breathtaking, and filled with far more stories that inspire and encourage and glorify the Lord. Let us do it together!

LIVING IN THE LINE OF FIRE

And so I say to each of you as you read this book and run your own race: ON WITH IT, whatever the cost, whatever the consequence. Lord, we delight to do Your will! You are worth it all!

Let's find out what He can do through vessels totally yielded to Him. Let's go for it while we yet have breath! IT. IS. TIME!

ENDNOTES

CHAPTER 01

1 See Michael L. Brown, *Go and Sin No More: A Call to Holiness* (Ventura, CA: Regal Books, 1997), 19-74.

CHAPTER 03

2 https://www.facebook.com/nancyie/posts/pfbid02zsoA2j9ebgk Pz5hir3KxN9Z8wwdCycEEajKuPqoMF75TX414Fq8U9edYbsU W3fTnl

CHAPTER 04

3 *Our Hands Are Stained with Blood: The Tragic Story of the Church and the Jewish People* (Shippensburg, PA: Destiny Image, 1992; second, updated and expanded edition published in 2019).

CHAPTER 05

4 Grand Rapids, MI: Zondervan, 1995.

CHAPTER 06

5 Jacksonville, FL: AWKNG Press.
6 Shippensburg, PA: Destiny Image.
7 All published by Destiny Image.

CHAPTER 07

8 Michael L. Brown, *The End of the American Gospel Enterprise* (Shippensburg, PA: Destiny Image, 1989), 3.

LIVING IN THE LINE OF FIRE

9   Michael L. Brown, *How Saved Are We?* (Shippensburg, PA: Destiny Image, 1990), 1.

10 Michael L. Brown, *Whatever Happened to the Power of God: Is the Charismatic Church Slain in the Spirit or Down for the Count* (Shippensburg, PA: Destiny Image, 1991), ix.

11 Michael L. Brown, *It's Time to Rock the Boat: A Call to God's People to Rise Up and Preach a Confrontational Gospel* (Shippensburg, PA: Destiny Image, 1993), xv.

12 I elaborate on these themes in greater depth in Michael L. Brown, *Seize the Moment: How to Fuel the Fires of Revival* (From Revival to Reformation: Book One; Lake Mary, FL: Charisma Media, 2024).

13 Now in Michael L. Brown, *From Holy Laughter to Holy Fire: America on the Edge of Revival* (Shippensburg, PA: Destiny Image, 1996), 265-266.

14 Cited in Michael L. Brown, *Revival Or We Die: A Great Awakening Is Our Only Hope* (Shippensburg, PA: Destiny Image, 2021), 11-12.

15 You can watch the part of the service I described at this link: Intercession for Our Schools: Brownsville Revival Service. 10-12-96 (youtube.com); accessed September 28, 2024.

16 You can watch some of that service by visiting this link: Brownsville Revival Lord Have Mercy II (youtube.com); accessed September 28, 2024.

17 Arthur Wallis, *In the Day of Thy Power* (Fort Washington, PA: CLC Publications, 2010).

18 Shippensburg, PA: Destiny Image, 1997.

19 Ventura, CA: Renew, 2001.

CHAPTER 08

20 "The Rev. Martin Luther King Jr. speaks from the pulpit on courage, Selma, AL, March 8, 1965"; faculty.etsu.edu/history/documents/mlkselma.htm; accessed September 25, 2024.

Endnotes

CHAPTER 09

21 *Seize the Moment*, 123-124.

22 Some of the areas where I needed to repent actually came to public attention in December 2024, twenty-three years after I had dealt with them before the Lord.

CHAPTER 10

23 Details in *It's Time to Rock the Boat* (1993).

24 Michael Brown, "America is in Moral Freefall," Salem Media, April 2, 2024; America is in Moral Freefall - The Stream; accessed September 25, 2024.

25 Grand Rapids, Michigan: Chosen Books.

26 This is an exact transcript of the recording.

27 Can you be Gay and Christian? Michael Brown vs Harry Knox (youtube.com); accessed September 25, 2024.

28 "30 New Activists Heading Up the Radical Right," *SPLC,* May 26, 2012; 30 New Activists Heading Up the Radical Right | Southern Poverty Law Center (splcenter.org); accessed September 25, 2024. Michael Brown, "An Open Letter to Mark Potok, Spokesman for the SPLC (Part I), Townhall.com, August 22, 2012; An Open Letter to Mark Potok, Spokesman for the SPLC (Part I) (townhall.com); accessed September 25, 2024.

29 "Choose from the complete list of GLAAD Accountability Profiles: Michael Brown," glad.org, April 21, 2023; Michael Brown | GLAAD; accessed September 25, 2024. Michael L. Brown, "The Left Wants to Eliminate Competing Ideas," ASKDrBrown.org, January 19, 2021. The Left Wants to Eliminate Competing Ideas | Ask Dr. Brown (askdrbrown.org); accessed September 25, 2024.

30 EXPORT OF HATE - Michael Brown (youtube.com); accessed September 25, 2024. Michael L. Brown, "The HRC Is Inciting Fear and Hate," ASKDrBrown.org, September 20, 2014. The HRC Is

LIVING IN THE LINE OF FIRE

Inciting Fear and Hate | Ask Dr. Brown (askdrbrown.org); accessed September 25, 2024.

31 In His Image: Delighting in God's Plan for Gender and Sexuality | FULL MOVIE (youtube.com); accessed September 26, 2024.

32 Tyra part 5 Transgender children and their parents speak out (youtube.com); Dr Brown on Piers Morgan with Ben Ferguson and Marc Lamont Hill (youtube.com); accessed both September 26, 2024.

33 Michael Brown, "Gay Is Good Or Bullying Is Bad? A Teachable Moment," *Townhall.com,* October 25, 2010; Gay Is Good Or Bullying Is Bad? A Teachable Moment (townhall.com); accessed September 26, 2024.

34 And this was the first one: "An Open Letter to SPLC Spokesman Mark Potok," *CharismaNews,* August 22, 2012; https://cn.mycharisma .com/opinion/an-open-letter-to-splc-spokesman-mark-potok/; accessed September 26, 2024.

35 Shippensburg, PA: Destiny Image, 2018.

36 Concord, NC: EqualTime Books, 2020.

37 Washington, DC: Vide Books, 2022.

38 Concord, NC: EqualTime Books, 2011.

39 "What Did Lincoln Say to Mrs. Stowe?" Harriet Beecher Stowe House, July 29, 2021; What Did Lincoln Say to Mrs. Stowe? - HARRIET BEECHER STOWE HOUSE (stowehousecincy.org); accessed September 26, 2024.

40 John Dart, "Billy Graham Recalls Help From Hearst," LATimes.com, June 7, 1997; Billy Graham Recalls Help From Hearst - Los Angeles Times (latimes.com); accessed September 26, 2024.

41 For the 0.5 percent, see Line of Fire Radio (podcast) - Dr. Michael L. Brown | Listen Notes; for the country by country information, see (via subscription) https://chartable.com/teams/line-of-fire-radio/ dashboard.

Endnotes

42 See "The Gay Rabbi and My Mother's Funeral" ASKDrBrown, November 28, 2016; The Gay Rabbi and My Mother's Funeral | Ask Dr. Brown (askdrbrown.org); accessed September 26, 2024.

43 You can listen to this entire call (or read the transcript) on The Line of Fire episode "Christian Working at Planned Parenthood Vows Never to Return: 'It's Not Tissue! They Are Babies!,'" YouTube video, run time 18:26, July 29, 2017, https://www.youtube.com/watch?v=BSmnPhAWU0c; accessed September 28, 2024.

CHAPTER 11

44 To read more about this, see Michael L. Brown, *Our Hands Are Stained with Blood: The Tragic Story of the Church and the Jewish People* (second edition; Shippensburg, PA: Destiny Image, 2019), 225-231.

45 *Answering Jewish Objections to Jesus: Vol. 1: General and Historical Objections* (Grand Rapids, MI: Baker Books, 2000); *Answering Jewish Objections to Jesus: Vol. 2: Theological Objections* (Grand Rapids, MI: Baker Books, 2000); *Answering Jewish Objections to Jesus: Vol. 3: Messianic Prophecy Objections* (Grand Rapids, MI: Baker Books, 2003); *Answering Jewish Objections to Jesus: Vol. 4: New Testament Objections* (Grand Rapids, MI: Baker Books, 2006); *Answering Jewish Objections to Jesus: Vol. 5: Traditional Jewish Objections* (San Francisco, CA: Purple Pomegranate Publications, 2010).

46 Lake Mary, FL: Frontline, 2012.

47 Lake Mary, FL: Charisma House, 2020.

48 Lake Mary, FL: Charisma House. For a powerful, five-minute video on this same subject, see: A New Jewish Proof for the Resurrection of Jesus (youtube.com); accessed September 28, 2024.

49 See The Gay Rabbi and My Mother's Funeral | Ask Dr. Brown (askdrbrown.org) for more of the story.

LIVING IN THE LINE OF FIRE

CHAPTER 13

50 I devoted a whole chapter on dealing with rejection in my recent book, *Hearts of Compassion, Backbones of Steel: How to Discuss Controversial Topics with Love and Kindness* (Grands Rapids, MI: Chosen, 2024).

51 See An Open Letter to Mark Potok, Spokesman for the SPLC (Part I), townhall.com; An Open Letter to Mark Potok, Spokesman for the SPLC (Part II), townhall.com; The SPLC Owes Me an Apology Too - *Charisma News.*

52 https://www.youtube.com/watch?v=lpGNVuYzGXI; accessed September 28, 2024.

53 https://youtu.be/L_NfmdWqmq0; accessed September 27, 2024.

54 "John Wesley: Letter to William Wilberforce," Asbury Theological Seminary (2012); Last Writing of John Wesley (a letter to William Wilberforce) (asburyseminary.edu); accessed September 27, 2024.

55 Karamchedu massacre - Wikipedia; accessed September 27, 2024.

56 You can watch the message at https://youtu.be/HMY1SVEpkY4; accessed September 28, 2024.

57 For more on Kanaka Durga and the "Jezebel spirit," see Michael L. Brown, *Jezebel's War with America: The Plot to Destroy Our Country and What We Can Do to Turn the Tide* (Lake Mary, FL: Frontline, 2019), 23-27.

58 Jacob Milgrom, *Numbers, The JPS Torah Commentary* (Philadelphia: Jewish Publication Society, 1990), 371.

CHAPTER 14

59 Dr Brown on Piers Morgan with Ben Ferguson and Marc Lamont Hill (youtube.com).

Endnotes

CHAPTER 15

60 Some of this account was excerpted from Michael L. Brown, *Hyper-Grace: Exposing the Dangers of the Modern Grace Message* (Lake Mary, FL: Charisma House, 2014), 2-3.

61 All About the Achiever StrengthsFinder Theme | EN - Gallup; accessed September 27, 2024.

CHAPTER 16

62 Lake Mary, FL: Siloam, 2017.

63 Isaiah 40:31; Psalm 103:5

ABOUT THE AUTHOR

Dr. Michael L. Brown holds a Ph.D. in Near Eastern Languages and Literatures from New York University. The author of more than forty-five books, including wake-up calls to the Church of America, scholarly monographs and commentaries on biblical subjects, a series of volumes on answering Jewish objections to Jesus, and much-discussed books on today's hottest cultural issues.

He has spoken throughout America and in more than 30 countries, and he hosts the *Courage in the Line of Fire* podcast. He is the Director of Spiritual Renewal and Apologetics at the Jerusalem Bible Institute and has lectured at numerous seminaries and Bible colleges.

He served as a leader in the Brownsville Revival from 1996-2000 and has taken the message of repentance, revival, and a gospel-based moral and cultural revolution throughout the United States and around the world.

He and his wife, Nancy, also a Jewish believer in Jesus, have been married since 1976 and have two wonderful daughters and four incredible grandchildren.

Check out
our **Destiny Image**
bestsellers page at
<u>destinyimage.com/bestsellers</u>

for cutting-edge,
prophetic messages
that will supernaturally
empower you and the
body of Christ.

YOUR Prophetic COMMUNITY

Sign up for a **FREE** subscription to the Destiny Image digital magazine and get awesome content delivered directly to your inbox!

destinyimage.com/signup

Sign up for Cutting-Edge Messages that Supernaturally Empower You

- Gain valuable insights and guidance based on biblical principles
- Deepen your faith and understanding of God's plan for your life
- Receive regular updates and prophetic messages
- Connect with a community of believers who share your values and beliefs

Experience Fresh Video Content that Reveals Your Prophetic Inheritance

- Receive prophetic messages and insights
- Connect with a powerful tool for spiritual growth and development
- Stay connected and inspired on your faith journey

Listen to Powerful Podcasts that Propel You into God's Presence Every Day

- Deepen your understanding of God's prophetic assignment
- Experience God's revival power throughout your day
- Learn how to grow spiritually in your walk with God

In the Right Hands, This Book Will Change Lives!

Most of the people who need this message will not be looking for this book. To change their lives, you need to **put a copy of this book in their hands.**

Our ministry is constantly seeking methods to find the people who need this anointed message to change their lives. **Will you help us reach these people?**

Extend this ministry by sowing 3 books, 5 books, 10 books, or more today, and become a life changer! Your generosity will be part of catalyzing the Great Awakening that many have been prophesying and praying for.

From
Michael L. Brown, PhD

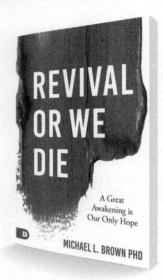

On the brink of collapse, our nation's only hope is a visitation of God's power and presence.

What will heal the deep racial, social, and political divisions that are tearing us apart? How can we stop the evil of human trafficking? What can turn the rising tide of opioid addiction? What will cure the epidemic of fatherless homes? Man-made laws and policies don't hold the answers. Social programs and initiatives fall hopelessly short. There is no political solution.

We must have divine visitation. We must have awakening. We must have revival.

In *Revival or We Die*, respected biblical scholar, bestselling author, and radio host Dr. Michael Brown calls the American Church back to God and His Kingdom purposes. He presents a prophetic "state of the union" address, offering a candid look at the United States and revealing why our only hope is a true spiritual awakening.

Written with the same passion and zeal that characterized his early books, *How Saved Are We?* and *Whatever Happened to the Power of God?*, Dr. Brown issues a fresh clarion call to every true believer in this generation.

The stirring message of this book is what every Christian must hear at this crucial moment. Our nation is at a tipping point, and *you* can play a pivotal role in the mighty revival that God longs to bring. Are you willing?

Purchase your copy wherever books are sold.

From
Michael L. Brown, PhD

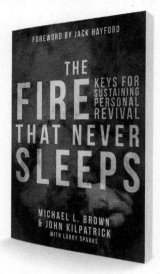

Get Revived . . . and Stay On Fire!

"I had such a powerful experience with God. He touched my heart so deeply... and after that one encounter, I wanted to live for Jesus every day for the rest of my life."

Then life went back to normal.

Sound familiar?

Perhaps you've had an encounter with God that powerfully impacted your life—where sin, addiction, spiritual dryness or other struggles simply faded away. If such experiences are commonplace when revival is happening, then . . .

How can I experience revival every single day of my life?

With guidance from the leaders of the Brownsville Revival and the Bay of the Holy Spirit Revival, you will **ignite and sustain your passion for Jesus** and learn how:

- Desperate prayer unleashes the supernatural power of God into your life
- Repentance is your key to enjoying unbroken intimacy with the Holy Spirit
- You can become a catalyst for great awakening in your church, city, and nation

Get ready to live passionately for Jesus, walk out God's divine purpose for your life, and enjoy His presence on a daily basis.

It's time to revive your fire!

Purchase your copy wherever books are sold.

From
Michael L. Brown, PhD

Every Christian must read this shocking account of the Church's history.

The pages of church history are marked by countless horrors committed against the Jewish people.

From the first persecutions of the Jews in the fourth century to the horrors of the Holocaust, from Israel-bashing in today's press to anti-Semitism spouted from the pulpit, this painful book tells the tragic story that every Christian must read.

In a freshly updated and expanded edition of this pivotal work, Dr. Michael Brown exposes the faulty theological roots that opened the door to anti-Semitism in Church history, explaining why well-meaning believers so often fall into the trap of hate... and showing how you can bring an end to the cycle of violence.

This generation can make a difference. Now is the time for change! Discover the important role you play in helping to shape a Church that will bless Israel rather than curse Israel.

Purchase your copy wherever books are sold.

From
Larry Sparks

Position Yourself to Experience Holy Spirit Outpouring!

"Ask the LORD for rain in the time of the latter rain." Zechariah 10:1

God is pouring out His Spirit and revival rain is falling across the earth. How should you respond? Ask for more!

How can revival impact your everyday life? Maybe you've thought revival is for "super-charged" Christians—not for everyday people going through everyday life. Wrong. God wants your every day to be overflowing with Holy Spirit power.

How thirsty are you?

Larry Sparks has assembled leading revival voices that will awaken your hunger to experience God in powerful new ways!

- **Bill Johnson:** Experience an increase of the Holy Spirit's presence.
- **Dr. Michael Brown:** Cultivate "holy discontentment" that births revival hunger.
- **John Kilpatrick:** Cry out for encounters with God's manifest glory.
- **Tommy Tenney:** Build your expectation for a great move of God.
- **James Goll:** Pray revival prayers that release Heaven's Power.

And much more!

God is seeking ready ground to pour out his revival rain on. *Are you ready?*

Purchase your copy wherever books are sold.

From
Frank Viola

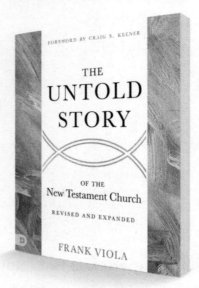

Experience the New Testament Like Never Before

One famous scholar said that reading the New Testament letters is like hearing one end of a phone conversation. *The Untold Story of the New Testament Church (Revised and Expanded)* reconstructs the other end so you can understand virtually every word.

Seamlessly weaving the narrative of Acts with the Epistles, you'll discover a coherent story enriched by intriguing details of first-century life. This unique and innovative presentation of the New Testament unlocks its epic story in a way that will leave you breathless and equipped to understand the Bible like never before.

Though it's non-fiction, this masterpiece reads like a cinematic experience and it will captivate your heart by putting you in the center of the drama. Drawing on the best of contemporary scholarship, Frank Viola includes background information about the people, cities, and places that are mentioned throughout the New Testament, all in an engaging narrative.

Prepare to be ushered into the living, breathing atmosphere of the first century so you can uncover the hidden riches contained in God's Word.

Purchase your copy wherever books are sold.

STAND STRONG IN A SHAKING WORLD: IGNITE YOUR FAITH IN TIMES OF CHAOS

Everywhere we turn, it feels like everything is shaking—evil is celebrated, and righteousness is ridiculed. The prophet Isaiah foresaw a time when darkness would be called light and light would [be] called darkness. We are living in those days.

But in these perilous times, God is raising up prophetic voices to speak clarity and truth in[to] the confusion.

For over 50 years, Dr. Michael Brown—a bestselling author, seasoned radio host, and biblical schol[ar]—has called the church to action, championing revival, Israel's redemption, and a Gospel-bas[ed] moral and cultural revolution. Drawing from decades of ministry and global outreach, he offers [an] unparalleled perspective on navigating tumultuous times with unwavering faith and boldness.

Prepare to embark on a life-changing journey as Dr. Brown invites you into the intimate moments [of] his walk with the Messiah:

- **Gain prophetic wisdom** from men of God like Leonard Ravenhill and David Wilkers[on] who personally mentored and impacted Dr. Brown.
- **Ignite your heart** with fresh fire as you experience the landscape-altering move of G[od] during the Brownsville Revival.
- **Receive divine impartation** to stand firm in a culture that is increasingly hostile [to] the truth.
- **Be inspired to leave a legacy** that will impact future generations for the Kingdom of G[od].

In this prophetic hour, God is calling you to rise up, stay the course, and burn with a passion that w[ill] set the world ablaze for Jesus. Don't give in to compromise. Don't crumble under pressure. And do[n't] lose hope for the future.

Dr. Michael L. Brown holds a PhD in Near Eastern Languages and Literatures from N[ew] York University and serves as Director of Spiritual Renewal and Apologetics at the Jerusalem Bi[blical] Institute in Israel and Chancellor of the CfAN School of Ministry in Orlando, Florida. The auth[or] of more than 45 books, he is the host of the *Line of Fire* broadcast where he serves as "your voice [for] moral, cultural, and spiritual revolution," and his syndicated columns appear on many Christian a[nd] conservative websites. He served as a leader in the Brownsville Revival fro[m ...] the message of repentance and revival around the world. Michael and his [wife, married in] 1976, have two children and four grandchildren.

WWW.DESTINYIMAGE.COM